The Doctrine of State

Friedrich Julius Stahl

THE PHILOSOPHY OF LAW

VOLUME I: *The History of Legal Philosophy*

1A: *The Rise and Fall of Natural Law*

1B: *The Recovery of Historical Law*

VOLUME II: *The Doctrine of Law and State on the Basis of the Christian Worldview*

PART I: *General Doctrines and Private Law*

BOOK I: *Philosophical Foundations*

BOOK II: *Principles of Law*

BOOK III: *Private Law*

PART II: *The Doctrine of State and the Principles of State Law*

BOOK IV

The Philosophy of Law
Volume II: The Doctrine of Law and State on the Basis of the Christian Worldview
Book IV

The Doctrine of State and the Principles of State Law

SECOND EDITION

Friedrich Julius Stahl

Translated, edited, and prefaced by
Ruben Alvarado

WORDBRIDGE PUBLISHING
Aalten, the Netherlands
www.wordbridge.net
info@wordbridge.net

German original: Friedrich Julius Stahl, *Rechts- und Staatslehre auf der Grundlage christlicher Weltanschauung: Erste Abtheilung, enthaltend die allgemeinen Lehren und das Privatrecht.* Fifth, unchanged edition. Tübingen and Leipzig: J. C. B. Mohr, 1878.

ISBN 978–90–76660–80–6

COVER ILLUSTRATION: "Die Huldigung der preussischen Stände vor König Friedrich Wilhelm IV in Berlin am 15 Oktober 1840" [The Ceremony of Homage by the Prussian Estates before King Friedrich Wilhelm IV in Berlin, October 15th, 1840]. Lithograph by Gustav Schwarz. This reproduction is in the public domain. Courtesy Wikimedia Commons.

TABLE OF CONTENTS

NOTES ON THIS EDITION

This was the most difficult volume in the series and the most in need of revision. That revision has been rigorous. In fact, the attentive reader will notice that the translation in many places has been rewritten. Why so, when such was not required for either the *Principles of Law* or *Private Law?* Quite simply, the difficulty of the subject matter. In the 15-plus years since I did the first edition, my grasp of both that subject matter and of the language in which it is couched have progressed sufficiently to allow for a significantly improved rendering.

Furthermore, whole chapters have been added to the translation which were not included in the original. These include:

- Author's Preface to the Third Edition
- From the Author's Preface to the Second Edition
- Part Three, Chapter 13: Territorial Representation after 1848

Similarly, §§. 18, 19, 23–26, 35, 158, and 163–168 have been newly translated.

Beyond this, the editor's preface has been substantially amplified and reworked.

Square brackets are used in the following cases: 1) for words in German which are susceptible to multiple meanings or the meaning of which was not entirely clear; 2) for interpolations to improve understanding or to provide supplementary material; 3) in the case of whole paragraphs, for paraphrases of the original text; 4) footnotes added by the editor.

Section headings do not appear in the original: they are of my own device.

Numbers which appear in bold between angular brackets (like this: <**1**>) are page numbers in the first edition. Unless otherwise indicated, references in the text and in the index to page numbers in this book use that page numbering.

With regard to specific terms, the following:

Ansehen: refers to the attitude of awe and respect with which majesty is to be regarded, and is an essential characteristic of state authority. It is here translated as "regard."

Konstitution: see *Verfassung* below.

Lands-, Landes-: something attached to the "land" or the "country," which in German history often refers to the territorial state such as Bavaria, Saxony, Hanover, etc. As such, it is usually translated as "territorial."

Obrigkeit: literally "overness" and is a general term referring to authority, usually civil. It is here translated as "ruling authority."

Polizei: see the comments in the Preface below (p. xxix).

Revolution versus **revolution**: where the context is clear, I have capitalized references to the French Revolution but have not done so for references to revolution in general.

Staatlich: literally "state-like," the best translation would probably be "statist" if that word did not already have such entrenched (negative) connotations. I translate it as "state-oriented," thus expressive of the character of the modern state.

Staatsrecht: usually translated as "constitutional law" or "public law" although neither of these is adequate, "constitutional law" because it leaves out administrative law, and "public law" because in Germany this included ecclesiastical law, church law, which obviously stands outside the state. "State law" is both the literal translation and the most accurate one.

Ständisch: literally "estate-ish," having to do with the phenomenon "estate" [*Stand*] which in German is something entirely different than it is in English. In German an estate is first and foremost a complex of vocation, class, and status; secondly, as "the estates," it refers to the body which represents these complexes taken as a group.

Subject: translates either *Subjekt* or *Unterthan*. *Subjekt* refers to "the person or self considered as a conscious agent" (Oxford University Press. (n.d.). Subject, n., II.8. In *Oxford English dictionary,* retrieved March 21, 2025, from https://doi.org/10.1093/OED/7487744047). *Unterthan* refers to a person subject to authority, as for example subjects of a king.

Verfassung and *Konstitution:* both refer to "constitution," but *Konstitution* usually refers to a written or at any rate a modern constitution, as opposed to a historical, received, unwritten constitution, while *Verfassung* is a general term embracing all forms of constitution. This explains the phrase "constitutional constitution," which is a translation of *konstitutionelle Verfassung.*

Weltanschauung, vision of the world, is translated in the accepted manner as worldview. Stahl was one of the original proponents of the worldview approach.

The notion of worldview took wing when, in the face of the rationalism which was predominant in the 18th century, speculative philosophy began to postulate the primacy of prerational vision, the presuppositional framework on the basis of which reason operates. This had the effect of making explicit the subjectivism which was already rampant but was left unexamined, lying hidden under the guise of rational objectivity. Worldview-ism certainly is a product of that turn; worldview could be and has been abused – converted into subjectivism – but the abuse does not negate the use. Stahl demonstrates as much as he outlines here the Christian worldview in its philosophical and scientific application.

GENERAL PREFACE TO THE DOCTRINE OF LAW AND STATE ON THE BASIS OF THE CHRISTIAN WORLDVIEW

<xv> Together with the *History of Legal Philosophy*, *The Doctrine of Law and State on the Basis of the Christian Worldview* comprises Friedrich Julius Stahl's magnum opus, *The Philosophy of Law.* This multivolume production provides us with the philosophical foundations upon which Stahl's career as a professor of state law, as a parliamentarian, and as a statesman in 19th century Bavaria and Prussia was based.[1] It is also unique: it is the only comprehensive work of legal philosophy produced by a modern, post-French-Revolution conservative, to wit, a follower of the pioneer in this regard, Edmund Burke.

Conservatism has always been in need of such a comprehensive philosophical system. For opposition to the Revolution did not necessarily lead to unity of worldview. Many conservatives were Roman Catholic and hence argued for a return to (idealized) pre-revolutionary conditions in church and state, thus for the primacy of the monarchy and the papacy – these generally bore the name Counter-Revolutionary. Others were Protestant, and thus perceived a need to move beyond pre-revolutionary conditions, albeit in a manner which maintained continuity with the political, legal, and cultural inheritance of Europe. Among the latter group Stahl was pre-eminent; he was the first of the so-called Anti-Revolutionaries, who in the Netherlands even formed a political party under the leadership of Guillaume Groen van Prinsterer and, later, Abraham Kuyper.

Stahl was a protege of Friedrich Carl von Savigny, himself the pioneer of the "Burkean" worldview in Germany. Savigny is best **<xvi>** known for his argument against codification and in favor of legal continuity, including the primacy of customary law, as contained in his *On the Vocation of Our Age for Legislation and Legal Science*. Such arguments were completely in line with what Edmund Burke had argued in his *Reflections on the Revolution in France* and elsewhere. Savigny

---

[1] For more on Stahl's life see Alvarado, *Authority Not Majority* (Aalten: WordBridge, 2007); G. Groen van Prinsterer, *In Memory of Stahl* (Aalten: Pantocrator Press, 2022).

founded what came to be known as the Historical School of Jurisprudence, perhaps the most influential school of legal science Germany ever produced.

The problem with this school was that it lacked a solid grounding in legal philosophy. Writing in 1901, James Viscount Bryce, the noted legal historian and diplomat of late 19th-early 20th century Britain, claimed that in view of its methodology it is "more applicable to the law of any particular country than to the theory of law in general, for the details of legal history vary so much in different countries that immense knowledge and unusual architectonic power are needed to combine their general results for the purposes of a comprehensive theory" (*Studies in History and Jurisprudence*, II, p. 186). Indeed, Bryce considered the task so monumental that he doubted it had ever been done, though it "may be done, and so will doubtless be done some day. Everything happens at last."

As a matter of fact, the task had long since been accomplished, even by someone "of the requisite capacity" as stipulated by Bryce.[2] In fact, Stahl had already published the first edition of his *The Doctrine of Law and State on the Basis of the Christian Worldview*, presenting a legal philosophy sprung from the loins of the Savignian historical method, back in the 1830s when he was a young law professor in Bavaria. Savigny recognized it as providing the essential underpinnings in eternal verities that he himself had failed to produce.[3] And in providing this service, Stahl not only gave the Histori- **<xvii>** cal School a philosophical basis, he gave the Burkean common law school of thought a basis as well, although the Anglo-Saxon world of jurisprudence was unaware of it, then as now.

The English common law has never enjoyed the philosophical attention that has been lavished on Continental legal systems. The reason is of course its being

---

[2] For more on the curious ignorance of Stahl on the part of future generations, see the preface to Groen van Prinsterer, *In Memory of Stahl*.

[3] For an alternative interpretation of this development, see John E. Toews, "The Immanent Genesis and Transcendent Goal of Law: Savigny, Stahl, and the Ideology of the Christian German State," *The American Journal of Comparative Law*, 37, no. 2 (Winter, 1989), 139–169; idem, *Becoming Historical: Cultural Reformation and Public Memory in Early Nineteenth-Century Berlin* (New York: Cambridge University Press, 2004), ch. 5: "The Tension Between Immanent and Transcendent Subjectivity in the Historical School of Law: From Savigny to Stahl."

a product of court practice without being made the continuous subject of scholarly analysis, as was done on the Continent. Even so, this did not preclude the development of a unique legal philosophy which, although it did not attain to the sophistication of Continental efforts, nevertheless developed into a full-fledged philosophical jurisprudence in its own right, inoculating the legal system from the challenge of natural-rights jurisprudence and enlightened-despot codification efforts the likes of which took over on the Continent during the 18th century Enlightenment. The common-law approach pioneered by Edward Coke, John Selden, and Matthew Hale (Coke and Hale were chief justices) provided the basis for Burke's political philosophy. And from this root came the Continental resurgence of conservatism, which had been driven out of business by Enlightenment rationalism.[4]

Regardless of the success this approach had both in preserving English common-law traditions and in reinvigorating Continental common-law traditions, in terms of legal philosophy it remained rudimentary. William Blackstone's *Commentaries on the Laws of England* (1769), which served as target practice for Jeremy Bentham and his utilitarianism, is paradigmatic in this regard. Indeed, from Bentham onward it might be stated that utilitarianism and pragmatism have been the leading philosophical approaches for dealing with the common law (e.g., Oliver Wendell Holmes, Roscoe Pound). And that legacy lives on into the present day (as witness its latest iteration, "Law and Economics," as exemplified in the work of Richard **<xviii>** Posner and Richard Epstein). The alternative is a natural-rights school of thought based essentially on John Locke and the *Declaration of Independence*, and which in consequence is constantly fighting a rear-guard action against French Revolutionary principles.

It might seem anachronistic that help on this front would come from, of all places, pre-Bismarckian Germany. But the sense of anachronism fades when one realizes the affinity between the pre-Revolutionary Continental and English legal systems. It is the divergence between these two which is constantly emphasized; but how is it, then, that Burke could postulate a fundamental legal continuity across Western Europe which was only ruptured by the French Revolution? Indeed, Savigny and his followers recognized in English common law a

---

[4] On this most interesting history, see Harold J. Berman, "The Origins of Historical Jurisprudence: Coke, Selden, Hale," *Yale Law Journal* 103, no. 7 (1994).

cognate legal system to the German pre-codification legal system. Which is what makes Stahl's legal philosophy so interesting to common-law legal science. Stahl provides principles applicable to the English common law as well as Continental law, for he draws upon the common inheritance of Western legal science such as described in part by Harold Berman in his *Law and Revolution*,[5] a legal science sharing essential characteristics, maintaining similar institutions, pursuing similar goals.

Stahl provides an understanding of the solid, unchanging foundations to the evolving, adapting thing which is the common law. Considerations of utility and pragmatism are made subordinate to principles of justice and what he calls providential purposes, within the context of historical development. Burke's partnership "between those who are living, those who are dead, and those who are to be born"[6] finds a distinct echo here, as does his conceptualization of rights as inheritance rather than *a priori,* a-historical givens. Likewise, rights are made subordinate to law rather than being the source of law as conceived by the natural-rights school. What's more, Stahl provides subjective right with a clear **<xix>** position and demarcation within the legal system, which is a feat in itself and, perhaps more than anything else, is needed in today's confused, rights-bloated jurisprudence.

The concept he uses to establish these foundations is that of a *doctrine* of law and state. In the introduction he provided to Volume II as a whole (see *Philosophical Foundations*, p. 1), Stahl explains this notion of doctrine: it is something other than jurisprudence on the one hand and legal philosophy on the other. Jurisprudence is the science of a particular legal system as it exists in a particular country at a particular time; legal philosophy is its opposite, bringing "law and state into connection with the highest cause and the final goal of all existence" (*Philosophical Foundations,* p. 2). The doctrine of law and state occupies an intermediate position. It generalizes from jurisprudence while it particularizes from legal **<xiv>** philosophy. It operates in terms of universals but fleshes out those universals in terms of the particulars provided by jurisprudence. In so

---

[5] Harold J. Berman, *Law and Revolution: The Formation of the Western Legal Tradition* (Cambridge, MA: Harvard University Press, 1983).

[6] Edmund Burke, *Reflections on the Revolution in France* (Oxford, England: Oxford University Press, 1993), p. 110.

doing it provides universal criteria out of which particular legal systems can be generated and by which they can be judged.

Stahl bases this doctrine of law and state on the Christian worldview: because historically the nations of Western civilization likewise were based on that worldview, and because every such universal doctrine must base itself on one worldview or another. "Every philosophical system of whatever name in the final analysis rests on a foundational presupposition that is nothing more than faith, no matter what claim it may make to so-called scientific certainty" (*Philosophical Foundations,* p. 3). So, ultimately Stahl provides us with a Christian common-law legal philosophy, in doing so epitomizing the Western legal tradition in its conservative variant.

PREFACE TO THE DOCTRINE OF STATE AND THE PRINCIPLES OF STATE LAW

"What might have been" is one of the games in which the historian enthusiastically dabbles. Usually this entails nothing more than something like a parlor game, although there are exceptions. Such as Operation Valkyrie in World War II: how differently would things have turned out if it had been successful? Something similar can be asked of the period with which this book deals. For it describes the form of law and government that was in the process of being solidified in Prussia prior to that country's transformation into what became known as the power-state of the German Empire. It outlines the blueprint which the King of Prussia, Friedrich Wilhelm IV, went about implementing during his reign, albeit with fits and starts. It held forth something vastly different from what would come. We will never know if it could have survived and prospered, because this process was terminated when Friedrich Wilhelm became incapacitated in 1857. At that point, his brother Wilhelm took over as regent. Already then, and the more so when he ascended to the throne upon Friedrich Wilhelm's death in 1861, Wilhelm brought with him the militarism and royal intransigence that his elder brother eschewed.

Everyone, it seems, saw that as a good thing. The standard interpretation we are given is that Wilhelm, through his Chancellor, Otto von Bismarck, transformed the Prussian system of government from Friedrich Wilhelm's rigid, romantic traditionalism into a flexible, executive-centered mechanism suited to the German Empire's needs. So goes the usual historiography. But what really happened is that Wilhelm transformed the Prussian system of government from Friedrich Wilhelm's *peace*-oriented, *confederation*-oriented monarchy *restricted* by Christian principles of right and wrong, war and peace, to Bismarck's *power-state Realpolitik* founded on sheer military prowess, eschewing no violation of the law of God or of nations to attain the self-imposed goal, Prussia's conquest of the independent German states and military defeat of rivals Austria and France, sowing seeds of enmity that would yield their pestilential harvest in less than 50 years. It was Bismarck's erstwhile mentor, Stahl's comrade-in-arms

Ludwig von Gerlach who exclaimed, "The Ten Commandments – he cannot bear them!"[7]

Indeed. And it is difficult for the questioning mind not to ask, how would history have been different if Friedrich Wilhelm had been granted the same lifespan as his brother, who died in 1888 and was only 1½ years his junior. For one thing, he would never have installed Bismarck in power. For another, he might have been able to implement and establish the form of government outlined in this book: a constitutional monarchy avowedly based on Christian principles, rooted in the Christian revelation, with no apologies and no crippling compromises. Such a government lodged in the center of Europe – a polity rooted in ethics rather than power – makes it difficult to imagine the series of events which culminated in two world wars and one "great depression."

But it was God's will to have things turn out differently. Apostasy has its consequences. At any rate, this book serves as testimony to what might have been. Even more than this, it serves as testimony to what we in our supposed superior wisdom have tossed aside – God's revelation and presence in public life. We know so much better! Things are so much more prosperous and well-arranged! Well now – by this time in the 21st century, we know differently.

Given all of this, the book you have before you constitutes a gauntlet thrown down before the modernist who cannot conceive of the state as anything other than the creature of the will of man, the construct of autonomous citizens. Even given its predilection for monarchy, it transcends the choice for monarchy versus republic. It is precisely that predilection which enabled Stahl to attain the depth it contains, for in defending monarchy in the face of a republican age, Stahl was forced to plumb depths of detail and philosophical penetration left unexplored by the self-assured ones who did not feel impelled by the same urgency to penetrate to the heart of the matter. For this reason, there is more to Stahl's discussion than meets the superficial eye.

For starters: the state for Stahl is, above all, a God-given reality. It is something which precedes the will of man, whether ruler or subject/citizen. Further-

---

[7] Quoted in Hans-Joachim Schoeps, *Das andere Preußen: Konservative Gestalten und Probleme im Zeitalter Friedrich Wilhelm IV* [The Other Prussia: Conservative Figures and Problems in the Age of Friedrich Wilhelm IV] (Berlin: Haude & Spener, 1981[5]), p. 66.

more, its existence is bound up with the existence of particular peoples and nations, for although it is a God-given reality, the state is also an expression of popular essence. This is the true popular character of law and state (cf. *Principles of Law*, §§. 2, 25) as opposed to what Stahl labels the revolutionary character of popular sovereignty as the ephemeral will of the people. This historical derivation is bound up with the God-givenness, and although the two cannot be equated, Stahl's high view of providential action in history dovetails with this profound respect for the received patrimony of an order of law and state which, to that extent at least, transcends the will of man.

<xxii> Does this mean that Stahl discounts this will of the people, the notion of the consent of the governed? No – rather, it means that his concept of sovereignty differs fundamentally from the modern Revolution concept, which makes the will, be it of the people, be it of the ruler, into a law. That will is thereby no longer subjected to any law, and in fact is a denial of the concept of a transcendent standard.

The transcendent standard is the first point of Stahl's conceptual framework. He then embeds this notion of transcendence within the concept of what he calls the ethical kingdom. This is the supreme category by which to understand human community. The ethical kingdom is "self-conscious, indivisible rule, in accordance with ethical-intellectual motives, over conscious, freely obedient beings, thereby also spiritually uniting them. Accordingly, it is rule of a personal character in every aspect, a *kingdom of personality*" (p. 1). The ethical kingdom is a kingdom, thus rule, over persons, but it is ethical rule, thus entailing the assent of those persons. Therefore, it is not rule over robots or slaves, but over freely-choosing, voluntarily submitting persons, by an ethically accountable, personal ruler, either individual or corporate. It is both law and personality; these are inextricably woven together; the objective, given order is intimately combined with the subjective, responsive act of free subjects.

The state is just such an ethical kingdom. It therefore partakes of the character of personality. In monarchy, this is evident in that the ruler is a physical personage; but it is just as much the case in a republic. For the ruling authority in a republic is likewise of a personal character, but in corporate form. This ruling personality stands over the people, otherwise it could not rule; this is its God-given status (Romans 13:1ff.; below, §§. 48–52).

The character of personality is crucial to Stahl's conception. Rule can never be of an entirely abstract, objective nature, as if natural laws existed which are self-evident and self-enforcing. Above all, God in Heaven rules over the affairs of men and makes His will known, and He empowers peoples and nations to participate in that rule, on their own account, and for their own benefit. As Stahl put it in the *Principles of Law:* **<xxiii>**

> Now then, in accordance with the self-reliance and unique originality that runs through the entire realm of personal being, the human community is to establish this order [i.e., the state], through which it maintains God's world order, *on its own as its own order*.... That is the high position and worth to which the human race is called. It is not simply to fulfill God's commands but also to establish and maintain this order as an instrument and vessel of world rule under God's influence. Man thereby assumes the godlike position of ethical steward, of lawgiver and judge.[8]

Both laws and persons are integral elements of the ethical kingdom. And the state is one form of that kingdom, a lower form given the fragmentary, irregular manner of its fulfillment of the ethical requirement, but nevertheless a full-fledged stage in the scale, so to speak, of ethical being.

The state is the form taken by human society as ethical kingdom: "the state is the *association of a people under a rulership* (*ruling authority*)" (§. 36 below). It is therefore more than just the government: it is the union of all the members of the nation into an ethical kingdom. Tellingly, Stahl distinguishes this from an ethical organism: "The organism contains determinate, various members, each of which mutually supplements the other, of which none have an independent existence, of which all, in fact, are required for the organism to exist (head, rump, two arms, legs, etc.). The kingdom, on the other hand, contains an unlimited quantity of equal, independent, existing beings, which neither mutually presuppose each other, nor are required for this concept the way they are in the case of the organism; they are subject to a higher rule" (§. 1 below). In other words, the state is not an organization; it is no group in which the members are subordinate and harnessed to the pursuit of a result; it is not a "command econo-

---

[8] Stahl, *Principles of Law*, p. 2 (1st ed., pp. 8–9).

my"; it is rather an association united by a general rule, both of government and of laws, wherein the members are autonomous and enjoy a relative independence while pursuing the common goal of a public ethi- **<xxiv>** cal order. Hence, "the state is... based not on the ethical vocation (ethos) of individual persons but on the ethical vocation of the human community (of the people) as a whole" (§. 36 below).

Accordingly, the state has two poles, which Stahl elsewhere characterizes as "institutional" and "congregational."[9] In the same way that the church embodies these two aspects, the state has an institutional, "top-down" element, which in monarchy is primary, and a congregational or associational, "bottom-up" element, which in a republic is primary. Both of these poles need to be accounted for in a properly constituted state, just as they exist in every form of ethical kingdom. It is not all subjection and it is not all autonomy and independence. Historically, the progression is for monarchy to be more fully supplemented by popular representation. But the latter is no end in itself; the state must ever remain a vehicle of order and authority, no matter the level of popular participation. And the ruling authority exists on the basis of divine right, regardless of the degree to which popular participation and the consent of the governed become reflected in it.

This is ultimately reflected in what Stahl (*Private Law*, §. 21) refers to as the "Two Poles of World Order: The Fear of God and Full Humanity." Contemporary society has taken on board the concept of full humanity, which constitutes its true claim to fame: the principle of humanity, the recognition of the rights of man, "the idea that the well-being, the right, the honor of every individual, even the most humble, is the concern of the community, which views each person in accordance with his individuality, which protects, honors, looks after him without regard for descent, class, race, gift, as long as he has a human face" (*Private Law*, p. 37). But in doing so it has forgotten the fear of God, the source of goals and higher principles, the elevating principle in life. "The state [in the modern conception] is based solely on human rights, not on higher goals; this is the sympathy for all opposition against all authority; it lacks the recognition of unconditional commands for the legal order. From this springs op- **<xxv>** position to the death penalty and in fact to any sort of punishment.... From this

[9] See my biography of Stahl, *Authority Not Majority*, pp. 29ff.

everywhere stems the revolt against all discipline, against all restrictions established for the fulfillment of a higher order of life" (*Private Law*, p. 39).

In terms of the state, this one-sided contemporary philosophy is expressed in a one-sided emphasis on law and freedom without any recognition of the concept of ruling authority. "The newer school of thought as it confronts us in the great multitudes and in the entire age, has appropriated essential aspects of the ethical kingdom (freedom, self-action of peoples and individuals, the law as the all-permeating necessity of public life, in contrast to arbitrary rule), but in exchange has forfeited the first and foremost of those aspects, the given higher real authority, the ruling authority, for and over the people, in which the people is to become politically unified" (p. 6 below). This one-sidedness leads to the loss of an understanding of law as anything other than a man-made construct. "Accordingly, it does not conceive of law as a given higher thing, as the law of the great institution that passes through the ages as one and the same, albeit in constant advancement; rather, for this school, the law is merely a self-made thing, the will of the then-living generation" (p. 6).

The times, then as now, are in need of the restoration of both of these principles together in a harmonious unity: "not the ongoing one-sided advance of humanity and the rights of man, but the restoration of the fear of God as the energetic principle in both hearts and public institutions, while in it and through it preserving humanity and the rights of man" (*Private Law*, p. 41).

If we do this, we will also recover the proper understanding of the *common good*. This is something entirely different from the sum of private goods, which is what modern political philosophy has made of it. But that is to compromise the common good altogether. Such a misconception is a manifestation of that "aggregationism" (p. 25) and "persons-representation" (p. 265) against which Stahl polemicizes, as if society and the state were composed simply of aggregated individuals without structure, order, or institutions. None of this, for the common good is distinguished from private goods and individual ends taken in themselves. It is the function of a collective existence, a collective personality which transcends individual existences, and has its own goals and purposes.

> The state is therefore based not on the ethical vocation (ethos) of individuals but on the ethical vocation of the human community (of the people) as a whole. Certainly, individuals everywhere pursue satisfaction in life and fulfilment of

> morals; both of these goods are the purpose of all human effort, and thus they expect assistance from the state in this task, which the state must provide. But this does not exhaust the nature of the state; it is not merely or primarily the means to satisfaction and morals of individuals, but it itself is *a kingdom* of morals and reasonable purposes through the shape and action which it has as a whole (pp. 75–76).

This common condition is distinct from the particular conditions and situations of private persons. As such, we see in this a circumscription of the action of the state. Such action is restricted to that common condition, so that the state is not to interfere in the legitimate private activity of individuals. "The state being the *fulfillment of the life-task of the nation* and not the fulfillment of the life-task of individuals, its rule is restricted to the common condition; the ordering and determination of one's innermost individual life is ever God's affair, not that of human rule" (p. 76).

This also suggests the sphere of the state's positive action. The state is called not only to maintain and uphold the law, but it also has activities to carry out for the common good. Here again, it is the *common* good that is determinative; the action of the state is neither to usurp the action nor further the ends of particular persons. This yields the area of public welfare.

In the continental legal-political tradition, this activity is referred to as the "police," which explains why Stahl uses the term *Polizei* for it.[10] It is not law enforcement, but all manner of activity carried out for the public benefit. "According to the nature and purpose of the state as discussed above (§. 39), only the *common life*, not that of the individual, can be the task of the public welfare, thus only the *common well-being*, not the well-being of the individual. The common life and the common well-being are not the life and well-being of all the individuals for themselves but in their communal life, hence of the individuals only in

[10] An interesting discussion in English of this activity is provided by Adam Smith in his *Lectures on Jurisprudence.* That Smith would use this terminology is explained by the fact that Scotland, his home country, has a Roman-law background which it shares with continental Europe, as opposed to England's common-law tradition, which does not share such a background. Apparently "police" (cognate terms include policy and politics) was an outgrowth of that tradition.

so far as they are members of the community, not insofar as they have an independent individual existence and destiny, an independent individual aim and pursuit" (p. 422). Included here are public morality, public education (which in Stahl's state must be confessionally Christian), public health, land-use planning, provisions for public safety, construction and maintenance of roadways, and many more such-like "common goods."

All of this befits the twofold nature of the state as ethical kingdom, with its law aspect and personality aspect. Stahl champions monarchy by highlighting, within this twofold nature, the personality aspect, precisely because in monarchy a real individual person embodies the power of the state in himself. Upon this basis he builds his doctrine of the **monarchical principle**, which is probably what he was and is best known for, certainly in his day.

In the monarchical principle, the prince

- possesses power to execute the laws
- controls the entire administrative sphere
  - public welfare regulation
  - administrative dispositions
- drafts laws
- sets the budget

For its part, the representative body

- has the right of consent to new legislation
- has the right of petition
- has the right of consent to laws affecting the legal sphere of the individual and affecting the constitution itself
- does not have the right of unconditional refusal of the budget
- does cooperate in establishing main categories of allowable expenditure
- cannot modify the budget and so force the prince to bow to its will
- can modify or cancel existing taxes, if they are not necessary to the government's functioning

In all of this, the difference with the parliamentary system as developed in England is evident. In the parliamentary system, it is the representative body which legislates, which sets the budget, which has the power to hold the king's ministers accountable to itself. In the monarchical principle, all these powers accrue to the monarch.

The difference between the two systems revolves around whether rule will be exercised by the prince or the representative body. If the prince rules, there is a balance between the prince and the representative body, as they form two independent seats of power, whereas in the parliamentary system, the balance is lost because the prince is entirely absorbed into the representative body. Stahl argues for a higher synthesis: "May the point in time arrive that energy toward both sides is possible, that a clear and full consciousness develops, and, thereby, a guarantee everywhere to defend the one bravely without overstepping the other! May the popular-rule party and the royal party be subsumed into a higher view of the state as the ethical intellectual kingdom, in which the ethical authority elevated over the people, which is the king, and the people itself as ethical community, take up their necessary and firmly delimited position" (pp. 291–292).

In one sense, Stahl's monarchical principle constitutes a continuation of the medieval doctrine of the estates. In that system, the representative body acts not as the primary government institution, the way it does in the parliamentary system, but as a control and a check on the primary government institution, which is monarchy. This check-and-balance function of the estates (something altogether different from the checks and balances of the separation of powers, of which more below) was maintained in Stahl's monarchical principle. But he also argued for its truly representative national character. The medieval estates did not act in representative fashion. Instead, they acted only in the interest of their own class, whether aristocracy or clergy or bourgeoisie. Stahl's estates were to act in the national interest, through proper representation of all the elements of society. Its powers, while not the center of gravity of the state, constituted a significant counterweight to the power of government and gave a significant voice to the nation at large.

The effect had by the monarchical principle differed depending upon the spirit in which it was conducted. During the reign of Friedrich Wilhelm IV, it was conducted basically along the lines Stahl sketched, whereby ethical, and specifically Christian ethical principles were adhered to, leading to governmental restraint, in particular with respect to foreign relations and the military. Wilhelm I and Otto von Bismarck stripped it of its ethical heart and used it to pursue unpopular and even unconstitutional policies in the face of an obstructionist representation. Bismarck resorted to unconstitutional methods to finance his military buildup, but when his policy led to victory over Austria in 1866, those budgetary resorts were retroactively approved by the representation, demonstrating hereby the proof of the adage, "nothing succeeds like success." It also demonstrated the vacuity of the liberal opposition, whose principles vanished in the face of the successful use of power.

What benefit can we derive from Stahl's monarchical principle? Just this: we can view it as an attempt to establish constitutional order, a true rule of law, over and above the political order. We can view it as an attempt to restrict politics to the area in which such practices which characterize the political process as horse-trading and logrolling are the appropriate means for arriving at decisions, while keeping politics out of the areas in which those methods are inappropriate, in which higher principles must rule. This is the true constitutionalism. Such constitutionalism must increase while politics must decrease, and in this the divine order, God's Word as the source of law and the ground of authority and the church as the public expounder of that Word, must all be readmitted to the public square. The monarchical principle accomplished just this; the parliamentary or representative system accomplished just the opposite. It became the vehicle of man-centered, God-denying power. Politics must be reined in by a transcendent law and authority. This is the crying need of our age, heirs as we are of unbelief and revolution.

The doctrine of the separation of powers was supposed to provide a competent substitute to this higher-law arrangement. However, it being a corollary of the parliamentary-representative system, it masked the fatal flaw afflicting this system. It purports to restrict power primarily by separating the legislative and the executive powers (an independent judiciary, being a part of the monarchical principle as well, is not a distinguishing characteristic). **<xxvi>** But in this separation it misunderstands the nature of law and the nature of government; failing properly to distinguish between these two, it ends up melding them together, in fact making law the creature of government, thereby rendering irrelevant the separation of the executive from the legislative. That separation only shifts the center of gravity from the executive to the legislative. And because the legislative power has complete control over the law, we end up precisely with the subsumption of law into power – the rule of will rather than the rule of law. Stahl's argument anticipates Friedrich von Hayek's in his seminal *Law, Legislation, and Liberty: Vol. 3: The Political Order of a Free People* (Chicago: University of Chicago Press, 1979). Having provided an extended discussion of **<xxvii>** this topic in my book *Common Law & Natural Rights: The Question of Conservative Foundations* (Aalten: WordBridge, 2009), I refer the reader to that work for further details.

The primacy of will over law finds further expression in a legal system in which codification has taken over and in which customary law is eliminated. This is the death-knell to the common law, which works not by comprehensive legislative fiat but by the adjudicatory process. Stahl refers to codification repeatedly in this book, but reference should also be made to his discussion in *Principles of Law* (§. 21). In line with the German "Historical School" of jurisprudence, of which he was a representative, Stahl viewed law as being generated primarily by custom and secondarily by legislation. This led, on the one hand, to his claim that the law was a distinct entity, apart from state power (the ruling authority). The two together formed the state's rule or dominion (§. 53 below). Accordingly, legislation corrects and adapts the received law without rewriting it. The hubris which presumes to generate a legal system out of its own resources is anathema to Stahl and the Historical School. The law as the expression of the "popular ethos" stands as a coordinate power in the state, conditioning and restricting the ruling authority. This is the case even in absolute monarchy (§§. 125ff. below).

An independent judiciary forms an essential element in Stahl's constitutional framework. And in fact he highlights its existence in the received historical monarchies, even those deemed absolute. But he also points out that the judiciary has only a limited role to play in determining the constitutionality of laws passed and measures taken by the government.

Stahl's discussion of federalism is also of interest. He does not devote an inordinate amount of attention to it, which is interesting in the light of various federalism-oriented projects under way at the time of his writing, envisioning a united Germany. Since he generally viewed the project of unification as a rather impracticable ideal, he did not devote much attention to the question of how it could be accomplished. But he did discuss federalism in the context of republicanism. In fact, he viewed federalism as the logical development of republicanism. For at bottom republicanism is a function of local communities which join together to form an associational union. This fundamental difference in origin explains why the U. S. Constitution is impracticable as a model for European countries. The divergence in origin is too great. The U. S. Constitution is tailored to the demands of a localist state structure, where power gravitates to the local community, and greater state unions are **<xxviii>** composite. This is fundamentally different from the organic union formed by European nations, which they have by virtue of having grown out of tribal structures (see §§. 87, 131 below).

One area which will strike modern readers is Stahl's effusive praise for government proper. These sections (e.g., §. 57) have the merit of highlighting the positive, indeed necessary, role government plays, in addition to merely enforcing the laws, national defense, and the like. But they also reveal the lack of experience with governments "gone wild" since then, governments which have gone far to create a sham citizenry focused on the proverbial bread and circuses, and looking to government to meet their every need and solve their every problem. In his defense, Stahl is quite aware of the dangers posed by mechanistic, centralized, bureaucratic government, examples of which are scattered throughout the text.

Another note of interest involves Stahl's discussion of written versus unwritten constitutions. His discussion complements nicely the current scholarly interest in what has become known as "common-law constitutionalism," [11] whereby the written constitution is viewed as being the main, but not sole, embodiment of the constitution, and where the body of the common law is viewed as likewise of the level of constitutional law, providing both context and additional content to the written constitution. Stahl's discussion, as contained in particular in §. 82 below, emphasizes the essentially unwritten nature of the con-

---

[11] For example, Douglas Edlin, "Judicial Review Without a Constitution," in *Polity*, vol. 38, no. 3 (2006), pp. 345ff.; Edlin, *Judges and Unjust Laws: Common Law Constitutionalism and the Foundations of Judicial Review* (Ann Arbor: University of Michigan Press, 2008). See also James R. Stoner, *Common Law and Liberal Theory: Coke, Hobbes, and the Origins of American Constitutionalism* (Lawrence, Kansas: University Press of Kansas, 1992); idem., *Common-Law Liberty: Rethinking American Constitutionalism* (Lawrence, Kansas: University Press of Kansas, 2003).

stitution, and provides helpful criteria for determining the proper role of written constitutions, which should be kept in mind even today, when written constitutions are considered the be-all and end-all of constitutionalism.

One subject of great interest is Stahl's discussion of the press. In our day the lack of objectivity and indeed partiality of the press is generally acknowledged. We have the idea that it did not used to be so. In Stahl's day, it was very much so. In the preface to the third edition, he complained of the lack of coverage given to the successes of the conservative party: "What this party has achieved is, of course, not mentioned in the daily press, which only celebrates what is of the press's own spirit; but its deeds and successes bear witness to it" (p. xlvii). Further down he names that spirit, which turns out to be bourgeois liberalism. "The propertied citizen class (*bourgeoisie*)... is the source of all the institutions [the press] advocate," including "the rejection of revealed religion, and the church founded upon it, in favor of the religion of reason" and "the complete freedom of the individual." It is this class which demands power in the name of the people, and it does it through the press, which for its part pursues its perennial object: ginning up unrest. "The daily press is generally nothing other than a daily call to action: let us take up the reins of government, let us bring to bear only our (the people's) will in the state and make the king into the bare executor thereof. Newspapers of contrary tendency have difficulty maintaining themselves in any decisive number if at all, because readers and customers wish to read about how they are to command, not how they are to obey" (p. 359). But of course, once this class gets into power, press coverage goes from activism to acquiescence. "Now that the reader of and buyer of dailies, the bourgeoisie, the gentry, themselves predominate in the government, the press must as natural law (to be marketable and to strike a chord) represent the existing order and not seek to overthrow it. In fact it is now the ruling class which is strongly inclined, not to give up freedom of the press in principle, which could be dusted off if needed for the sake of the political position, but in practice to restrict it as much as possible" (pp. 359–360). Press restriction is then pursued, this time against the up-and-coming "proletarian" press, which however does not have the resources to pose the same kind of threat to the new establishment – at least, not at this stage. "The danger of the Chartist and proletarian press is not of the same degree to the power of the possessors as is the liberal press to the power of the monarchy; for, on the one hand, the proletariat cannot provide its press with the same level of income and recognition, and, on the other, the propertied… themselves as mass are much more secure vis-à-vis the proletariat than is the monarch, who over against the citizenry has nothing other than faith in his authority" (p. 360).

There is much more, both of theoretical and of historical interest. In particular, the discussion of the historical growth of the **<xxix>** ancient estates-systems into modern representative bodies (§§. 101ff.) is of the utmost importance to understanding the history of representative government. Of course, the critique of the French Revolution and its spawn retains its relevance, as the progeny of that revolution continue to pursue dominance in today's world. Stahl's work is a powerful antidote to such thinking. If it is not applicable in its entirety, it is at least thorough in its appraisal of the underlying issues, which is more than can be said of most such treatments. And it records a most tantalizing "what might have been."

AUTHOR'S PREFACE TO THE THIRD EDITION

The third edition of the *Doctrine of State* which I hereby offer to the public has been greatly expanded besides being thoroughly checked. The expanded chapters are mainly: on the community (§§. 7–9) – on the estates and society (§. 14) – on the nature of the state (§§. 36 and 38) – on the constitution of the state (§. 83) – on the press (§. 141) – on popular sovereignty (§§. 147 and 148). Chapters have been added on the governmental rights of the landowners – regarding the distinction between constitutional and other laws – the oath to the constitution and the cure of destructive constitutions – territorial representation after 1848 – absolute monarchy – the republic – the declaration of rights – of the right of the people to rebel. It was my intention to add a fifth part, on the relation of the state to religion and the church, but that would have overly expanded the volume. I therefore reserve the right to publish the details of this in the near future.

In terms of the system of this work, the *Doctrine of State,* like the prior edition, follows the three books which form the remainder of the second volume (*Philosophical Foundations – Principles of Law – Private Law*), as the fourth book (state or public law). The quotations from the first volume (on the history of legal philosophy) are therefore referenced by book and section. But although the doctrine of state forms a supplementary part of *The Philosophy of Law* as a whole, it is nevertheless a *self-contained work* on the state, independent of all the other parts of the entire opus.

It is especially with regard to the doctrine of state that I, with this third edition of 1856, stand before the public in an entirely different light than with the second edition in 1846, since my entire parliamentary career lies in the interim. It comes with the heightened significance and increased responsibility which attend the actual deed. The principles which it professes, or principles related to them, have become, through the cooperation of men and events, the program of a party which is great and, through its influence in the country, powerful; they have become a factor in the public condition; my responsibility has become a shared one. But with the increased prominence has come increased hostility. I have neither contempt for nor indifference to this hostility, for I do not consider the old common ground of moral and scientific judgment to have been so demolished that one need not concern oneself with those on the other side. But I do have a calm consciousness with regard to it. I have not provoked the opinion of the time, I have not sought wantonly to embitter it, but rather I everywhere seek understanding with it, as far as possible. Yet in opposition to it I could not help but uphold the truth I had recognized, in all its acuity and determinacy, and if this annoys anyone, it is not my fault. In particular, however, I have the reassurance that it is not merely false judgment but mainly false statements and insinuation by which I am opposed.

If it is a reproach that I have defended the divine right of the authorities, legitimacy, the monarchical principle, the Christian state, the historical order, as I have done in my published work for a quarter of a century as well as in my activity as a statesman, then I gladly take this reproach upon myself. But I have as little denied the love of constitutional order, the guaranteed rights of land and subjects, in the one as in the other. I and my friends have resisted the repeated efforts to establish an unrestricted form of government by legal means; we have everywhere preserved the rights of the representation of the country which are compatible with monarchy, and if the fullest energy has not been expended for the development and guarantee of even well-founded new freedoms, it must be borne in mind that after the explosion of 1848 had caused such shock and destruction, with liberalism having prevailed for more than a century in doctrine and more than half a century in the measures of governments, the primary requirement was and still is first of all to consolidate the true foundations of public order, and then to strengthen the government which maintains them. The inviolable right of the person, and the freedom of thought and of intellectual movements, is no less an object for us than for the Liberal party, although we do not permit ourselves to strive for it with equal ruthlessness and exclusivity; while the danger of being oppressed and silenced, as experience shows even under the most favorable circumstances, is much greater and nearer to us than to them. Truly, then, arbitrary government, absolutism, oppression by mechanical powers is neither our ideal nor our interest. But we have nothing at all in common with advice to establish order and the possibility or perhaps merely the convenience of governing by violence and the violation of law and oath, nothing in common with the exaggerated loyalty which holds that the more complete the denial of everything that for a century has been striven for as free and good, the greater the political correctness. It is a deplorable error to think that the catastrophe of 1848 was merely the result of a small oversight, that an impotent popular uprising was not put down with the requisite energy of bayonets and cartridges, and that the same thing could not happen again since Cavaignac and Changarnier discovered the military means by which to counter the barricades, and statesmen came to the realization that they should not make concessions. That catastrophe – call it a riot or a revolution – was a divine judgment, and a judgment not only on the sins of the people but on the sins of the authorities as well. The very fact that such insignificant forces caused such a convulsion that the thrones of kings and emperors, themselves supported by armies, fell before a handful of laborers and students is a confirmation of this. It is, of course, a sin on the part of the authorities to give away the authority God gave them out of fear or in pursuit of popular favor, and it is only too true that this was practiced to the fullest at that time. But it is no less a sin of the authorities to disregard right and oath, to take the self-chosen path of violence, or to exploit the office consecrated to the public good as a domain for self-will and self-ends, rather than the God-ordained path of legality, which requires patience and perseverance. It is no less a sin of the authorities to surrender the honor of the true God and His revelation and the right of the churches founded on them to the temporal will of men, or to play high-handed games with things sacred; and it is the height of the sin of the authorities to commit wrongs against men and then to desire to counterbalance the resulting disfavor via wrongs against God by consorting with unbelief. I have never knowingly abetted any of these sins of the authorities, either by word or deed, inside or outside of Prussia, in my public or in my private actions.

My and my comrades' only approach to *the German affair* is to apply the principles of authority and of a law that stands above the people and the present generation. It is not based on particularist isolation, nor on a lack of sense of unity and greatness of the German nation. We were "not angry with the German cause, but only with the revolutionary cause." The uprising of 1848 was not primarily a national but a democratically liberal uprising, for if a completely unified Germany under an absolute monarchy, or at least under predominantly princely power in the manner of the German Empire, had been on offer, the present state of a fragmented Germany with its Baden-Württemberg-Hessian chambers still would have been preferred. It therefore placed itself from the beginning and through all stages on the foundation of popular sovereignty, and its plan and work was only the execution of the general template of the revolution. The *basic rights of the Germans* were the principles of the *French of 1789*. The constitution of the Reich was a republic – a democratically constituted republic under the name of the empire. Only through the deliberate breach of the oath by the King of Prussia could it become capable of governing, if that were possible at all.

Moreover, true and lofty as the idea of German unity is, the manner in which it was carried out, the plan of a German *constitutional federal state*, as I have already shown there, was an impossibility.[12] Such a composite and yet unified body of government as was aimed at under the name of federal state can only be either an association of princes, like the German Empire, or an association of sovereign popular assemblies, like the North American Union; it cannot be an association of both princes and assemblies of subjects, so must either be monarchical or republican, but not [in this sense] constitutional. That the subjects of the German territorial princes should turn around and, as members of the German national representation, have legislative power over their territorial princes, is a political monstrosity. The authentic German Empire had the insight that he who is a tenant of a territorial prince [landsässig] could not be a member of the imperial estates [reichsständisch], and he who is a tenant of a local lord [hintersässig] could not be a member of the territorial estates [landständisch]. The inauthentic German Empire could not have had this insight, it having abandoned the concept of ruling authority upon which it rested; and because this latter is the basis on which the undertaking took its start, the consequence would certainly have been the loss of ruling authority altogether. Even mechanically, a constitutional monarchy that was to consist of constitutional monarchies was a union of all the poles – royal center, unified representation of the people, multiplicity of sovereign princes and provincial representatives – an insoluble problem, and such a complicated and impossible constitution would have had to be transformed into a simple and possible one, and that, since safeguards against it were refused, would have become the sovereignty of the unified representation of the people. But even the Erfurt Union Constitution sought to solve this impossible problem; it did not provide any safeguards against a transition to a republic, and in fact destroyed monarchical sovereignty in principle

---

[12] See my pamphlet *Die deutsche Reichsverfassung*, p. 23, and my speech in the Erfurt Second Chamber, April 12th, 1850.

by establishing a jurisdiction over royal law. Nor was the directorial project[13] in the least a corrective to this. It might have prevented all the other princes from coming under one prince, but it would have made all the more certain that the entire body of princes, through internal rivalry, would have come under Parliament, and, moreover, would not have guaranteed the desired unity.

Should it now be considered a lack of national spirit that we did not consent to the destruction of the institutions and goods of the German nation, and that we did not want to let the state itself, which is a center of German civilization, a bearer of German glorious history, perish in the chaos from which, as gullible hope would have it, a unified, powerful Germany should arise? Should it be due to a lack of national spirit that we resisted the disloyalty of the Frankfurt resolutions, that we joined the Erfurt proposal only with hesitant caution and only under restrictions and conditions? That although we were by no means opposed to the constitutional federal state, we insisted on an institution of it according to which, in the event of its inevitable alteration and transformation into another form of state, the monarchical power and the Prussian kingdom would be secured as the fixed and unchangeable point? If the honor and power of the German nation, which can only be achieved through unity, really is the supreme consideration, then the liberal party might renounce its idol of popular power in favor of it. A monarchically unified Germany, as under the old empire and with even stronger royal power than had existed since the Hohenstaufen, is at least a possible form of government, and it might therefore perhaps have been achievable. But just to say that would have been considered madness or impudence. Is it merely because of our lack of national spirit that we have not renounced our conscientious conviction regarding the right of existing legitimate authorities, and our political conviction of the necessity of a monarchical constitution? And if we had relinquished it, and they who were to make the decision had relinquished it, would the desired unity have been secured, would it even have been probable? Would the Republic, with or without a constitutional façade, have provided a guarantee for it? Is not the jealousy among the German territories [Stämmen] at least as great as among the German princes?

Our position in the Eastern question is also determined by these principles. To be sure, our immediate motive was the *power-relation of the states*, that

---

13 [A reference to a proposal by Austria to appoint a ruling directorate of seven princes.]

Germany should not promote a preponderance of either the Western powers or Russia. But it was also our motive that the *power-relation of principles* should ensure that the Revolution, which proceeds from the West in an interrupted but recurring thrust, should not establish its undisputed empire in Europe, that Germany should retain a proven alliance with Russia against it, which, according to its natural conditions, is the bearer of monarchical authority, of historical order, of ecclesiastical state foundations; and it was our motive in particular that Germany should not draw her sword in a war for the integrity of the Mahomedan empire over Christian subjects. And has not the outcome already confirmed our opinion only too well? Has this Mahomedan empire really been taken up into the community of Christian states, that it may order and rule the condition of Christian Europe with them? Has it really been out of tenderness for the unperturbed sovereignty of the Sultan, although he now rules over his Christian subjects only with the help of Christian powers, that these Christian subjects been left to his mercy, without protection and guarantee under international law?

On the other hand, it is a false slander that we would like to achieve or even tolerate a shaping of our conditions according to the Russian model, or an interference of Russia in our internal affairs, or a leadership of Russia in Europe which Germany would serve as a henchman. Our personal independence will certainly not be denied, even by our opponents. But in the same spirit, we are also jealous of the independence of our fatherland. The kingdom of order, customs, and culture, as it stands before our souls, as we testify to it in word and deed, can no more flourish under the influence of Russia than under the influence of France; only our native rulers and the spirit of our own people in their full freedom can ground it. It is not because of our idea or the governments which shared it, that Germany did not take the highest position in Europe as an arbiter over the warring states in this entanglement – which we stated from the outset to be our goal – but instead reaped no other fruit from its firm resistance to the demands of the Western Powers and the liberal-democratic onslaught than that of its own preservation from the evils of war – which should not be underestimated.

Be that as it may, the German question and the Eastern question are of a transient nature, and so is everything that is connected with them in terms of displeasure or reproach.

But strangely enough, the accusation against me on account of the monarchical principle, by which it used to be thought that I would be morally annihilated, has also receded into the background. After anti-monarchical sentiment so obviously suffered shipwreck in 1848, it is now prudently assumed that the monarchical power had never been opposed – as if it had not been a question of monarchy and republic, of real monarchy versus constitutional sham monarchy, but as if the whole struggle had been directed solely at an aristocracy which not only suppressed the people but sought to bring the monarchy under its own control. Since then, the accusation against me is no longer directed at the representation of the monarchical interest, since the liberals themselves pretend to be the most zealous royalists, but at the representation of aristocratic interests, the union with the Junkers.

I do not deny this. I represent the *interests of the aristocracy* – more precisely the knighthood – and already represented them in the first edition of this book, in 1833, when I stood far from the public arena and might have expected my absence to be permanent. Nevertheless, I do not represent their interests in general but only certain of their interests, only those which, like every true estate interest, are at the same time the interest of the country. They are: the great share in the territorial representation which is due them, the administration of the local public welfare, the continuity of property in their families; and this latter I also strive for with regard to the peasantry. On the other hand, I represent with no less emphasis the interest of the *general citizenry*. With the exception of this narrowly defined position on the part of the aristocracy, I have never taught anything other than the equal rights of all citizens, especially in the punishment of crimes, in the adjudication of damages, and above all in the appointment to public offices. In particular, I have everywhere and most definitely denied any position of the landlords by which the rural population would be placed in a subordinate relationship, thus all patrimoniality of magistrates, all other subjections except that to the king (speeches of February 1st, 1854, and March 11th, 1856). I am not the patron speaker of the *spirit of Junkerdom*, of caste pride, of the idle, arrogant consumption of a position received without merit, of the naked demeanor of self-interest, of dullness with respect to idealistic aims, the relentless zeal for the political order with its privileges, in fierce resistance to the ecclesiastical order with its discipline and strict morals. Rather, I testify – and I had to testify especially in that period of leveling – to the *noble spirit* of reverence for family memory, of the tradition of high profession and high duty, of knightly honor and custom, of protection and assistance for the less well-to-do rural population, of personal loyalty and devotion to the king. These ethical motives of earlier times should not be lost when the latest ethical attainments – civic duty, loyalty to vocation, legal order, pursuit of the common good, and general national community – are gained, but together with them they should permeate the population as the fullness of civility and support of the social condition. While there is also a high national spirit running through our army already by virtue of universal conscription, yet at the same time there is a trait of the old chivalry and feudal loyalty, and precisely in the permeation hereof consists its moral excellence. The aristocracy itself, therefore, must not renounce these genuine aristocratic institutions, since they condition their public profession. Nevertheless, it behooves him who does not belong to the class to stand up for them, since they are essential conditions of the general welfare, and since the doctrine and way of thinking of the time endanger them, to the general detriment. Just as the territorial representation must now vouch for the right of monarchy, just so should the citizenry vouch for the right of the aristocracy. This is precisely what the present national spirit requires, in contrast to the earlier estate spirit.[14]

There is no danger of *aristocratic interference with the general rights of the people.* Where are the privileges to be found in Germany, and especially in Prussia even before 1848, which not without reason caused the bitterness of 1789? Apart from a few insignificant and scarcely applied provisions in the general law of the land, which progressive legislation has (as it were) forgotten, on the whole every privilege of birth, and consequently every real privilege of class, had ceased. The rights of the district and provincial estates, the landlord's jurisdiction and the public welfare belonged to the citizen proprietor just as well as to the nobleman. There was no legal nobility, but only a knighthood with free and

[14] "I hope that the knighthood," I said on January 27, 1852, "will one day do for those who do not belong to their class, just as those do today who likewise do not belong to *their* class – stand up for them so as to establish their permanent position (through entails). I hope that the knighthood will stand up for the class that is particularly recommended to their representation, the class of small landowners." Such was accomplished this year (1856) by the representatives of the knighthood in the House of Lords (motion of Count Itzenplitz) with equal emphasis and equal care and attention.

equal entry for all. In particular, however, in the leading German states, Austria, Prussia, Bavaria, etc., a public career was and is open to ability and merit without restriction, and it is an honor due to the citizenry that commoners attain the highest offices without being ennobled. This well-founded equality, which the French prince with such pride justly praised in France, in his speech at the Industrial Exhibition at Paris, has also been gained in our fatherland without it being revolutionized, and stands high among its goods and honors; and justice and wisdom, indeed the very interest of its princes and their governments, guarantee that it will not be curtailed.

Nor is there any danger of *aristocratic mastery of royal power* in our country. The comparison, especially with the French nobility under the Restoration and with the *chambre introuvable* (which has been repeatedly made) is without any ground. Our situation since November 1848 has been quite different from that of the French Restoration. In Prussia the monarchy did not re-establish itself as it did there, by the aid of foreign powers, but by its own strength; it was not an ally of an enemy invasion, and its adherents had not deserted the fatherland, nor had they strengthened the enemy's armies. On the other hand, revolution in our country did not crown the nation with glory and power, as it did there, but only brought impotence, humiliation, and disgrace upon it. Royal sentiment did not range itself against patriotic sentiment; all patriotic memory and patriotic enthusiasm attached themselves to monarchy, and the army in particular had sympathy not for the revolution against the legitimate monarchy but for the legitimate monarchy against the revolution. Moreover, with us the antecedent state of affairs did not exhibit deep and intolerable evils, as it did there, the removal of which, in spite of all accompanying horrors, was nevertheless thanks to the Revolution, the recovery from which was to be accomplished by the Restoration; nor did our revolution provide us with acquired rights in the form of national goods, as did the Revolution there in its short inglorious course; it did not yield us any firmly established greats such as those French generals and statesmen, nor a new generation with a new way of thinking. And in the wake of this, the aristocracy, because of its participation in the restoration of full royal power, stood not in opposition to the nation, like the French, but precisely in the center of the nation.

To this more favorable situation, it also added a better attitude. The French aristocracy made a great mistake when it sought to consolidate its power even in opposition to the monarchy, and so sought to extend the rights of the chambers against the crown in general. It was caught up in the delusion that even now, as in former centuries, it was something separate from the crown, on its own, a power in the country; it entertained the delusion that it was only maintaining its old medieval position and would suffer no other consequence if it took its place under a modern charter and in a modern chamber, as it once did under the constitution of the *états généraux*. It was an encouragement but perhaps also an excuse for this, that the imperialist phase of the Revolution preceded the Restoration. This meant that, by virtue of a natural law, reaction was directed even more strongly against bureaucratic despotism than against democracy. Thus effort was directed to establish the power of the representative body sufficient to displace the liberal bureaucracy even against the will of the crown, without considering that such power would altogether deprive the crown of its power, opening the way for it ultimately to fall into quite different hands from its own. Nevertheless, the *chambre introuvable* was the only element that represented the historical order; and great as its fault was, yet the complete destruction of it on the part of the king was still greater.

But this attitude of the French aristocracy is directly opposed to that of ours. Nor has ours any traditions at all, such as theirs do, of great lords (*seigneurs*) with their own military and political power independent of the king. Ours, however, has this in common with the Chamber of 1815, and must have it in common, that it also represents the historical order – that it is not governmental and ministerial but conservative, and therefore combats liberal bureaucracy. But the inviolable power of the crown was, and always is, the first and foremost thing for it in comparison with any regard to its own righteousness. It wants to appear strong only together with the crown, not in opposition to the crown. The termination of the former absolute monarchy is not its work, and its restoration was not its vocation. That it should have simply steered world history back in the proper direction, namely by artificially bringing about a breach of the 1849/50 constitution, is declared by one honorable albeit isolated voice to be its duty, and the failure to do so as its inexpiable guilt, on the basis of which it is said to have no more of a monarchical ethos than the constitutional or democratic party. But however incessantly and with such rare self-confidence in one's own statesmanlike insight this is repeated, in truth it had neither reason nor right to tread on any other ground than that assigned to it by Providence, and on this ground it has only proved itself monarchical. Since 1849 it has never shown any desire to strengthen itself against the crown by strengthening the chambers, but on the contrary – in each chamber under different leaders – has itself refused the power offered to it in order to maintain the strength of the crown. Would the *chambre introuvable* have renounced the right to authorize taxes, would it have rejected the law of ministerial responsibility introduced by the government itself, this best remedy against a ministry-Talleyrand or -Decazes? In the *chambre introuvable*, could a spokesman of the aristocratic party have said, to the applause of the aristocracy: "If we succumb today, we do not succumb to our opponents but to the government of His Majesty, and we shall celebrate even our defeat as a triumph, since the power of His Majesty's government is thereby demonstrated"? And conversely, would our First Chamber, notwithstanding its well-founded jealousy of the bureaucracy, not only moderate an electoral law, like the *chambre introuvable*, but reject it on the ground that it gives the state government a considerable influence over the elections?

We do not have a *party of the nobility* but a *monarchical-conservative party* of manifold elements as well as of manifold factions and hues. The aristocracy is an important element of it, a powerful tribe and fulcrum. What this party has achieved is, of course, not mentioned in the daily press, which only celebrates what is of the press's own spirit; but its deeds and successes bear witness to it. It has strengthened the power of the authorities, has first and foremost relieved the government of the necessity to take unlawful measures after a revolution, has made it possible for the continuation of territorial representation in an independent state of Europe, has given the first example in Germany of chambers which do not pay homage to liberalism nor even moderate it but rather pursues the dissolution thereof (*le contraire de la révolution*) with all its energy, who are a support instead of an attenuation of the government, who combine loyal devotion with complete independence and make a system of corruption as impossible as it is unnecessary, who resist individual measures of the government but are the protectors and guardians of the rights and prerogatives of the same government. It has not broken the power of the government at any point; it has paved the right way of true principles for it against the obstacles and inducements of false opinion; and when it refused its consent because it did not approve of the government's course, it never denied its loyalty. If one wishes to call this aristocracy, it is not my decision – I stand together with this aristocracy, for it is my like-minded comrade and confederate. "If it were a question of an opposition of the aristocracy to the crown, I would be the last to appear in their ranks. I am not devoted to the crown for the sake of the aristocracy, I am devoted to the aristocracy for the sake of the crown. I have no personal interest or social relations with the aristocracy, I am only *politically* connected to the right side of this House, where the aristocracy is an important element. It is the *army in which to this point I have served*."

After all this, I considered it particularly advisable in this volume — the Doctrine of State — to refer whenever relevant to my speeches in the First Chamber or the House of Lords,[15] as well as to discuss in footnotes the events in which I was involved, partly because in the speeches, in consequence of the uplifting and exciting power of the situation, my principles are often set forth much more vividly and emphatically than is possible in a literary work, partly to show the consistent agreement of my scientific doctrine and my active conduct, to justify my doctrine by the test of application, my active conduct by fidelity to convictions long before proclaimed.

Berlin, May 1856

[15] I have published a selection of my speeches in the past: *Reden von Stahl* [Stahl's Speeches]. A complete collection of them has now been published apart from my participation: *Parlamentarische Reden von Stahl* [Stahl's Parliamentary Speeches]. [Another edition of Stahl's speeches was published in 1862: *Siebzehn parlamentarische Reden und drei Vorträge* [Seventeen Parliamentary Speeches and Three Lectures].]

FROM THE AUTHOR'S PREFACE TO THE SECOND EDITION

My political convictions have remained essentially the same as in the first edition. I proceed from the divine right of the ruling authority, from the legitimacy or sovereignty of the prince; nevertheless, it is precisely through the deeper significance of these foundations of all state existence that I arrive at the state (or constitutional) principle, i.e., the principle of public necessity in constitution and administration, and at the development of the activity of the estates in the newer, national uniform character. I do so in opposition to the movement of the time which pursues these institutions only on the basis of popular sovereignty and therefore without internal measure, as well as in opposition to the reactionary doctrine which rejects it. I desire authority and freedom — which is what everyone wants – but not so that order and authority are the product of freedom (the will of the nation) but so that they are original, prior to and above freedom; and yet I also desire freedom. For this reason, I do not place freedom in self-government, in the rule of the nation, but in self-active obedience, i.e., in the co-representation and co-creation of its legal condition. In this I find myself in decisive conflict with the basic attitude of the Liberal party; on the other hand, I seek not to repulse but only to purify and delimit various important results of their system, which are often reckoned by those who think like me to rank among the absolute aberrations. To the reproach that I thereby participate in the political apostasy of time, I have only to counter with the question as to whether it is possible to designate to me a point in time (*terminus a quo*) at which the apostasy begins, a political state of affairs that would have been worth retaining? If not, then the constructive instinct of the present with its peculiar forms must not be rejected but only corrected. It does not escape me that, according to the law of nature as well as according to all historical experience, a so-called "center right" has no foothold, and that everywhere the Gironde is overwhelmed by the Mountain. But an articulated view independently developed from a principle is not a mere "center right"; it is one thing to abolish the legitimate authority and then set standards for a will of the people that has been let loose, and another to hold fast to legitimate authority above all else and to call forth from it the participation of the people within a certain limit. That this is feasible in itself must be held as an ethical postulate, even if at present the predominant tendency, since it lacks reverence and modesty, is a great obstacle to the fruitful execution.

For two centuries, the principle of individual freedom and the power of the people has prevailed exclusively in science, which developed in accordance with all the consequences hereof, and finally also was fully realized in life as the absolute emancipation of man from divine revelation and the divine-human historical order. Then the slumbering sense of the obliterated truth at last reawakened, and the other pole of human existence, that which stands above man, again came into its own; the great spiritual conceptions have since borne a quite different character, and the course of history proceeds towards a different goal. Above all, the Christian faith, which had gradually been completely swallowed up, returned to the minds with all its vitality and evident growth. The short-sighted consider these first beginnings of a world-historical revolution to be the idiosyncrasy of a small handful, while they view the contentless foam that roars on the surface, the vacuous mass of a past process of purification, as the fruitful germ of time. For many, and above all for its own consciousness (which is the most essential thing), monarchy has again become a moral power, not as the people's appointed bearer of executive power but as the authority to which the people are subject by virtue of God and right. There is again a sense of the life-vocation of the estates and its corporate cultivation, of acquired rights, of laudable discipline and restriction for the preservation of material and spiritual goods. All this is a great act of restoration which God's providence is accomplishing in the consciousness of the age, and it will not be denied even in the actual events of the future. If we rebuild that which that movement destroyed, we must not destroy what it has built: the right of man, the free initiative of the nation, the constitutional order, the spiritual power of public life.

* * *

These principles are clear to me beyond all doubt; they are based on our deepest fundamental ethical conception. The implementation is something else. This goes into the realm of external mechanical results; it depends on the fullness of knowledge and experience. In this I may err in many ways, conceding too much here, cutting off too much there, misunderstanding the formative germ of development or the conditions of factual relations. I am happy to be content with that. I do not boast of being the right helmsman who could lead church and state safely through the cliffs and storms of this period, but I believe that my compass is the right one, and that I sail in the direction in which the land lies.

Berlin, December 12th, 1845

INTRODUCTION: OF THE DOCTRINE OF STATE IN GENERAL

§. 1. Concept of the Ethical Kingdom

The doctrine of the state, as put forward in this book, is grounded in the concept of the *ethical kingdom*, which is: self-conscious, indivisible rule, in accordance with ethical-intellectual motives, over conscious, freely obedient beings, thereby also spiritually uniting them. Accordingly, it is rule of a personal character in every aspect, a *kingdom of personality*.

The idea of the ethical kingdom, upon which we found the doctrine of the state, is the supreme ethical concept. This idea runs through all relations, and exists under all circumstances of the human condition; it is the general and absolute purpose (τέλος) of that condition. Hence, it pertains equally to the religious, the moral, and the legal sphere. The kingdom of God, which the Christian religion promises to us in the beyond, is the completed realization of the ethical kingdom. In the kingdom of God, it is the supreme personality, God, who rules men, and He does so in accordance with His perfect holiness and wisdom, as well as in perfect freedom, that is, internally fulfilling them in the same way that He externally maintains them and keeps them in order, so that they may be one spirit and one will with Him, and therefore with each other (Book I [*Philosophical Foundations*], §. 27). Yet even on Earth, the moral world (the inner life and the free action of men) is an ethical kingdom, even when not visibly manifesting itself as such.

For the real power of God effectuates in us regard [Ansehen] for the moral commandment and the fulfillment thereof, to the degree that it is obeyed. It effectuates the particular ethical conceptions of peoples and times; it effectuates the natural consequences of sins and vice; it effectuates <2> Nemesis, perceptible only as foreboding, in the life of men and in the history of the peoples. It is not so that people in absolute isolation, as if shut off in their innermost being, obey or infringe an impersonal ethical law, a dead rule. Rather, there is a bond over them to the common ruling power, which surrounds everything everywhere, but only in the beyond will be revealed. Ethics nowhere exists as a bare law and a fulfilling individual; it exists everywhere as conscious common demand and compliance, in accordance with a common purpose; it exists everywhere as a kingdom.

The civil order, then, likewise is an ethical kingdom. Here as well, there is rule established over men, rule of a personal character, i.e., conscious of itself and with control over its own actions, having a real power over men; only here, the rule of a real natural personality is replaced by the organized institution (the state organism); and the perfect, or at least ordered, natural condition, is for it to have its innermost center likewise in a natural personality (the monarchy). Here as well, it is rule of ethically understood purposes, and here as well, men are freely to obey, while the ethical rational order, which stands over them, is likewise their true essence and will, and only realizes itself through them and in them; they are to be united under it, through compliance with this order and its spirit. That an artificial institution erected by men, and not a higher personality (God), exercises rule, is certainly an entirely different kind, a much lower stage, of the ethical kingdom, for which reason the civil order is ruled in accordance with faulty human insight and mores [Sitte]; it is also a lower stage of the ethical kingdom, in that the ruling real power and the law are not inseparably one, but can be split apart, and, also, because the inward filling of the subjects with the spirit of law and order, which is the requirement, in reality scarcely exists.

But the concept of the ethical kingdom, and those general characteristics of the ethical kingdom, are the same here as there. Its concept is our most general and inward perception, because it, everywhere, is the purpose established by God for the ethical world. Accordingly, we derive the norms of the civil order not from the archetype of the future kingdom of God, nor from the moral world as it exists in the here and now, but from the essence of the ethical king- <3>
dom, which in like manner appears both in the here and now and in the beyond, as something general. We do not build upon parallels and analogies from other ethical areas, but on the characteristics which each ethical area contains in itself, in accordance with the archetypal law of the ethical world.

This concept of the ethical kingdom provides the deeper (philosophical) foundation and guarantee both for the political order and for political freedom. For it counts among its characteristics the need for an authority elevated over men, that is, a claim to obedience and respect, obligatory (hence the principle of legitimacy, in contrast to popular sovereignty) not merely to the laws but to a real power outside of them, the ruling authority (state power). Likewise, it includes the need for an ethically reasonable content, which therefore also forms the restriction on this authority, that is, the need for laws of the state, which, being passed down through history, stand over prince and people and can only be changed in accordance with those laws' own requirements (constitutional principle in the true sense). Finally, it contains the recognition of the nation (the subjects) as an ethical community, therefore as being independent and thus freely obeying, being subjected to the laws only as the expression and obligation of their own ethical essence (Book III [*Private Law*], §. 10), from which those laws originally arise through custom and tradition, and against which, in later ongoing development, by means of the consent of the representative body, those laws are assayed (representative principle in the true sense).

Deduction from the will of men, be it individuals, be it the collective whole, be it either their arbitrary or their rational will, does not attain to a simple elevated real authority, and therefore, in its innermost ground, is always revolutionary, whether harsher or milder, revealed or hidden. Deduction from the acquired rights of a ruler, or from the necessity of unified leadership, or from the divine establishment of rule (when one adheres to this alone), does not procure the independence and (independent) entitlement of the people. Only the perspective of the ethical kingdom yields the eternal order of the state, containing all its principles and elements in harmonious unity. When, in reality, this is difficult to bring about – be- <4> cause governments in actual power do not easily elevate the people to independence, and the people in actual power do not easily allow for the elevation of princely majesty; actually, given the untrustworthiness of men, each staves off the yielding of something of their power as if it were a sort of state of emergency – nevertheless, the ethical kingdom unshakably remains the ethical-political archetype and standard of judgment and action.

In particular, this is the duty and purpose which accords with the Christian life-valuation, in that the idea of the ethical kingdom in all its stages suits the Christian worldview, and only it. The true Christian life-valuation corresponds neither to the revolutionary doctrine of the old Scottish Puritans and English Independents, nor to the doctrine of absolute power and unconditional obedience as represented by the adherents of the Stuarts (Filmer et al.), nor to the political indifference of older German Pietism. It can lack neither the regard of the given ruling authority, nor the development of political freedom and entitlement of the people under this regard, nor inward ethical-legal lawfulness and necessity.

Understandably, Kant's and Fichte's overarching ethical [ethischer] concept of the ethical [sittlichen] world-order is a different one from this concept of the ethical kingdom. For them it is a rule, a law, that the personalities are to follow, not a personality (or some other real power), who encompasses and unifies all of them. Such a power can at most (as Kant in fact postulates) only externally supervene in order to ensure the fulfillment of the laws and restore their violation – thus, fulfill the role of a judge; that power itself (God or the ruling authority, as the case may be) and its rule (its permeation in men and their union in it) are not the essence and fulfillment of all mores.

The matter is the same with the concept of the absolute, or rather objective, Spirit, which, in the philosophy of Hegel, takes the place of our concept of the ethical kingdom. Hegel's concept differs, in that it is not a living union of many personalities with and in the one supreme personality (God – king – ruling authority), but the absorption of the same in the Substance (the concept, the idea, the <5> world spirit). Of course, this is not, as with Kant and Fichte, a bare rule (an ideal); it is instead to be a reality; nevertheless, even assuming this, it is in any case an impersonal functioning power, unconscious of itself and therefore acting, not out of awareness, but in accordance with a bare rule (dialectic). This is not the place to demonstrate that such a concept regarding the eternal relations of men leads to despair. In terms of politics, it leads only to the formal authorization (the dotting of the i) of that which is logically self-derived, with the personality of the prince allowed no material influence; therefore, despite all efforts to resist this on the part of well-meaning persons, it leads not to an original real authority (prince-legitimate republican government) as such, but only to the recognition of an impersonal Reason, the "power of the idea," over the people.

In theory, such is certainly better than the (subjective rationalistic) doctrine of Rousseau, which allows only the will of individuals, or of the multitude, to be the ethical power on Earth. In practice, however, it has the same effect. For the idea as such is neither authentically made known in some way, nor does it have any power; in this case as well, therefore, it is human consciousness (the people) which itself constructs the idea, and, in accordance with that idea, establishes and commands its ruling authorities, rather than having the ruling authorities over it, allowing them to rule over it. Hegel's monarchical or, much rather, governmental [gouvernementalem] standpoint inevitably has sunk to the democratic standpoint of the newer school. For the monarchical power, and indeed the power of any ruling authority, as taught by Hegel, is itself only the result of laws of thought (dialectic), that is, a power that nowhere wills in a personal, self-conscious manner except in me (in the individual), over which, therefore, I (the individual) or, above all, the multitude of those in whom the Spirit has come to consciousness, the people, also have the supreme judgment and judicial authority. In the same manner in the area of morals, the followers of Hegel have substituted genius for the ethical law, which for Hegel had an objectivity. In this manner, all higher ethical order dissolves finally into so-called self-consciousness or free spirit, that is, in the thought and will of men, which then loses all content, <6> but in impudent capriciousness only destroys what it finds. One must, however, recognize that this conception of Hegel's, in that it postulates both an objective power and a subjective appropriation and fulfillment as distinct and nevertheless unified aspects, scientifically prepared the way to establish a truer standpoint (that of the personal world cause), derived from the true understanding.

The newer school of thought [Bildung] as it confronts us in the great multitudes and in the entire age, has appropriated essential aspects of the ethical kingdom (freedom, self-action of peoples and individuals, the law as the all-permeating necessity of public life, in contrast to arbitrary rule), but in exchange has forfeited the first and foremost of those aspects, the given higher real authority, the ruling authority, for and over the people, in which the people is to become politically unified. The newer school, therefore, everywhere revolves around two abstract concepts, freedom and law, and cannot entertain the possibility that these do not exhaust the matter; it has no clue that it lacks the most essential thing: the original ruler and the original collective purpose of rule, by which alone the multitude becomes a kingdom. Accordingly, it does not conceive of law as a given higher thing, as the law of the great institution that passes through the ages as one and the same, albeit in constant advancement; rather, for this school, the law is merely a self-made thing, the will of the then-living generation. This is the source of the truth and the error of public opinion.

On the other hand, the few who maintain this aspect of authority in living consciousness have the habit partly of maintaining it in such one-sidedness that they yield, or at any rate subordinate, that other principle, the more so because the manner in which that principle is generally asserted scandalizes them in the highest degree, as it ought to. From this stems their aversion to all that is constitutional, their aversion to political freedom. The overarching concept of the ethical kingdom, in its full amplitude, is therefore the true proper middle way, that is, the articulated higher view, in which the <7> motives of the combating parties together find their genuine satisfaction.[16]

The concept of the ethical kingdom is distinguished from that of the ethical organism, in the same way that kingdom and organism are distinguished in all cases. The organism contains determinate, various members, each of which mutually supplements the other, none of which have an independent existence, all of which, in fact, are required for the organism to exist (head, rump, two arms, legs, etc.). The kingdom, on the other hand, contains an unlimited number of equal, independent, existing beings, which neither mutually presuppose each other nor are required for this concept the way they are in the case of the organism; they are subject to a higher rule. It is in this sense that we speak of natural kingdoms. The plant kingdom is a plant kingdom, even when this or that specimen, in fact this or that kind or genus, is lacking, and the one plant does not require the other. But we also call the concrete manifestation of like natural things [Naturgebilde] a kingdom because a higher ruling spirit is perceived in all these existing beings, thereby ruling them; because all rule is the absorption of the thought and will of the ruler into the being of the ruled. We must consider

---

[16] When I, here and in the following, combat the standpoints of the parties, I in no way deny the achievement of the writers of these parties, which is true and good in certain results. Even less do I find myself in opposition to those who, apart from any ethical-philosophical standpoint – simply the general sense of the good and right in the background – exclusively apply the perspective of external result, experience, and history as standard. This manner of treatment will of course always have its great shortcoming, because an ethical-philosophical standpoint, like the rudder of the investigation, cannot be lacking, and therefore always will include such philosophical grounds for determination, only less investigated and conscious. But on the other hand, it has the advantage of an impartiality in the treatment of results, which someone of general scientific viewpoints, be they proper and clear as you like, does not entirely preserve. Both methods of treatment are therefore necessary and suitable, mutually to purify each other.

the divine Spirit to be active in the moments of creation, in a manner such that His thoughts are incorporated in matter, in a systematically advancing, mutually <8> adapted way, such that matter is filled with those thoughts, in order truly to recognize that Nature comprises kingdoms and is itself a kingdom.

It is the same with ethical relations. For example, marriage is an ethical organism. The rule of the state, when it is not, as in despotisms, a mere personality, is an ethical organism, in that personality everywhere can only be substituted for by organism. Prince, estate, judiciary, the orders of officialdom, all supplement each other; state rule is not entire when one or the other is lacking, and, where they are not lacking, it is complete in itself.[17] But the state itself, i.e., the mass of men in its ordered rule, is not an organism, but an ethical kingdom. Though millions be added to it, it does not require any of these individuals for it to be a state; all are ruled by the same power and order, and therefore are

---

[17] Taking state rule to be an organism in no way leads to the conception that it must have the same or analogous organs as the human body, in the manner of the parallels drawn by Bluntschli in his book *Psychologische Studien der Staat und Kirche* [Psychological Studies on State and Church]. The many unacceptable results contained therein need not be held to be a refutation of a great scientific conception; but what is precisely scientifically certain (*a priori*) is that such a parallel cannot exist; for when the state has this in common with the human body, that both organisms are instrumental facilities, it is still obvious that the instrumental facility serving the purposes of an individual life (facilities for breathing, eating, procreation) must be something other than the facility for the rule of a number of independent personalities (facilities to maintain justice, to develop a joint power, to promote common mores, etc.). Even if, therefore, the doctrine of that adventurous philosophy of the sixteen basic organs of the human body were more than a simple game, even then it does not follow that the state must have the corresponding organs – on the contrary, it follows that it cannot have them. As untenable as this new doctrine of state is, to that degree is it rich in detail in instructions and apt results; yet this is not the consequence of those notions but of the personal insight of this capable writer and statesman. It is similar to how, in earlier times, superior and mentally excellent men worked with an adept to obtain some real gold in the adept's wonderful laboratory, and actually also obtained it – only it was gold which was previously deposited, not produced by the charlatan.

united in it, and the union of these individuals under this order is the purpose of the state. <9>

On the other hand, the concept of the ethical kingdom is also to be distinguished from the local community or congregation [der Gemeinde].[18] In the congregation, the higher rule emanates from the will of the united persons, while in the ethical kingdom it emanates from a power and authority prior to and over them. Thus, the Christian congregation as such (even when considered as the collective congregation of all living Christians) recognizes no other law and regard than the will and the conviction of the collective members in their unity. By contrast, the kingdom of God derives its law and regard from God himself, and the Christian church, which also is an ethical kingdom and, as such, is to be distinguished from the collective congregation (even when comprising the same persons), derives a law and regard from God-established institutions, and from the constitution added to those institutions in history, with its authorities. The jurisdiction to forgive sins is granted not to the congregation (not even the collective congregation) but only to the church in this sense; though the congregation elects its pastor, the pastor does not derive his authorization through the congregation (persons cannot grant such), but through the church, through the pre-existing ecclesiastical ruling authorities and offices, which the current generation did not give, thus through the institution, which stands over the congregation of collective living members. Even terminologically, the congregation is composed of persons, while the church, i.e., the house of the Lord (κυριακόν), is something institutional [Anstaltliches] standing over them. It is the same in the area of politics. The local community rules itself (self-government); its constitution is therefore also republican, in accordance with its nature (self-elected ruling authorities, etc.). By contrast, the nation is to be a state, and thus an ethical kingdom. As a rule, therefore, the nation is to be governed by a given higher authority, by a king, while it itself – the nation – is only entitled to the free adoption of the laws.

Should one grant this concept of the ethical kingdom, in particular also the given real authority which is the primary aspect of it, <10> one must then also grant the entire political conception as carried out in the remainder of this work.

---

[18] [*Gemeinde* in German signifies both congregation and local community or municipality. It thus denotes "bottom-up" government.]

In the same way that Rousseau's book is nothing more than the implementation of the concept of the "general (human) will" as the principle of public life, mine is nothing other than the implementation of the concept of the ethical kingdom as an order and power over men, who nevertheless belong to it as free self-acting members.

§. 2. Dimensions of the State

The doctrine of the state comprises a spectrum of relations which taken together fulfill the entire task of the state: to wit, the state in itself, the relations between states, and the elements and smaller spheres under the state. Each of these relations has its characteristic concepts and providential purpose (τέλος), but they all finally flow into the one concept of the ethical kingdom.

By the state we understand firstly the closed association of a large number of persons under a supreme independent (sovereign) power. Its providential purpose is rule for the *totality* of the human common condition [Gemeinzustandes] and common purpose [Gemeinzieles]. For this rule, the human community is ordained an institution through which it exercises power over individuals as one will and acting subject [Subjekt], as a consciousness identical with itself. The state is therefore in its innermost essence a personification of human community. To this end, it is however also essential that this ruling will is to be rooted in a mental determinacy, an individuality (Book I [*Philosophical Foundations*], §. 9), in order for its rule to flow from an ethically rational, in itself unified view of life. This is why the state is the task of a *people* [des Volkes] and not of mankind in its entirety. By virtue of the unity of its descent or its history, and by virtue of its organizational development and the connectedness of its activities, this unity of consciousness and appreciation of life, both in general terms and specifically with regard to the common condition, exists in the people. Only the people therefore has the energy of <11> common consciousness and the pervasion of its conditions that are needed to constitute a state capable of acting as true personality.

Collective mankind has no business ruling life as a subject, but it does have the task, as a community of peoples, of embracing and supporting as basis the rule exercised by the people (the state). This is the *law of nations* [Völkerrecht] and *diplomacy*. The providential purpose of the community of nations is the conservation of the peoples and states in their existence and their rights, and consequently the care for general interests which make up the shared basis of the condition of individual peoples, such as e.g. the freedom of the seas, world trade, and finally, in the case of higher development, even the maintenance to a certain degree of generally recognized political principles, which governments are to lay at the foundation of each state.

World history starts from the condition of the most extreme division and animosity among the peoples, the consequence of the confusion of human consciousness. First the Christian deliverance of humanity restored the possibility of a bond of inner conviction among the peoples. From there outward, there is an approximation in the community of nations to a "kingdom" (rule of a personal character) over the individual states in terms of form and content. In terms of form, in that instead of isolated negotiations between individual participating nations, a constitution-like, all-encompassing bond is more and more to be produced, by which the affairs of the peoples are being ordered as one undivided association of nations; in terms of content, in that more and more unity of political estimation is to be generated among the states. Should this latter become complete – which on Earth will not occur – then humanity instead of the peoples would have the vocation to be a state. But that would mean the end of world history. The medieval emperorship was an anticipation of this situation, which is why it existed more in the idea than in reality.

On the other hand, it is an undeniable truth that the collectivity of the peoples has the vocation to support the most basic foundations of ethical political order when they are lacking on the part of a specific people. This was the intention of the Holy Alliance. It would be one-sided to look for this foundation purely and simply <12> in monarchical power. An intervention establishing the monarch in his full power but which does not help the people against the dissolution of reaction or to secure truly founded rights and the restoration of a lawful condition cannot engender ethical veneration and satisfy the public consciousness. It therefore is only an ephemeral external restoration, without establishing the fundamental attitude which alone is capable of durably securing the restoration. When the powers of Europe, or Germany as the case may be, step in as a higher authority to protect the ruling authorities of a country against its subjects, they thereby assume the obligations of higher authority, to preserve law and justice and even quarter and pardon, and to facilitate a return of calm, while on the other hand the government which in this manner is supported by foreign help has to that degree forfeited its right to entire independence. Great difficulties at any rate accompany such maintenance of justice and order against the contemporary revolutionary movement, which is aimed not at certain individual rights but at the ruling authorities and the entire legal order. But that does not relieve the duty. Accordingly, *nonintervention as a principle* is erroneous; but intervention should only occur in rare cases. The actual, regular vocation of the community of nations is therefore only the ordering of international relations.

Outside of the community for the totality of life purposes, which is the state, the people also develops communities for *particular* purposes, firstly *local communities* (municipalities), then *vocational communities* [Berufsgemeinschaften] (estates). As their purpose in the final analysis is always a component of that total purpose, so are the elements and members of the state; but in accordance with their specific nature and their own interests they are separate from the state; they are not mere appendages of the state but are their own institutions with an independent position in the state. As such, they must also have a rule of personal character, to be constituted as a single, conscious acting subject – this is the municipality and the *estate community* [Standesgemeinschaft] (corporation [Korporation]), or when, in the case of landownership, relations of superiority and dependency exist and are legally exercised – *manorialism*. These smaller communities, to the degree that they serve the mutual satisfaction of needs and not the purpose of common rule in accordance <13> with higher concepts, comprise the sphere of "*society*" [Gesellschaft] in distinction to the state in the strict sense or the sphere of politics.

Accordingly, the ethical kingdom which men are to construct has its center and final fulfillment in the state, that is, the single cohesive association, but it derives its full subject matter and content from the life and work of the smaller spheres, municipalities and estates, and it is supported and borne, and for certain of its highest tasks even supplemented, by the mutual security and reciprocality of the peoples.

Correspondingly, the doctrine of *society* and that of the *community of states* is essential to the *doctrine of state*. It encompasses the strictly *political*, the *social*, and the *international spheres*, while only all three together in inseparable unity are the state in accordance with its entire full significance.

The sphere of the state in this extent is juridically expressed as the sphere of *public law* according to its secular side, thus in exclusion of the church. For these are the two great institutions for the rule and education of the human race, the one according to the earthly, the other to the eternal purpose, church and state, which we include under the concept of public law as opposed to private law as the sphere of the fulfillment of individual existence (Book II [*Principles of Law*], §. 45). The state exhausts the sphere of secular public law; municipality and estate are elements of the state; the law of nations is a relation among states.

§. 3. The State as Personality

From the discussion thus far we may therefore derive the legal type of the state, or, what is the same thing, the type of public law, both in itself and in distinction to that of private law, and valid for the church as well to the degree that it exists as an external, legally-ordered institution.

Public law comprises all human communities, all human rulerships for the fulfillment of human common existence; private law comprises all relations for the satisfaction and fulfillment of individ- <14> ual existence. Public law rests on the concept of the ethical kingdom, in the same way that private law rests on the concept of personality, and in all its institutions it has a double principle of development, just as does the latter (Book III [*Private Law*], §. 1), namely *first* the *providential purpose* (τέλος) of the concerned institution, that is, the material and spiritual tasks of common life, and *second* the *personal character of rule*, as we have discussed it. The ethical kingdom is the general type of public law, just as the personal character of life is that of private law.

The characteristics of public law thus are:

1. *Power (imperium)*, to which the members are subordinated; this is not a power of the ruled which is transferred by them, as is *associational power* [Gesellschaftsgewalt], nor is it a power for the sake of the personal satisfaction of the ruled, as is *domestic power (potestas)*, but rather power inhering in the institution itself and serving to fulfill its requirements. This concrete factual foundation and meaning of power distinguishes public law from private law. Should one conceive the power exercised in public legal institutions, namely in the state, as mere associational power or as patrimonial power, in either case the concept of public law is eliminated, leaving only private law.

2. The ordered connection [Zusammenhang] of men according to specific positions, and therefore the arrangement of the institution which is the subject [Subjekt] of rule – the *constitution*.

3. The range of necessary purposes and ordered tasks to achieve those purposes – the *administration*. This legal necessity of purposes and tasks likewise

distinguishes public-legal institutions from private ones, and the true public principle from the patrimonial.

That peculiar character which is the principle of development of public law (§. 2.), that of the *personality of rule*, is realized through these characteristics. It therefore permeates all the institutions of public law. The state, the municipality and corporation (even the church as external institution) have as one of their essential traits, that with regard to rule they are personalities. This trait is not to be confused with the concept of the *legal person*. Instead, one may characterize it as the concept of the *political person* in contrast to the <15> legal person. The legal person is a figure of private law and only entails the capacity to be a bearer of assets [Vermögenssubjekt], while the political person is public and entails the capacity to be the subject of action and rule. The state, for example, in that it adjudicates, rules, etc., is not a legal person but has a personality in a much higher sense, such as is lacking in e.g. a foundation.

The question as to whether the state is to be considered a moral person, in particular whether the monarchical state is a person separate from the prince and is the actual subject of power, is to be decided on this basis. The state is in no way a moral person in the usual legal sense; only the fisc is that. The latter is most certainly separate from the prince; the prince can in this respect form a moral person from his income (Civil List), distinguished from himself as well as from the treasury. By contrast, the state is a person in the sense given here; as such, it is to be distinguished from the prince, in that yet other organs outside of the prince together constitute this artificial person; but it is never to be separated from the prince and recognized as an independent subject apart from him, because its personality has its center in the prince and hence could not exist without him. If, for example, the prince were to issue a judicial decision or, in a constitution with estates, pass a law without the approval of the estates, this would be no act of state but merely of the prince (actually, only of the person who is the prince); this manifests the distinction between state and prince and the justification that it be asserted. However, the estates cannot do anything without the prince, nor can the judge enforce anything in the face of his obstruction; the state therefore can factually and legally execute no act without the prince, and is nowhere a personality apart from the prince.[19]

In consequence of these considerations, the essence of the state and all institutions of public law consists not in substance (im- **<16>** personal necessity) acting through it as a higher power over personalities, as in Hegel's conception, but quite the opposite, in the community itself becoming a personality. The former conception does nothing less than contradict the character of the state. It would only answer to a condition in which no concentrated acting power (*imperium*) existed, but in which collective persons of themselves followed a higher rule. In actuality, the entire shape of the ethical world confirms the personality perspective and refutes the pantheistic perspective (Book I [*Philosophical Foundations*], §§. 6 and 7).

---

[19] Throughout Maurenbrecher's book *Die deutschen regierenden Fürsten und die Souverainität* [The German Ruling Princes and Sovereignty] he confuses the state's legal personality and its political personality, while also confusing the *distinction* of state and prince with the *separation* of state from prince.

PART ONE: THE SOCIAL ELEMENTS OF THE STATE

Chapter 1: The Municipality

§. 4. The Territorial Principle Applied Locally

The general rule of common obedience under a superior places everyone, apart from his will, in subjection to the soil: that is, it subjects him to the structured community of those others located with him on the same soil. The municipality is founded on this principle, as is the state; neither of these suffers anyone in its midst who is not willing to honor this principle, and whosoever enters their spatial sphere, enters the sphere of their rule. The characteristic bond of the municipality is the community in the *narrow space* that man is capable of ruling with his bodily presence. It brings about the continuous contact of persons and the immediate proximity of things. There is nothing in it corresponding to the state, which, although sharing territorial interests, pursues them in greater extension. Object and purpose (τέλος) of the municipal bond, therefore, is that which becomes a common affair through such proximity, the *local interest*. This above all includes activity in support of livelihood, production of goods, thus foodstuffs, construction, care of the poor and sick, protection against the elements, care for the locality itself (cleanliness, health, beautification, road connections) and the like, and finally the municipal wealth as means to accomplish all of this. These are the actual municipal concerns. On the other hand, the interests which transcend locality, which concern the national condition or the higher ethical ideas of common life, are the object and task of the state, e.g., the military, national taxation, national public welfare, higher education, judiciary, etc. **<18>**

But apart from the fact that local and national interests often permeate each other, or that the boundary lines between them are fluid, a twofold modification underlies this distinction. On the one hand, municipal interests sometimes undoubtedly can be taken care of more effectively by state officials, by virtue of impartiality; on the other hand, matters which actually are the concern of the state can to a certain degree be reasonably taken care of by the municipality at the lowest level, especially those which require particular application at the local level, such as public welfare administration in many branches, and even the courts. That the municipality be *commissioned* for this is not an entirely appropriate way of speaking, because such has the appearance of arbitrariness. It is true, however, that the community in these instances is only the organ of the state. This entails significant consequences: in this case, the municipality stands under the leading of the state, while in the case where the state acts in strictly local affairs, the municipality acts only in terms of state *supervision* or *trusteeship* [Kuratel]. Trusteeship is a care for another regarding his private affairs, purely for the sake of that other person's interests; therefore, municipal trusteeship is always only of a negative, restrictive sort, and is a limitation of municipal disposition under consideration of local, and not state, interests. Furthermore, in the case of state functions, municipal officials alone are the organ, while in the case of local functions, it is likewise also the entire municipality or its representatives.

§. 5. The Forms of Municipal Association: City and Country

The business of sustenance being the supreme local interest, two main classes of municipality are distinguished in terms of it: the *rural community* [Landgemeinde], the sustenance of which is based in agriculture, and the *civic community* [Stadtgemeinde], the sustenance of which is based in industry and trade. The distinguishing effects of this are sweeping. The rural community is simple community, while the city community is composed of various associations of equals [Genossenschaften], in that various forms of occupation are in it. The farming community cannot obtain <19> great expansion, and, within its small space, the people are not so heaped together, while each requires a broad substrate in his possession, and must seek the proximity of benefit-conferring nature, not of people; they live in *villages*. The industrial community, on the other hand, multiplies and crowds in the *cities;* for that is where everything is sought and found in reciprocal communication, and more restricted space is sufficient for everyone to do their work. Finally, the culture [Bildung] that the active life, the multiplicity of viewpoints, and the development of special occupational groups [Stände] for intellectual [geistige] interests, engender in the city, cannot arise in the countryside, given its uniformity of relations, lack of interpersonal contact, and restricted incomes. These distinctions of necessity are expressed both in the form of constitution and administration of the municipality, and in the manner in which the state rules over it.

Formerly the boundaries were sharply drawn which disallowed the pursuit of urban sustenance in the countryside. The abolition of this prohibition has made the boundary fluid. But the distinction itself has not ceased, and ought not to be abandoned legally. Approximations and transitions, as well as the possibility of the exchange of city law for village law and vice versa, have occurred at all times. The current large-scale factory establishments in the country could be the basis for modifications of rural association or particular associations, but not for the equality of city and countryside. It is, however, not even desirable that, factually, the distinction be eliminated, that villages, these seats of steady, quiet, and simple life, be gradually transformed into cities. The distinction between city and country is the foundation of sound social conditions.

§. 6. The Secular and the Ecclesiastical Community

The civil municipality is not separated from the ecclesiastical.[20] The same local nature is binding for the secular as for the spiritual <20> task. In fact, in that the spiritual task is the foundation upon which collective life rests, historically it was often the ecclesiastical association (parish) which was first, to which the civil municipality was joined. Apart from affiliation with the parish, no municipal right can be exercised (Hamburg). Continuous development, and, mainly, the confessional split, has caused the civil and the ecclesiastical communities to maintain a separate existence, which nevertheless ought not to be without connection. Here as well, though, the distinction between city and country is manifest. In the country, with its simple relations and lack of elements of education outside the church, the pastor and the school generally form the center of the entire community.

§. 7. Municipal Constitutions

The constitution of the municipality in general is *republican*, because in the final analysis it is concerned with the interests of men and not a higher ethical order, while in contrast to the state it embodies a streak [einen Zug] of society. Even so, here as well the establishment is a function and power over men, and the

---

[20] [To repeat: in German, the same word, *Gemeinde*, is used for community, municipality, and congregation, which is why Stahl speaks here of municipality and congregation in the same breath.]

ruling authorities representing it therefore must enjoy an independent, strong regard.

The constitution of the city community is based on a *collegial* [kollegialen] *ruling authority* (magistrate, senate, narrower council), at the head of which is the mayor, and on a *city representation* (select committee [Ausschuß], local councillors, broader council). The magistrate properly emerges from election by the citizenry or its representation, yet the cooperative effort of existing magistrates with the citizenry is appropriate here (such as e.g. according to the constitution of Frankfurt of 1816). Pure self-replacement (cooptation) of the magistrate corresponds more to the older half-sovereign, state-like relations of the city than the purely communal relations which now obtain; nowadays the prerequisite of inherited higher stations such as used to be afforded to the city patriciate is lacking, and the participation of the community is in itself appropriate. On the <21> other hand, the members of the magistracy, after having been elected, retain their offices for a long period of time, the mayor for life, both in order that they conduct them with the interest of a life occupation, and that they be independent from the voters. For where there is ruling authority, there must also be independent regard. In particular, the office of salaried mayor, once imparted, ought not be removable through periodic election. It runs contrary to the essence of the ruling authority that the bearer of the highest ruling authority over the community is himself dependent upon the community for his living. The consequence is also that the most competent do not devote themselves to such a precarious position, for which reason the office of mayor, especially in smaller cities, where honor and remuneration form no attraction, falls into the most untrustworthy hands. These removable mayors are also first and foremost a product of the French Revolution. The older establishment did have alternating discharge of office among various mayors or periodic elections from lifetime councilors, but not removal of mayor from the magistracy by being voted out of office.

The constitution of the rural community, absolutely simple and natural, on the one hand rests on a *personal ruling authority* (constables [Schulzen]), with the support of a few assistants, on the other hand on the *personal voting right* of the collective (fully entitled) members of the community, and this simplicity is the salutary condition of the rural community. The artificial installation of collegial officials and representation [der Repräsentation] conflicts with its nature. This simplicity is also consistent with the office of constable being attached to landholding [einem Gute] or being appointed by a higher authority. Cooperation by the community in the latter case is in itself appropriate, but in our conditions of democratic agitation and the lack of historical instances, it is not without reservations. Yet even the free right of election of the rural community, where it is historically founded, and thus especially in originally free farming communities, is a blameless institution.

The corporation [Körperschaft] of the municipality or its representation must, in either form of community, preferably be **<22>** founded in production of sustenance – on the one hand industry and trade, on the other agriculture – as that which is the substance of the municipality, the rural community in particular on the possession of land and soil, in that there participation in the ordering power everywhere is based on such. Accordingly, in the city the representation of the citizenry, in terms of its chief families [Hauptstammen], will arise from the associations of industrial and trading estates, to which other elements appropriately join themselves. In the country, the deciding community assembly will likewise be composed of the farmers (first and foremost the actual farmers, then, as less-entitled classes, the tenant farmers [Kossäthen], cottagers [Büdenern], etc.). A class structure according to taxation is an effective replacement in the cities, in view of the dissolution of vocational associations, in order to obtain conservative officials (e.g., the Prussian threefold property classes); but for the rural communities, such displaces the yet factually existing natural classes based upon the various forms of property and destroys the estate consciousness of these classes which is based thereupon. It therefore ought only to make its appearance in the most extreme cases, in which, in consequence of the complete change of property (dismemberment and consolidation), such a real factual situation can no longer be maintained.

Membership in the municipality (*home town*) as a rule ought to be oriented to *origin*, not *residence;* the latter ought to be the exception. Increased commerce and overpopulation could lend residence the weightier consideration over origin. However, in this one may reach the extreme – and we are close to it – in which municipalities are virtually nothing else than way-stations for the great migration of working classes in search of sustenance. It is necessary that this be reduced in every way, for the healthy community relation is not merely a spatial bond but a personal one, and therefore ought not immediately be discontinued and exchanged when a spatial change takes place. **<23>**

§. 8. The Municipality as Integral Member of the State

The municipality is related to the state as a *member* and therefore must be characterized both as an independent entity and by the totality of the state. It arises from itself, like the state does, and together with the state; its constitution develops by means of natural growth and therefore is peculiar to each local community. However, it is appropriate to indicate state-statutorily certain principles of public necessity, and thereby uniformity, which hedge about these individual structures. The proper approach here is to leave these historic preexisting individualities alone and only in certain points to subordinate them to a few common, newly determined necessities. Nevertheless, in most states the opposite was done: first all the existing and particular elements were eliminated, then an entirely new constitution was drafted, and only then was each municipality permitted, even ordered, to develop within this general framework, from that point forward.[21]

The constitution of each and every municipality, in particular each city, is not to be an isolated untouchable privilege of that community but a part of the state constitution, yet nevertheless valid as the law of those communities, both individually and taken together, and therefore providing, apart from the protection afforded by the collective national representation, if not absolute veto power, nevertheless a power of protest which cannot lightly be ignored. The individual municipal right of citizenship is to exist, along with the freedom of domicile within well-defined boundaries, according to lawful requirements. The municipality is to have an independent administration, although on the basis of national laws and under the <24> supervision or the leadership of the state government (§. 4). The cities are to elect their own mayors, although subject to the approval of the sovereign. The municipality is thereby a unique unmixed body in the state, albeit permeated by the unity of the whole; self-acting for its specific municipal interests but not withdrawn from higher moderating factors.

---

[21] The Prussian City Ordinance of 1808 did allow a statute to each city, i.e., an epitome of individual regulations partly to be maintained, partly to be established; but itself it is so detailed in its uniform regulations as to leave no particular significance for such a statute. In this the preserved city constitutions have the advantage that the multiplicity of historic constructions are recognized and are only subordinated to a common higher principle.

§. 9. Revolutionary Destruction of Municipal Integrity

The older municipal constitution arose *naturally-historically*, and therefore *individually*, each in every municipality, and had a most sharply expressed *estate-oriented* [ständischen], *autocratic* and therefore *autonomic* character. An estate-based gap existed between city and country by means of the prohibition on the conduct of urban trades in the countryside, and no less strict were the restrictions on non-guild members from representation in the city assembly (the broader council), while in the country the smaller landholders (tenant farmers [Kossäthen]) were excluded from the local assembly. The municipal authorities went about their business without any input from the community: in particular, in the cities the magistrates ruled from their own power, their offices were for life, and they added to their number by means of cooptation. The individual city was independent, even closed off from the totality of the nation. It had its self-contained constitution resting on special privilege and historical development and was inaccessible to national legislation as a matter of acquired right. Its exclusive right of citizenship could be acquired by other subjects of the territory not by fulfilling legal requirements but only through the free gift of the city itself. It had an approximately complete and to that degree exclusive range of political competencies, provided for the common welfare and the courts, formerly even its own armed forces as a matter of city right. In this manner, each city was a small state.

In consequence of the expanding pursuit of means of subsistence, advancing education, and the general trend toward higher levels of community and self-action, these characteristics, appropri- **<25>** ate to the times and a picture of fair, sensible, and organic structure, had to be tempered; the insularity in all relations had to move forward to a bond of unity. Until the French Revolution, however, nothing had been done about this except that the old autonomy was restricted by the territorial lord to an almost excessive degree.

Rather than conceding such expansion, moderation, and development toward unity, the French Revolution destroyed the entire natural order of the municipality from the bottom up. On December 14th, 1789 the Constituting National Assembly abolished all received municipal constitutions, replacing them with a new one based solely on this law[22], one and the same for all municipalities in France. Each municipality had a mayor (*maire*), a restricted and a

---

[22] [Decree on the Constitution of Municipalities.]

broad council (*conseil municipal* and *conseil général*) and a syndic (*procureur de la commune*, formerly *defensor civitatis*). These officials were elected for two years, drawn from the entire group of collective municipal members with a very narrow property qualification. The constitution granted a general unlimited freedom for settling or nullifying all previous special entitlements from the civil law, even property entitlements. The principles of *codification*, *uniformity*, *popular sovereignty*, and *aggregationism*, upon which the municipal constitution is built, stand therefore in complete opposition to the previous characteristics. The Directory government (*5 fructidor an III*) now also abolished the local community itself, in its place putting cantons with urban municipalities, making local communities mere municipal agents implementing the decisions made by the municipality. Although under the consular government the local communities (*mairies*) were restored in place of the cantons, it nevertheless remained the case that local communities often were merged into a collective community (mayoralty, *mairie*). Finally, in reaction to democracy the consular government (*28 pluviose an VIII*) abolished the influence of the local population to appoint the ruling authorities but likewise abolished all municipal independence. The mayor was appointed by state officials for a five-year period, the *corps municipal* selected from among the most heavily taxed, the mayor also received his orders from the state officials, and the *corps municipal* **<26>** everywhere only had an advisory vote and assembled only once per year apart from any special appointment of the prefect. This is the municipal constitution of the empire, which formed the final stage of the revolutionary development. This was constructed, again in extreme contrast to the older character of autonomy, upon absolute *centralization* and the *pure bureaucratic principle*. These various phases of municipal order in the Revolution are those which since then have also been pursued and imitated in Germany, with greater or lesser moderations, emphasizing either the democratic or the bureaucratic character. It has been the same way in England since 1835.

The error in the conception of the Revolution, here as in relation to the state, is twofold. The first (formal) error is that the municipality is made a construction of human effort rather than something given by nature. National legislation hereby erects communities as if none ever existed; it gives them constitutions, as if they never had had any. The municipal ordinances issued along these lines are appropriate for men such as those which sprang from the stones of Deucalion; but for men with fathers and thus a history and a relation to the past, they are inappropriate. The other (material) error is that the community is viewed as a mere voluntary association of equally entitled human wills, and not as an objective necessity and higher task over these wills; accordingly, it is not the requirements founded in the essence of the municipal association that are taken into account, but only the equal entitlement of all persons. The consequence of this error is general leveling. For then the different occupations of the urban and rural community according to their productive function, the different occupations of the individual people in each community according to property and employment, and finally, what is the core of all community life, the necessity of the local connection itself, all these things disappear. Thus, no power over the common members grounded in the institution can exist; decision-making power can lie only with them and their will in equal competition. The result of this constitution is general dissolution and destruction.

Here as everywhere else, codification destroys the consciousness of restraint (II. [*Principles of Law*] §. 21). In particular, the population of the coun- <27> tryside loses the attachment to tradition and the naive belief in the necessity for this immediate order of life, and, once consigned to the written law of today, which, moreover, will be replaced by another tomorrow, is challenged to ask why it is so and not otherwise, namely why not more to our (the questioners) advantage?

The mixing of city and countryside causes the rural community to be based not on landownership, in accordance with its nature, but to have artificial establishments and the complex administration of the cities imposed upon it, and given that the farmers are not equal to this, they become forced to seek leadership from bureaucratic elements of the worst sort, mostly compromised in other careers, who in turn compromise the farmers' condition and spirit.

Participation of all local residents in municipal representation and the rural community assembly puts community business in the hands of the unbidden and the unconcerned, from which partly arises the poorer care for that business, and partly a wavering between apathy regarding community affairs and revolutionary agitation for questions of general political principles rather than zealous occupation with local, particularly acquisition-oriented interests. In the countryside, to wit, the agricultural estate, when it no longer exclusively or predominantly forms the community, and does not hold onto its individual right to vote [Virilstimmrecht], loses its entire estate feeling, which is one of the first levers of a steady and solid sentiment and condition.

The lumping together of many local communities under a mayoralty destroys the sense of community, which of necessity is local, and quite easily damages the particular interests of localities.

Finally, rulership from below to above, this foundation of all offices on election and ever more frequent elections (*fréquente amovibilité*), and precisely in the spirit of the predominance of the municipal representation as bearers of municipal sovereignty over the magistrate, destroys the concept of ruling authority and revolutionizes the entire sentiment of the population. The concept of popular sovereignty, once it has lodged in the smaller circles and daily application, will be difficult to keep from the broader circle of the state. The public nature of town councilors' debates, the public <28> thronging to hear piquant questions, are then the supplementation in this general education of and unfolding of all moral forces for the system of revolution.

The imperialistic phase in the municipal constitution of the Revolution has now put an end to the democratic disorder and revolt in the municipality, but has put an end to freedom as well. In place of the rule of the head count have come the biggest taxpayers and the almighty prefects. With the destruction of inward organic structure, the municipality can only be held together by the external glue of property qualification and the iron brace of state power. This phase is therefore characterized by bureaucratic despotism over the municipality. This does not contradict the spirit of the Revolution. The Revolution did desire the freedom of municipalities, but conceived it as the emancipation of the municipal population from its municipal ruling authorities and not likewise as the freedom of the city, this communal whole, over against central state power. The resistance against magistrates founded on birth, family prerogative, or cooptation, was thus the inalienable core of the new viewpoint, from which it has not deviated. By contrast, there was no awareness of any infringement against freedom when, even after the constitution of 1789, the municipality could be overwhelmed by any influx of new settlers, the Reign of Terror reigned supreme through the National Agent whom it appointed to replace the city procurators, in which, finally, in accordance with the consular and imperial constitution, the municipal ruling authority was appointed by state power, and the community had virtually no say in the administration of its affairs.

Abstract freedom and equality of all individuals and abstract governing mechanism extending outward from the supreme authority with its despotism are goals which stand not in a sworn deadly animosity but instead are both children of the same modern culture. The irreconcilable animosity now extends to all privilege of birth apart from the sovereign, and to a given (not continually elected) power of the ruler of a small circle. One puts up with the despotism of an emperor – that is enlightened – but one cannot tolerate the mild rulership of an independent magistracy or lifetime mayoralty. The **<29>** superimposing of local, provincial, and national representation, such as pursued already by Turgot, and lauded in the initial period of the Revolution, albeit generally speaking correct, in this constitution is completely unorganic, in that the municipality, province, and state are conceived as equal, all as mere masses of people. Neither the material variance in tasks nor the variance in constitutional principles for these various spheres receive their proper and complete valuation. We place the institution of the state with its task of higher ethical order and its given authority, the monarchy, over against the municipality, with its task of care for its own (local) interests and with a self-elected ruling authority. In the other case, though, everything is the rule of the people in the interest of the people, and there is certainly no reason why twenty million Frenchmen, or even the one recognized as their representative, should not give orders to the few thousand in individual municipalities.

For this reason, in France and in most cases in Germany the bureaucracy exploited the democratic municipal constitution for itself. Those collective municipalities, just as the cantonal municipalities during the Directorate, arose merely in the bureaucratic interest; it was felt that the local communities did not have enough capacities to implement the ordinances of the state government, for which the municipality was to be a mere means. The individual voting right in the rural communities had to give way because the officials could more easily complete their task with a single form of representation. Uniformity thus pressed the stamp of the administrative mechanism on all municipalities; and finally, the nonsense which is never absent from a democratic establishment grants title for the state administration to arrogate to itself exclusive rule in the municipality. The freedom of the municipality is the slogan with which the movement began, and governmental absolutism is where it has ended.

So did the Revolution in every aspect falsely complete the task. Instead of invigorating the municipality as a structured whole, so that even with increased self-reliance the members remain linked to and united by the vocation of the whole, it completely destroyed its interleaved [gliedliche] character. According to it, the municipality is a mere mass of persons and indeed a **<30>** fluctuating one, given its unrestricted freedom of movement, powerless against movement from inside and pressure from outside, powerless against the centralized power of the state. A forceful municipal entity is not attained by dissolving the municipality into atoms but by concentrating it as an institution, by appointing to rulership the elements which by nature have the strength and capacity of rulership, by bringing to predominant influence the interests upon which the municipality by nature is founded, thus by fostering the estates of vocation (the civil and agricultural aristocracy) and strong independent ruling authorities. Only thereby does the municipality attain that which is its true freedom, a steady and secured satisfaction of its needs, and only thereby does it maintain its independence against state power. Dissolving the municipality into a mere aggregate of equally entitled wills also dissolves the entire national population into a general aggregate which only can be divided and ruled by the general state government.[23]

§. 10. Centralization and Localism

Centralization is a necessary step in particular for the relation of the municipality to the state, yet one which the Revolution wrongly accomplished (imperialism). The older system of autonomy preserved during flourishing times the general advantages of freedom and self-reliance, to wit, active participation, public spirit, greater development of forces, the sense of civic honor, the expectation that the orders issued from the municipality answered to its <31> sensibilities and needs. On the other hand, it disrupted the unity of the state, restricted the implementation of large-scale measures for the country as a whole, and led, when the power of the cities and thereby the blossoming of enthusiasm finally gave way, to the opposite, to narrow self-interest of the municipality and its rulers – to philistinism [Spießburgerthum]. Therefore, it was appropriate for its time: in a certain period of state development, the municipality had the vocation of being the carrier of state functions, as in yet earlier times and in other ways the family had that vocation (the patriarchal age). How much did the Ger-

---

[23] Compare my speeches in the first chamber on 3 December 1849 [*Parlamentarische Reden*, pp. 333ff.] and on 7 January 1853 [ibid., pp. 364ff.], and the one by von Gerlach on 4 December 1849. The speeches of 1849 articulated resistance to the government's drafts of municipal, circle, and provincial order taken over from the promises of 1848. We only had 17 votes against out of 180, and the law was therefore promulgated in 1850. But after many vain attempts at implementation, it was abolished again in 1853. The final above-mentioned speech was given in favor of this abolition.

man cities of those days achieve in the area of public welfare, when the states (territorial lords) as yet had no capacity and no incentive for it!

But just for that reason it is no longer appropriate, since this period has passed. The French system of centralization controls the abuses of the earlier autonomy, providing the unity and force of the ship of state. But it provides it only through mechanical effect; its successes prove themselves only in the material sphere (railways, streets), and on top of that, to the same degree that the state increases in force of implementation and transformation, to that degree it loses the force of preservation, in that the innovation stemming from the central government does not first have to test itself against the resistance of independent corporations; and movement against the government, revolt, when it comes, once having penetrated to the central seat then sweeps the country along with it. On the other hand, this centralization deadens all living impulses and all peculiarity of municipal association, and thereby everything in the community of an ethical bond and ethical spirit; in fact, in terms of its essence it is nothing other than the destruction of the municipality. While in the older system the municipality was a smaller state within a state, here it is a mere administrative district, a geographic division for the implementation of state orders; there are indeed no longer any municipalities but only mere localities. This system of centralization is therefore reprehensible at all times. But the proper satisfaction of the necessary advance is for the municipality to be subordinated to the unity of the state and its rulership, yet neverthe- **<32>** less to be maintained in its independence and self-reliance as a true corporate body [körperschaft].[24]

Independence in the smaller circles is the foundation of all truly free constitutions. It is unnatural that the people participate in the joint rulership of the state when participation in or attendance upon their nearest interests is taken away from them. Territorial estates ought not to administer, but municipalities, districts, and even to a certain degree provincial associates are to administer in their sphere. Möser, if I have rightly understood his spirit, placed public freedom predominantly in this self-administration of the smaller sphere. A similar thought is also given by Tocqueville when he distinguishes between *governmen-*

---

[24] The Prussian city ordinance of 1808, often used as a model in Germany despite having a destructive effect internally in the municipality, yet has the advantage of preserving a sphere of independence over against state power.

tal and *administrative* centralization, recognizing the former as necessary, characterizing the latter as an evil, particularly in France.

Progress in history from earlier autonomy to true centralization is an advance from lower to higher organism. In terms of the older situation, the members of the state, the cities and corporations as well as the manors, certainly were borne by the whole, but not determinable by it, not ruled with certainty and set in motion, but entirely independent – such is the character of the merely organic, or the *lower organism* (similar to plants). In terms of recent principles of state, these members are certainly to retain an independent free sphere of activity, but to be subordinated to the single state rule, enclosed by it and *determinable* by it, which is the character of *higher organism*, the *body* of a single spirit, i.e., a *personality* or an *ethical kingdom*, serving as bearer, and therefore itself possessing full unity, central governance of its members.[25] This *higher organic* (the body) is only <33> apparently akin to *mechanism*, which contains a similar unity but only by destroying the life of the parts, degrading them to mere means and instruments. The former, which is a vocation of the times, is true centralization; the latter, which has been implemented since the end of the previous century, is false. By contrast, the aspiration to return to the old autonomy is based on the error of holding the merely organic to be higher than the corporeal and personal, as unification for and into an ethical kingdom.[26]

---

[25] These are not mere figures of speech but concepts. If it is permitted to transfer the concept of the organism, which belongs to the physical world, to the ethical world as a general concept, as it is used by everyone nowadays, then it must no less be permitted to transfer the distinction between mere organism and body, which no one can deny for the physical world, and which exists no less for the ethical. Organism, mechanism, and body are the deeper scientific expression for those three systems, the illumination of their innermost essence.

[26] The municipal constitution of North America (usually I have New England in mind) is based of course on entirely different principles: the most extreme *democracy* and the most extreme *independence from the state.*

The collectivity of municipal members does not merely have sovereignty but exercises it itself, which outdoes the constitution of 1789. It has no representation which decides in its place, but itself formulates the decisions in general assembly through one man, one vote [Virilabstimmung]. It also has no magistracy to which it transfers power, only mere functionaries. To wit, it annually elects municipal officials, partly for general business (the selectmen), partly for special business (tax distributors, tax collectors, supervisors of public places, commissioners of care of the poor, schools, roads, fire, etc.). But all these officials have no independent power of order, they conduct their business only in terms of instruction from the collective community, and where such is not given by general regulation, observance, etc., they must apply for a special decision. The administration is therefore concentrated only in the collective community, not in any official; in particular, the officials for special business are not subordinated to those for general affairs (selectmen), as the technical officials are subordinated to the mayor in our communities, but directly to the collective community. Indeed the members of the community thus administer the collectivity.

But likewise the independence of the municipality vis-à-vis the state runs to the limits of the possible. It administers not simply the actual municipal affairs without any intervention, supervision, perusal by the state, but itself in the same independence provides for actual state affairs, for example sanitation [Sanität], public morality, schools. In fact it nevertheless within its sphere provides for even that which of necessity and inseparably pertains to the state, for example military needs, state taxes, and is liable as a whole to the state, it provides for ammunition supplies, allocates and levies state taxes.

The entire municipal constitution is based on the peculiar relations of North America, in particular that there the entire social condition was derived from the municipality (not the nation) and still yet is based on the municipality, it is based on the peculiar spirit of North America, in particular the churchly spirit of Independency, the principles of ecclesiastical constitution of which are actually reflected in the political establishment. For this reason, imitation elsewhere is simply impossible; in fact, the question is whether it can be maintained in America when the population becomes as dense as it is with us.

Chapter 2: The Estates and the Economy

§. 11. The Estate as Life Vocation

<35> The people develop various forms of activities for the various goals which make up their common life, which in turn mutually condition and supplement each other organically into a kingdom of rational goals, a common goal of their existence. In accordance with this, people separate themselves into classes for each of these activities – the *division of labor*. Attendance to this becomes their special life vocation and hence determines their *position in life*. These are the *estates*. Hence *an estate is the particular life vocation for the sake of common life, which also determines the life position of those who apply themselves to it*. The purpose (τέλος) of the estate is the *complete provision* of each activity necessary to the common life, but no less is it – by virtue of the principle of personality – the derivation of *satisfaction* and *worth* from that activity.

Accordingly, only that occupation forms an estate which has a direct and regular effect on the whole, which is a co-bearer of the general condition, so that through it one's entire position in the community is enduringly determined. An activity which does not affect and ought not affect the common life, e.g. a private tutor, does not form an estate. But likewise, only the main forms of activity in which the popular life develops as an objective shared thing, and which for this reason enduringly exist and are conducted by a larger number of people, are capable of forming an estate and estate vocation. The individual vocation follows on the basis of this, and for this reason does not carry anything general and enduring in itself but is restricted to the life of the individual (see, e.g., Niebuhr's *History of Rome*). Only the former belong to the objective, legal order; the latter, by contrast, belong to the moral. <36>

The concept of the *estate in the legal sense* therefore also entails that this particular life position, resulting from a particular life vocation, is not merely factual but also established legally. The large landowners, for example, factually always form an estate in distinction to the industrialists [Gewerbtreibenden]; but legally they only form such when special legal stipulations are valid for them. It is the peculiarity and the advantage of Germanic law, that it conceives people in the distinction of their life vocations, and thus their estates, and attaches legal consequences to them. In this manner, a *law of estates* has been developed, i.e., both various political rights for various estates, as well as, in yet more extensive manner, various private-legal determinations, as they are applicable to their life vocation. Roman law only contains regulations for specific activities, such as trade, brokerage, the carrier business, while Germanic law contains regulations for persons having these activities as life vocations, e.g., merchants, brokers, carriers, so that such do not accrue to other persons even when they carry out the same activities – and such by right, since these activities, as regular and declared estate-activities of a person, truly merit a different legal valuation and treatment.

§. 12. The Equality and Inequality of Estates

Such a division of human activity, resulting in the estates, inheres in the idea of human-earthly existence. But the actual condition of the estates is determined not simply by the division of activity but also by another cause, by the struggle of man with nature – the curse on labor (Genesis 3:19) whereby, i.e., the external world and even one's own inner forces of human intent stubbornly resist, and only with difficulty can be made serviceable. "In the sweat of thy face shalt thou eat bread" holds true not only for baser activities, the production of bodily necessities, but more or less for all human pursuits. There is no goal which does not have to be pursued in the sweat of one's brow. Even in intellectual areas, in art and science, each possession is gained only through exertion. From this comes the defectiveness of the social condition: firstly, the *particularism of the* <37> *estate*, predominantly determined both in its formation and its life position by the one-sided character of the estate rather than by the universal essence of men; secondly, the *separation* of human society in two classes, the one devoted to the higher intellectual activities, the other allotted to bodily labor for maintaining one's own existence – the foundation of the distinction between honorable and disdained castes in the Orient, the nobility and the people in older Europe, the higher and lower estates everywhere and at all times; finally, pauperism.

This situation does not correspond to the idea of human existence. For one's own activity and product is certainly a joy and an honor; but this hardship, this lack of success, and the stunting or at least restriction of numerous classes of men is neither the one nor the other. This condition should therefore increasingly be overcome so that the particularism of the estates is tempered by the higher universal human essence (the all-roundedness of culture and insight, the general civic right) and the lower estates are elevated both personally through mores and culture and in terms of their estate through the awareness of higher consecration lying in every human vocation, which ethically ennobles everyone who conducts it in this sense. This is also increasingly attained by Christianity and Christian civilization. But as long as earthly conditions endure, it cannot be eliminated. It is therefore one of the deceptions of the Revolution that it attempted to eliminate the distinction of classes, thereby desiring to go beyond earthly circumstances and eradicate by means of human action, i.e., legal establishment, that curse on labor which only God Himself can remove. Its intention that the various vocations no longer determine life position but only exist in a variety of activities (a general, a minister, a shoemaker, a tailor, a hairdresser all being citizens plain and simple) is really only attained in form and title, not in fact; for the various estimates of worth of each form of vocation are ineradicably founded in nature and in truth, and even when the nobility is abolished, the distinction of wealth and poverty confirms ineradicably the cleft between two classes. Moreover, though, it is a reversal of things – the caricature of the Christian idea – when the estate of the mechanical laborer is conceived, in extreme <38> contrast to previous times, precisely as the higher, as the actual people, to which even still today the liberal opinion, in fact even the celebration of poetry in France, is often directed.

It has been regarded throughout all of history that the higher estate should be relieved of bodily exertion and lower forms of labor. This is based on the deep truth that the original and eternal purpose of man is not labor of this sort but free spiritual existence and activity. The only activities then considered worthy of man are the ethical-intellectual activity of war and government or religious ceremony [des Kultus], and effortless landholding. The ancient world demonstrates to us the extreme of this conception. Hence Aristotle held that a well-constituted state ought not grant manual laborers full rights of citizenship; likewise Plato excluded the laboring class from the government. In the same manner, the nobility throughout the entire Middle Ages was held to be an elevated estate with exclusive full honors over the citizen estate, and this has continued in tempered fashion up until this century. As Christianity atoned for sin, so did it also remove the dishonor from labor. In fact, it made the condition of labor and exertion, which from the perspective of eternity should not have come into existence, into a means for a yet greater probation of man's ethical strength. An enlightened viewpoint, which gradually arose from the bosom of Christian civilization, imparted to manual labor its proper valuation. Even trade and industry entail, in varying degrees, spiritual, partly intellectual, partly artistic activity, and the motivation of providing a family's upkeep and satisfying the needs of fellow citizens, finally to manufacture excellent commodities, is no less ethical than is defending and providing advice to the fatherland. General civic entitlement and honor is therefore a requirement of true Christian civilization.

Yet even if all occupations are honorable, still there are higher and lower occupations, and while civic right is equal for all, the distinction cannot and ought not cease in social custom. The mere mechanical occupation, and the lack of culture [Bildung] which accompanies it, effectuates a factual subordination by virtue of natural laws, and there is by no means an ethical-political requirement <39> artificially to terminate it by force (égalité, fraternité). In terms of Christian civilization, this distinction is not to be preserved legally, but factually, effectuated by nature, and men are to be equalized through free act, i.e., by means of a deeper valuation ignoring this and everywhere only considering the person; in terms of the revolutionary civilization, this is to be mechanically terminated, obviating the need of humility on the part of the higher. Similar to distinctions of wealth in Christian civilization going together with the rich having the duty to share with the poor, in the revolutionary (i.e., in terms of consistency, communist) civilization, equality of wealth is to exist from the start, ruling out sharing. For this reason, in terms of Christian civilization it is an obligation of the rich to give and on the elevated to forget their higher position, while in terms of the revolutionary civilization it is an authorization of the poor to take, of the lesser to make themselves equal. The person pursuing the lesser occupation can in his humility stand much higher than he who pursues a noble one, and God looks gladly upon the humble; but that is yet one more proof that in himself he is the lesser. Christ's birth was revealed to the shepherds – not the priests! – but it does not follow that the shepherds' estate is higher than the priestly, but rather the contrary.

In modern estimation, the Christian "even though" becomes "because." The (mere mechanical) laborer insists that he is the one who is truly entitled in society, precisely because he is a laborer. In this manner, the deepest truth is overturned into the most extreme error. That the highest honor is due labor is only correct when, by labor, one understands not exertion but productive activity; the former lays claim only to our sympathy, not our esteem. An intellectual can invoke only the value of his work, not his late nights at work; and one would scarcely value more highly the drudge who makes the greater exertion than the supervisor and, above all, the principal, who provide to labor the intellectual leadership. In the same manner, it is proper that production be granted the higher honor than mere consumption, when by production one understands the advantageous influence on the commonwealth, and not merely the material influence thereon. Occupation with government or war is not an <40> unproductive condition in this sense, and why the landlord living from lease and rent payments is any less productive and estimable than the tobacco industrialist living from the sweat of his laborers' brows is not clear. That which underlies such a valuation is not merely the thought of equality but also the materialistic sense which values most highly goods for material enjoyment, and therefore their production as well. Resistance to the mere consuming classes had its grounds and its justification when a class privileged by birth had the prerogative to spiritual activities, to civil and military offices or estates-oriented representation, and where a legal distinction of honor existed. Where this has been eliminated, such an opposition is of no more benefit than is an overestimation of material goods and material production.

The question raised by Aristotle as to whether perfection could better be attained in individuals through well-rounded harmonious education, or in the commonwealth through men in one-sided, and therefore more intensified, development, has been factually answered in our time. In terms of his *being* and *essence*, man is to receive a harmonious education, in that, as personality, he is an absolute goal in terms of his being and essence; but his *activity* and *skill* is exclusively to be directed to one specific part of the common activity, because that activity has the whole as its goal. These goals, therefore, no longer stand in contradiction, but on the contrary, they require each other reciprocally.

§. 13. Public and Private Estates

The estates are divided into two main classes, *public* and *private;* the former's activity has a direct effect on the commonwealth as a whole, in particular in its leading, and therefore also takes place in the name of the commonwealth and is determined by it; the latter's activity has an effect, firstly in particulars and upon other individuals; only mediately, in terms of result and by and large, is it a supplementary member of the commonwealth; therefore, it proceeds from, and <41> in accordance with, the free motive of the individual.

The public estates (officialdom, clergy, military) do not form any system in themselves, while each has its origin and existence independently of the other, in the institution or sphere in which it is to serve. These will therefore first be spoken of in those places. The private estates, however, do form a system, a whole enclosed in itself, in that they serve one and the same purpose: the *satisfaction of life requirements*, in this regard especially the *creation of wealth*.

Human community itself creates its wealth, the means to meet its needs, through its own activity, and yet, as with all human activity, it does so on the basis of material which nature provides. The system of private estates is therefore the real[27] progress of this activity extending from this basis. It is simply the following:

1. The extraction [Gewinnung] of natural materials through the cultivation of nature – *landholding* and *agriculture*.

2. The shaping and processing of these materials through human action, by which they are assimilated to human use – *industry* [Gewerbe].

3. The *control* [Beherrschung], i.e., distribution and circulation, of these goods among the human community for needs – *trade* [Handel].

These are the basic estates of society. On their basis stand the estates which through mere spiritual, i.e., non-material, activity serve the needs of their fellow citizens: doctors, lawyers, teachers, artists.

§. 14. State versus Society

The private estates in their reciprocal augmentation are the *civil association* [bürgerliche Verband] or, as it is now termed, *society* <42> [Gesellschaft] as distinguished from the state. Although the concept and expression "society" comes from France and, indeed, from the communist-socialist doctrine, it is well-founded when purified of the errors of that doctrine. Society, in terms of this concept, has as its purpose the reciprocal satisfaction of human needs, while the state has as its purpose the maintenance of higher commandments, the fulfillment of higher ideas about men. Production and processing of goods for human

---

[27] Hegel developed this from a logical progression, the categories of the substantial (landholding), the reflective (industry and trade), and the union of both (general estate, i.e., officialdom). As this development itself does not have the specific nature of the estates as its foundation, it arrives at the inappropriate result of joining the private estates and a public estate as members of one system.

enjoyment, doings and dealings, that is society; maintenance of divine commandments of justice, punishment of crimes, upholding of discipline, majesty of public power, that is the state. The former is the *economic* [wirthschaftliche], the latter is the *ruling* [herrschaftliche] association of the nation. The former is the essence of reciprocal augmentation, exchange; the latter is the unity of higher regard, ruling authority, and obedience.[28] <43>

Society and state, the social and political fields are only distinguishable, not separable. They are only the different aspects of one and the same national

---

[28] Entirely different from this is Hegel's distinction between "civil society" and the "state." By "society" we understand, in line with the French concept, simply the distribution of activities, life vocations, and human positions deriving therefrom, while by state we understand the higher rule in terms of ethical-reasonable goals, in which, of course, the order of society itself is also included. Hegel, by contrast, understands by "society" everything which intends or extends to the advantage of people; indeed, everything whereby people as individuals are conceived, in opposition to the state, the concept of which is discovered in people being subsumed in the whole (the substance). Accordingly, in his "civil society" he includes not only the civil association in our sense but also the entire administration ("public welfare"), indeed the entire legal constitution (*Grundlinien der Philosophie des Rechts* [Baselines of the Philosophy of Law], §. 157 and §. 258), in that these have, as their task, the well-being and rights of people (thus, people conceived as separate subjects). (Still, even this could not be applied to the administration of penal law.) As "state," then, there remains for him, by his own clear statement, nothing beyond the constitution, i.e., the organization of power, in that here and only here does the individual disappear, and only the whole is brought out. This distinction is derived from mere determinations of logic, and thus does not get to the matter in the way the other mentioned above does, but is altogether unnatural. In terms of it, the construction of the state is "state," its activity is "society." This is to be a correction of the earlier natural law approach, which put the entire concept of the state in the protection of rights, thus in the administration of justice. But even though it might be proper for the state not to consist exclusively in the administration of justice, still, the administration of justice is one of the essential aspects of the state, it being the realization of the idea of justice, and law can by no means be considered to be a *social* institution; legal transactions [Rechtsverkehr] are a mere *private* activity, but the administration of justice is a *state-oriented activity.*

existence and task. They therefore permeate each other everywhere, without a clear boundary, and everywhere stand in reciprocal action. Thus, for example, the local community, the guild, the nobility, the teaching estate [Lehrstand], the relation of masters to journeymen and apprentices, all have their social and their political aspects. The social element, the character of estates and their economic coherence, has a necessary influence on the political element: on the formation of the territorial representation, on the constitution of the judiciary and public welfare, on the establishment of administration (autonomy, patrimonial power, bureaucracy), even on the position of the king and royal court. And vice versa, the social element, the entirety of economic activity, is determined by the political element, the position of the ruling authority of the local community, labor union [Innung], squirearchy [Gutsherrschaft], territorial authority [Landesbehörde], and is absolutely conditioned by the legal protection of the state. The state and its constitution have their substrate in society, and vice versa, society is only held together by the state. State and constitution therefore must be considered to be under the influence of the social condition, although not the mere consequence of it. They have an independent significance, do not exist simply for the production of wealth and satisfaction of needs, and thus have an independent principle of formation which is not given by the form of social conditions, but instead initially determines that form. For this reason, the social sphere cannot be separately judged in itself, and aid for the current difficult conditions in that sphere cannot be sought there alone. Thus, in particular, the warding off of pauperization depends particularly on political (ruling-authority) relations, on the establishment of fixed authorities, on discipline and obedi-
<44> ence. It is always an error to separate the social from the political.

The communist-socialist school, from which the concept and expression originated, indulged in this error to the utmost. With them, this separation is the intention and goes so far as entirely to absorb the state by society, which means the abolition of both the higher tasks and the higher regard over the people, leaving the common production of goods and common enjoyment. But even those who are far from the socialistic standpoint are of the opinion that the "social question" ought to be dealt with in complete isolation from the political, as something that can be resolved by itself. Likewise, the attempt is made at state philosophy as a general "social theory." That is a path to illuminate new aspects, but not to hit and to exhaust the core of the matter. In the same way that, up until lately, the constitution was simply deduced from ethical and legal principles apart from any consideration of economic elements, now the tendency is toward another one-sidedness, to view the constitution as the mere consequence of economic conditions. If this error of separating the social from the political is completely given up, the distinction of the two relations, and the more careful cultivation of the former, is a gain for the knowledge of the state.

The distinction between the social and the political aspect corresponds to the distinction between *civil* and *political* rights, in the manner customary since the treaties of the Rhine Confederation. To wit, among civil rights, in addition to pure private rights, one includes participation in economic activities and positions in the people, thus the capacity to acquire landed property, to belong to trade associations, while among political rights one includes participation in the rulership positions in the nation [im Volke], the capacity for civil office and territorial representation. That is to say, only full citizens who are a part of the entire ethical element of the nation, in particular its religion, may participate in the higher ethical task which the state serves; on the other hand, others can certainly also participate in the satisfaction of their own needs and thus the needs of their fellow citizens as a whole.

Something entirely different from this concept of civil rights is <45> the concept of *social rights* in the sense of the socialistic doctrine. By this, it understands not the participation in wealth-creating activity but participation in wealth itself, a portion in existing or produced goods. This concept presupposes the abolition of property or the private economy [Sonderwirthschaft].

§. 15. Economic Theory and Its Shortcomings

The creation of wealth, as it proceeds from these estates, as provision for national needs, is the object of the science of economics [Nationalökonomie].

The order of this creation of wealth, and the science of it, has its supreme (philosophical) principle in the ethical meaning of material goods. We have sought scientifically to explain that these are not mere means for the fulfillment of ethical duties, but have an independent value in themselves as satisfaction – a natural and ethically confirmed pursuit of personality – and yet, their value is always subordinate with regard to ethics and spiritual bonds, they ought not be the absolute goal, the supreme satisfaction, but must remain in connection with and under the rule of higher goods. The natural human temptation is to descend to satisfaction through tangible goods (practical Epicurianism, as well as the ethical systems in which sensual enjoyment, or satisfaction in general, is made the principle of ethics). The effort to safeguard against that, to maintain freedom over those tangible goods, often led astray in another direction, namely, making the severance from those goods, which by all means is required as an inward act of liberation, into a requirement for the permanent external condition, and so entirely rejecting satisfaction through material goods (Stoicism, monastic asceticism). The full free human position is to derive satisfaction while yet standing over it, with the entire spiritual ethical existence. This is the Christian, and especially the Protestant [evangelische] life orientation. John the Baptist neither ate nor drank, but the Savior both ate and drank. The pursuit of the acquisition of tangible goods, therefore, goes hand in hand with the pursuit of satisfaction through them. The <46> one is ethically justified or commanded, as the case may be, in the same measure and in the same manner as the other, and the room which it takes in men's life activity depends on their degree of ethical advancement.

The ethical meaning of goods for individuals is of necessity the same as it is for the nation. Therefore we see here the same oppositions. The ancient world gives us the example of the rejection of the possession and enjoyment of national goods in order to keep the higher political life from being infringed upon by them; satisfaction ought to be sought only in love of the fatherland, glory in war and the like, not in possession and private enjoyment. The most recent social theory takes this to the opposite extreme, viewing the enjoyment of tangible goods as the highest, absolute goal of the human race, and considers all ethical relations, marriage and the state, as mere means to this end. This is no longer a mere one-sided doctrine but one entirely devoid of ethics. But even apart from the social theory, at least the production of material goods (thus in the end, even when unspoken, the enjoyment thereof) is considered to be the decisive consideration of the nation, in terms of which the shaping of the civil and political world is to be directed. Here as well, however, the proper ethical relation is: the means of material satisfaction are good and are a goal in themselves; their multiplied production is therefore a task which in itself has no limit; but they must remain in relation and subordination to the ethical political common existence of the nation. But this consists in the individual families and the wealth-creating estates being maintained in a condition in which they conduct an ethical life and can fulfill their vocation for society and the state in a worthy manner.

Accordingly, it is not the wealth of the nation in the abstract but the secured livelihoods of specific families which is the end, and not the endless increase of the production of goods but likewise the appropriate distribution and, above all, the sustainability of the producing classes. Hence these producing classes must come into consideration in terms of their entire personal existence, i.e., not merely in their wealth-creating activity in itself alone (the economic side), but likewise the conviction and the power <47> on behalf of the commonwealth which is connected with it (the political side).

Should the supreme ethical principle of wealth creation lead us to this result, so does it no less confirm it through its own organic law. For according to this, the point cannot be that of producing the greatest possible amount of goods, but likewise that of preserving the organs of production, i.e., the families and the estates, in a lasting manner. Such infinitely increasing production, torn from all other considerations, when it exhausts in increasing degree the producing classes (the steadily widening contrast between plutocrats [Geldfürsten] and proletarians), must end in there no longer being any market, and production itself ceasing.

The development of the science of economics, which attained its fulfillment with Adam Smith, brought to light the great insight, entirely foreign to earlier ages, of the natural laws of goods production. But it conceived of wealth (merely material) in isolated fashion as an absolute goal and in the abstract, as wealth created by society for society. In this respect, it is one and the same whether one seeks national wealth in *money*, i.e., in the maximum amounts which annually flow into the country after balancing imports and exports (mercantile system), or in *natural production*, the maximum amount of natural products yielded by the soil (physiocratic system), or *labor*, the maximum mass of goods put into the world through human activity (industrial system). From this viewpoint, the goal becomes the interminable increase of production and, as means, the unrestricted freedom of production and commerce, in that the latter, through competition, harnesses to the greatest degree the forces of production. The mercantile system as the crudest beginning of abstract economic doctrine did not progress to this result, which is the necessary consequence.

Economics is thereby relieved of the ethical and therefore also the true political principle. That the self-interest of individuals is restricted for the benefit of others' equal opportunity of acquisition, which recent economics often views as the ethical principle of its science, is as little an ethical principle as is the restriction of individual freedom for the equal freedom of others (maxim of coexistence) <48> in relation to law. The result from the realization of this doctrine, firstly, is certainly a greater surplus of goods among the people, yet with reciprocal overbidding and conflict, the accumulation of those goods in the hands of the individual wealthy, and the impoverishment of the larger mass.

This is the contemporary, generally dominant standpoint of economics, just as liberalism is of politics. It is an entirely erroneous one. It is already self-contradictory to seek the well-being of the nation and to be indifferent to the well-being of the persons making up the nation. But it also no less contradicts clear ethical requirement. Even in economics, goodwill and love to persons (individuals) must be the principle. The point is not whether the multiyear statisticians discover that so many masses of commodities were produced, but whether the people who produced the commodities were in a state of affluence or misery, in steady income or in constant fluctuation. It can be of no use that society builds an industrial palace the brilliance of which outshines any that ever existed, which is to proclaim the unity and greatness of the human race, similar to the Tower of Babel of yore, when the people who are the tools of such an industry languish en masse. Goods production is for the sake of man, not man for the sake of goods production. It was therefore a significant correction when Sismondi asserted that the point is not merely the amount of produced goods but also their proper distribution. Yet neither did this gain the proper viewpoint of national economics and exhaust its full range of vision. For in accordance with it, the starting point is still the production of goods, and goods in the abstract at that, and only then are people sought to be understood, instead of beginning with people in the entire personal position in which they bring about production. The proper task and treatment of economics, which has already begun (if in weakness), is therefore the organic conception of how the national wealth arises from an arrangement of specific organs, to wit, the estates, and how in the maintenance of these organs, namely the ethical and economic force of these estates and the families of which they are composed, it has <49> just as much its purpose as its means.[29]

---

[29] The ethical viewpoint which this development of economics left out of consideration has been asserted by distinguished writers. "Patience, labour, sobriety, frugality, and

Accordingly, it is a healthy condition both economically and ethically when the great mass of the people form a *middle class* [Mittelstand]. Thus the maintenance of an estate of independent farmers capable of conducting a life which, while restricted, is not stunted, in opposition to large landowners and day laborers, likewise the maintenance of an industrial estate of small well-to-do master craftsmen in opposition to factory lords and factory workers. This is the goal, and since it cannot be attained of itself, it must be brought about through legislation, be it implemented as carefully as possible. Certainly by virtue of the individual freedom that is valid for the sphere of property (III [*Private Law*], §. 29), *no* individual (subject [Subjekt]) can be prescribed the form or measure of production, consumption, or possessions, as occurred in the ancient world and as the latest social theory weaves in its dreams. But the (objective) *organization of profit-making businesses* [Vermögensbetriebe] ought and shall be arranged in accordance with the public common goal of the economy [Volksökonomie], for which goal the individual is to be restricted. Such a restriction for public prosperity and the <50> healthy arrangement of wealth-creating estates is no violation of rights and justice; indeed, the converse is true: it is a violation of rights and justice when the ruling authority, neglecting its vocation, leaves the entire activity of acquisition to itself and thereby protects no one in the sphere of his

---

religion, should be recommended to them; all the rest is downright *fraud*." Edmund Burke, *Thoughts and Details on Scarcity*, p. 4. "The number of well-to-do families must be measured according to an entirely different standard than national wealth, and this standard is none other than possession of an unencumbered secure property for the greatest possible number of citizens and an income amply sufficient for true needs, since affluence necessarily depends upon frugal mores. Should the number of those who are affluent in this manner decline... then such a people has declined in prosperity, even when riches rise immensely, when the means for manifold enjoyment have increased with all classes which are not impoverished." Barthold Georg Niebuhr, *Römische Geschichte* [History of Rome], vol. 1, p. 395. To investigate the degree to which this true advance has either been appropriated or forfeited in recent economics does not fall within the scope of my studies. Regarding the development of national economics starting from the one-sided viewpoint, and in connection with the development of philosophy, Brüggemann has said much that is instructive in his writing against List. I of course must dispute his assertion that Kant (the perfecter of the abstract viewpoint) contains the true ethical viewpoint. Kant is not the correction to Adam Smith but his parallel.

acquisition, abandoning the weaker to the superiority of the stronger. One can no longer have any doubt about this, that the objects of human satisfaction, extant prior to and apart from any human activity, are destined by nature to meet the needs of the community, not merely individuals, of the succession of generations, not merely the now living, e.g., forests and mines governed by publicly secured regulation, which – left to the caprice of individuals – would be squandered apart from this. The same viewpoint is no less valid for landholding and for industry; here certainly, individual caprice does not effectuate the destruction of the object, but it does effectuate the destruction of its contribution to the subjects (in mutual consumption), and the one is just as necessary to society as the other.

History everywhere shows us such protective, restricting regulations in varying manners and with various motives. The institutions of many Greek states, like the suggestions of many Greek philosophers, are based on abolishing or at least reducing tangible goods and their satisfaction, thus did not consist in restriction of commerce but in restriction of possession, e.g., the prohibition on money, the establishment of a maximum beyond which no one might possess, and the like. The Jewish year of Jubilee, by contrast, contains the idea of property distribution in its full profundity (even though not in a universally valid and universally implementable shape), namely, the concern that each family maintain an independent existence in secure fashion. The ancient world's pursuit of elevation over the sensorial is utterly foreign even to the German institution, which did not have a restriction and limit on possession but only on alienation, in order to protect the family. But Germanic law did not protect every human family, in divine aprioristic fashion, but only those in possession, in positive historical fashion. In the Jewish case, there was a distribution to each family, and an eternally repeating relapse to them; in the Germanic, only a prohibition on alienation or <51> division. Thus, those who happened to be in possession were maintained therein, while for the others it was even more difficult to acquire. Such an abuse, especially with larger populations, called forth its opposite, the liberal principle of free alienation and competition, so that a greater number might participate. This however leads to a no less disastrous result, the entanglement of the weaker by the stronger, so that no family is protected any longer. At that point along come the social [i.e., socialistic] theories, that is, society's laying claim to everything, in turn constantly allotting to each their lot and their labor.

The unfeasibility and reprehensibility of these theories is not difficult to fathom. But this does not justify the other principle. Instead, in the same way that the true constitution is not simply the possibility of establishing future rights (principle of the French Revolution), but above all the protection of specific existing acquired rights (English principle), just so must economics not merely open the possibility to future wealth in the abstract but above all seek to maintain the existing livelihoods of owners.

This forces us to return to the original Germanic principle, but also to expand it, namely, to maintain those in possession but to connect to this an attendance to those not in possession. For the maintenance in a state of possession of those already in that state has the priority over the provision of such a state to those not yet in it. This is the problem facing science today. I do not possess the technical knowledge to implement it; that which is given in the further sections of this chapter may therefore contain much that is weak and bare. This cannot however unsettle the truth of the indicated line of thought.

§. 16. Agriculture

Agriculture has a character of special sanctity among the branches of livelihood, in that here nature is the provider, man is the receiver of God's blessing in continuous dependence and expectation on powers over him, giving result to his labor. It is therefore the estate of greater simplicity, subordination under a higher governance. **<52>**

The purpose (τέλος) of agriculture is on the one hand the greater yield of the soil for the purpose of increased common satisfaction, on the other the maintenance of the estate itself, the specific families in their livelihood and their sense of vocation; the latter consists in love for the individual character of the property. The increase in yield is the economic motivation for legislation regarding landed property, while the preservation of specific families and this sense of vocation is the political and ethical motivation. In accordance with the latter, the supreme principle is the *continuity of property*, i.e., the greatest possible maintenance of these families, and the greatest possible maintenance of the complexes from which a family is capable of making a living.

[This was the motivation of earlier institutions by which families, both noble and common, were bound to the soil. In recent times these institutions became too restrictive, leading to the contrary principle of free division and alienation. This has led to the ruin of the farming estate and accumulation of property by the wealthy. A solution to this problem is difficult to determine. There must be restrictions placed on divisibility, the goal being to maintain landed property at the level at which it can support a family. An appropriate order of succession is also needed, preserving the property intact to the next generation. Furthermore, hereditary leaseholds should be encouraged. Such divided property creates an organic bond between wealthy landowners and propertyless laborers. Full freedom of property, whereby such relationships are ruled out, does nothing to help the propertyless class, which does not possess the wherewithal to acquire ownership: in this manner, the land comes into the hands of the rich. Patrimonial power is something entirely different. Here the bond is political and personal, and is a legacy of feudalism, unlike hereditary leasehold.]

§. 17. Industry

In the *branches of industry* man forms matter for his use, through which he imparts to it meaning and ideas. Therefore the ethical mainspring which leads activity here is not love for <53> the thing (individual property) but love for labor: diligence, reflection, skill. The task (τέλος) of industry in its entirety is on the one hand provision for the public, to which end abundance, efficiency, and cheapness of production, on the other hand provision for laborers and their sense of security, together with the maintenance of a sense of ethics and loyalty, to which end turnover.

[The older form of attaining these goals was the guild, which for moderns was akin to the feudal bond; recent times has substituted for it unconditional freedom of enterprise. The latter makes the individual laborer into a means for the public, while the former made the public into a means for the laborer. Unrestricted competition does not bring long-term benefits, in that it destroys the integrity of the laboring estate, undermines its security. In former times the guild guarded against this, but at the expense of sacrificing the public interest to an acquired private right. Nowadays it will have to be the public, i.e., the state or local community government, which will have to regulate competition. This could lead to the bureaucracy serving its own interest. The better method is indirect, through setting stricter requirements and conducting inspections, than the government directly trying to determine the capacity for generating livelihoods.]

[The introduction of machinery into the production process has been advantageous to production as a whole, but disadvantageous to the distribution of wealth and the maintenance of a sound middle class. In place of craftsmanship, it has reduced labor to something unspiritual and slavish, and its labor-saving takes away jobs. To this point, the use of machinery in production has been disastrous to the human race. The key now is to transform this negative into a positive. First and foremost, a healthy trade and industry estate [Gewerbstand] should not be sacrificed to the new factory lords. Where the new system already is established, the workers should be ensured a non-atrophied existence. The means: protective legislation and cooperatives among laborers (care for widows, the sick, unemployed, for the acquisition of necessities of life in order to maintain prices and meet the needs of individuals, savings banks). Nevertheless, an estate incapable of maintaining itself is unsuited to form a political estate.] <54>

§. 18. Trade

Trade, finally, is what energizes, impels, and connects the entire world of wealth. As ruler of material commerce, it carries the spiritual on its back, the way the state does the church. Culture goes from people to people via trade and navigation, and the expansion of scientific knowledge takes the vocation of bookselling as its means.

If the task of landownership is continuity, and that of industry is wealth and secure sales, that of trade is secure connection, the power of trading, bringing near the most distant thing, in order to provide the one thing for the other at any moment, with ease. The nerve of this power is *credit*. The ethical motive of the trading estate is therefore the *unshakeable and punctual observance of obligations* [Verbindlichkeiten]. This, as sense and practice of the trading estate, is a much higher standard than the extent of activities and the size of exchanged sums and commodities. Bills of exchange [Wechselobligationen] and government bonds form the pure credit relations and thus correspond to the pure thought forms and thought determinations in the human spirit, for which reason they will always be filled with that content and exist for its sake. But just as in our time the forms of thought by abstraction have been severed from content, in order to become thought in itself, so also has the trade in bills of exchange and government bonds become severed from their content, commodities, in order to become a trade in itself. Trade in this form (agiotage) is the same thing in the area of wealth creation that rationalism is in the area of science. Impoverishment, dessication is the consequence of both.

Freedom of trade, that is, the removal of barriers to import and export, is the stimulus of trade. For it is the precondition for that power of turnover, for the possibility of sending the surplus on one side to the deficiency on the other. Customs duties create a barrier that keeps need on one side and the means of satisfying it on the other, without allowing them to come together. Human prosperity suffers as a result, but especially the class that makes a living from bringing these two things together. Nevertheless, freedom of trade cannot be demanded unconditionally. If a production, to which domestic forces naturally turn, and which therefore cannot be replaced by any other activity that feeds families, cannot maintain its market against foreign countries, then the deciding factor must not be the cheap satisfaction of the public but the preservation of these producers (of the particular families). Free trade throughout the world, as theory demands, would indeed have the effect that more goods would be produced in the abstract because weaker production, which cannot withstand competition, would be eliminated, making way for the more powerful and energetic. But through it, these multiplied goods would then accumulate in the hands of the predominating nation, and the less favored would not even retain what they would originally have had, in the case of the reduced wealth of the human race in general which would have resulted from the protection of its industry.

This freedom of trade over the whole world has as its reason and its success a relationship between humanity and nation that is similar to that of unlimited freedom of trade and fragmentation of property between the nation and the individual family. In the latter case, large factory owners and buyers of estates arise along with day laborers; in the former arises a world-dominating industrial nation that virtually turns the others into helots. Protective tariffs for branches of industry on which a country really depends are therefore quite justified, and not just as a temporary measure until domestic industries have grown from weak beginnings to be able to compete with foreign countries, but, depending on the circumstances, even if they never attain that level. The point of view of the particular state, and not the cosmopolitan one, applies. The demand for freedom of trade carries far more weight when it is not presented as a general theoretical principle, but rather, conversely, **<55>** as the need of a particular country to raise its agriculture by means of the free export of its products, and not to encourage a proliferating factory industry which brings down the whole generation. In this case, too, an abstract maxim, whether free trade or protection of industry, can never be the deciding factor, but only a concrete technical examination of the particular production and the overall circumstances of the particular country.

§. 19. Balancing Freedom and Restriction of Trade

The contemporary theory of unconditional divisibility of landed estates [Gutszertrümmerung] and unconditional freedom of enterprise is based *firstly* on the *abstract legal-philosophical principle* of individual freedom according to which, on apodictic grounds of justice, no restriction of any sort is allowable outside of the protection of the freedom of other individuals, thus, in particular, none for the maintenance of the public welfare, the sound collective economic organism; *secondly*, upon the *abstract economic principle* according to which the intensification of forces of production via the greatest possible competition counts as supreme in that it brings about the greatest amount of wealth in the abstract for the nation, although neither the ethical motive inherent in each estate nor the complete economic result, in particular the proper distribution of goods, is taken into consideration. It is as if the mere sound of the word "freedom" places a wicked spell on the age.

How long ago it was that enlightened science and public opinion proclaimed absolute freedom in all these matters as the undoubted good and accused every sceptic of obscuring the light. This should make us a little more cautious about all such slogans of enlightened public opinion that are passed off as apodictic. However, the abstract principle of freedom should not be countered by an equally abstract principle of restriction. Rather, this must be determined in each case according to the sphere in question. Thus, especially for trade and commerce, since they only entail the individual's use of his own activity, freedom must form the rule, restriction the exception; on the other hand, for land ownership, since it refers to a given object that serves the whole community according to the natural order, restriction must prevail over free disposal. But there is something else in addition to all this. It is the genuine wisdom of the state in all cases to follow the specific need as the sole task: where there is overburden, to relieve it; where there is wealth, to enable acquisition; where free property does not meet the need, to allow encumbrance; where fields and meadows are needed, to clear the forest. <56> But the more recent theory, instead of dealing with the needs of the individual, attempts to draft a plan for the entire economy. In this way it masters nature: there should not be so much forest instead of field and meadow, there should not be any encumbered property. In a word, it is a *codification of the national economy.* The exaggeration that lies in this undertaking has taken a heavy toll. But for that very reason, one must also be careful not to attempt a similar codification based on other, albeit correct principles.

§. 20. Right of Authorship, Invention: Intellectual Property

[Provision for the public's higher intellectual needs is also an object of property acquisition to those who apply themselves to it. Chief among these activities is authorship. Hence the prohibition on reprinting. But since literary activity has as its goal to be generally accessible, and since the writer receives his ideas from God, there can be no timeless, unrestricted right to an author's productions. Similar to this is the right to a technological invention, which can receive protection through monopoly and privilege, but only for a specific amount of time.]

[The right protected by the prohibition on reprinting is expressed as "intellectual property" [geistiges Eigenthum] and therefore is considered under the heading of property. But then it would have to be timelessly existing, like other objects of property are. But property in anything other than a physical object is absurd. Objects of property serve only the owner, while the productions of writers and inventors serve all. They should therefore be considered not as property but as acquisition by intellectual attainment. Their systematic position and determining principle are therefore properly found in business law [Gewerbrecht] rather than property law (law of things). Another principle than acquisition is now being used to justify the prohibition on reprinting, that of the recognition of authorship as such. But this underlies the prohibition on reprinting as little as does the other principle, regardless of whether one views it as dishonoring the author or as interference in his right of disposition.] <57>

§. 21. Guild, Corporation, Association

The common vocation of members of estates also requires their union for its cultivation – the *fellowship* [Genossenschaft], the *corporation* [Korporation]. This union exercises a power over individuals, precisely by virtue of the vocation of the estate which obligates each. This distinguishes *corporation* from *association* [Association]; the latter is a convening at will for a self-chosen individual goal, the former a given unity for an organic vocation of the people, to which the participants belong with their entire life position. Farmers are to form such fellowships (the rural community), then the individual industries (guilds, with nothing of the old guild coercion [Zunftzwang]), the merchants, the large landowners, and, within reason, other estates as well (artists). The object of the fellowship's activity is the representation of the estate's rights, the estate's interests, the estate's honor, inward as well as outward.

[The fellowship exercises a moral influence on honorable trading which lies outside the reach of the state. It combines mores and honor, upholds quality of craftsmanship, holds court over violations, ensures work for all members; the lack of guild life is painfully apparent. Regardless of the abuses of previous times, the guild function needs to be recovered. Legislation cannot accomplish this but it can foster its accomplishment. For its part, the association cannot replace the corporation. In fact, in normal situations the corporation should be much more widespread than the association. But in the contemporary situation with the destruction of corporate life, the association can serve as a stopgap until the shortcomings thereof are recognized.]

Chapter 3: The Newer Social Theories[30]

§. 22. The Common Denominator: Socialized Wealth Creation

The *social theories* which in recent times have arisen in England and France, and have been systematically developed in the latter in particular, strive for a reversal of the entire form of national wealth creation and distribution such as has hitherto existed. Their common character is the *destruction of the system of separate individual enterprise* through a *collective economy of human society.*[31] All these theories have this as their innermost essence, and therefore jointly form a contrast with actual conditions and the existing life valuation. But they are sharply distinguished from each other by the *form and degree of communality* [Gemeinsamkeit] they require of the economy. *Communism* desires an ongoing *equalizing* [gleichheitliche] distribution of all goods in society, hence the abolition of property. *Distributism* (a term I believe appropriately describes St. Simon's or rather Bazard's economic theory) does not wish for an equalizing distribution but rather a continuing *just* one, namely, devolution of all property vacated by death and the distribution thereof in terms of industrial merit, i.e., to the most active and industrious laborer, thus that capital goes to the most fruitful for the society (only such can serve as reward in such an industrial state), hence retention of (lifetime) property but abolition of the right of inheritance. *Socialism* does not wish for community of property but only community of wealth creation [Vermögensgewinnung], <60> i.e., common labor ("organization of labor") and distribution, thus no abolition of individual property or inheritance but abolition of *individual acquisition of property.* Here as well, wealth-pursuing activity of the individual will therefore proceed not according to his will and judgment but according to the leading of society, and it will not gain wealth for him directly but only for society, which will then apportion to him his share according to its valuation. The above-mentioned innermost

[30] Stein, *Der Socialismus und Communismus des heutigen Frankreichs* [Socialism and Communism in Contemporary France].

[31] This is merely the precise characterization of the general spirit [Genius] of these theories. Even though socialism does not adhere to the abolition of property or inheritance, it is also a species of this form of economics.

essence therefore is shared by socialism with communism and distributism. One may thus summarize these three systems, since they all only recognize a society economy, jointly under the description *social theory.*

§. 23. Leading Principle: The Autonomous Individual

Should one seek to reduce these doctrines to their deepest life principle, it is entirely the same as that of the political revolution, namely, that *the individual person* is made into *the supreme basis and goal of things, apart from a higher order and necessity* over him. From this springs all the parallels between these social theories and the political theory. That the social theories, at least communism, are the consequence or parallel of the revolutionary postulate of *equality* is generally recognized and, in particular for the Germans, has been comprehensively laid out by Stein in his valuable work. Assuming the absolute equality of men as goal, it cannot be of help that they are made equal only in the formal and legal sense and not in the material, factual sense as well, i.e., so that they attain satisfaction of life, enjoyment, and education in equal degree; the former is merely equality of possibility, by which the greatest number, for whom it does not become reality, is not served; only the latter is true equality. Another parallel of the social theory with the Revolution, the necessary accompaniment of the equality postulate, is the *apriorism* or revolution as such, i.e., the non-recognition of the entire result of the past and the dissolution of the human common condition from its historic unity and continuity into mere atoms of generations. When the constitution as it existed up until 1789 is held not to have existed, but only those are considered valid which the nation established in 1789 purely out of its **<61>** world-ordering reason, why should the distribution of property and wealth, which to that point had been the product of human action, have a greater claim to validity? And to be consistent, this must be repeated in every moment. This parallel in the social sphere should bring to their senses those who do not wish to admit the reprehensibility of revolution and *a priori* construction in the political sphere! Finally, the social theory shares with the Revolution, in particular Rousseau's doctrine, the complete *collapse of the private sphere into the public sphere,* or *pandemism,* as one might call it, and this parallel is valid not primarily for communism, as are the other two, but also for social theory in general. Rousseau makes freedom, the will of the individual, into the goal, but only believes it achievable through the individual alienating his will to the general will unconditionally. Just so does the social theory make the individual's means of enjoyment into its goal and believes this can be achieved only by destroying individual enterprise. It is the curious equality of outcome. When man recognizes no given order over himself, to which every individual is joined in his own way, but instead makes each individual into the absolute center, then the final result is that the individual falls into a yet more slavish subservience, under a common order, than that from which he wished to free himself.

But the peculiar principle of social theories, which at first glance shows no relation to the Revolution, is materialism. They all rest on the view that sensory pleasure is the highest good, the goal of human life, and that for this reason society exhausts its activity in the attainment of this good, and every individual must achieve it to the greatest extent possible. On closer examination, however, even this materialism has the closest affinity with Rousseau's political theory. Rousseau makes man's pure, naked, independent will the principle of the state, not reason, not a moral commandment. This essentially distinguishes him from Kant; it is the character of the empirical direction that extends through England and France, in contrast to the German rationalist one. But what could be more akin to each other than my arbitrariness as the principle of the legal system and my enjoyment as the principle of the property system? On all of these principles, social theories are the product of a completely erroneous evaluation of life, which, with the breaking away from Christian truth, necessarily also had to be revealed. But their origin lies not only in the development of a false principle to its logical conclusion, but in the existing actual conditions and their challenge, in the enormous disparity in the distribution of wealth that the present offers, especially in England and France, and the stunting of a large class of people as a result. On the basis of this factual and well-founded motivation, social theories, despite their false point of view and their scientific fallacy and moral wrongness, nevertheless contain at least an impulse for true insight and correction of the received economic doctrine. A closer examination of the same should reveal its factual impracticability, its moral reprehensibility, and this aspect of its truth. **<62>**

§. 24. The Unfeasibility of the Social Theories

The social theories are factually *absolutely incapable of being implemented.*

The mechanical obstacles that stand in the way of their realizability have been asserted most frequently. They will win laughs all around, but that will only challenge the well-meaning, the earnest, and the consistent to try to remove these obstacles than to abandon the entire path. But since their impracticability is also based on ethical grounds, failure is certain from the outset (*a priori*), without the need for empirical tests.

Above all, it misunderstands the sinful nature of man. The indestructible truth expressed in Scripture, "the imagination of man's heart is evil from his youth" [Genesis 8: 21] is not only not taken into account here, it is flatly and consciously denied. The founders of the doctrine as well as the common creeds almost all expressly state that man is good by nature, that evil has its origin only in the present social condition, the improper distribution of goods and the resulting pressure of poverty, that even temptation must cease when, by virtue of proper sociability, all desires will be satisfied. Therefore, the administration of justice has no place in this system of human community, and Fourier, for example, confidently teaches that the authorities of his industrial state would not need the sword (guards and weapons) because no crimes would be committed. Such gross, palpable folly, yes, such madness is what the human mind falls back on when it breaks away from divine truth. Sin and crime have their origin not in external want, but in the innermost personality of man himself. Want is only one of an infinite number of temptations and is never a necessity. Would the passions of sexual love and ambition disappear if that economy were introduced, with the hoped-for economic success? Would arrogance, scorn, anger, and vindictiveness cease if man had enough to eat? Yes, would contempt and favoritism and jealousy among the sexes give way if, according to the most extreme party, marriage ceased? Given the evil inclination of human nature, the impossibility of those teachings is evident from the outset.

Above all, the authorities in whose hands the distribution of wealth (the total income according to communism, the reverted inheritances according to distributism, the proceeds of labor according to socialism) and the allocation of the work must be placed, will not proceed along lines of pure justice and wisdom, but equally, or even predominantly, in selfishness and partiality and ignorance. Yet proper allocation is, after all, the foundation stone on which the whole undertaking is built. As much complaining as there is now, under all forms of government, about the filling of public offices, that much more will be the case when the measure of prosperity and the daily labor requirement or the freedom to work is assigned by human beings! There will be just as few stewards of the common economy (Phalange) of the kind that are needed under socialism – with the requisite unselfishness on which Fourier bases the cheapness of this common economy – as there are such landlords now. Finally, not everyone will work and work diligently, even if they are allowed to choose the type of work according to their inclination. For it is true that every person has an inclination for some kind of activity, as Fourier assumes, but it is by no means true that this inclination is for a productive or generally praiseworthy activity, and not for card playing or the like. Indeed, the constant and strenuous activity on which the production of goods is based is not naturally pleasant for most people but is wrested from the reluctant inclination towards leisure and unproductive activities only by the necessity and love of gainful employment. Expectations of greater production through socialism must therefore be disappointed, if only because the most powerful incentive for work, the certainty of gain for the worker, is abandoned, even if the right of inheritance is preserved. No one will readily exert the efforts of physical labor or inventive thought that now increase our production, for the uncertain prospect of having their industrial merit properly appreciated and rewarded by the social authorities. If human nature were as pure and unselfish as it is everywhere assumed to be here, there would be no need for any reform of society; everything would be as happy and as rich under the existing system as it is dreamed of here. And such purity presupposes a theory that declares sensory pleasure to be the highest purpose in life.

Another fallacy of social theories rendering them infeasible is the failure to recognize the limitations of human intelligence, which are closely related to the ethical nature of man. Even if people's wills were as pure as is assumed, they would still fail due to the inability of the human mind to calculate in advance the total needs and total output of labor in all their circles, and then to order industrial activity accordingly. Industry regulates itself according to its own laws through the power of nature, through the result of labor, sales and their reciprocal effect. The authorities may curb or guide it here and there, but to establish it purely on the basis of calculation by removing the natural effects and reactions that the individual entrepreneur senses and acts upon is a task that no human being is capable of. And how all individuals suffer when the rulers miscalculate. It is something similar to modern codification, which likewise expects human insight to calculate all cases and possibilities in advance, to exhaust human life and cover it with legal provisions.

Finally, social theory is based on a misunderstanding of the natural order, according to which human activities are not equal in value and honor but are of higher and lower rank. This hierarchy cannot be undermined by a conventional declaration that they should be accorded equal respect. Fourier believes that, out of natural inclination, there would be as many child minders as needed, probably also as many sewer cleaners as needed, and no more goldsmiths, painters and scholars than are needed. To accept this now requires unusual naivety. Therefore, the lesser occupations will have to be assigned against one's will, which is a tyranny as bad as the oriental caste system.

§. 25. The Ethical Reprehensibility of the Social Theories

Ethically, the social theories are *totally reprehensible.*

Above all, they destroy the *primeval right of personality*. Property and inheritance are primeval rights [Urrechte] of man, and such primeval rights, which he already possesses, and which do not need to be won through a revolution, are sacred institutions ordained by God (III. [*Private Law*], §§. 23 and 90). To have one's own hearth, to found a world on one's property and its use as is the imprint of one's own innermost being and will, is the most indispensable satisfaction and the first right of man. Freedom consists above all in this; it is not possible without property. Likewise, to give those to whom one has given existence the satisfaction of existence, and to extend, as one's own personality, this entire circle of private existence in one's descendants is the primeval satisfaction and the primeval right of man. Precisely that which is the highest and purest human satisfaction is rendered impossible by this theory of satisfaction. But even if property and inheritance are left alone and only the individual acquisition of property and the separate labor and consumption arrangements cease, as under socialism, the actual meaning of property, the individual shaping of one's way of life, is abandoned. How dissatisfied we are now that the authorities monitor our every move for the sake of security, cleanliness, sanitation, and public culture, and such is only a negative, a restriction of our activity; here, the entirety of our activity is to be positively guided by an authority, the social (heads of the phalanges, etc.). Our daily work is not to be done according to our own impulses, but in rank and file in military order, and even our enjoyment of life, the reward of this work, should be under the same guidance; we should live in a general building, in the place assigned to us, eat from a general kitchen, etc.

This freedom and entitlement of man likewise does away with the *ethical consecration of property,* for such consists only in serving the manifestation of individuality and the care of the family. It loses all ethical significance if it becomes merely a means of subsistence and enjoyment, even if it is enjoyed equally. For even in such a communist or socialist order, there is no production of wealth out of love for one's fellow human beings; each person's activity and production is always only for his own good, just as in a mercantile society, and thus in truth only out of self-interest and the desire for enjoyment. If human nature were such that in such a communal production people would predominantly have the common good in mind, not their own share in it, then, as we said before, these new institutions would not be needed, but all evil would be eliminated under the present ones as well.

Moreover, not only the ethical significance of property, but the *ethical significance of the entirety of human life* is undermined by this social theory, which makes *material satisfaction the highest, indeed the only purpose of life.* There is no ethical motive left at all. Fraternity, i.e., the endeavor to give the same enjoyment to others, is not an ethical motive. All debauchees likewise possess this virtue. This is merely animal sympathy. This loss of the ethical basis of life, the innermost root of the theory, is also the basis of the destruction or complete desecration of the marriage bond, which some preach openly and unabashedly (Babeuf in a brutal way, Enfantin in a disgustingly sentimental way), others less crudely without aspiring to it any less (e.g., Fourier, who wants to introduce a whole assortment of different sex connections in order to derive the greatest possible enjoyment from each according to the degree of sympathy); and finally some may well reject it without realizing why. Just as the individual no longer has an ethical goal in this way, neither does the community and communal life. This is the essence of the industrial state that is demanded here. The state is not supposed to establish an ethical order, which the means of material enjoyment, and thus industry, only serve, but industry as the means of material enjoyment is itself the ultimate and only purpose of the state. Therefore, according to St. Simon, the highest task is to make the owners and the officials serve the workers. May all one-sided promoters of industry be shocked by this pure and sharply defined image of the orientation to which they themselves unconsciously belong, and come to their senses. May they recognize what it means to separate the economy from higher purposes and make it the sole aim, whether for the individual or for the nation; what it means to supplant and destroy the nobler motives that still exist in public life in the pursuit of greater profits.

When a right honorable German writer on social theories (Stein) finds the seat of this aberration only in the fact that enjoyment and not also knowledge is regarded as a good, and therefore also derives the origin of social theories from the fact that the French lack the German philosophical direction, the logical "conception of the I" (acknowledgment of logic as the supreme world cause and supreme world law), the "idea of knowledge," i.e., knowing for the sake of knowing, then this is not merely insufficient, but is also quite beside the point. In fact, if it were only a matter of these theories dispensing with, even excluding, the good of German philosophy, the logical world view, then one could not argue with them. The English also dispense with it and exclude it, especially for the sake of church and state, and we do not for that reason wish to exalt ourselves against them. Indeed, one might perhaps not even blame a vigorous people if it gave preference to the pleasures of the eyes and the senses over the formulation and study of German-philosophical systems, especially if it held the material [sinnliche] well-being of the *whole* of humanity in higher esteem than those treasures of the mind from which even the majority of our scholars are withheld by a sacred aversion.

It is not logical knowledge as a goal in life that is the principle opposed to the sensorial enjoyment put forward by the social theories, although perfect knowledge is one side of the highest good and all true knowledge is a good and goal of man, but simple *morality* [Sitte] and the deeper ways of *religion*. The fulfillment of the sacred commandments under which human life stands, love for the ethical order and devotion to it, love for personalities not as companions in pleasure but in things spiritual and moral, and in the case of a true and conscious state of man, devotion to God the will of whom is what these commandments are, the work of whom is the beauty of this order, that is the goal and in truth also the highest satisfaction, enjoyment in the truest sense. Material enjoyment is only a part, and a subordinate one, of the purpose of life and of the satisfaction of life, and knowledge is either imbued with this ethical atmosphere or it is also only a more refined form of enjoyment. German philosophy – in this respect essentially different from French philosophy – has indeed retained the venerable ethical seriousness in its luminaries, but this is rather a consequence of the general culture of the nation, which in turn supports it (likewise with Schiller's poetry), than of its particular scientific (logical) point of view. It is therefore not the lack of German philosophical education (indeed, the most recent philosophical school of Germany and the communists are very much alike in their philosophical world view), but the detachment from the living personal God that evokes such phenomena.

The logical forms and laws cannot be held as the ultimate purpose of life and will not be so held; such did not last for a generation with us either. If we do not have the presence of a personality, a living holy will and conscious all-wise spirit with whom to be one and remain one forever – that is what gives peace and joy, behind which everything else disappears like fog and smoke – then our own material pleasure and the pleasure of our fellow human beings, with whom we have an animalistic community, must be the highest good.

French materialism is what generates social theories – there is no doubt about that. German rationalism certainly forms a contrast to it, but not an eternal, irreconcilable one. Its eternal contrast is the Christian worldview and morality [Gesittung]. They are clearly aware of this. It has not escaped them that a religion which demands self-denial, i.e., renunciation of pleasure, and devotion to God and His unbreakable commandments, makes their entire point of view impossible. The overthrow of Christianity and the founding of a new religion were considered by Saint-Simon, Fourier, and Cabet to be their indispensable task. Some of these sects have even developed their new religion into a dogmatic pantheistic or atheistic creed. But all of them have established, with the clearest consciousness and intention, a new practical religion in opposition to the Christian one. It consists in nothing other than the doctrine that enjoyment and not morality is the absolute measure and commandment for man, that the contradiction of human nature, according to which the flesh lusts against the spirit and the spirit against the flesh, must be resolved not by subjecting the flesh to the spirit, as Christianity erroneously wills, but by the flesh dominating the spirit (morality). It is the absolute emancipation of sensory pleasure. This is the reason for the affinity between communism and German writers who aspire to this emancipation in the fields of philosophy or fiction. What motivates them is not compassion for suffering humanity, as they claim, but the new religion that is to be founded, the worship of the flesh.

§. 26. Their Element of Truth

All this notwithstanding, the social theories, like every error, are not without a grain of truth. Above all, they are based on the ethical truth that every individual is an absolute end in himself, and that therefore the circle of the wealthy who hold power both factual and legal must not abandon the mass of non-owners to their fate. Just as it is the ethos of the individual to take upon himself the fate of the destitute, so it is also the ethos of society. It is, however, a false axiom that every man has a claim to equal enjoyment with others. Enjoyment is something incommensurable in the first place, and even assuming that it is measurable, this axiom rests on the assumption that enjoyment is the highest purpose in life, for only for such is equality a requirement – not for subordinate goods. God makes rich and poor, as He makes healthy and sick, strong and weak, talented and untalented, and man cannot and should not equalize these inequalities of gifts and well-being; it is only the highest good that God determines and offers in equal and absolute measure.

But everyone has a right to enjoyment in general and without comparison with others and in the true sense, that is, to satisfaction in life and to an external existence as the basis of ethical life, and society has an obligation to provide everyone with such things. Much more correct than the communist demand for equal enjoyment is therefore the socialist demand for a minimum for every human being, to some extent a *Congrua*, as is recognized for salaried priests in our country. However, given the infinite diversity of living conditions and thus of the necessities of life, this minimum cannot be calculated (expressed in figures and measurements) in a general way, and on top of that the complete allocation of it always fails because in many and perhaps most cases the need is the result of fault [Schuld] (sloth, fornication, gluttony, extravagance), since to compensate for this, to remove the punishment that nature has placed on them, lies neither in the power nor is it the vocation of human society. The only task that remains is to offer everyone the opportunity (i.e., not just the legal opportunity, which is of little help, but the actual opportunity) of a satisfying existence, provided they have not forfeited it through idleness and vice. Society has to solve this task in three ways: through direct support of the needy (charity), whereby poverty on a mass scale is met by, and indeed demands, sacrifices by the rich on a mass scale; then through the internal regulation of the conditions for the needy classes (§. 17), and finally, by regulating the ways of earning a living by means of measures and institutions that come to the aid of the natural powerlessness in which the destitute are abandoned to the rich. In this respect, social theory is also based on a highly important and profound economic truth.

It is through them that insight has been gained into the fallacy of the principle of free competition (*laissez faire*). Out of this principle the newer economics has emerged from all its schisms and schools (disregarding the incorrect and limited restrictions of the mercantile system, the crude beginning of science). Therefore, it can be called *liberal economics* and is the analogue of Kant's philosophy of law. In contrast, the social theory, since it does not start from wealth in the abstract but from the need and the satisfaction of a particular class of people, finds that this principle leads to the ever-increasing oppression of the destitute by the rich. The struggle for wealth is a struggle of man against man; if it is released from control, the strong will necessarily overcome the weak and subjugate him, dictate to him the even less favorable conditions of the future struggle, and so on to infinity. How could the small landowner survive the competition against the large one with his consolidated economic structures, his systematic distribution of labor; how could the tradesman survive against the factory owner and his machine power; how can the laborer, who can hardly live for a few weeks without employment, survive the labor boss who can survive years without employment? Laissez faire therefore means nothing other than: Let the wealthy oppress the poor. It is the same as if one were to abolish the usury laws, this protection of the needy against the rich, because natural need would find the right balance. This gain owed to the social theory is an invaluable, if only negatively critical one. It is not that the social theory was the first to express this view, or even the only one to do so; the conservative political and economic party has been asserting it for a long time. But the social theory has found it from a point of view for which the age is still receptive. When it is demonstrated from the organic order and public prosperity, it is ignored; but when demonstrated from the equal enjoyment of the individual, it makes an impression.

If we now abandon the principle of free allowance, two paths open up: the direct path and the indirect path, i.e., the path of guidance of income-generating activity and the path of restriction thereof, or, to put it another way, the regulation of subjective gainful activity and the regulation of objective income-generating paths, and here we must again distinguish ourselves from the social theories. They want the direct route, with productive activity assigned to each individual and positively directed by the social authorities.[32] The truth, however, is to ensure objective earning conditions through legal order, as we have explained.[33]

---

[32] The socialist idea was already expressed by Mirabeau on Aug. 10th, 1789, in an improvised apology to the clergy. "Je ne connais que trois manières d'exister dans la société ; il faut y être mendiant, voleur ou salarié. Le propriétaire n'est lui-même que le premier des salariés. Ce que nous appellons vulgairement sa propriété, n'est autre chose, que le prix, que lui paie la société pour les distributions, qu'il est chargé de faire aux autres individus par ses consommations et ses dépenses, les propriétaires sont les agens, les économes du corps social" [I know of only three ways of existing in society: you have to be a beggar, a thief or a salary earner. The owner is only the first of the salary earners. What we vulgarly call his property is nothing other than the price paid to him by society for the distributions he is responsible for making to other individuals through his consumption and expenditure. Owners are the agents, the bursars of the social body].

[33] Heinrich Wilhelm Kaiser gives an incorrect idea of socialism when, in his commendable historical account *Die Persönlichkeit des Eigenthums in Bezug auf den Socialismus und Communismus im heutigen Frankreich* [The Personality of Property in Relation to Socialism and Communism in Contemporary France] (Bremen, 1843), he describes socialism as all *indirect* efforts to achieve public prosperity through the organization of channels of commerce [Verkehrswege], such as those which can be found in world history (e.g. the Jewish jubilee, the German ancestral domains) and thus combines them with *direct* efforts. The concept of socialism is simply to achieve general prosperity *directly* through the direction of individual activity. Therefore, it is not (as it seems to Kaiser) together with those wise institutions the true principle, in contrast to communism, but together with communism the false principle, in contrast to those institutions. Furthermore, one cannot agree with Kaiser that the true fulfillment of the socialist principle (i.e., the concern that all partake of goods) is found in the removal of barriers to communication, because that would make it possible for everyone to acquire property. This would not be the fulfillment but the opposite of the socialist principle. Existing socialism regards unregulated competition precisely as the system it combats, and true socialism, if we are to use the word that way, must do so no less because competition provides only the abstract possibility of general participation in goods while preventing the reality of it. The "logical progression of the concept," from which the

Accordingly, we have two contrasting systems: the abstract system of political economy, which is represented in particular by Adam Smith, and the materialistic system of the newer social theories. Between these two opposites oscillate the higher scientific attempts, until they arrive at the entire truth (I. [*Philosophical Foundations*], §. 22). As its principle, the former has abstract abundance, the number of goods, while the latter has the sensory enjoyment of the individual. True and complete economics, on the other hand, must have as its principle the person (man in his entire ethical-spiritual as well as sensory existence) and the ethical kingdom, the ethically ordered and ethically guaranteed common existence and common rule of men, of which material goods and material satisfaction are necessary vehicles.

---

author draws his results, does indeed present unrestricted alienation as a step towards the general participation in goods, but the real result is precisely the opposite.

Chapter 4: The Nobility

§. 27. The Idea of Nobility

[Nobility is defined as a class which is politically privileged on the basis of its own, inherited right. It owes its origin to the need for rulership positions, and to the original status of birthright as entitling one to such a position. There is always a need for subordinate positions of rule under the supreme ruler, be it monarchy or popular assembly. Nobility first seems to have arisen from a right of the firstborn over the remaining members of the family (Israelite tribes, Athenian nobility from the first family of each phratry). Later it came through one tribe subjecting another. The enduring basis for nobility is warfare: capacity for war-making and offering protection is by natural law connected with right of rule. Therefore nobility is everywhere the ruling class. Leisure which enables one to devote oneself to callings other than those involved in subsistence accompany this. Other necessary attributes are wealth, mainly in landholding, and ennobling education and mores (παιδεία). Connected to this is maintenance of noble sentiment, consciousness of nobility. Not having to labor for subsistence and accompanying momentary concerns, the nobility can devote itself to cultivating a higher awareness extending back into history.]

[Nobility has ever involved the suppression of the other classes. Therefore, the movement in history today is the emancipation of those classes. In the ancient republics, the triumph of the people over the nobility was the point at which the state began to decline. In the Germanic states, the attributes originally attached to the nobility have been separated off and attached to other classes, especially the civil service and the military. Landholding has shifted towards the wealthy citizenry. Higher education likewise is shifting **<66>** from nobility and clergy to the wealthier classes in general. This has advanced the emancipation of the people, which will be completed with the idea of human and civil equality, resulting in the total displacement of the nobility as ruling class as an unequal estate. Yet nobility may continue to exist as a special vocation and estate, to wit, as the first estate among the wealth-creating estates, albeit primus inter pares. This is its natural and enduring position.]

§. 28. The Continuing Function of the Nobility

[The aristocratic element is advantageous to, if not necessary for, the social condition. I understand hereby a class of large, distinguished property owners with a legally established position, by which it forms a concentration point of popular power over against state power and bureaucracy, as well as being a guarantee of the state and government against dissolution by the popular mass, and maintains the identity of its own interests with the maintenance of the existing order and the national honor. Such a class rests on two bases: landownership and historical continuity. The landowning class is the only propertied class that does not have to worry about maintaining its wealth. It therefore can focus on higher ideals and the public interest. Landownership leads to the identity of interests with the national interest. It is also the natural basis of all wealth creation and all social cohesion. Continuity of possession also enables maintenance of class consciousness and history.]

[The legal position is expressed in participation in the national representation. It should have an independent position in the assembly apart from consideration of number. It is also expressed in its being used by the government as mediator of state power to the country. The class is maintained through continuity of landownership. This can be accomplished through primogeniture, coheir communities of property, substitution, inalienability of possession without indivisibility. This continuity is even more important when the aristocracy does not have the government or offices in its hands, as these provided wealth or subsistence. This possession is important not only as a means of subsistence but because these estates are the <67> source of national sustenance and bearers of political power and political sentiment. Nowadays such a landed aristocracy must be open to entry from outsiders, as long as these meet certain requirements, mainly acquisition of such an estate and restoration of the manner of inheritance where such has been removed. Thus will the nobility be, not a ruling estate, but a distinguished estate in the territorial representation, and not a closed aristocracy of birth, not a mere landed nobility, but a landed and estate-oriented nobility by virtue of familial continuity. This is the position and essence of the contemporary landed gentry.]

§. 29. The Legitimacy of the Old Nobility

[The general idea of a nobility may be accepted by many today, but what they find more difficult to accept is the continued existence of the "romantic" nobility, the currently existing nobility with roots in medieval times, specific characteristics and manners, specific political traditions. This nobility ought to be eliminated from public and social life. But this is unjust. For one thing, one cannot accept something in the abstract and reject it in its concrete manifestation. This nobility's traditions are interwoven with the nation's. It has a significance for the nation: personal devotion to the prince, specific notions of honor and noble customs, which we designate as "chivalry." These traits have spread to other sections of society, such as the military, higher echelons of social life, but they have their origin and base in this nobility. They do not belong only to bygone times. What bothers people about the nobility is not this but the tendency toward polished emptiness of form. But other classes are just as likely to exhibit deformation, such as the citizenry, which instead of exhibiting civic virtue displays mere pride of wealth and thinks that its money buys it esteem. This class should be left with its titles and its honors, rather than have all of these legislated away. But it should no longer be politically privileged.]

§. 30. Illegitimate Aspects

[What truly runs contrary to the times are the following: 1) Institutions elevating the honor of the nobility over other classes: mixed marriage where this has legal consequences (not being presentable at court), differing punishments, depending on whether a violation is committed against a nobleman or not, separate education at genteel academies, ennobling of all who enter into higher offices, etc. 2) All privileges not grounded in an objective vocation and not balanced by similar privileges with other objectively determined vocations, such as e.g. tax exemptions, exemption from military service. 3) Privileging of the nobility in public offices.]

Chapter 5: The Governmental Rights of the Landowner

§. 31. The Basis of Patrimonial Relations

[The natural relation is for the social position to provide the basis for the political position, thus that those who through large possessions have power over others also are the bearers of governmental power over them. This is especially true regarding the land. Upon this basis rests manorial lordship and the institution of linking public offices to landholding, such as the justice of the peace in England. The origin is partly in personal dependence and partly in material dependence. This approximation of authority and property is what distinguishes these patrimonial relations. Authority over persons is treated as a private property right. Nowadays the personal subjection is entirely removed, the office is bestowed by the sovereign on the landholding, the office is performed entirely in a public manner, the landholding being only the precondition for exercise. There is a great advantage to this institution: regard for the ruling authority rests on a prior natural regard, and the one exercising the office lives under the same conditions as those over whom the office is exercised, and exercises it at his own expense, which gains him respect and devotion. The abolition of this form of office in favor of bureaucracy is the replacement of organic relations with mere mechanism.]

§. 32. The Enduring Significance of Manorial Lordship

[Manorial lordship in the old fashion is no longer feasible. The previous preconditions have disappeared: obligations of service and <70> payment, hierarchical property rights; the only natural dependence is that of tenant farmers of large landowners, often the memory of earlier bonds of obedience and piety. The principle of general full citizenship has now arisen, which overrules all the older forms of patrimonial rule.]

[The English institution of justice of the peace is an excellent one, exemplary, appropriate to the times. But it cannot be everywhere implemented, especially as a replacement of manorial lordship. In terms of the English institution, the officeholder is chosen and discharged at the pleasure of the government without a specific landholding being attached to the office, which fits English conditions but not ours. Besides public welfare, the justice of the peace is also involved in the administration of criminal justice. Here his position is more elevated than that of the executive (the sheriff), and he is less constrained by a formalistic legal system than in Germany is the case, making this institution better capable of implementation there than here.]

§. 33. Modernizing the Manorial Institution

[Thus, where the patrimonial relation has been replaced by a bureaucratic one, there may the English justice of the peace be introduced; but where such a relation has not been replaced, it should not be so but rather "inoculated" with the truth of the English institution, thus taking the relation of manorial lordship as a basis and purifying it, transforming its character from patrimonial to official. One important step in this direction would be the elimination of manorial administration of justice, leaving only public welfare and accompanying penal power. Not that there is such a hard and fast line between the two, but their separation is carried through elsewhere in government, while with manors it is even more significant in that property in land is much more closely connected to public welfare arrangements than it is to the administration of justice among local inhabitants. Furthermore, the function should be exercised not as the extension of property but as a royal office, permeated with the notion of <71> duty of office.]

§. 34. The Public Status of the Manor

[Aristotle already made the connection between property relations and political relations, although he went too far in making the former determine the latter. But his viewpoint is valid at the local level, especially regarding landholding on the part of the rural population. Haller likewise is correct in pointing out that the state not only has local communities but also manorial dominions as its members. The current drive to have every person and every property be part of a local community is misplaced. The local community is an association of equals which regulates community affairs through common decisions. But where there is a large landowner who has other community members residing on his property, there can be no question of a community of equals. On the other hand, Haller denies the need of progress to eliminate all villeinage, to achieve general direct state relations unmediated by other authorities, and to establish the state-official character of public functions.]

§. 35. The Maintenance of Mediating Structures

The social relation [der sociale Verband] in particular is to be brought out of its medieval state by the newer movement of the times. The Revolution is moved by two basic impulses: there should be no particular interest of small circles, but only the one general undifferentiated interest of the whole nation and the individual as such; and property and the conditions of acquisition should not be the basis of ethical, i.e., political ties. Therefore, the Revolution destroys all internal organization of society; it tolerates no association of trades, no association of any kind; even local communities are only dependent and weak-willed instruments of the state for it, and every relationship of manorial lordship is completely abhorrent to it. Thus, there remains only a state organization and dealings between individuals. The reprehensibility of such a political structure is now being recognized more and more. But the real task of our time, which is misunderstood when judged by those motives, is to achieve the *full political personality of the individual.* Above all, this includes his direct position under the state power. While it precludes his entire personal position from being subordinate to some other, intermediate authority, like the older manorial or corporative authority, it does not preclude the existence of superiorities and agreements that, in certain precisely defined relationships, issue a regulation [Vorschrift] to the individual or [bez.] set a limit for him. **<72>** It precludes relations of property and acquisition from becoming independent bearers of political power, but does not preclude such relations from wielding power for property and acquisition, especially when subject to the higher supervision and influence of state power. Furthermore, it is part of full political personality that the social (not the political) organization, which formerly rested almost exclusively on *bonds of superiority* (landed gentry, urban birth aristocracy), now also rests more and more on *bonds of commonality.*

Not that all manorial relationships should cease, or that the lord of the manor should not have authority over or at least possess a preponderance in these relationships, or that the lords of the manor should not be allowed to be used as organs of the state administration; but the rural community will have to be elevated more and more, so that it takes over the arrangement in the broader scope instead of, or together with, the former. Likewise in the cities, the power of the magistracy must not be weakened; even so, the old family aristocracy, that innate superiority, cannot hold its own before the principle of modern times, as little as can a magistracy and administration that is completely divorced from the community as a whole. All of this points to progress towards a higher, fuller personality of the individual, and thus towards the transformation of the whole from an organism into an ethical community, an ethical kingdom. To help this endeavor of the times along, so that it does not, in the sense of revolution, discard all internal structure, the social structure which in earlier times was purely monarchical-patrimonial in the countryside and aristocratic by birth in the cities should in a certain sense be republicanized (communified) while retaining a center of gravity in the great landowners or in the municipal magistrates as well as in the wealthy and prominent in every trade. Perhaps this would be the true statecraft. It requires creative organizing power. By contrast, the wrong approach is to evade the Revolution by taking all political power out of the social structure and creating a mechanism of mere bureaucratic government. This finds itself on precisely the same ground as the Revolution.

PART TWO: THE GENERAL DOCTRINE OF THE STATE

Chapter 1: The Essence of the State

§. 36. The State as Ethical Kingdom

The human community, in terms of the large units in which it unfolds – the peoples – is to be an ethical (ethical-intellectual) kingdom: it is to govern its common condition in accordance with the commandments and purposes that characterize such a kingdom, and is to rule after the manner of personality, as a single will and mind, as a single acting subject. An institution [Anstalt] of governance is organized and ordained to this end, and that institution is *the state*. Thus, in accordance with the manner and form of its existence, the state is the *association of a people under a rulership* [Herrschaft] (*ruling authority*). In terms of content and significance, it is an ethical kingdom. It is quite simply the *ethical world* (I. [*Philosophical Foundations*], §. 25), i.e., the ethical-reasonable shape of human community in itself, in accordance with all its conditions, relations, and purposes, to the degree that these are its own work and vocation (apart from union with God – religion and the church). More deeply considered, it is the human order and regime through which human community maintains God's world-order, and is to serve His leading as instrument, in God's empowerment and on His behalf, albeit in independent manner, in accordance with its own free plan, and according to its own regard, thereby, as a unity, demonstrating both its obedience to God and its assumption of the high "godlike position of ethical steward, of lawgiver and judge" (II. [*Principles of Law*], §. 1). It is an ethical kingdom of people that has a ground and purpose in, and an invisible connection to, the true ethical kingdom, the kingdom of God; it is to <74> serve that kingdom, albeit in the infirmity and within the limitations of earthly conditions (I. [*Philosophical Foundations*], §. 48). The ethical kingdom in all its stages and sorts has the threefold purpose: the welfare of people, the manifestation of the profusion of creative and form-giving thoughts, and the rule of holiness and justice, all three in inseparable unity and mutual permeation. This is why the state unfolds an activity according to three aspects: the protection and support of people – the completion [Vollendung] of national existence – the maintenance of a desirable order of life. It provides protection outwardly, peace inwardly, defense against natural damage, means of subsistence [Ernährung], education, civilization. It completes the national existence through the unfolding of all natural and ethical powers (armed forces, wealth, culture), through the manifestation of the innermost spiritual individuality of the nation, through its own completed construction with the manifold institutions of mechanical efficiency or ethical commitment. It maintains a desirable life-order: law and justice, punishment of criminals, discipline and honorableness, the ethical shape of the family, the validity and regard of religion and the church. And these various aspects of the action of the state are not separated but mutually permeate each other everywhere. For instance, the administration of penal law is at the same time the protection of men, a manifestation of the nation's justice, and a vindication of the God-ordained order. Self-preservation, life-satisfaction, the improvement of people, and, again, the maintenance of people under God's commandments and the maintenance of God's commandments and God's tribunal over them, and finally the vivid completion and ethical glory of this human kingdom of the nation itself – all of this in particular is the act and the purpose (τέλος) of the state. Such a profusion of relations and such unfolding according to various, even contradictory directions, which nevertheless merge back into one undivided grand effect, is precisely the specific essence of the ethical kingdom.

The state is therefore based not on the ethical vocation (ethos) of individuals but on the ethical vocation of the human community (of the people) as a whole. Certainly, individuals everywhere **<75>** pursue satisfaction in life and fulfilment of morals [Sitte]; both of these goods are the purpose of all human effort, and thus they expect assistance from the state in this task, which the state must provide. But this does not exhaust the nature of the state; it is not merely or primarily the means to satisfaction and morals of individuals, but it itself is *a kingdom* [Reich] of morals and reasonable purposes through the shape and action which it has as a whole. The union of the many into one ordered common existence – the establishment of an ethical authority and power, with its grandeur and majesty, and the devotion of subjects – the life satisfaction, which does not isolate individuals, but is granted to the nation, and to individuals only in the nation, to wit, the consciousness and the uplifting feeling of belonging to this ordered commonwealth and this nation with its spiritual significance – the characteristic ethos, which consists not in ethical life, in the fulfillment of commands, but in ethical rule, in the establishment and upholding of commands, in the realization of ethical ideas of rule, power, wisdom, justice – these are the characteristics which comprise the innermost essence of the state, and which have their foundation, not in individual life, but in human common existence.

Even so, it is not the promotion and development of common human existence for which the essence of the state consists; the improvement of human conditions is only one side of this essence. Rather, the essence of the state is likewise, in fact primarily, the maintenance of commands established by a higher power (God) over human conditions. So, for example, it is certainly not the mere promotion or perfection of human existence for which the state maintains the holy ordinance of marriage (prohibition of incest, divorce) and obedience of children to parents, for which it punishes criminals, exercises discipline against immorality and disrespect, but the viewpoint of an inviolable command assigned to it; and it is a deep decline when consciousness of this has been lost sight of, and it is considered a matter of mere human statesmanlike consideration as to whether it is beneficial or not. The state, the ruling authority, is not merely the promoter of corporeal and spiritual goods; it is also the guardian of holy ordinances. This is its first and noblest meaning. **<76>**

The state being the *fulfillment of the life-task of the nation* and not the fulfillment of the life-task of individuals, its rule is restricted to the common condition; the ordering and determination of one's innermost individual life is ever God's affair, not that of human rule. Even so, the state's rule of the common condition must, in terms of its idea, be of a truly ethical sort – it must require complete ethical character of actions, to the degree that they affect the common condition – the ethical shape of the common condition and individual morality must mesh with each other without limit and homogeneously (I. [*Philosophical Foundations*], §. 45). This is what the most ancient state formations strove after, each according to its conception of ethics; this was the case with the first scientific doctrine of state, as sketched by Plato, likewise even with the fractions of the Protestant church, which melded state and church into one undivided, life-ruling theocracy.

If in this manner, however, the rule of the state is to be of an ethical kind, its fulfillment by people, in line with this, must be no less of an ethical kind, i.e., it must everywhere result from free will and inward motivation.

Now then, under the given conditions of the human situation, we do not always and everywhere realize the good, but have a choice between good and evil (and so, by the back-and-forth between the two within us, in our innermost being, we are to be fortified into the certain grasp of the good (I. [*Philosophical Foundations*], §. 40)). Furthermore, because the rule of the state is conducted with anything but pure will and unerring intelligence, this freedom and personality of man comes under threat, and even gets suppressed. Despite this, individual freedom and personality is not to be restricted; rather, it is to be confirmed and elevated so that the community may be elevated to an ethical kingdom, and even, in a certain sense, to a personality. To promote this, then, the rule exercised by the community is only to be *external*, i.e., only of a *legal* sort. As such, the state is an ethical kingdom in that it realizes *ethical ideas* – justice, public decency [Ehrbarkeit], purity of the family bond (e.g., prohibition of incest), etc. – and indeed its very existence, this union of the <77> nation and founding of a higher regard, is an ethical idea, it being borne by an ethical conviction [Gesinnung]. But it realizes these *ethical ideas* only in the *manner of law*, to wit, through external, in the end coercible commands and institutions [Anstalten], and precisely for this reason in restricted, only negative extent (II. [*Principles of Law*], §. 6), while the full and positive realization of ethical ideas is an affair of the freedom of individuals and the common ethical conviction. This latter is the work of a higher suggestion [Hauches]; the state cannot engender it, but neither can it afford to leave it to life, nor can its existence as an ongoing institution be maintained by or be dependent upon this ever changing, and to that degree arbitrary, common conviction. Moreover, the innermost life and will of the individual is already in fact removed from the community [der Gemeinschaft], both the knowledge of it and its effect, and should the community attempt to intervene in this sphere, the nature of which is only to be the result of inner impulse, then it builds on unknowable conditions and realizes uncertain, indeed often counterproductive results.

Therefore, the state is merely the institution [Anstalt] *for the external order and promotion of social life.* However, just as, according to its eternal idea, it ought to be truly and completely an ethical kingdom, thus to realize ethical ideas in kind and extent fitting to it, so the goal always stands above it, to approach more and more closely to that kingdom, i.e., not itself to be such a kingdom but to bring that kingdom forth constantly as its fruit, as its spiritual emanation in human common life.

Accordingly, it lies in the essence of the state to be both of these: a kingdom of law, "law-state" [Rechtsstaat], and a kingdom of ethics, an *ethical community*, which by virtue of the deeper unity of law and morality (II. [*Principles of Law*], §. 6) is no contradiction.

The state is to be a *law-state* – the shibboleth of modern times, but also, to speak truly, its developmental impulse. Both the paths and limits of the state's activity and the free spheres of its citizens are to be precisely determined and unassailably secured, and the ethical ideas are not to be realized (enforced) by authority of the state, thus directly, beyond what is appropriate to the sphere of law, i.e., the most <78> necessary minimum. The concept of the law-state by no means is for the state merely to maintain the legal order without administrative purposes, or, moreover, merely to protect the rights of individuals; this concept does not signify the purpose and content of the state at all, but only the manner and character by which the latter are to be realized. The law-state, therefore, above all is contrary to the *patriarchal*, the *patrimonial*, the out-and-out *welfare* [Polizey-] state, wherein the ruling authority seeks to realize the ethical ideas and the purposes of utility in their full extent, in terms of a moral, and thus arbitrary, valuation of each individual case; it is no less contrary to the *people-state* [Volksstaate] (Rousseau, Robespierre), as I call it, in which, by authority of the state, the people expects complete and positive political virtue from every citizen, and recognizes no legal restriction on its own particular ethical appraisal – conditions the first of which, in accordance with nature, is a beginning which only hereafter must be overcome, the last of which is an absolute error.

But the state is not less to be an *ethical commonwealth* [Gemeinwesen]. The ethical idea of all life relations and public endeavors, e.g., family, church, school, should be the principle of the legal order; this order should be borne by the ethical common conviction, which for its part should rule life in a spiritual manner, above and beyond the limits of the legal order. In this manner the sense [Sinn] of the nation is to recognize in the state and its action, in the maintenance of law and public order [Zucht], no mere external establishment for security and utility, but the deeper ethical and God-ordained order, albeit within the limits of what pertains to law. Power is to reside not merely in the legal authorities but, each in its way, also in the ethical or [bez.] political common conviction. The obedience of subjects is to rest not merely on lawful duty but on piety and faithfulness respecting the prince and on devotion to the community. The moral life of individuals, even though it is not to be determined by the state as institution, yet should be determined by the development of public moral judgment. Such power of the ethical spirit, although it cannot be effectuated directly, still remains the supreme purpose and gauge for all institutions and measures, far more than material utility; and its existence, or lack thereof, is the supreme standard for passing judgment over the prosperity of **<79>** a state.

The opposite of the state as ethical community is the *mechanical state*, whether it has a monarchical, constitutional, or democratic form, even, in fact, if it has absorbed a few ethical impulses – for instance regarding political freedom – while, beyond that, it has closed itself to the remaining ones, such as purity of the family bond, public decency, regard for the monarchy or other given ruling authority.

As such, the notion of the law-state and the notion of the ethical-kingdom-state are not in conflict with each other; on the contrary, they condition each other. The mechanical state cannot be the true law-state, and the patrimonial state, like the people-state in the above-mentioned sense, cannot truly realize the notions of an ethical kingdom. The steady improvement in the ethical and religious content of the state institutions, and yet the unshakeable legal order and the inviolable law and life-sphere of individuals, which for the sake of religion or morality cannot be intervened in using external force – these are two purposes which should be, and can be, pursued jointly.

Earlier natural-law theory divested the state, as indeed the law itself, of ethical ideas, viewing both as mere protection of the individual will. Hegel's great achievement is that he, following Schelling, asserted the *ethical content* of the state. But Hegel ignored the bare *legal character of its activity* and therefore conceived it absolutely "as the realization of the ethical idea." This is the untruth, or at least the unclarity, of his concept over against the Kantian, against which even the simple mind immediate takes umbrage.[34] From this, <80> therefore, arises that apotheosis of the state which one finds already with Hegel himself but in much greater degree with many of his followers.

From this concept of the state arises its inner coherence, its purpose, extent, and relation to underlings and other institutions – in further detail in the following manner:

§. 37. The Public Institutional Character of the State

The state is an *institution* [Anstalt], a *commonwealth* [Gemeinwesen] (*res publica*), i.e., an original whole, carrying within itself its grounds of determination, the power and the law of its existence and its activity. It is a kingdom of realized and to-be-realized ethical ideas and rational purposes, which is given in the ethical world-order, to which persons as subordinate members belong automatically.

It is not a mere *society* [Gesellschaft] (*societas*), which derives its existence and its law through the will of its individual members, but a power and a subject for and over them. Being the people constituted into a personality, it has a grandeur over the natural people, the latter conceived either as a mere aggregate of individual people or even as the organic unity of its various estates and classes.[35]

---

[34] Moreover, should one delve deeper into the context [Zusammenhang] of the Hegelian doctrine, one discovers that Hegel finds the ethical content of the state to lie not so much in its ordering of conditions in accordance with ethical ideas as in its being the unity of the substantial and the subjective will; and therefore its mere existence as state is the realization (reality) of the ethical idea, i.e., the logical unity of the aspects of universality and particularity. "Considered abstractly, reasonableness in general consists in the mutually permeating unity of universality and particularity, and here concretely, in terms of content, in the unity of objective freedom, i.e., the general substantial will, and subjective freedom as the individual will and its particular-purpose-seeking will" (*Grundlinien der Philosophie des Rechts* [Baselines of the Philosophy of Law], §. 258).

[35] This is likewise Aristotle's conception, that the state is there prior to persons in the same way as the whole before the parts. This is right, not merely regarding the concept but also regarding every individual person in time, and is the most genuine corrective to the recent natural-law theory. But Aristotle errs in viewing the person as a mere member of the state not merely in the political sphere, which is an affair of the

Therefore, it is not an *immediate personal* or *private rule* having its origin and the law of its existence in the will and rights of the ruler, nor the arbitrary mutual agreement between ruler and subjects – not even in a monarchical constitution. The power the prince has originates not in his person but in the essence of the institution, and therefore not by his private will and unto his private purposes but restricted and determined by the purpose of the institution and in accordance with **<81>** its laws. The relation of the people to him is not a mere relation of personal subjection but one of subjection as under the head precisely of the legally ordained community which it helped to shape. To this degree, but only to this degree, can one say with Rousseau[36] that the state is republican under all constitutional forms and that only the republican state is legitimate. The state is a public affair through and through. All regard and all power in it are grounded in its order and necessity, not on the will of the people, nor on the private relation to the regents. This equally rules out both the popular-rule and the private-rule conception.

The center of this institution, however, the first and most essential in the concept of the state, is the *ruling authority* [Obrigkeit]. The ruling authority is that through which, and in which, an institution of rule, thus the state, exists. One therefore cannot first establish a state and thereafter arrange its ruling authority. The state does not exist prior to the ruling authority. The state, then, is a given power (grounded in the essence of the institution, not from men set over it) – it is a public power, i.e., serving higher commands and purposes, and not (firstly) the particular gratification of the possessors [des Inhabers] – it is a power ordained by God and performing His work – it is, at the same time, the unity of the people and the regard over the people.

Grotius was the first to articulate scientifically the principle of the state as a commonwealth existing in itself as distinguished from mere princely power, and this is his great significance, which characterizes the new era in the area of legal philosophy and politics. But in so doing he inserted a false aspect. To separate the state from the person of the prince, he grounded it on the will of the citizen, thus making it into the product of his contractual union. This spurred the later

---

commonwealth, but in general, and in terms of his entire essence, thus as a derivative, secondary being; this is the Greek one-sidedness.

[36] *Social Contract*, IV. 6.

philosophers ever more strongly, culminating in the full development of the *social theory* [Gesellschaftstheorie] (will of individuals) in Germany, and the doctrine of *popular sovereignty* (will of the entire mass) in France. In order to counteract the latter, Haller returned to the pre- <82> Grotian conception of the monarchical state as mere personal bond, with the rejection of any institutional character for it. That which once was lack of development, lack of clarity of consciousness, and therefore in any case a mere lack, now with Haller has become a decisive error.

The doctrine of *popular sovereignty* did, however, contain the truth that the state in the final analysis indisputably rests on the will of the people, and only thereby is it an ethical kingdom of the community. But this popular will is, firstly, itself an original spiritual element which permeates individuals rather than being the result of the *will of individuals* (II. [*Principles of Law*], §. 24); furthermore, it is no *arbitrary will*, but instead a power determining the will, a consciousness of ethical necessity, and therefore also not a momentary will but a continuous ethical-legal will which to that point had already realized itself in the formation of the state and which, therefore, is also bound to the received laws and authority;[37] finally, it is only the *basis* of the state, and, as such, conditions, restricts, and influences the institutional (constitutional) authority, without however being itself the *subject* of acting, ruling power. The *error* of the doctrine of *popular sovereignty* consists in muddling these matters, either separately or taken together.

§. 38. The Purpose of the State

The purpose [Zweck] of the state is the realization of the ethical kingdom. This entails, on the one hand, *rule* as such, the establishment of ruling authority over people, existing by virtue of the ethical bond and regard, not merely by virtue of natural power; and on the other hand, the *purpose of rule:* protection and promotion *of people,* development of the *nation's* condition, maintenance of *God's* commandments.

This means that the state does not exist merely for the sake of the purposes of individuals but also for the sake of the purposes of <83> the nation, the fulfillment of the common (objective) condition. It should as a whole fulfill tasks

[37] In this there exists an analogy with the conscience of individuals (I. [*Philosophical Foundations*], §. 35).

which in no way can be tasks of individuals, as for example penal justice; it should as a whole be the expression of higher conceptions, the development of gifts and powers of the nation in its unity, and, to that end, it should demand the devotion and sacrifice precisely of individuals. Indeed, the goods of individuals – their welfare, education, morality – are not the immediate purpose of the state; those are just the life-task of individuals, while the state is the fulfillment of the life-task of the nation. The state preserves people only in the possibility, the means of these goods – this is protection and promotion – not in the goods themselves, and it strives after these goods to the degree that they have a relation to the whole, that they have a characteristic of commonality, and this indirect promotion of individual people in their free pursuit of those goods is for their part again a side of the fulfillment of the common condition. That is the marvelous depth of the ethical world: everywhere the higher power and order has people as its purpose, no less than they have it as their purpose.

For this very reason, moreover, the purpose of the state is not merely to provide for the conditions under it, but at the same time for its own existence. Its value consists not merely in that which it *effectuates*, but, above all, in that which it is. As the hero or the wise man is not a mere means for other people whom he protects or promotes, but is himself a purpose in the economy of the ethical world – in the same way are institutions. The bravery and power of the army, the wisdom of the administration, the majesty of the ruling authority, the obedience and devotion of subjects, are purposes in themselves, not mere means to protect against the enemy and to satisfy needs and maintain order. In all this, in fact, lies the fulfillment of national existence. But this fulfillment is not a mere *artistic* fulfillment, the impression made on the beholder (Schelling), nor is it a mere *logical* fulfillment, the complete explanation of abstract categories of universal and particular (Hegel), but it is *creative* and *ethical* fulfillment. It comprises the range of national powers and their uniform rule, the range of ethical bonds, and the <**84**> depth of ethical sentiment characteristic of each.

Finally, the purpose of the state consists not merely in the improvement of human conditions but above all in the maintenance of divine commandments, not merely in freely pursuable goods but in obedience to inviolable ordinances. In the same way that the concept of the state is the highest aspect of the ruling authority, so is the concept of the ruling authority the highest aspect of this maintenance of God's commandments.

The noblest purpose of the state is *law* (in the objective sense)[38] *and justice.* Law is precisely the most important component of the commandment assigned to it, it is "the life-order of the people for the preservation of God's world order" (II. [*Principles of Law*], §. 1). However, law in this, its true meaning, no less than morality, has the Ten Commandments as its content and essence (II., §§. 4, 6). It is the free human application of these commandments issued by God to individuals and for individual acts, to the order of the common condition and the institutions. When the state, through its legal order, supports the true worship [Kultus] (regard of the church, Sunday observance), protects life and property, upholds the pure order of marriage and obedience to elders and ruling authority, it indeed does nothing other than apply the Ten Commandments (not to the individual, but) to the public life of the people. In this sense one may say: the highest purpose of the state – and the core in the position of the ruling authority – is to be the upholder and avenger of the Ten Commandments. It is, as the ancients said, the "guardian of both tables."

Freedom and the right of individuals are already included in this, for they are an essential component of the legal order. But one may also justifiably consider them to be a particular independent aspect of the purpose of the state. Because absolute freedom, the secure sphere of independent action and choice [Schalten] of the people comprising the ethical kingdom, is part of the essence of that kingdom. This is a **<85>** no less essential element of it than are its commandments and ordinances. One might say that these commandments and ordinances, as well as the goods of the nation and the individuals who produce them, are the matter of the ethical kingdom, while law and the freedom of individuals are the necessary form of its existence; only that here the form, in turn, is just as essentially matter. Both together are the one indivisible purpose of the state, since in both together the concept of the ethical kingdom is realized.

In accordance with all of this, the purpose of the state is certainly by all means a *uniform* [einheitlicher] one, yet not a *simple* [einfacher] one.[39]

---

[38] [As opposed to law in the subjective sense, or rights (see II. [*Principles of Law*], ch. 6).]

[39] Similarly, we had to recognize a dual purpose regarding marriage (III. [*Private Law*], §. 66).

The objectivity of the purpose of the state is the high merit of Plato's doctrine of state, albeit with the sacrifice of the gratification and entitlement of individuals, which in fact are necessary to the fulfillment of the whole. But this insight disappears from Plato onward. Already Aristotle placed the purpose of the state in happiness (τοῦ εὖ ζῆν ἕνεκα), hence [bez.] the virtue of individuals. In the same way Cicero[40] with his *honeste beateque vivere.* The entire Middle Ages followed Aristotle, although, in consequence of the Christian confession, with the modification that the state targets earthly virtue and the earthly good, while the church targets heavenly virtue (grace) and eternal salvation. In this manner Thomas Aquinas, Dante,[41] et al. Bacon, in Aristotelian fashion, still viewed the purpose as *bene vivere.*[42] From Grotius on, however, the *right* of the individual was asserted to be the primary purpose of the state, while the good, which Grotius retained, was therefore conceived materially, as utility rather than virtue. It continues in this fashion through the development of natural law, until the good was completely eliminated by Kant, and only the right of the individual remained as purpose of the state. In this **<86>** manner, the purpose of the state everywhere was placed in the objectives of individuals, and the controversy of the most recent period revolves solely around the question as to whether utility, virtue, or freedom are the same as law. In the same manner the English, with Locke at the forefront, sought the purpose of the state only in the protection of life and property, chiefly the latter. Finally Rousseau, although entirely annihilating the will of individuals under the *volonté générale,* content-wise provides for the latter, as well as the *bien public,* nothing other than the good of the individuals, and his deduction of the state, as Sidney's and others, therefore proceeds like this: "What do men seek in the state, given that they give up their natural freedom? A higher good; *thus their greater advantage.*" So stated, finally, Mounier in his lecture regarding the constitution of July 9th, 1789, on behalf of the committee with the approval of the National Assembly: "Les droits du roi et de la nation n'existent que pour le bonheur des individus, qui la composent" [The rights of the king and the nation exist only for the happiness of the individuals who make it up]. It is the vocation and therefore the inner drive of the

[40] *Laws*, II. 5.

[41] *On Monarchy*, Book III at the end; Thomas Aquinas, de regim. princ. lib. I. cap. 14.

[42] *The Advancement of Learning*, Book VIII.

entire epoch to bring out the truth that man, thus each individual person, is an absolute end [Zweck] of the state, and that the protection of rights is not one of many tasks, but an actual independent principle of the entire political institution. It was precisely the one-sidedness and exclusivity of its emphasis that enabled this essential aspect of the purpose of the state to attain a certain powerful awareness which fills the age. By contrast, the perfection of the common condition, the higher ethical order of life relations, which is no less an aspect, in fact the first aspect, of the essence of the state, vanished entirely from this viewpoint. It is understandable, then, that here the overall valuation of the state in all its relations must necessarily be one-sided and faulty.

Schelling was the first to return to Platonic objectivity, thereby founding a new epoch for the philosophical view of the state; the standpoint he gained received greater extension and confirmation through Hegel's more developed doctrine. Accordingly, while the ancients viewed the state as a mere means for conditions **<87>** outside of it, in fact perhaps as a necessary evil; Schelling[43] viewed it simply as an end in itself; its purpose is simply "to be the state (i.e., unity of universal and particular etc.)." Similarly Hegel,[44] who therefore also considered the constitution to be the state; but the administration, thus the entirety of state provision for conditions, he consigns to the humbler sphere of "civil society." This however goes too far to the other side. The effect of the state on conditions, above all the protection of rights and the administration of justice for example, is no less significant and elevated as is its own structure [Bau]. But the idea of enforcing the prescribed ordinances [Ordnungen] is everywhere lacking.

Montesquieu's view, which occasionally is accepted even by later writers, whereby every state has its own special purpose, e.g., the Romans conquest, the Indians religion, the citizens of Marseille trade, the English political freedom, and where, excepting mechanical indispensable self-preservation, there is no general state purpose, is something like a denial of natural law. Certainly, in accordance with the individuality of the age and the peoples, this or that endeavor

---

[43] *Vorlesungen über die Methode des academischen Studium* [Lectures on the Method of Academic Study], 10th lecture.

[44] *Grundlinien der Philosophie des Rechts* [Baselines of the Philosophy of Law], §. 258 (pp. 311, 312).

will predominate in the state; even so, the state has a significance for human life which is the same everywhere.

§. 39. The State Restricted to Common Life

Accordingly, the activity of the state comprises the totality of human common life. It is not *an* association [Verein] for *a* purpose, but simply *the* association for *the* purpose of community; it is social order and rule. Within its range, therefore, fall all relations and purposes of human life: security, welfare, protection against the elements, mores and decency, education, etc. There is no reason why any of these relations, e.g., public education or morality, should be excluded from the range of the tasks of the state, unless one assumes, completely arbitrarily and in denial of the purpose of all of human existence, **<88>** that man has been created for absolute external freedom and isolation by nature, and can only be restricted for the sake of the purpose of this freedom. On the contrary, each of these relations and endeavors of human existence promotes the community of men and leads to such; for each, it is necessary that the common action of men be ordered, both to reveal the higher rule of that action, and to promote it for the sake of community.

But the state does not comprise these relations in every respect.

Firstly, in accordance with the above, they are the object of the state only to the degree that they are purposes of the community and not merely individuals. For the task of the state is not the totality of human *lives* but only the totality of *human common life*. It is not the concern of the state that the individuals A, B, and C be well-off, educated, moral, but only that *national* wealth, education, morality exist. Therefore, in the state the totality of private life and private aspiration remains intact, albeit restricted and permeated by the demands of public mores and welfare.

Moreover, the state does not, even to the degree that it is concerned with them, have the task of their positive inner fulfillment, but only their *external order* and guidance, and so, when they are of an inward spiritual nature, only their *indirect* promotion. So, e.g., the state is not to lead and determine the development of science in the nation, but only *indirectly* to promote it through its institutions. The state is not social life itself, but only the bearer, orderer, promoter of it.

Here lies, on the one hand, the justification of those actual states, which, through all of history, have not restricted their activity to mere legal protection but have drawn the entire life of the people within their ambit, and on the other hand the prophylaxis whereby the freedom of individuals is not absorbed by external state leading [Staatslenkung] in the way that national development and endeavor is.

Religion alone, in itself and in the final analysis, lies outside the assignment of the state, in that it does not concern the fulfillment of the human condition in itself, and according to its earthly existence, but rather the union of men with God and the life beyond. In **<89>** this peculiarity and heterogeneity with the purpose of the state, religion is accorded its own institution, the church. And yet, on the one hand the state has religion as its determinant, it being the supreme standard of everything ethical; and on the other, by virtue of a deeper unity which exists between these two purposes, and, therefore, also between church and state, religion also becomes, at least indirectly, a task of the state, i.e., through the protection and promotion which it grants the church.

The restriction of the state to legal protection and, to that end, the protection of individual rights to the exclusion of all other spheres of life and ethical ideas, began with Thomasius ("pax externa") and was fulfilled with Kant ("external freedom"). Thomasius had already perfected the most significant aspect, in that he vouchsafed the ecclesiastical power no other purpose than to guard against reciprocal disturbances of the peace. This conception, as insipid as it is untrue, was terminated by speculative philosophy, which restored the totality as well as the objectivity of the purpose of the state. But speculative philosophy, in turn, gravitates towards another danger. It overlooks or ignores the aspect of externality and conceives of the state as itself being social life, instead of as the mere bearer and orderer of social life, and, accordingly, allows the state more and more either itself to assume the purpose of the church (Rothe), or entirely to subordinate it as negligible (Hegel). So does it come to an apotheosis of the state, and thereby to a convolution of all of human life and aspiration.

§. 40. Indispensable Role of the State in Morality and History

When, accordingly, the state has only *external* order and the promotion of *social* life as its immediate activity, it is nevertheless indirectly the bearer and safeguard of the inner morality of individuals. Although the ethical commandment extends to inner conviction and free will, the person who is to fulfill that commandment nevertheless belongs with his entire existence to the external world as well and is dependent upon that world's effects on his body, upon its impressions on his mind. Therefore, even if the indi- <90> vidual ethical decision of a person, by virtue of his freedom of the will, is entirely superior to everything external, the morality of people as a whole and in the long run still cannot exist apart from order in external relations, the state. By this, which is its order, it preserves room for ethical aspiration, keeping such from sinking under the confusion and struggle of mutual self-defense, as well as the ongoing revelation of ethical concepts in all life relations, so that they not disappear from human consciousness. For although the manner in which the state upholds faithfulness and honesty in commerce, purity of marriage, deference of children to elders, etc., is by no means adequate to the deeper ethical demand of these relations, it is through such constant observation of rules and morality that one nevertheless is made aware of those deeper demands; the ethical will of the individual within is awakened and strengthened by the exercise of the ethical will of the individual without, and ethical knowledge is perpetuated through times and among masses lacking in personal penetration of morality. Without this – with unrestricted continual infringement – even the consciousness of the ethical command would in the end be lost. In this manner, the mores of people are conditioned and supported by the state, even though this cannot be its direct task.

In the same way, the state is also a means and instrument of history. Of course, the latter proceeds through inner impulses. Its factors are the, to us imperceptible, divine instigation and distribution of talents and human free decisions and acts. But these acts can only have a result and lasting effect on the community through the enduring and secure bond of the community. Everything, therefore, which is effected through history, not only in the shaping of external relations but also in the progress and expansion of culture [Bildung], occurs through the state as means. The state ensures the mutual contacts, the mutual effects on understanding and will. It brings thereby the events and acts of people to a general result, so that they do not vanish fruitlessly in the chaos of bustling activity; it renders every event, every perception into a shared good [Gemeingute], it renders the work of an age into the enduring possession of all ages. On the other <91> hand, it is an exaggeration when one considers the state to be the only purpose of world history. It is only one of those purposes; the higher spiritual kingdom of ethics and culture, of which the state is the bearer, and the individual person, who participates in the same, are no less purposes of world history than the state.

It is only through these relations of the state – the direct ones to external conditions, the indirect ones to the morality of individual persons and the leading of the human race – in their indissoluble unity as its total purpose, that the essence of the state and its significance in the divine world order are completely exhausted.

§. 41. Resistance to State Power

As the institution for the rule of the collective human common condition, the state is the *sole, supreme, sovereign* power on earth. Men and their aspirations, other institutions and communities, even the church as far as her external existence is concerned, are subordinate to it. The state judges them without being judged by them or justifying itself before them, there being no authority and no judge over it. This is the proper significance of the doctrine of "the omnipotence of Parliament," and to have restored the state in this power is a true advance of the times. But the ethical and natural, or more deeply considered, the divine order of things, ever stands over the human kingdom of the state, which in fact is to serve it. In consequence of this higher order, people in their personality (innate right) and acquired rights, as well as other communities, above all the church, are entitled subjects, in the sphere of which the state cannot intervene without committing injustice.

Therefore, the state, although *sovereign*, is not the *absolute* power on earth. *Formally,* its power is *unrestricted; materially,* it is not. This material restriction of the right of the state is above all a determining factor for the state, that is, for those who hold power, that it everywhere respects rights – natural-ethical rights unconditionally, positive-legal rights in the highest possible degree – and keeps from infringing them. But the state still asserts itself even when such infringements do take place. Thus, if the state abridges the **<92>** freedom, the advantage, the rights, of individuals or communities or of the church, in the sphere which generally is subject to its order, this may constitute an overstepping of its reasonable limits, an inner injustice for the case at hand; yet still, the act is binding in every way, even for the injured party. So, for example, when the state, within the limits of its *jus eminens,* expropriates things without actual ground, or abolishes rights (e.g., nobility, municipalities), or when, alongside the received state church, it allows for another, etc.,[45] the parties may complain about the unfounded curtailment of their rights, and yet they must obey. On the other hand, if the state abridges people, communities, the church, in the sphere in which they, in accordance with that higher order, are independent of the state, then the act is *non-binding* for them. Active resistance against state power is of course not allowed, nor can any court of law or state administrative body refuse to comply with such acts,[46] but protestation and passive resistance are open to the parties. So, for example, when the state forces subjects into a vocation (trade, clergy), or entirely removes from them the education of their children, or commands of them, as in the time of the Terror, a certain political persuasion; or when Protestant soldiers are enjoined to genuflect, or Catholic priests to unconditional consecration of mixed marriages. So did the Scottish church long protest against state decrees which prescribed patronage in a manner which, according to its doctrine, it held to be religiously inadmissible, and it had (to the degree that such truly was its doctrine) the complete right to consider such a decree to be non-binding for it.[47] **<93>**

---

[45] For this reason alone, the papal protestation against the Peace of Westphalia cannot be justified, it being mainly directed against the reception of the Protestant church; besides, it is not a mere legal *protestation* as a materially entitled subject vis-à-vis the imperial power, but an *annulment* as a formally higher power over it.

[46] The judge who identifies a law of king or Parliament as contrary to the divine order may resign from his office of judgeship before applying it; as judge, however, he cannot refuse to apply it.

[47] Mere positive-legal, constitutionally guaranteed entitlements are also a restriction of the omnipotence of the state which have the same effect in the case in which the infringed parties, precisely by virtue of the constitutional guarantee, themselves are an integral part of state power; they therefore do not have to recognize the infringing act as an act of the full entire legitimate state power. So, for example, the nobility and clergy in France, when the right of special curia and veto were taken from them. But, as a rule, such acts, by the power of circumstances, have a universal-historical justification and confirmation, against which all resistance collapses. Things took a special turn with the abolition of princely claims of succession by the present constitutional power. This will be treated first in the doctrine of monarchy.

One might consider such acts, which the judge must recognize as lawful, and which the person concerned rightly considers non-binding, to be mere infractions of the ethical duty of the state; even so, with these kinds of infractions the subject [Unterthan] has no other remedy but remonstration and the duty of sufferance and obedience, not protestation and passive resistance. Instead, they are violations of the legal sphere of state power, thus violations of its legal obligation, even though no objective verdict and no objective judgment have been issued in that regard. One is to behave toward the state which exceeds the ethical limits of its activity in the same way as the people are to behave toward a sovereign prince who violates the constitution (II. [*Principles of Law*], §. 31).

The form of public condition in which the state does not recognize such material entitlement as rooted partly in the nature of things, partly in the positive constitution, but considers its will to be the law on earth plain and simple, which can do no injustice, we call *state absolutism.* This is to be distinguished from princely absolutism, since the parliament (prince and estates together), in fact even the democratic assembly, can also exercise such absolutism and violate the right of individuals, minorities, the church. State absolutism thus has its origin primarily in the removal, from over the state, of a higher (divine) order, in which all the rights of men and institutions have their root, making the human will, be it the individual will, be it the common will, into the lord on earth. This was the state absolutism of Hobbes, of Rousseau, and to a degree Hegel as well. Conversely, the barrier against state absolutism is the commitment of the public consciousness to that higher order, thus the living civility [Gesittung] and religious conviction [Gesinnung] of the people. In <94> this consists a factual power vis-à-vis the state, which cannot have a legal one over it. But since the ethical conviction cannot anywhere be upheld without the religious, the collapse of faith leads in its final conclusions to state absolutism. Accordingly, public freedom has its deepest confirmation and most secure guarantee in such conviction of the nation, regardless of the particular form of the constitution. An energetic consciousness of inner necessity and independent motives in all life relations and endeavors, in marriage, upbringing, trade, science, church, as likewise an energetic consciousness both of law and the value of people and citizens, as well as of acquired rights, and finally and above all, a habituation and resolution "to obey God rather than men," these are the pillars on which all state absolutism founders. A richly articulated political constitution, in which the various entitled elements have strong representation, affords a mighty support for this; no less so does a free church constitution, i.e., one independent of the state, such as possessed by, e.g., the Catholic or the Scottish Presbyterian church. Should, however, the latter be inwardly hierarchical, though it provides protection against the state, it itself becomes an absolutism of external power.

Hobbes gave insight into the notions of the single and sovereign power of the state in his exposition that the state is not merely connection and assembly ("consentire"), but union ("unio"), through which all are made into one will, so that a new person arises. This is the notion of centralization in its final and deepest significance. In this aspect Hobbes, like Grotius in another aspect (namely the notion of the state in contrast to the princes), was the herald of a new epoch. But, separated from that higher order, he conceives of this union abstractly, without a determinate moderating content, and only sees the silhouette of the state, without the inward living articulation and movement. In this, his view regarding the state is similar to Spinoza's regarding the universe (I. [*Philosophical Foundations*], §. 22). Hereby he arrives at unbridled state power ("imperium absolutum"), in which the subject has no right, property, not even conscience, no judgment of his own regarding good and evil, and to which even the church with its doc- **<95>** trine is to be entirely subjected.

Rousseau's concept of the general will (*volonté générale*), which can do no injustice, is entirely the same in this,[48] only with the modification that Rousseau

---

[48] Thus Hobbes de cive V. II: "Quae potestas et jus imperandi in eo consistit, quod unusquisque civium omnem suam vim et potentiam in illum hominem vel concilium transtulit. Quod fecisse nil aliud est quam de jure suo resistendi decessisse" [Which power and right to rule consists in the fact that each citizen has transferred all his force and power to that man or council. Which to have done is nothing other than to have renounced his right to resist]; Rousseau, *Social Contract,* ch. I. 6: "De plus, l'aliénation se faisant sans réserve, l'union est aussi parfaite, qu'elle peut l'être, et nul associé n'a plus rien à réclamer" [What's more, since the alienation is unreserved, the union is as perfect as it can be, and no associate has any claim to it]. Likewise II. 6: "Il ne faut plus demander, si la loi peut être injuste, puisque nul n'est injuste envers lui même" [It is no longer necessary to ask whether the law can be unjust, since no one is unjust towards himself]. (Thus, since the people, *la volonté générale,* cannot do any injustice against

vindicates this common will inalienably for the majority of the people, while Hobbes transfers it to a king or an assembly. Rousseau unites popular sovereignty and state absolutism. In this manner he realized the French Revolution. Had this extreme not been realized, still the times gravitate to state absolutism,[49] and current Catholic writers are conducting a well-grounded polemic against it worthy of all consideration. But the meaning by which they combat the "absolute state" and the "omnipotence of Parliament" is to assert against the state other powers as independent and equally entitled *formally* as well. They place *absolute individual entitlement* against the *absolute state*, so that the state (king and Parliament) can never abolish the acquired right of a person, a city, a corporation, and such abolition is to be held as formally unlawful. They declare war on the *absolute* state and conduct war against the *unified* state, only to disperse it into independent unsubjected manorial estates and corporate entities [Körperschaften]. Instead of the *independent* **<96>** church, which has authority and power in herself and her sphere for herself, they aspire to the *sovereign* church, which does not need the authorization of the state even for its legal civil validity and is not subject to its supervision. Such an establishment of a secular sovereign church, its liberation from all legal subordination under the state, must of necessity lead to the subordination of the latter, as in the Middle Ages. Would it really be gain if the omnipotence of the church, and in particular of the Pope, to whom the king is subject, were to take the place of the omnipotence of the state?

---

itself, it cannot do any against a minority either!) Kant (*Metaphysische Anfangsgründe der Rechtslehre* [Metaphysical Elements of the Doctrine of Law], p. 165, §. 45) repeated after Rousseau, without being cognizant of the import of this statement.

[49] Hegel certainly had a concrete determining content for the state, in the entire development of the Idea in its aspects up to the state. But because for him the state is the highest realization of the Idea, because for him it in fact is the graphically revealed God, so is there, when the subordinate stages are ignored, no higher consideration that moderates it, and, in particular, faith and church assume such a subordinate stage under the state, and so little value is attached to acquired rights, that at any rate all real elements of power are lacking vis-à-vis the state.

Chapter 2: Nation and Land

§. 42. The State is the Vocation of the Nation

<97> Because the purpose of the state encompasses the whole of human existence, it is the task of the *people* [des Volkes]. For only the people contains the tendencies and means of human existence as a whole, together with a common consciousness. Only it, therefore, has the power, the distribution of activities, the common ethical standard, which are requisite for the state. A more restricted sphere does not possess the means, while an alien multitude does not possess the unity of consciousness, of order and purpose. The people are already the natural power and community, which the state is to elevate into a legally ordered one.[50]

Humanity taken as a whole has neither the community and unity of natural needs, nor the unity and individuality of ethical consciousness. Therefore the state is not the vocation of collective humanity, in order for it to construct a universal kingdom; the state is the vocation of the people. Each people is to manifest the total picture of human life in accordance with the particularity of its external existence, in its particular fashion. And history leads every people along its own path; each is allotted a special arrangement and capacity, and a special work and portion in the plan of the whole, be it an insight **<98>** or skill, be it a custom or institution, which it develops undisturbed in itself, which in short order becomes a common heritage. Therefore, the state as orderer and bearer of that life, as instrument of this leading, must fall specifically to each people.

The establishment of a universal kingdom would in no way lead to a higher condition – perfected human nature allowing of no races – for in restricted,

---

[50] Even the city (πόλις, *civitas*), which Greek and Roman antiquity identified with the state, is not the true subject of the state. It does not possess sufficient means, self-sufficiency (αὐτάρκεια), which even Aristotle typified as the essence of the state. Those city-states were a double-being of state and municipality, and partly they needed dependent regions whereby a numerous population was politically subjected, and partly the confederation whereby they first together became a true state. The state is not a *city* (*civitas*) but a *kingdom* (*imperium*).

temporal conditions, the disparity of characters [Anlagen] of necessity prevails; the particular characters and capacities of peoples would be suppressed, and each would be hindered in fulfilling the vocation specially assigned to it. In that case, not only would the foreign general government simply not understand how to value and promote a particular people's special needs and endeavors, and not strive for them, but the particular spirit of the people would thereby die away, because its preeminent expression, which is what the shape of the state itself is, would be withdrawn from it. For the universal kingdom to be the appropriate one, the separation of human consciousness in peoples and languages, the particularity of needs according to place and individuality, would have to end. But then history itself would have ended, and its bearer, the state, would no longer be needed.

§. 43. The Nation Originates in Blood, Continues as Ethical Union

The people originates through a strong individuality (personality), a patriarch, having a large number of descendants, who bear this individuality within themselves, and likewise through their numbers are capable of isolating themselves and uniting themselves together into a whole.[51] The testimony of the most ancient documents con- **<99>** firm this: thus Israel, Edom, Ishmael, etc. The unity of descent and thereby the imprint of a personality is the primeval concept of the people. With it is given the unity of spirit, of mores, of language. Mixtures of peoples might arise, which however does not abolish this concept of the people. For the mixture of peoples already assumes pure peoples as original, and is based on large-scale intermarriage (*connubium*), resulting in unity of blood in later generations, even though from a dual source. Thus the contemporary English and French, the ancient Romans. Such mixture and supplementation of two or more people-individualities is by no means to be considered a lesser condition. On the contrary, the third product can end up being the higher one. The first and original concept of the people, accordingly, is the natural one: the unity of blood (initial descent or later mixture through

---

[51] I would not derive the original formation [Bildung] of the peoples primarily from the disturbance of the religious consciousness in and of itself, but from the natural separation of descent. The religious separation directly took hold of this natural separation, through which the mere variation of individuality proceeded until there came about complete dissimilarity, in fact even sharp contrast.

intermarriage), and, in consequence of this, the unity of disposition, of natural temper, of the spirit, of mores, of language. The latter are what are important to the state; the unity of blood is only the basis for it. The ethical kingdom of the state demands unity of ethical consciousness and ethical life relations.

As the people forms the basis and condition of the state, so for its part is it itself conditioned and acted upon by the state. Already the family, from which the people arises, is not merely a *natural* community of blood but also an *ethical legal* community of *regard.* The patriarchal power, which is the original state, precedes the family, just as it has the family as its condition. Just so the state with regard to the people. It is no less the case that a strange mix of people over time become a people when they together lead a common life and, finally, are united through a political power; and conversely, the descendants of a people lose the actual, or at least complete, character of being a people when they, entirely dispersed from each other, live among strangers, even though unmixed. The effect of the political association on mixed races, thus new peoples, as well as on ethnic groups [Stämme] preserved unmixed is to effectuate a unity of consciousness, of language, culture, ethical valuation <100> [Würdigung] within them, in scarcely less degree than the unity of descent. One might designate the one as the *natural* popular union [Volkseinheit], the other the *historical.* Beyond the fact that the union of political association brings about a natural popular union, in itself it is an essential aspect in the concept of the people. For the inner purpose (τέλος) of the people is precisely the idea of common interest, the cohabitation of people in mutual satisfaction of needs, in mutual spiritual influence, in common ethical rule of their lives. When, as a result, language, mores, life valuation are the decisive aspects for the concept of the people, behind which the unity of blood recedes as mere basis, much more so is the final realization of common interest: the shared formation of a state. Hereby arises a second, to wit, a *legal* concept of the people, in contrast with the natural and historical: the unity of political power. Accordingly, "people" is every multitude subject to a state power.

For all *legal issues,* of course, only the legal concept of the state comes into consideration. Law and the regard of states over subjects do not depend upon the latter being distributed among them in accordance with their natural or historical popular relations, and the contrary does not justify war or rebellion.[52] For *political* issues, however, the natural or <101> historical concept of the people is decisive: whether the unity of national consciousness, mores, language, is given by blood or by history. The people in this sense is the natural basis of the state, and is the necessary prerequisite for a healthy and vigorous state. With new distributions of land, therefore, the leading consideration should be whether the people-association [Volksverband] is natural or historical, to the degree that existing rights do not hinder this. When a nation, such as the German, is divided into clan-states [Stammstaaten], a higher state union is to be pursued, and the stronger the better, within which the common national consciousness receives its manifestation and security. When several peoples of sufficient number are united under one scepter, their individuality is to be preserved, for which reason an independent constitution is granted each of them.

---

[52] Since this was first written (1846), this legal principle has become especially clear. For a chief object of the movement of 1848 was the contrary one: *a new constituting of the European state system* [Staatenbestandes] *according to nationalities* (that all Germans must form one single state for themselves, all Italians, all Poles, etc.) and *abolition of all contrary treaties and rights of rulership.* This enterprise is *contrary to law,* it destroys for political purposes well-founded rights regardless of how praiseworthy they might otherwise be, it destroys the law of nations for the future as well, because according to it no cession [Abtretung] and no subjection is valid anymore, and with such destruction of the law of nations it might come down to the victorious people only finding security in the genocide [Ausrottung] of the vanquished. There lies, however, in the *unlawful* establishment of nationalities at the same time an *ethical outrage:* man overcomes God's counsels [Rathschlüsse] and divine judgments, wishes to do away with His leading of the peoples, in order to assume it himself. This is a parallel with communism, which in the same manner aims to establish an allegedly rational, i.e., humanly conceived distribution of goods through the destruction of all existing rights. But even factually this enterprise demonstrates itself to be *impracticable* and *chimerical,* because the nationalities do not just remain in their places of origin (a German population residing in Poland, a Danish population in Schleswig), and one cannot liberate the one without oppressing the other.

§. 44. The Territorial Nature of the State

Now in order to form the state, the people must have the same place of residence. The entire life of men being connected with the soil of the earth, the order of the state likewise assumes unity and stability in the relations to the soil. Only the land preserves the unity of needs, the solidarity of means for their satisfaction – stability of relations, institutions, interests – the love for ordered existence, and the rulership which is to be obeyed. The land therefore is an integral part of the state, as essential to its content as is the people. Thus, a migratory people is not a state in terms of the complete concept, and every prince rightly takes his name from the land. In this, he expresses not that he has property in the land but that the state, whose prince he is, is a stable kingdom firmly fixed to the native soil of the earth in enduring order. On the other hand, designation merely after the people, as took place in 1789 and again in 1830: "King of the French," as with Clovis "King of the Franks," **<102>** or Attila "King of the Huns," fits just as well with a nomadic horde. It brings back the picture of the barbarians. It is based on that persuasion, peculiar to the Revolution, of breaking loose from everything prehuman-given [allem Vormenschlich-Gegebenen], to which the land also pertains. The language designates state, people, and land together extremely aptly as *kingdom* [Reich]. The fully equivalent designation of a king is, therefore, after the country over which he rules, e.g., of France, Austria.

But the land also imposes certain conditions and requirements on the state, through climate, its own particular sources of subsistence, etc. It therefore helps to determine the state's institutions, and lends it its imprint, similar to the individuality of the nation, albeit not in as great a measure.[53] In the way that every man is given, by God, not merely a certain peculiarity of his nature, but likewise, in agreement with it, a certain peculiarity in the relations surrounding him, so is every people allotted a specific land; and the spiritual direction of the people, and the condition of the land, are geared to each other, in order for each people to hold its corresponding land in accordance with its special vocation. One can thereby explain world history as little by geography as vice versa, but instead consider popular disposition and the condition of the land as belonging

---

[53] In recent times it has become customary to overemphasize the influence of the character of the land. Montesquieu in particular is representative of this.

together in a single higher plan of divine providence (I. [*Philosophical Foundations*], §. 15).

Since the land in this fashion is a supplementary part of the state, the state also has a *right to land* – i.e., both over the spatial area of the land, and the soil itself – *territorial right.* By virtue of this right, every state encloses itself over its area and tolerates no landholding [Grundbesitz] and no persons who do not pay homage to its rule.[54] Precisely on this right are founded various regalia, such as the roadway regale, the shipping regale, and, on the other hand, the possibility of state servitudes [Staatsdienstbarkeiten] in foreign territories, then the extensive expropriation of immovables, and the like. Of **<103>** course, one may by no means attribute a supreme property in land and soil, i.e., a right that generates wealth [Vermögensbefriedigung] like property does. If this were so, the state or the prince would appropriate the prime yield of the soil, as is the case in several oriental kingdoms. But the territorial authorizations mentioned above are not to be derived from the mere power of the state over the persons of the proprietors, thus from the mere obedience of subjects, for it is not exercised in the same measure over the movable holdings of subjects. On the contrary, these authorizations are the consequence of a specific political or state-legal power over land and soil as such. Land and soil are not merely its perimeter, but also its object.

"Natural law" does not at all bring the concept of the people into connection with the concept of the state. This higher, of necessity unifying, of necessity ruling bond, lies outside the appreciation of natural law. It must recognize as a state, indeed as a rationally grounded state, every aggregate of persons who unite themselves to protect their rights. Nor does its abstraction include the relationship to the land in its representation of the state.

---

[54] Natural law is totally incapable of setting this out (Vol. I, p. 375 [*The Recovery of Historical Law,* pp. 37ff.]).

Chapter 3: The Origin of the State; The Foundation of the Duty of Subjection

§. 45. The Organic Origin of the State

The state arises through *historical events* – i.e., the position into which descent, necessity, lot, and acts bring men – in a particular people, in a particular area, and through the *ethical-legal idea* which accompany those men. It does not arise through outward convening but through inward development; it does not arise through human intention, but through higher Providence. The first state is the patriarchally ordered family (Aristotle). Here the relations are all packed into a bud which further develop into separate existence – family, estate, state, church. Then the family expands into a people, bequeathing privileges of birth, bringing with it the practice of the worship of God passed down from the ancestors, adding common protection outward, common satisfaction inward, a relation of regard and dependence, rule and obedience following upon victory and subjection. In this manner, suzerainty [Obergewalt] arises through birth, gifts, superior strength, partly in gradual habituation, partly in voluntary subjection or through assimilation. All these events and conditions, however, are accompanied by the consciousness implanted in men of having to establish and maintain such order; and so, they lead to the comprehensive and confirmed institution which we call the state. Such are the causes through which, everywhere in diverse ways, in gradual development, states arise. As with the peoples, so with and in them the states, and as the individuality of the peoples is determined by the community of ethical – at its innermost, religious – consciousness, so also is the shape **<106>** of their states.[55]

---

[55] Certainly there are general natural laws which influence formation into monarchy, aristocracy, democracy, as Schleiermacher sought to determine in his treatment of state forms, that namely an "individual horde" leads to democracy, a greater majority to aristocracy, an entire nation to monarchy. Even more extensive results are provided by Schmitthenner, Sybel, etc. But the individual life-valuation of a specific people is no less a decisive aspect for the original formation of the state and its constitution than are those general laws. The endeavors of the Schelling-Hegelian school are devoted to this aspect.

The state is never the work of choice and intent, nor does it arise through the agreement of men, who, hitherto outside the state, now come together to establish it; never does its basic form arise from their reflection. Men find themselves in it before they reflect on it, and a traditional way of viewing things, which stretches across the generations and individuals, had already given it the specific character of its institutions, which afterwards may be changed through free decision, but never can be destroyed without consequence. The will of men is certainly an essential factor in the foundation of the state, but that will does not found the state on its own, nor does it found the state directly. The state arises neither through the will of individuals, nor through the will of the people as a whole, since it does not arise through a deliberate act at all, as little as does the original law; nor does it arise through the spirit of the people. But there is an even higher factor than the human will, which is historical Providence, which brings the innumerable acts of innumerable people to one single result, one in which the state arises and does so in a specific manner.

§. 46. The Role of Contract in State Formation

In this manner the state arises factually, and in this manner it comes to be binding legally. Its regard rests on its mere existence as such. It is an original regard inherent in itself, and subjects therefore have the duty of obedience immediately, not in consequence of their prior approval, by way of an underlying contract of union and subjection. This obedience is not voluntary and dependent upon approval, but rather <107> necessary, similar to the obligation to parents, to the nation, etc. In fact, it is the original legal obligation, no less original than the legal obligation to keep contracts; for the state is itself the realization of the legal order, and the question: "upon which legal ground is the state based?" at bottom is therefore the same question as "upon which legal ground is the law based?"[56] Nor are the specific position between princes and people or the

---

[56] The right of emigration, which certainly ought to be granted subjects and is granted in most states, does not contradict this. The possibility and authorization of parting is certainly no evidence that a connection was not there prior and originally; and where no usage is made of emigration, this cannot, as an implicit approval, be the ground of the duty of subjection, for such already begins where no decision was yet possible, and even the necessity itself either to declare oneself a subject or to allow oneself to be

specific institutions of a state contractual relations, but the consequence of an activity proceeding through the institution (i.e., its appointed organs) and according to its laws, in consequence of a higher vocation. The contract [Vertrag] is often the means and form of its origin; it can lend a personal seal of good faith [Treu und Glauben] to the bond, in itself already holy, between prince and people, and more specifically determine, freely, the institutions the principles of which are recognized necessarily. But when historically they have has *arisen* [*ent*standen] in this manner (as e.g. the Magna Charta in England, German coronation charters and estate freedoms), so in their *existence* [*Be*stande] they are not to be judged as contracts, but as higher public laws and institutions. For that reason, in particular, they are neither promulgated unilaterally, as with the case of the party in North America that wished to cancel the Union because it was a contract, nor are they, when one party (prince or estates) violates it, thereby non-binding for the other. In fact, precisely the opposite. Whereas the natural law teachers treat the entire state, which ever historically arises in unintentional development, as a contractual relation, the reality is that even those parts and determinations of its constitution **<108>** which truly did arise through agreement must nevertheless be viewed as if an authority standing over the parties had established it.

§. 47. The Contract Theory of the State

The theory of the *state contract* and of *transferred power* was – leaving aside traces in medieval writers (e.g. Marsilius of Padua) – firstly, and on principle, proposed by Grotius.[57] Hobbes then developed it further; out of the state of nature,

---

viewed as such already presumes a prior state power. Emigration is furthermore nowhere unconditionally free, and rightly so. At the very least, prior obligations to the state must be fulfilled.

[57] "Deinde vero, cum juris naturae sit stare pactis ...., ab hoc ipso fonte jura civilia fluerunt. Nam qui se coetui alicui aggregaverant aut homini hominibusque subjecerant, hi aut expresse promiserant, aut ex negotii natura tacite promisisse debebant intelligi, secuturos se id quod aut coetus pars major, aut hi, quibus delata potestas est, constituissent" [Further, seeing that it lies in the natural law to keep agreements... the laws of particular nations spring from this same source. Because he who bound himself to any community or subjected himself to one or more men, had either expressly agreed to this,

people found the state through contract, and a dual contract at that: the union of the multitude, and the transfer of power to one person or a deliberative assembly.[58] To these, Pufendorf then gave the technical names *pactum unionis* and *pactum subjectionis*. Rousseau finally rejected the *pactum subjectionis* in the sense in which it was understood until then, the majority of the united multitude itself inalienably retaining power. According to his doctrine, the mere establishment of the state is a contract, namely, a mutual contracting of all with one and one with all, whereas the establishment of the government is no such mutual contract but a legislative act of the entire mass as sovereign, through which it determines, firstly, the form of government, then the persons for it, so that these receive merely an assignment, an office (commission, *emploi*), not a contractual right. Sieyès follows him in this. Kant, in turn, is undecided.[59] **<109>**

But the contract theory is absolutely untenable. Firstly, it is in contradiction with all reality and possibility, in that no one is asked, nor can be asked, for his approval. It also leads to the conclusion that the existence of the state must

---

or from the nature of the case is tacitly assumed to have promised to acquiesce in what the community, either the majority or he to whom the power had been entrusted, had decided]. Grot. *de jure belli et pac.* Proleg. §. 15. [Cf. Alvarado, *The Debate that Changed the West: Grotius versus Althusius,* p. 201.]

[58] "Itaque intercedentibus pactis, quibus singulis singuli obligantur et juris donatione, quam ratam habere obligantur imperanti, duplici obligatione civium munitur imperium, ea, quae ad concives, et ea, quae est ad imperantem" [Wherefore what by the mutual contracts each one hath made with the other, what by the donation of right which every man is bound to ratify to him that commands, the government is upheld by a double obligation from the citizens, first, that which is due to their fellow-citizens, next, that which they owe to their prince] Hobbes *de cive* VI. 20 (the translation is Hobbes's own: *De Cive or the Citizen,* ed. Sterling P. Lamprecht, 1949, p. 86). Compare also VII. 11 and the entire deduction. Pufendorf is wrongly held to be the discoverer of the doctrine of this dual contract.

[59] He speaks (*Metaphysische Anfangsgründe der Rechtslehre* [Metaphysical Elements of the Doctrine of Law], pp. 165, 170) entirely in the sense of Rousseau, that this united people ever remains lawgiver, the prince is mere *gouvernement* (executive power), and nevertheless on p. 176 dispossesses the people of lawful resistance against the prince as lawgiving head.

continually depend upon the will of the subjects, who can leave it at will, and that the state can have no other power over subjects [Unterthanen] than which they contractually can establish over themselves, thus, in particular, none over their life and freedom, in that these are their inalienable right, which would mean that the entire penal power, without which no state can exist, must cease. The chief argument in favor of the contract theory, which Sidney already had in view and which Rousseau made into the foundation of his entire political system, that no man in himself could have regard above "his equal" without that person's consent, overlooks the fact that it does not concern the regard of a person as such and in himself, but the regard of an order and institution in its ethically necessary and historical existence, found everywhere before any of us. Similarly, one might also assert that man cannot be subjected to the regard of law in general, thus also the binding force of contracts, and the regard of ethical commands, when he has not agreed to it voluntarily. On the other hand, the contract theory is based on the truth that man be in the state by consent, that he is to recognize it as the postulate of his own ethical will. But this subjective aspect is only secondary. Man, come to awareness, makes the state his own, but he does not produce it.[60]

[60] One often believes he finds the contract theory historically confirmed in the most ancient conditions of the Germanic peoples, in that the allegiances [Gefolgschaften] were voluntary, and the dukes and kings originally were elected. But the form of election is not a contractual principle. However, that every individual was subjected to the majority of the people or its districts [Gaues], that he stood under the judgment of the popular courts, participated in popular wars, that he had to obey the leaders set up by the majority, none of this rests on his consent. All of this demonstrates nothing more than that the state formation, and, in particular, the monarchy, was initially only in an embryonic state. By no means does it demonstrate the modern contract theory.

Chapter 4: The Divine Institution of the State

§. 48. The Divine Decree in the Formation of the State

<111> Although the state initially manifests itself as an ethical kingdom of the human community, it nevertheless, considered more deeply, is likewise a *divine institution.*

The *regard* of the state rests above all on the *decree* (authorization, appointment) of *God.* This is the final ground of the (as described in the previous chapter) "original regard inherent in itself" [p. 106]. Its entire legitimate order – law [Gesetz], constitution, ruling authority – derives its binding power from this. In particular, the ruling authority has regard and power from God. It is by the grace of God. "The powers that be are ordained (τεταγμένη) of God" (Romans 13:1). Of himself, no man can have authoritative power over another man, not even the collective over the individual. Nor can men ground authoritative power through contract, in that they do not dispose over their lives and their freedom, for which reason one cannot grant that power. This is the divine right of the ruling authority.[61] It has its validity in all forms of state, for the committees and magistracies in the republic no less than for the king in monarchy, whether elective or hereditary. For even when the persons who are to exercise the ruling authority are designated by election, the office and regard themselves are not based in the will and authorization of the elector, but only on God's commandment and authorization. The <112> divine institution of the state and its ruling authority merely means that its regard is based in God's *commandment and order,* not God's *immediate act* (intervening in nature); the complete freedom of men (nation) to live in this or that constitution therefore continues unrestricted. But such divine institution, in turn, does not *merely* mean that the state is God's commandment *in general,* but also that everywhere the *specific* constitution and

---

[61] The opposition of *authority* to *majority,* which I made use of in my answer to an entirely unexpected attack from Bassermann (Erfurt, April 15th, 1850; cf. my *Parlamentarische Reden,* p. 135) has since then been the catchword even for the opposing parties, a sign that it hit on the focal point of the political struggle in our time. Yet this had its final ground in nothing other than whether the ruling authority is from God or from men.

the *specific* persons of the ruling authority have God's sanction. It is here that the main assault against the divine institution of the state is directed. One retorts that God and His order only allow of the deduction that men in general are to live in states, not however that they exist in particular states, with a particular constitution, with particular princes. As all of this obviously is neither prescribed directly by God nor effectuated by Him, but ever proceeds from men, and therefore can ever only depend on the human will. For this reason, obedience to a particular constitution, to a particular king, James or William, cannot be based on God's sanction but only on the free consent of men. Thus Rousseau[62]; the Jesuits as well.[63] In response, it should firstly be considered that the particular state (France, England), the particular constitution, the particular dynasty, of course arose *by means of* the human will, yet not *through* the human will, but as the unpredictable result of many intersecting wills, which, individually considered, aimed at something entirely different, and which assume a higher effectuating cause, which, if not senseless chance, is precisely *God's Providence* [Fügung] which, in turn, is to be distinguished from an immediate act of God intervening in nature. But even allowing for the fact that the human will effects all of this, it does not yet follow that its regard also rests on and depends upon the human will. While the particular state, the particular constitution, the particular <113> dynasty is founded by the human will, it immediately separates therefrom and becomes *the state;* and as the state, precisely because the state is a divine ordinance, it puts under obligation those who established it no less than the descendants who come along afterward. Certainly, as long as nothing yet exists, man has unconditional power and right [Macht und Fug] thereby to establish this or that constitution, to make James or William king. But, as soon as this occurs, then this constitution is the state, James is the king and all of this has become the God-ordained authority over them, so that they ought not

[62] "Il n'est pas clair, que Dieu veuille qu'on préfère tel gouvernement à tel autre, ni qu'onobéisse à Jacques plutôt qu'à Guillaume. Or voilà de quoi il s'agit" [It is not clear that God wants us to prefer this government to that, or to obey James rather than William. But this is what it's all about]. Rousseau, *Lettres de la Montagne.*

[63] This is comprehensively and beyond doubt set out in my *Der Protestantismus als politisches Princip* [Protestantism as a Political Principle], pp. 24ff., and *Die katholischen Widerlegungen* [The Catholic Refutations], pp. 8–14.

change the constitution unless in accordance with their own laws, and not remove the king unless in accordance with his own will.[64] This is likewise expressed clearly in the saying, "the powers that be are ordained of God." In similar fashion marriage as well is the ordinance of God, and although here as well it is neither prescribed nor decreed from God that a young lady marry James or William, once she has married James, then her marriage bond with James is God's ordinance and commandment. The state, however, it being the work not of each individual person but only of the *community* as a whole, is made into the shape of God's order, in which it is fashioned through the *community*, either in conscious act, or in mores and custom.[65] **<114>**

§. 49. The State as Servant of God

The vocation of the state also rests on the *service of God*. It maintains God's commandment for common life – justice, discipline, mores – and it establishes God's rule. The ruling authority, in accordance with the saying of the Holy Scriptures (Romans 13), is not merely "ordained of God" but also "God's servant" (θεοῦ διάκονος, *dei minister*). Here as well, this does not mean that the orders of the ruling authority themselves are to be considered God's commandments, but that it is their office to uphold His commandments. The ruling authority is therefore from God, not merely in the general sense that all rights are from God, but in the entirely specific sense that it attends to the work of God. It exercises its right not merely *in accordance with* God's order, as with the proprietor or the father, but it exercises it *for the sake* of God's order. It is not a question merely of one's own right, one's own possession, but of a divine mission. The power over the lives and freedom of men with the purpose of establishing a

---

[64] Sidney's argumentation is based precisely on this mix-up: *Discourses of Civil Government,* ch. I, sec. 6.

[65] The question as to whether rebellion is allowable by way of exception, that is, in violation of the principle, in cases of extreme need and oppression, such as where the human organ James violates in the deepest way the divine order which he was to serve, is of an entirely different order. Here we treat only of the principle as such. Although here is not the place to deal with this question, it can be answered in the affirmative, as did for example Burke, without thereby founding the state on human will, just as by way of exception divorce can be allowed without thereby founding marriage on human will in principle, without regarding it as a contractual relationship [see §. 153 below].

higher ethical order, cannot merely be one's own right over another, as is the right of spouses over each other, of fathers over their children, but a right exercised in office from God. Only as the "servant of God" is the ruling authority "a revenger to execute wrath upon him that doeth evil." Therefore, the ruling authority is also clothed with *majesty*, for majesty is the specific attribute of God, as the absolute real and ethical power and revenger of the law. This is the ultimate ground of that generic distinction between public power (*imperium*) and all private power, whether it be societal power [Gesellschaftsgewalt] or domestic power (*potestas*) (§. 3), and the final grounds for the thoroughly public character of the state (§. 37). Only because the state exists for the service of something higher, for the service of God, must everything that is personal, private, merely human, be subordinated, while that which is institutional [das Anstaltliche], truly organic, must come to the fore – only for this reason do the ruling authority and people jointly stand under a higher necessity, to which their authorizations and activities are directed. Accordingly, the purpose of the state is **<115>** not merely the fulfillment of ethical ordinances but also a service and obedience to the *person of God*, and the establishment of a kingdom for the *honor of God*, and so should the ruling authority and the people consider it.

§. 50. God's Action In and Through the State

Finally, the *activity* of the state indeed rests, albeit in concealed manner, on the *influence of God*. Certainly, the mutual permeation of God and the human race, according to which the divine and human kingdom would be in inseparable unity, is impossible in the earthly condition of distance from God. Even so, it is the divine breath which forms and preserves the states, and the state is a tool in God's hand. God puts into men's hearts – in accordance with each age and each people – the order they establish, the purpose they pursue. Should, then, individuals and multitudes, rulers and subjects, resist it, the power of the community over individuals, the power of institutions enduring through the generations, gains the victory, and, however men inwardly stand vis-à-vis God, with regard to the general outward condition His commandment must more or less be fulfilled. God gave men the unlimited freedom to follow the ethical commandment or not, and for this reason He also confirmed the establishment of this power, to act as a restriction against the most extreme collapse of the entire human race. Similarly, when the state, as we have seen, serves that Providence in history which in artistic and providential ways brings the conditions and the culture of the human race through the peoples and epochs up through the final unfolding (I. [*Philosophical Foundations*], §. 15), so does it hereby serve the living God, who guides history, and so does it stand under His influence.

And so, after human guilt led God to withdraw His personal and immediate activity from temporal existence, nevertheless, in miraculous manner, did He establish this institution over men, form it out of men, albeit clothed with His regard, and open to His influence, in order that in His name it would rule over the entire outward condition. Accordingly, the state is the institution of God <116> for the sake of this condition. In God's stead, it is to order and promote it, punish violations of order, yet thereby also preserve the ethical-rational will of human community; its obedience is to establish God's order, and its own insight into the wisdom of that order. To that end, the state is furnished with the majesty of God and His omnipotence on earth. It is, albeit in the most obscured fashion, ever a *divine-human kingdom.*

§. 51. The Divine-Human Character of the State

If, then, the regard of the state in its deepest ground rests on the divine authorization, it comes to the state in *entirely independent* manner, by virtue of the independence granted by God to all His creations and institutions and the withdrawal of all immediate and visible activity of His from temporality. This regard is initially and immediately inherent in the state, and remains in the state unconditionally, even when the state uses it against the purpose for which it was imparted (I. [*Philosophical Foundations*], §§. 35 and 45). Now then, by virtue of its origin, the state has a boundary where the *immediate* commandment of God speaks; the ruling authority is not to be obeyed when it commands the violation of apodictic religious or ethical rules. True, the *legal* ground of the state is by no means to be sought in the divine authorization, for that it has in itself, it being the realized legal order. It is *its* law, not the law of God, which legally binds subjects. But the deeper *ethical* ground for the state, as well as for the law itself, lies in the divine authorization. This is also why a command of the state which conflicts with God's commandment, albeit ethically non-binding and ethically exhortative of non-obedience for all who recognize God's commandment, is by no means unlawful, for the state itself is the source of all lawfulness. Therefore, a people entirely divested of religion still ever retains a recognition of the state as a higher authority grounded in itself, and, conversely, a people who have preserved the faith should not lose sight of this independence of the state authority.

At first sight, then, the struggle regarding the divine right of the ruling authority appears to be more a religious and philosophical one <117> than a legal-political one. For law and politics in and of themselves merely have to do with the principle as to whether the state or [bez.] the king have their regard from themselves and not through the subjects; as to whether, on the contrary, this regard grounded in itself stems from God or from the world substance or from a mechanical necessity is, legally and politically, initially not in question. On the one hand, the task of the state seems entirely different when completely separated from the person of God, but on the other hand the regard of the state cannot factually be preserved where faith in the divine sanction has vanished, for in that case everyone has the urge to assert his will, and the people to assert its, i.e., the multitude's, will, as the source and guideline of state power. For this reason, the divine right of the ruling authority is nevertheless not merely in the religious interest, that the human life-order be directed toward God, but also in the political interest, that the state and its constitution retain this deeper confirmation and guarantee.

The human regard of the state ought never (theocratically) be *commingled* with the divine regard, but it must necessarily (religiously) be *grounded* in the divine regard.

In all of this, the regard of the state by no means is grounded on the fact of revelation but on God's order and authorization, of which our conscience already testifies, and which revelation only makes more certainly and completely known, and expressly corroborates; and because the commandments and ordinances of God are nowhere dependent upon human knowledge thereof, nor on the means to this knowledge, so is the regard of the state and the ruling authority valid where the Christian revelation is unknown, or where unbelief has liberated itself from it.

§. 52. The Various Presumed Grounds of State Authority

The Greeks, in impartial observation, understood the state to be a given ethical authority. This, while not a denial, nevertheless was a lack of recognition of the deeper ground of that authority, as an essential aspect in the meaning of the state. The Middle Ages exaggerated the God-ordainedness of the ruling authority into a <118> theocratic conception. The Reformation recognized the divine institution of the ruling authority in its purity.[66] The newer legal philosophy (from Grotius to Kant and Rousseau) deprives the state of independent authority, grounding it merely in the consent of its members, from which a state and an authority cannot arise. Speculative legal philosophy (Schelling and Hegel) restores the independent authority of the state to awareness, but does not receive it, like the Greeks did, as a given, instead basing it upon the state itself being made into God – namely, into one stage, and precisely one of the highest, in God's development. [67] That is also, presupposing the entire pantheistic worldview, consistent and concurring; but precisely the untenability of this entire worldview is demonstrated in this work. [68]

---

[66] Augsburg Confession, art. 16. Gerh. *Loci* (loc. 25 p. 1. ch. 3. Sect. 1); my *Der Protestantismus als politisches Princip* [Protestantism as a Political Principle].

[67] "It is not a construction of the state as such but the absolute organism in the form of the state, the immediate and visible picture of absolute life." Schelling, *Academischen Studium*, p. 235. In the same way Hegel, *Grundlinien der Philosophie des Rechts* [Baselines of the Philosophy of Law], §. 257. "The state is the ethical spirit as the substantial will intelligible to itself," i.e., God. Hence "the state is the spirit, which stands in the world" – "the state is the *course of God* [der Gang Gottes]" – "one must instead consider the idea of the state, *this actual God,* in itself" §. 258 summary. "The state is the divine will, as present spirit developing into the actual form and organization of a world" – "God is the general idea, and in this (the religious) feeling of the indeterminate, which has not ripened to determine what it is in the state as developed." Note to §. 270. From here comes Hegel's polemic against those who derive the divine authority of the state or [bez.] the prince from a God outside and over the state, instead of understanding the actual God to be in the state itself. §. 279, remark at end.

[68] The vulgar conception, in particular even in the textbooks of positive state law, still to this day – after the rationalistic philosophy has run its course – runs most decisively against the grounding of the state on the ordination and authorization of God. One no longer ventures to counter with the grounding from contract, which is rejected as revolutionary, or the grounding from emanation of the world spirit (the impersonal God) in decisive denial of God. One counters by grounding, simply and apart from any discussion of why and how, *from reason* ("postulate of reason," "rational cognition," "rationality of the state"). That is a Proteus; for reason is taken in such diverse meanings

that one has difficulty holding onto any of them. Philosophers understand by reason the pure law of thought from which, as they demand, the moral law must be derived. The non-philosophical writer, on the other hand, understands by reason anything but the pure law of thought, instead simply the (innate in us) moral law, to which, however, the consideration of suitability is added, usually in a certain chiaroscuro, namely that our reason (understanding?) says to us, we can lead a secure, satisfying existence answering to our purpose only in the state, and we for that reason recognize ourselves morally and legally bound to be members of the state and to obey it. With all the vagueness of the concept of reason, the core is everywhere the same: a purely human principle independent of God, a law inherent in man and arising from human nature (thus only immanent, not transcendent), that in the same way exists and binds even when there is no God, which is why, with this as a basis, one believes he can assume a neutral position with regard to belief in God or the denial of Him. Such is done in the interest of releasing the human order from God, to found the ruling authority on mere human consciousness and mere human relations, to consider the improvement (rationality) of human conditions to be the only vocation of the state, rather than obedience to God. For this reason, one takes up a position against the "religious foundation" and everything that could be "only the affair of faith, not of rational cognition," of course without examining what of the state remains when everything which is an affair of faith is stricken from it. To be consistent, one would also have to change the title "king by the grace of God" to "king by virtue of reason" (or "the rational conviction of the citizen of the state") and the oath which holds the state together (oaths of fealty, constitution, office) to be sworn by reason rather than by God. In this it makes no essential difference whether one combats the "religious foundation" plainly and simply or whether one eclectically pays it the tribute of a certain recognition as "a very worthy view regarding the relation of state power to subjects" and as a "proof" of the necessity of a "rational justification of the state over the mere fact," thereby however finding the actual ground of the state and ruling authority not in the ordination of God but in "rationality," "necessity of reason" (Zöpfl, similarly already Maurenbrecher).

Such emancipation of the human life-order from God, and such neutrality toward faith in God is from the religious standpoint inadmissible, but this grounding in reason is likewise untenable from the standpoint of science. The state itself, its authority and power over people, cannot be derived from human reason; only an order (a "postulate") for men to establish or [bez.] obey the state can. Accordingly, it ever first required that men themselves (each and every one) be convinced by the order and freely agree to its fulfillment. The grounding of the state on reason therefore is impossible apart from the *mediation of contract.* In this way all careful thinkers (Kant, Rousseau) have viewed the matter: reason postulates the state, but that a particular state could bind and coerce particular people first required their free act, the contract, through which they might fulfill that postulate. Apart from it, the compulsion which the state exercises over men, even when they did not wish to agree to it, remains unjustified, a mere factual power, a historical condition. Moreover, the derivation of the state from human reason does not provide the explanation for those of its powers and its ethical impressions which overtop the reach of relations among men, such as decisions over life and death, the majesty of the ruling authority, nor does it provide the explanation for its factual power, which it nevertheless preserves over men despite their unreasonableness.

It is entirely unthinkable that a commandment or the binding regard of an institution be grounded on our reason. Our reason can provide testimony of a commandment and of the binding regard of an institution, but cannot itself be the ground of this commandment or regard; it cannot itself be what is binding. Only a power over ourselves which is likewise the ethical and real primeval power can lay a commandment on us, can confer to an institution majesty over us (I. [*Philosophical Foundations*], §. 34). One therefore must either deny God and ground the state on an impersonal world power – matter, substance, reason in the sense of the power binding the universe (and from this, too, there can only come a compulsion, not an ethical order); or else, when one believes in the living personal God, so must one recognize the ethical law to be His commandment, and ground the regard of the state on His sanction. Whatever lies in between is a groundless third. Therefore, when it is said: "the legal doctrine of the state can as little be grounded on the religious commandment *be subject to the ruling authority* as a doctrine of penal law can be grounded on the commandment to avoid *sin,*" actually exactly the opposite holds. A legal doctrine of the state in the final analysis can be grounded in nothing else than on the commandment: "be subject to the ruling authority" and a (philosophical) theory of penal law can be grounded nowhere else than on the commandment: "avoid sin." Apart from the former commandment, no subject would be bound to obedience to state power, while apart from the latter, no criminal would be punishable.

It is, furthermore, no way out when "upon *common conviction* of the members of the community, resting on rational cognition" one makes "mutable legal conviction" the foundation "of both law in general" and the government (Zachariä), and likewise adds or substitutes either the principle of rationalistic philosophy, reason, the principle of the Historical School, or the popular consciousness ("according to Puchta"). This is insufficient both for law in general (II. [*Principles of Law*], §. 20) and for the ruling authority in particular. For the question is, what is the ground of this "common conviction" regarding the ruling authority, property, law of succession, etc., and what is the proper legal conviction, whether, e.g., the "mutable legal conviction" of the French people, that it be allowed to pass judgment over the king, was the proper one. *Contract* or *reason* are a false foundation for the ruling authority; *popular consciousness* is no foundation at all.

Chapter 5: State Power

§. 53. Law and State Power

<121> As an ethical-intellectual kingdom, the state is a real and free controlling power, yet one which is founded upon an ethically reasonable order. Its dominion [Herrschaft], therefore, has a dual element: the *ruling authority* or *state power* [Staatsgewalt] (*imperium*), i.e., the power exercised by men, and the *law* [Gesetz] (*lex*). The former is the power of a personal will (be it a natural personality, a prince, or an artificial personality, a constituted assembly); the latter is an enduring conviction [Gesinnung] which must undergird the truly personal will (I. [*Philosophical Foundations*], §. 7), "the ethos" of the state (Niebuhr), as emanating from the national life-valuation (§. 3). Given the nature of the state as an external institution, this life-valuation can only be made known for the state in external demarcated rules. Through both of these united, therefore, the dominion of the state has *the full character of personal dominion.*[69] Law and state power, then, relate to each other the way in which, in individual persons (I., §§. 39–41), character relates to will (power of decision). The law is the ground and presupposition of state power, through which state power is state power (laws of form of government, succession to the throne), and it is partly restriction, partly the positive determinant of the exercise thereof; the latter must not overstep it and must execute it. On the other hand, state power is the ground and presupposition of the law. The law is valid because of the regard enjoyed by state power; that power <122> can also change the law and further develop it, and, within the law, state power rules freely in a broad sphere. As is the case with personality (I., §. 4) and with things organic, there is mutual presupposition and interaction between law and state power without either compromising its own independent sphere. By contrast, when state power is viewed as the primary thing plain and simple, state absolutism is the necessary result even if exercised by the sovereign people (*volonté générale*) (Hobbes, Rousseau; see above, §. 41).

---

[69] Ruling authority and state power mean the same thing, the former more the personal and ethical, the latter more the institutional and mechanical side. In terms of the task of this chapter, therefore, the latter is the more appropriate.

The law becomes the product of state power rather than being accepted as an equally original extant power.

§. 54. The Powers of the State

In terms of its essence, state power is indivisibly one, the way each personality is one, each will is one. It cannot be divided into several powers and among several subjects, but it must be one subject, one personality (prince, or organized assembly, or both together as one subject). In this unity is *sovereignty* [Souveränetät] (state supremacy [Staatshoheit], plenitude of power [Machtvollkommenheit]). But in terms of exercise, various conditions underlie state power, and there are various organs under the sovereign which are more or less independent with regard to it. This diversity rests on the diverse relation of its tasks, either to the law as the other power in the state, or to the rights of individuals. To wit, state power changes or enacts the law – *legislation;* or it rules in accordance with the law or within the law – *government* [Regierung]; or it intervenes in the legal sphere of individuals to restore the violated law – *administration of justice* [Gericht]. The *division of state power* is based on this. Even so, these are ever only tasks of one and the same state power, located in the sovereign; it is inappropriate to treat them as powers in their own right.

The basis of for a division of state power can only be this inner content of its activity. By contrast, a division according to its diverse organs (by which one must distinguish a power of the king, *pouvoir royal,* of the minister, of the estates, the municipalities, the courts of law, the military) or according to the external form of its activity (where one must distinguish between a regulating, resolving, deliberative, <123> restricting, subsuming, implementing, supervising, distributing, electing power) is generally not feasible, since all of this is only connected to the specific institutions, and would be idle and pointless.

§. 55. Sovereignty

So *sovereignty* is the first, original, and supreme power, which conditions and *encompasses* all organs and tasks, either positively determining them, or at least negatively restricting them.[70] It is the will of the ruler, present and active across

[70] Sovereignty therefore is not merely the supreme power, the higher power over others (that would also be, e.g., the supreme court over lesser courts, the German Confeder-

the entire range of the state, the innermost personality of the state. The sovereign therefore *represents* the state inwardly and outwardly. He alone *prompts* all tasks of state power, and so appoints the organs, at least the supreme ones, to that end; he alone imparts validity and authority to them; he *exercises the supreme supervision over them.* No less does he determine their *content,* to the degree that special restrictions are not set on it.[71] A sovereignty which existed in the empty power of formal initiation and authorization (e.g., Sieyès' Great Elector of the Empire) is an absurdity, in the **<124>** same way as is a will which cannot decide anything. The restrictions may consist in his being bound by consent, in his having to make use of certain organs (civil servants) for implementation, even leaving the application of individual cases to them without interference (judges). He himself cannot be coerced into anything, nor can a power exist alongside the sovereign *which could effectuate anything positive for the entirety of the state.*[72]

---

ation over the confederated states), but also the original power, conditioning and determining the others. So, e.g., in accordance with the Sardinian Synod and its confirmation by Valentinian, the Pope had the supreme power (*primatus jurisdictionis*) in the church, in that appeal might be made to him from provincial councils, but still not sovereignty. For the bishops and provincial councils did not yet rest on his authority and appointment, etc. This he received much later.

[71] In the monarchy this is exercised by the monarch in person; in the republic, to the degree that this is possible, by the popular assembly. That here much which belongs to sovereignty cannot be exercised by the popular assembly itself (e.g., initiative, overall control, above all the government itself), is precisely a shortcoming of the republican constitution. Here the sovereignty, which according to its nature ought to be indivisible, nevertheless is divided in certain degree between the popular assembly and the magistracy.

[72] The estates merely restrict the sovereignty (negatively) but cannot (positively) accomplish anything against the will of the king (e.g., in England the unconditional royal veto), and the judges have no power over the entirety of the state. Thus, in Athens as well, the courts could nullify the decision of the sovereign popular assembly but could not force another one upon it.

§. 56. Legislation

Legislation is the *establishment* [Feststellung] of *legal principles* [Rechtsgrundsätze] (norms for the legal condition, actual laws). It is by no means the first expression of state power either in terms of time or of concept, which the other expressions must presuppose. The laws [Gesetze] must certainly precede those other expressions; but the laws already existed, through custom and tradition, as a given law [Recht], apart from, and long before, legislation. By contrast, legislation presupposes the legal condition and the other tasks of state power in full exercise, and only comes on the scene when the right basis for these has been established. Nevertheless, in terms of power and effect it is the first: it determines these without itself being determined by them; it is the highest expression of state power.[73] For this reason, it can only be exercised by the sovereign. In the republic, the people's assembly (not the magistracy) is the direct legislator, while in the monarchy, only the prince in person (not civil servants) is the legislator.

The laws (legal principles) as the ethos of the state have (materially) their origin and seat in the national consciousness, as they (formally) have their validity through the sovereign (compare II. [*Principles of Law*], §. 23). They are the common basis both of ethical, spiritual com- **<125>** munity and of the ruling authority. For this reason, legislation is not merely an affair of the sovereign but also of the people. In a democracy, both coincide. On these grounds, in the developed monarchy the consent of the territorial assembly is required for law, and even in the absolute monarchy, at least consideration of the popular conviction is required. The prince as sovereign of course always remains the subject of the legislative power, but, even so, he is to assay the laws against the public consciousness.

In general, however, stricter conditions for its exercise often underlie legislation precisely because of its importance, both to attain the maturity of decisions and to secure the regard of the received laws and the interests of the existing legal condition. To this first and foremost pertains the consent of the estates themselves; then, in several states, the prior examination by the council of state; in Athens, the defense of existing laws before the Nomothetes.

---

[73] Which is why Kant confused it with sovereignty itself.

§. 57. Government and the Distinction Between Laws and Decrees

The government [Regierung] *is the actual, immediate, and concrete provision* [Versorgung] *of conditions* [Zustände]. Therefore, the execution of state power must be continually and uninterruptedly active; in this consists the normal activity of state power; the other elements only arise because of a special cause, the courts through committed injustice, legislation through lack of agreement between the laws and life. As the immediate provision of conditions, it requires many organs, and a hierarchy of them, from the center of sovereign power outward – the *civil service* [Beamtenhierarchie], and it promotes, in every single case, concrete appreciation and concentrated vigor; it is, thus, an affair of personality and not of public consciousness. The prince, and, in the republic, the supreme magistracy, thus exercises it according to his own judgment, apart from popular consent, and does well to allow the civil servants at all levels a suitable space of independence.

In terms of its concept, government is limited by the law, and the organs of its exercise are therefore rightly under obligation to the law; but the manner and measure of this obligation depends upon **<126>** the relationship of subordination.

Provision by the state comprises: firstly, the implementation of existing laws (administration of the constitution as well as other laws, excepting the administration of justice) – *execution;* secondly, pursuit of purposes not prescribed by the law (e.g., enactment of a school curriculum, a mail- or passport-ordinance) – *government in the strict sense*. The former is positively determined by the law, while the latter is only negatively restricted thereby. Omission grounds a legal complaint in the case of the former, but not of the latter. For both, the government consists both in forming decisions and in executing them, both in taking temporary and particular measures and in giving enduring and general orders. It therefore expresses itself in *measures* [Vornahmen], in *decisions,* in *decrees* [Verordnungen].

This yields the distinction between law [Gesetz] (laws, statutes, *lois*) and decrees (proclamation, *ordonnance*), which is so momentous for the doctrine of state and state law. This distinction is grounded in the essence of the state, and therefore is found among all forms of government, although it first came to full clarity and great significance in the developed monarchy. Decrees, namely, being mere acts of government power and therefore not requiring the consent of the estates, are certainly general rules, just as are laws; yet they are fundamentally distinguished from laws, for laws comprise *legal principles*, while decrees only comprise a leading of common activity to realize *purposes*. Therefore, that which in itself counts as necessary belongs in the sphere of law, either as an integrating part of the public legal condition or as the guaranteed right of persons; but that which belongs in the sphere of decrees is that which exists as mere means toward ends, and, therefore, in itself has the trait of being treated differently in accordance with changes in circumstances. Regulations in the sphere of the constitution and the administration of justice therefore will largely be laws, while regulations in the sphere of public welfare, finances, the military, will largely be decrees.[74] **<127>**

Accordingly, laws are usually lasting, decrees more mutable. For duration corresponds to the inner necessity, to the character of law, while movement corresponds to that ongoing pursuit of the better, the more beneficial, which is the character of government. Nevertheless, decrees are by no means restricted to having to serve the execution of laws, which is the common doctrine. For that is only one side of the government; on the contrary, the essence of actual government is to bring about, independent of laws, something new, something positive, in free, creative activity, to promote conditions in accordance with purposes. The attainments of government (excluding execution in the strict sense) are not means for the law, but for purposes apart from the law. The first impartial look at the content of most decrees, such as are given for the promotion of agriculture, industry, trade, for the improvement of education, security, health, water and fire hazard, for amenities and beautification, etc., should convince one that they by no means are promulgated to serve the fulfillment of preceding laws, but are directed toward a purpose and a result in real life, and toward means called for by circumstances; and that the government's peculiar task consists precisely in these purposes, and its peculiar activity in this free choice.

§. 58. Administration of Justice

The administration of justice (judicial power) is the *restoration of violated law to the individual,* through intervention in his *legal sphere,* either to uphold the

---

[74] This is the motivation behind the separation; more detailed determination is, of course, the business here as everywhere else of positive law (tradition, state practice, analogy). Regarding German constitutional state law, compare below, ch. 12.

rights of others, or for the regard of the law itself. This peculiar activity has its root simply in the essence of justice; it therefore is led, on the one hand, by the demand for the steadfast validity of the law, and on the other by the inviolable independent right of the person, which it is to fulfill, apart from any consideration of the public weal. Given that the essence of that independent right necessarily entails the power of *self-vindication,* state power as the administration of justice cannot just proceed in accordance with *its* consider- **<128>** ation of individual entitlement, but must allow the *self*-defense of the one against whom proceedings are to be taken.[75] This is *procedure,* which is found only in the administration of justice and in no other activity of state power.

Accordingly, the administration of justice consists in a balance between the law and self-vindicating personal entitlement, i.e., verdict and enforcement [Vollstreckung]; these together form the concept of the administration of justice.[76] The administration of justice is not a connecting link between law (or legislation) and execution [Vollziehung], but an independent, specific task alongside execution. The latter is geared to the *public* (state and common welfare); the administration of justice is geared to the fulfillment of the law toward the *individual,* in accordance with justice. In terms of its nature, the administration of justice is ever only directed against a specific individual person (physical or moral), and for a past case, namely, ever in order to restore a violation of law. Executions and orders for *the whole*, the establishment and interpretation of a legal rule for *future application,* do not pertain to its purview. It is, furthermore, ever directed against the person in the sphere of his independent entitlement, his bodily freedom or his assets, to the degree that these are guaranteed as inviolable with regard to public considerations. The restoration of the law against the disobedient or the violator where such entitlement is not recognized does

---

[75] Whether the procedure of the court is initiated by the state or by request of another party (criminal or civil justice) is one and the same here.

[76] It is possible to think of subsumption [see the following footnote for an explanation] under the law separately from the reality of the proceedings (compelling the individual to self-defense, indication of venue) and enforcement (as in Rome, roughly, the *praetor* existed for the former and the *judex* for the latter); nevertheless, only both together form the complete concept of the administration of justice. It is therefore subsumption, albeit real rather than logical.

not pertain to judicial activity, thus also not to the subsumption[77] of the individual case under the law, either for restoration or other legal execution. Hence, the administration of justice has its place in the sphere of the judiciary. **<129>**

The administration of justice, dealing as it does with justice, can only be determined by the immutable rule of the law, not free personal rule, and requires, in that it is directed to personal entitlement, an impartial power between the latter and state power. Therefore, it must be exercised in independence of the sovereign, by organs bound merely by the proper application of the law. This is not contrary to the unity of state power, since the administration of justice is ever restricted to the individual case and the individual person,[78] and is a subordinate task, namely dependent upon, and determined by, legislation.

§. 59. Separation of Powers

The first and already entirely comprehensive investigation of the division [Eintheilung] of state power with an eye to assessing the constitution in those terms is found in Aristotle.[79] In terms of the view of Greek constitutions, Aristotle divides state power into the deliberative (assembly of the people or the aristocracy), the executive (magistracy), and the judicial. He assigns the power of ruling on capital crime to the first and considers the executive power to be entirely subordinate to the deliberative.

The investigation retained its great practical importance on into more recent times, since Locke, and, following him, Montesquieu, proclaimed the doctrine of the necessary separation of the legislative and the executive power as the foundation of political freedom, thus subordinating monarchy as well to that theory, abstracted from Aristotle's republic. Accordingly, the division into *legislative,*

---

[77] [Subsumption is the application of the syllogism in legal science. In *The Rise and Fall of Natural Law* (p. 186), Stahl describes it like this: "It is based on there being, apart from the rational rule, which is the major premise, also matter separate from it, as the minor premise. Scientific activity brings both together and draws a conclusion."]

[78] If the courts are empowered to interpret the constitution for the future, this would certainly be a violation of sovereignty and against the nature of the judicial power. In the same way the English Parliament in ancient times rightly complained that the kings had constitutional principles established through the judge.

[79] *Politics,* IV, 14ff.

judicial, and executive power took shape as textbook theory. This division is in many respects erroneous. <130>

Already the concept itself is not delineated sharply enough, in that it is founded on the external form of activity – norm, subsumption, and execution – rather than on its content; for the innermost concept of the legislative power is not that it issues norms, but that it determines the legal condition, while that of the administration of justice is not that it subsumes but that it decides legal controversies.[80] Otherwise one would have to reckon, e.g., a command not to smoke tobacco in public places, in the same way to the legislative power as the penal laws regarding murder; one would have to reckon the allotment of taxes, the location for the examination of candidates for the civil service or the evaluation of police officers, the question as to whether, in accordance with general decrees, a pass may be issued in a specific instance, just as much to the judicial power as a criminal case or the location of a bankruptcy case; one would have to consider the enforcement of a judicial sentence to be an expression of the executive power in the state and, to be consistent, attribute it not to the courts but to the sovereign and the ministries.

With this tripartite division, one is consciously or unconsciously led by the parallel of logical conclusions (major premise, minor premise, conclusion).[81] But then one would, as in the case of those conclusions with the three clauses, so also with every public act have to arrange the three powers in this super- and subordination, i.e., everywhere the law coming to execution through the medium of the courts, while in fact they, excepting the judiciary, everywhere run only parallel to each other: all laws (e.g., the constitutional laws) are applied

---

[80] The English division into legislative and executive power is based on the simple and undeniable distinction between the ideal power of the rule [Regel] and the real power of the actual implementation. But this is none other than the above-mentioned distinction between law and state power; when applied to the internal workings of state power, it is not exhaustive and precisely delineated, for the reasons there given. Beyond the legislative and executive power, Locke assumes yet a federative power, i.e., the power of war, peace, and treaties, which he nevertheless declares to be of the same kind as the executive.

[81] Consciously and expressly by Kant, *Metaphysische Anfangsgründe der Rechtslehre* [Metaphysical Elements of the Doctrine of Law], p. 165 (§. 45).

apart from the administration of justice, and <131> most execution (administration) takes place without a law. The division of state power cannot possibly be discovered from logic (the nature of thought), but only from the state and its specific nature, that it reigns as a kingdom according to rules and through personality, and has independent persons under it.[82]

This doctrine furthermore overlooks the actual free power of government and assimilates it to the executive power, i.e., the mere enforcement of given laws. In the current praxis of constitutional states, this has the disadvantageous consequence that every standing order not issued in consequence of a preceding law, thus not mere execution, as for example a school ordinance, is viewed as a law and thus requires the consent of the estates. In this way the state presents itself as a great lawmaking machine, and each part of the entire mechanism meshes with each other only in order to make laws and apply those that are made. Decrees are either for the laws or against them, but by no means independent within the bounds of the laws. This view is expressed clearly even in German constitutional documents, when the right of "decrees conducive to the enforcement and maintenance of the laws" is conferred upon the king.[83]

Finally, it eliminates the unity of state power, in that it leaves the concept of sovereignty entirely outside of its sphere and directly assigns the legislative and executive power to different subjects, the popular representation and the king. Rather than being the sovereign, the latter is then the holder, more appropriately the organ, of <132> executive power. This is the core of the so-called *constitutional theory,* which is something entirely different from the true constitutional

---

[82] The same objection therefore also hits home with Hegel's division, taken from his logic, into legislative, executive, and princely power, as universality, particularization, and the unity of both. This theory does have the great advantage over the older one that it restores the unity of sovereignty, but in return it loses sight of the so essential distinction between judicial and executive or administrative power.

[83] e.g., Württemberg Constitutional Charter, II, §. 89; Hessian, §. 95. Even in the constitution of 1814, the king was not attributed the governing power, as would be just, but the executive power as his exclusive right. The Proceduralists [Prozessualisten], on the other hand, ever have properly opposed the affairs of the judiciary to the affairs of government. The more recent exponents of the doctrine of state have now rightly replaced the concept of executive power with governing power.

constitution [konstitutionelle Verfassung]. Montesquieu, who brought it to predominance on the continent, yet had enough practical insight to preserve for the prince, in accordance with the pattern of the English constitution, a negative share in legislation. But in his doctrine this only appears as an external bonus, in that the concept of the prince has nothing to do with legislation, and in fact as executive power forms the exact opposite to it. The consequence of this doctrine therefore developed further into the complete exclusion of the prince from legislation. So has it been set up as an ideal by later exponents of the doctrine of state (e.g., Behr's dyarchy), and attempted in reality in the French Revolution (intentionally in 1795, in fact already in 1791) and the Spanish Cortes (1812).

Nevertheless, this separation is not possible because the executive power, when entirely divested of the legislative, ceases to be a power and becomes the mere tool of the latter. The consistent implementation of the doctrine of separation therefore frustrates the original intention to secure the position of the citizen between two opposing independent powers. What it achieves is entirely the same as what Rousseau, the declared opponent of the doctrine of division, wanted. For he no less demands the division, in that the subject of execution (*Gouvernement*) is to be separate from that of legislation (*Souverain*), only he does not wish the former to be a power. The factual result, finally, is then the simple conversion of monarchy into democracy – and this is implicitly given from the start, with popular delegates considered to be the legislative power. Later French politicians (Clermont Tonnerre, Benjamin Constant) attempted to mitigate the evil by adding a *pouvoir royal,* a power of final decision (yea or nay), but that again is only one power among others, not the unity of the collective state power. Contrary to this, Hobbes expressed this unity of state power or the concept of sovereignty in complete certainty and clarity, albeit with the erroneous intermixture of absolute power. Rousseau (while combating the doctrine of the division of powers that had since emerged) followed him in this. But Rousseau, in insight in this area far short of Hobbes, does not attribute sovereignty, as Hobbes does, **<133>** to the ordered state ("rex" or "concilium") but to the unconstituted multitude, at most the majority. According to his idea, the Revolution expresses the unity and indivisibility of sovereignty, which falls to the people. That is then an indeterminate concept; on that basis one can make the national representation into undivided power just as well as attempt a division according to Sieyès, but always with the disadvantage that, with all constitutions, the revolutionary masses stand above the constitutional authority, as something over it.

Nevertheless, Locke and Montesquieu did attain the great truth, which redounds to their immortal fame, that the participation of diverse elements (the people, the civil servants, the judges) in the exercise of state power, each according to the three tasks, truly is the foundation of civil or political freedom, and conversely, where only one and the same subject (prince or popular assembly) provides for all functions alone, despotism is the unavoidable result. So it is in oriental states, where the prince issues laws, rules, and judges, everything in person if he likes, and things are no better when this is assumed by, e.g., a democratic popular assembly. However, they falsely make what is merely the participation and cooperation of various subjects in the exercise of state power under the sovereign (or at any rate the collective possession of sovereignty) into a division of state power itself among various subjects [Subjekte], of which the prince is only one, in fact in some degree subordinate to the others. The former is the organic development and articulation of state power from original and ongoing unity, the latter is mechanical assemblage. Yet more than this: freedom is guaranteed in the truest manner not merely when *other subjects* participate in the above-mentioned tasks of state power, but when these also are truly *diverse elements.* Should all comprise one *similar* element, freedom is not as well secured. Even in the case of the popular element, which (as e.g. in North America) forms the legislative assembly, the senate, the jury, and public opinion, then the individual or the minority is delivered over to oppression (Tocqueville). Herein lies the incomparable worth of the real constitutional constitution [konstitutioneller Verfassung], that various elements – kingship, landed aristocracy, independent judges, indispensable civil servants, people, and public opinion – partici- **<134>** pate in power and share influence. Precisely because of this, however, the so-called constitutional theory misses the mark because it accepts neither true kingship nor true landed aristocracy but instead turns the king into an individual entrusted with executive power and the peers into a mere counterweight in the legislative assembly; all participants in public power thereby again become one homogeneous element.

Chapter 6: State Constitution and State Administration

§. 60. Constitution and Administration; Elements of the Constitution

As a kingdom, as an institution for the rule of people, the state has two sides – constitution and administration. The structure of the human community, through which the state as institution exists – thus the coherence of institutions, the distribution of provisions, the formation of organs for rule – is the *constitution;* the rule which it exercise in terms of this arrangement over human conditions is *administration.* The former therefore is a condition, the latter an activity and a sphere of tasks. In the former, people appear as complementary parts of the state, it being formed from them; in the latter, as subjects facing it.

Accordingly, the content of the constitution is the formation of diverse communities in terms of the joint connections of public life into legally ordered institutions of rule over men, and the formation of these communities themselves, in turn, into one comprehensive rule of the state. It orders:

1. rule of the general (national) community of the state as such – (determinations regarding form of government, territory of the state, establishment of an army, basic establishment of courts of law and civil service);

2. the relation of individuals to the state (determinations regarding residence, right of citizenship, right of emigration, guarantees of personal freedom and entitlement, for instance freedom of conscience, habeas corpus acts, etc.);

3. spatial and vocational communities (determinations regard- **<136>** ing the formation of municipalities and corporations, and their place in the state, regarding the nobility, civil and agricultural estates);

4. the religious community in its relation to the state (determinations regarding state religion, tolerance, recognition in the constitution of public churches, law of protection and supervision over the church).

The constitution of the state, accordingly, has various distinct elements, namely, an actual political element, an element of personal freedom and entitlement, an estate-corporative, and a religious-ecclesiastical element. They still condition and permeate each other mutually, e.g., the political element (popular representation, local administration) is conditioned by the estate-corporative element, etc.

§. 61. Elements of Administration

The content of administration is the realization of ethical ideas and rational purposes in, and by means of, the activity of subordinate people. Its purposes and thus its sphere are:

1. the *physical power of the state,* which protects its order against resistance and attack from outside or inside – the *military;*

2. the *pecuniary means of the state,* to maintain it in its condition and its activity – *finances;*

3. the *common weal,* that is, the promotion of conditions and pursuits of individual persons (not merely of the public establishment), to the degree that they are common – *administration of public welfare* [Polizey].

4. justice [Gerechtigkeit], the restoration of violated rights of individuals or the violated regard of the legal order itself against the criminal – *the judiciary* [die Justiz].[84]**<137>**

These spheres are determined and ruled by the ideas of power, of wisdom, of justice; their proper provision is the disclosure of these ideas in human common life. Therefore, the meaning (τέλος) of administration is both for the specific result to be attained in all its spheres, and for these ideas and the fulfillment of human community to be displayed through it. The meaning of the military is not merely that the enemy or rebel be kept from overthrowing order, but also actually that the nation proves itself in its power, as a hero. The meaning of public welfare is not merely that agriculture, industry be promoted, public health [Sanität] be safeguarded, storm damage be prevented, etc., but also that the idea of wisdom be realized, and that in this provision the community shows itself as an intelligence. It is the meaning of the judiciary not merely that justice be done for the individual person, but that the human community be an ethical power ruling in terms of the idea of justice. The state is not merely to seek purposes outside of itself, it is itself to be a kingdom of power, wisdom, justice. This is the true objective recognition of its essence. Power, wisdom, justice, are however the

---

[84] Yet another peculiar sphere of activity for the state is grounded in its relation to other states. This however no longer belongs to administration per se, as we have delineated its concept, in that it is not and does not have as its purpose the direction of subjects and their conditions. It does not even arise from the purpose of the state, but from that of the community of states.

eternal idea of the *ethical* kingdom, i.e., the kingdom through which the human community is a completed whole in itself, thus the state; while faith, hope, love are the ideas of the *religious* kingdom, i.e., the kingdom through which the human community is to be related to God, to be united with Him personally (I. [*Philosophical Foundations*], §. 25).

§. 62. Relation of Constitution and Administration; Scope of the Constitution

Incidentally, constitution and administration are only two sides and relations in the existence of the state, not two totally separated spheres; in most relations, the one blends with the other without any determinate boundary, and the one permeates the other. So, for example, the establishment of an army (whether mercenary, vassal, **<138>** conscript, or general citizen participation) is a part of the constitution, while the organization of the army (battalion, weaponry, war-making, rations) is an affair of military administration.[85] The duty to pay taxes on the part of subjects is part of the constitution, while the order for specific taxes and their distribution is an affair of financial administration. Regulations for trade belong on the one hand to the constitution, to the degree that the organization of the trade and industry estate [Gewerbstand] is based thereon, and on the other hand are expressions of the administration of public welfare. The arrangement of offices pertains to an administrative relation, because in this consists the provision for the specific branches of administration, and indeed the organism becomes most apparent by considering these branches of administration, since they exist for its needs; yet on the other hand, these branches necessarily belong to the existence of the state, in particular in its main features; as part of the organism, they are prior to actual tasks, and are partly of a general character, comprising many branches of administration, in fact partly of the sort that not only serve the branches of administration but even the execution of the constitution, as with the ministries. As such, they pertain just as much, or even more essentially, to the constitution. For this reason, science can only make clear the essence of the constitution and administration; it cannot draw a sharp dividing line where one does not exist in real life.

---

[85] Therefore the former is usually seen to by the ministry of the interior, which is responsible for implementing the constitution, the latter by the ministry of war.

The concept of the constitution can also be more narrowly defined in terms of positive law, namely by those provisions set up under the strict guarantee of the basic law which at the same time are considered to be an inviolable right of those to whom they apply. These commonly include the form of government, the state religion, privileges of rank [ständischen Privilegien] etc., but not always the constitution of the civil service. Finally, common usage often understands by constitution in the strict sense merely the form of government. But never in that case is a concept intended which in addition to the ad- **<139>** ministration is to exhaust the entire state.

The definition often given of the constitution describes it as the relation between the subjects [dem Subjekte] who rule and those who obey. But the constitution is not a mere mutual relation among men (rulers and subjects [Gehorchenden]) but the relation of an institution over them, the coherence of this institution in itself, in terms of which the legal relation between regents and subjects first arises. But this definition of the constitution is also much too restrictive. It does not include, e.g., determinations regarding state religion or the relation of estates to each other, which nevertheless emphatically belong to it. One comes to such unsatisfactory conceptualizations because one considers the entire content of the state to be something arbitrary, where, therefore, the first alleged act, in which a compelling power is produced (constitution) once and only once, is essentially distinguished from all institutions and basic laws of the state. But the state religion, the relation of the estates, etc., are historically and legally just as original as the institution or the existence of a supreme power. The ruling authority certainly may be the center of the constitution, but it is not the whole of the constitution, and it is not such merely in the rules regarding the personal powers of the right of the ruler, but also in those regarding the objective limits and duties of it.

PART THREE: THE CONSTITUTION OF THE STATE

Chapter 1: The Forms of the Constitution

§. 63. Monarchy, Aristocracy, Democracy

<141> The concept and supreme distinction of the forms of constitution rests on the *subject of sovereignty* (the highest ruling authority). This is either a person or [bez.] a family (dynasty) – *monarchy;* or a specific estate – *aristocracy;* or the collectivity of the people – *democracy.* Should sovereignty rest in an estate or the collective people, then an artificial subject must be formed for it at the assembly itself, which gives rise to the peculiarity that the same people who rule as members of this assembly, obey as individuals. In this, aristocracy and democracy together form an opposition to monarchy – the *republic.* In turn, monarchy and aristocracy for their part have this in common as against democracy, that the subject of rule stands over against the obeying multitude.

Monarchy is of two forms. The monarch has sovereignty either as the head of a dynasty by its right, or through conferment by a republican assembly – *hereditary monarchy* and *elective monarchy.* In the latter case, the electoral assembly which calls him to rule is to that degree a higher power over the prince. The elective monarchy, therefore, is a cross between monarchy and republic; it divides sovereignty in terms of time and object, so that, up until occupation, the electoral assembly is entitled to it, afterward the prince; because of this, elective monarchy is an unnatural form of government, even in general. The (Germanic) *confirmation monarchy* [Bestätigungsmonarchie], as one might label it, is a mixture of hereditary and elective monarchy, <142> namely, that the right of lineage appoints to the throne, but the one appointed nevertheless requires the free recognition of the people as well. The appointment of princes by predecessor or by lot are as seldom as they are inappropriate surrogates of hereditary monarchy.

Aristocracy varies according to the estate which has rule; either the historic estate, the nobility, which, as with the dynasty in the monarchical constitution, passes on its right through birth – *actual aristocracy,* or the estate of wealth – *timocracy,* etc. When the ruling estate is another tribe which has subjected the ones serving but itself is democratically constituted, it contains only another basis for aristocracy, not another form of constitution. Now when the ones serving are without rights, an enslaved mass, as for example in Sparta, this is not aristocracy, for here the latter is no part of the people anymore, and therefore the ruling estate is no estate but itself an entire people.

Democracy is the rule of the people under equal participation of all estates and classes, albeit always only in ordered assembly.[86] When all individual citizens are joined in one assembly to exercise the most supreme rights of government, in particular the legislation and the arrangement of the magistracies, as in the Greek states, it is *direct democracy;* when they elect representatives who exercise these rights in their place, as in the current Swiss or North American constitution, it is *representative democracy*. The same distinction also holds for aristocracy. The relation of direct and representative democracy is similar to that between hereditary and elective monarchy.

§. 64. The Idea of the Mixed Constitution

These are the forms of government in terms of the subjects of sovereignty, and with that the main forms are exhausted. But with regard to the elements which under the sovereign participate in the exercise of power (§. 54), there arise various sorts under these main forms themselves, and mixtures and transitions are <143> possible up until the level of imperceptibility. The subforms are indeed so manifold that they do not allow for an exhaustive division, but only for an individual characterization; even so, certain more general concepts can be determined, in particular, for the monarchy with regard to those functions of state power (§§. 54f.). Accordingly, there are to be distinguished:

1. *monarchy in the strict sense* from *despotism* – its concept is for the *judicial* power to be exercised by independent judges;

2. estate-based or *representative* monarchy from *simple* – its concept is for the *legislative* power to be bound to the consent of a popular-representative body.

The essence of monarchy in distinction to despotism is the inviolability of *private rights*,[87] attained through the independence of the administration of

---

[86] The Greek notion of democracy is rule of the poorer class in opposition to the rich.

[87] This is the concept of monarchy as characterized by e.g. Boehmer *introd. in jus publ.* p. 250, and *Maximes du droit publ. franc.* p. 84 and others. Montesquieu's characteriza-

justice; and the essence of estate-based monarchy by contrast with simple is the *political entitlement* of the people, the influence of its judgment on the public condition, attained especially through cooperation in the changing of laws.

With that, however, only the most extreme abstractions of these forms of state are given. The specific shape of it, even of the general type, e.g., the older territorial estate-based and the newer constitutional, ever remains a historical individuality. In particular, the entire register of institutions which customarily are reckoned to the concept of the constitutional state: ministerial accountability, freedom of the press, estate initiative, trial by jury, separation of the judiciary from administration, etc., is absolutely unsuitable to describe a genus or category of constitution. <144>

Under *mixed constitution* is not to be understood those in which the various elements which participate in power are different merely through their number (single, college), not through their specific sort (hereditary or lifetime rule – privileged estate), such as in the North American constitution, and altogether when these elements do not even have an actual entitlement to power, but merely a function, as, e.g., the generals in Athens. In this inappropriate concept of mixed constitution, Cicero finds a monarchical element in the Roman consuls, and Sidney the ideal mixed constitution in Cromwell's English state establishment. In this sense must all republican constitutions be more or less mixed, in that the people cannot possibly exercise all functions of power themselves. But by mixed constitution one more legitimately understands only the institution in which various specific elements, an actual king, an actual preferred estate, have a legal share in power. So, e.g., the Roman republic was a mix of aristocracy and democracy, the medieval feudal constitution a mix between monarchy and aristocracy, the current German constitutional monarchy a mix between monarchy, aristocracy, and democracy. One may however understand the mixed constitution in an even more restricted sense, namely, for the constitution in which, under a sovereign element, other elements not merely have a share of power but

---

tion in bk. 2 ch. 4 of the *Spirit of the Laws*, which in this connection speaks of *lois fundamentales* [fundamental laws] and claims for the *corps politiques* a *dépôt de lois* [custodianship of the law], is false. The former criterion too broad, because even oriental despots are restricted by fundamental (e.g., religious) laws, only not by rights of subjects. The latter is too narrow; surely one cannot designate simple monarchy without territorial representation as despotism.

have a share in *sovereignty itself.* Thus, the German empire was a mixed constitution in this specific sense, for the sovereignty itself lay in Kaiser *and* Reich. The emperor and the estates had a *condominium* in it, and the emperor nevertheless was truly a monarch, which cannot be said of the Roman consuls. The same is the case with the current English constitution, albeit perhaps not in the same degree as the German Reich in terms of law, yet so in terms of fact. In this sense the old constitutional document of the city of Hamburg expresses as fundamental principle: "that in this city the κύριον or the highest law and power exist in a noble council and the hereditary resident citizenry *inseparabili nexu conjunctim* [inseparably linked] and jointly, not however *privative* [privately] in this or that part." Sovereignty in a mixed constitution of this sort is by no means divided, because it cannot be so, but has a *composite subject.* <145>

§. 65. Inadequate Attempts at Classification

The division of constitutions, the foundation of which can be attributed already to the Greeks, in particular Aristotle, appears now to be shaken by the new doctrine of popular sovereignty. For when sovereignty everywhere and necessarily lies with the collective multitude, there cannot be different constitutions according to the powers of sovereignty. Therefore the perfecter of this doctrine, Rousseau, actually maintained that one could distinguish monarchy, aristocracy, democracy not as forms of constitution but as forms of government (*Gouvernement*), i.e., in terms of the subject charged by the sovereign people to administer it. Should one take the doctrine of sovereignty in the strict sense of Rousseau, that namely the people also of necessity must exercise sovereignty, i.e., that the legislative power itself must be exercised in the collective mass, not through representation, and unrestrictedly, without a veto, and that it may revoke its contract for *Gouvernment* at any time, then all distinction among forms of state constitutions will indeed be eliminated, and popular sovereignty and democracy will then coincide as one and the same, for the accidental and provisional form of administration of affairs (of the *Gouvernment*) is of so little importance that it does not constitute a form of government. Should one, however, take the doctrine of popular sovereignty in the sense in which it is realized in France today (1846), so that the people may not exercise the least act of the sovereignty ascribed to it, and every power, king, chamber, judge, is legally established above its will, then it does not signify a characteristic of the constitution at all but is only a principle, the guideline for endeavors of state power and norm for the decision in extreme cases of conflict; it then signifies not a relation of the state in itself, which is what every constitution is, but the relation of the people (the mass considered as dissolved and unconstituted) to the state.

Just so would our systematic outline of state constitutions collapse if Montesquieu's doctrine were correct, according to which sovereignty in general and everywhere is left out of consideration and state power only comes into consideration according to its two completely separated components, the legislative and executive **<146>** power. In accordance with this Montesquieuian conception, Kant[88] distinguishes the form of government (monarchy, aristocracy, and democracy) from the form of rule, namely: whether state power is divided in terms of content, which he calls the republic, or undivided (be it in one person or in an assembly), which he calls despotism; and others, for example Behr, divide the constitutions entirely in accordance with the latter consideration and not the former. This is precisely the consistent application of the erroneous doctrine of the division of state power. Forms of government are then distinguished in terms of two entirely separate, unrelated viewpoints.

The distinction of states in accordance with the activity of the estate which predominantly fills the life of the people, and includes the state's major financial resources – thus according to the basis of the state instead of its rule – as nomadic, agricultural, trade, military, priest states, and the investigation into the influence of this basis in popular life on political institutions, as conducted by Leo, is of great scientific value, and can rightly be labeled the "natural doctrine of the state."[89] Through it, a new aspect in the essence of the state is illuminated, although it cannot be considered to be the complete viewpoint of the doctrine of state and the scientific classification of states; and, likewise, it appears not to have been intended as such by its creator; for it contains only individual powers [Potenzen] in the popular life, through which it explains only a few traits of

---

[88] *Zum ewigen Frieden* [For Eternal Peace], p. 25.

[89] Leo, *Studien und Skizzen zu einer Naturlehre des Staates* [Studies and Sketches Toward a Natural Doctrine of the State]. Only "ideocracy" in my view does not fit in this system. The orientation of sacrifice for a higher concept does not belong to the natural elements but contains precisely in itself the character of its ethical manifestation, although the concept of the Idea-state, which is equally to include the Jewish temple-state, the Lycurgean war-state and the Robespierreian reason- and virtue-state, is much too general to yield something fruitful for institutions.

organization, and not the constitution in accordance with its entire arrangement. Indeed, it could not be expected to, if for no other reason than that the constitution rests much more on ethical valuation than on <147> the natural basis.

Just so are things with the, incidentally entirely arbitrary, division of states on a psychological foundation, in terms of the life-aims of peoples, as, in particular, Mohl has attempted (naive life – patrimonial state; sensual enjoyment – despotism; preparation for the next life – theocracy; rational development of men – law-state). Furthermore, these purposes in life are not the exhaustive, nor even the proper,[90] ground of the given constitutions. At the least, such divisions should come in the place of the old natural division according to forms of government. The constitution is something independent in itself, and, therefore, must have a principle of division into various sorts in itself, and this is, as was shown, sovereignty. The constitution is, however, so much the essence of the state-as-state that the foundational division of states must simply remain that which is in accordance with forms of constitution. Certainly the constitution itself is determined by the deeper underlying orientation of the people; but this determining factor is not a predominant activity, a predominant purpose of life, but the totality of the popular consciousness in accordance with its entire determinate content and the total task of the people in the plan of world history. Should one therefore consider the state in accordance with the deeper principle of the constitution, one therefore must not consider it according to such abstractions as "sensual enjoyment," "preparation for the life hereafter," but precisely in accordance with the specific concrete course of formation of humanity; one must distinguish between the oriental (including, as an entirely unique species, the Jewish), the classical, the medieval, and the new state, and then in turn distinguish the various stages of formation and national character in each; this, however, is not a division of states and a consideration of states <148> in itself,

---

[90] For example, the Jewish people, as is generally known, were not directed toward the next life, and yet had a theocratic constitution; one cannot conceive that the oriental peoples, the Romans under the Caesars, therefore the peoples of despotism, had sensual enjoyment as purpose in life in greater and in different degree than the present or the ancient times of the Germans, or that the latter were of a more naive, simple life and judgment regarding life and state than the ancient oriental, despotically ruled, etc.

but a division of history and consideration of states in their coherence with the historical development of humanity. This, then, certainly forms the cornerstone of the scientific description of the state, in that it is the basis of any science at all. Any other divisions than this, apart from the simple self-contained one according to form of government, is more or less arbitrary.[91]

---

[91] Schleiermacher's astute investigation *Vorlesungen über die Lehre vom Staat* [Lectures regarding the Doctrine of State], contains highly estimable contributions to the natural history of the states, namely regarding the factual conditions and the stages of state formation, among which democracy, aristocracy, monarchy are possible or [bez.] necessary. But his dialectical solution to these (Hellenic) conceptual definitions is entirely ungrounded. That a state can exchange these forms and nevertheless remain the same state and retain a basic leaning to the one or the other, that interminable mixtures and transitions are possible among them, and in fact arise of necessity, all of this is an objection to the concept itself. A confusion between that which is factual influence and result and that which is form of constitution and legal competence or inner purpose runs through the entire treatise. Thus, he considers it to be a distancing from pure democracy, in fact to be actual aristocracy, when someone through "knowledge of affairs and the power of reason" becomes the "spokesman," and then this "popular leader" has "similar successors among his followers." Equally when he, in order to demonstrate that only two forms of power exist (legislative and executive), declares the administration of civil justice to be a mere component (a supplement) of legislative activity in that it "determines" this "doubtful law," as then "the hearings and results of the administration of justice everywhere provide the basis to explanations and improvements of the codex" (thus entirely overlooking everything characteristic of the administration of civil justice, the application in certain concrete cases, the effect on the specific free entitled person, the commitment to an existing legal norm). It is, however, altogether an emphasis on abstract, irrelevant relations, rather than concrete decisive character of the thing, when he puts the administration of criminal justice together with warmaking, in pursuit of the same purpose. "Regarding the administration of criminal justice, it is, like warmaking against the domestic foe, just as essentially a part of the executive power as the warmaking power is against the external foe," etc.

Chapter 2: The Standard of the Constitution

§. 66. The Criteria for Evaluating the Constitution; the Conservative Imperative

<149> The constitution is only one aspect of a people's existence and must agree with the other aspects. For this reason, each state must be constituted according to its own peculiar relations; the constitution must correspond to the needs, the received relations, the mores and disposition of the nation, and to realize this is the most essential requirement it has, which ought not be sacrificed to the ideal of a constitution perfect in itself. Furthermore, the actual formation of the state produced in each age, according to its own stage of development and its mental orientation, as for instance the Middle Ages, should be recognized as being necessary and complete in itself, even though the next generation must branch off and fulfill the task set for it both for life as a whole and for the constitution. Nevertheless, while the purpose of humanity in highest and final fashion is in fact one and the same for all men and peoples and times, because the essence of the state is general, for this reason, a common, thus absolute perfection must also exist, not of course a certain constitutional code which would be the most perfect, but certain basic relations and characteristics in which the perfection of the constitution exists. We therefore must distinguish a threefold standard of the constitution: an *absolute,* a *relative,* and an *individual.*

The *absolute* standard consists precisely in these relations and principles which are given by the essence of the state and its significance everywhere for all human life, apart from any particularity. There is partly (negative) absolute requirement, partly (positive) absolute advantage. The *relative* standard consists in the appropriateness to the given conditions which are <150> decisive for the feasibility of those principles and, in particular, those advantages; it therefore has precedence over the absolute, for exactly that which in itself is perfect can be ruinous if its preconditions are lacking. The *individual* standard refers to the specific manner of implementation of general constitutional principles; it does not, like the relative, form an opposition to the absolute but is only another side thereof (II. [*Principles of Law*], §. 11). For this implementation proceeds from what is innermost in the *popular individuality;* therefore, there is no judgment with regard to what is the higher, better individuality, and no comparison with the creations of another individuality. In this manner, one state has an advantage over another by virtue of constitutional establishments which in the latter are either impracticable in terms of relative conditions, or the implementation of which has been neglected; but every state has a side to its constitutional condition according to which it simply cannot be compared to other states. Already the general distinction between monarchy and republic scarcely allows a judgment about which is higher and more perfect; for when on the one hand monarchy is the normal, generally appropriate form of constitution, on the other hand there are states which decisively have the vocation of the republican form, and then develop advantages which the monarchy for its part cannot attain; both, then, are so much the simple expression of the most inward particularity as to rule out comparison and ranking. This individual side of the constitution is, however, the product not merely of the original particularity of the *popular predisposition* [Anlage], but no less as well its entire *history* up until then. The latter is also a power of irrevocable effect which impresses a specific individual stamp on both the temper [Sinnesart] and the social conditions of a people.

Already from this individual standard arises the untenability of those theories which set up a fully realized constitutional blueprint (the so-called constitutional system) as the norm and ideal for all states or indeed a state law already in force, or which transfer from foreign constitutions, e.g. the English, not merely certain general principles but all the details to their own states; likewise the untenability of the so oft-mentioned question as to whether this <151> or that people is ripe for the constitution of another, reading into it the relative standard, while ignoring the individual. But even the *absolute standard* of the constitution, which we must recognize, should by no means be considered an *absolute constitution,* such as this theory always presumes, i.e., a constitution which, in its form, is simply the true, unique, complete one, and as such to be pursued by all states. To believe in such is to deny the conditions of human existence. Because the state on Earth always rests on an imperfect condition, its constitution is always and must always be adapted to that condition, and therefore it cannot be a picture of absolute perfection. The absolute constitution could only be the expression of an absolutely perfect life condition; but this lies outside earthly boundaries. But certain features of perfection which can be pursued through a multiplicity of means in a multiplicity of ways will more and more show themselves to be universal, and for this reason the shrill diversity of constitutions will also abate as the level of culture becomes more elevated. Let one compare the contrast in mores and arrangement as shown by the ancient world or the Orient with the conditions of Christian Europe: to the same degree must the constitutions of more recent times come to more agreement between each other than did those of the Middle Ages, without the individuality of the peoples thereby having to stop being characterized in them. This follows not merely because of a lack of strength to bring forth, which certainly also declines, but just as necessarily from the gathering of peoples into a higher inward community. It is also the case with the constructions of nature: the higher the kingdom, the greater the agreement, up until, finally, the level of men. Nevertheless, for the reasons given, the field of public life has not yet reached such a degree of perfection and uniformity that one type of constitution could or should be adopted as a universal model. Accordingly, the doctrine of state has likewise the task, not to set up a closed, self-contained constitution but only to determine the significance of the various elements of the constitution – kingship, territorial representation (in the case of the republic, the magistracy, popular assembly), judiciary, civil service and their mutual relation, and even then, only in the sense that this **<152>** significance and this mutual relation in turn be individually given shape in every specific constitution, and this individual shape – e.g., the predominance of Parliament in England, of kingship in Prussia – not be a reprehensible deviation from a normal constitution, but instead the innermost soul, the life and strength of this constitution.

Finally, the excellence of the constitution is not the same thing as the excellence of the public condition. Attitude and mores have even greater significance than the form of government. If it is erroneous only to believe in an absolute perfection of form or to consider such to be the ultimate purpose, then it is no less erroneous to expect that with a yet properly grounded improvement of form, the content of public life would necessarily also be improved, that, e.g., through a better popular representation, the material and spiritual interests also of necessity would be advanced, or that a reform of the constitution could alleviate overwhelming evils (e.g., pauperism). As a rule, it is not the goodwill of those in power which is lacking when it comes to remedying such evils but the insight of the age, and it does not follow that, e.g., the extension of voting rights will be accompanied by this insight. In general, all action is of higher value than mere arrangement [Einrichtung]. A state in which the true living law of justice and wisdom is preserved acquires for itself greater respect, its subjects are happier, it itself is a higher, more worthy manifestation, than a state with a more perfect form yet lagging in these advantages. But the task is both: the arrangement and the action. It is imperfect when, in the properly constituted state, the mind of the government or of the people is not the right one; but it is also imperfect when the most properly ruled state does not also have a well-developed constitution. And the arrangement has the special value that once it is pervaded with the true spirit, it serves as the indestructible foundation for the proper fulfillment of the same in the future, while an outstanding government which is not based on institutions [Institutionen] is dependent in certain degree on chance, so that it can vanish as quickly as it arises. In any case, the subject matter of the doctrine of state can only be the arrangement.

The two truths here gained – that the perfection of the consti- **<153>** tution consists not in an absolute constitution but in certain characteristics and basic relations, and that each constitution must have an aspect of individuality which is incommensurable and immeasurable, of at least as great an extent as the principially necessary aspect – lead to this, that the progress of the constitution to a higher, more perfect shape [Gestaltung] will occur in no other way than through *continual historical development,* not in the way of the demolition of the existing to start anew. If the perfection of the constitution consisted in something finished in itself, as a mere system of principles ("constitutional state law"), separable from all specific conditions formed by free act and fortune [Schicksale], then the opportunity and the task would be to abandon all that exists and establish this perfect constitution. Should, however, the perfection of the constitution consist only in certain characteristics and basic relations which a specific individual condition appropriates in its way and which only then gain an actual existence, then the specific condition should certainly not be destroyed in order to establish them. The demolition-oriented, *a priori* start-over method of constituting destroys that which was formed from the innermost spirit and the history of the nation, therein precisely destroying the *material itself* through which the true characteristics might obtain their true shape. Even the perfected ethos is not a mere system of rules for individual persons, which one is to establish even unto the destruction of his entire individuality, but the discipline and direction of will of an individuality which is to incorporate these into itself; as such, a convert is only to imbibe the new life principle, not give up his individuality in order first to gain one from that principle. The received constitution, accordingly, must always remain the subject which there is furthered; new ideas and principles must be realized in it as in their real material; they must not begin a new constitution outside of it. This is true not only of the entire constitution, but also for each individual component.

Connected with this insight, and, in particular, in opposition to an age which is overly enamored with revolutionary overthrow, is a certain predilection for the existing, and an aspiration for a slower rate of change. This is the *conservative principle.* It is nothing less than stability; it in no way excludes the most thorough reforms, where <154> they have been introduced, nor the greatest energy against abuse and evil; and the most diverse political tendencies, those for expanding political freedom as well as those confirming authority, can pay it tribute. It does not consist in the old principles being maintained, but in the material being retained. Its opposite is the lust after novelty, radicalism and destruction. The destructive tendencies are the sort that have their final purpose in simple devastation and negation, e.g., leveling instead of organic construction. But where that is not the case, where a truly grounded purpose is pursued, it is reprehensible to destroy the existing first in order only then to carry out the good. Christ did not first abolish the Jewish laws, then to give His pure spiritual doctrine, but He allowed the former to exist, and gave the latter; it then of itself purged the false. Luther would have acted similarly if the Roman church had not expelled him, so robbing him of the received material. If this holds for the spiritual sphere of religion, how much the more for political and social institutions. The English constitution shaped the existing medieval material according to new true principles; the French Revolution destroyed everything in order to build a world from mere abstract notions without any given material; which became a better, more sustainable building? Therefore, they merit little thanks who have set for themselves the task of divesting, at all costs, our German condition of that which is medieval, regardless of what follows, as if it would take care of itself.

The conservative principle rests on the *true ethical* sentiment, namely on the devotion to a higher divine leading which passes through the ages and simply calls each generation to take part in the work, while radicalism rests on the presumption that the current generation would, on its own and for itself alone and for always, give shape to the common condition in its entirety; and it leads to the true *political achievement,* that the nation has an identity in its condition and consciousness through its entire history, a complete possession of its past in the present, while according to the radical principle the nation of today is an entirely different one from the one of yesterday or of tomorrow. When the state is recognized as an ethical kingdom, the conservative principle is made sure, for the given real power and the divine ethical order over the people contain in themselves a <155> continuity through the ages; but if it is considered to be resting merely on the will of men, then the condition of the moment is separated from the past as well as the future.

§. 67. Requirements and Priorities of the Constitution

The nature of the state puts these *absolute requirements* on the constitution: fixed authority and rule, i.e., a *secure and strong government,* the opposite of which is complete or approximate anarchy; a *specific legal order,* whether more or less developed, whether its power lies in an organized representation of the country or merely in public morals [Gesittung] and opinion; and *civic freedom,* i.e., the protection and the independence of the citizen in the sphere of individual life, thus the protection of rights, general human rights as well as acquired rights. These and similar requirements can be asked of every constitution; there is no condition which excuses their absence.

Absolute advantages of the constitution are external expediency [Zweckmäßigkeit], concrete [plastische] fulfillment, and political freedom.

Expediency consists in the mechanical appropriateness of arrangements for an external result, and in this external result, for which it is a mere means, lies its sole value, e.g., the concentration [Koncentrirung] of government, the rapidity of the administration of justice, ready availability of military and financial powers.

Concrete fulfillment consists in the rich unfolding of the constitutional elements, and, thereby, the rich expression of the idea of the state: the majesty of the kingdom, historical generations with traditional political outlook, a corps of juridical and administrative intelligence, a clearly defined legal order for the various branches of administration, a strong secure citizenry entitled to self-reliant participation in the public condition, etc. This manifest fulfillment is to be distinguished from external functionality, it having its value in itself, in the unfolding of these elements in itself, not in a result external to it. In this sense, Plato required beauty of the <156> state, namely that manifold forces unfold and be harmoniously ordered; in the same sense, Schelling finds the value of the constitution in the "energy of rhythmic movement and beauty of public life," and combats the standard of mere external functionality. It is not, however, the mere sight of beauty in which the priority of such unfolding consists but, at the same time, no less the unfolding of the ethical motive which corresponds to those elements and ideas, the devotion to personal authority and majesty, the historical conservative sense, faithful carrying out of duties in office [Amtstreue], the sanctity of the laws and acquired rights, the consciousness of freedom and security in the private sphere, the corporative sense. How much richer in this is, e.g., the European condition than the North American! The wealth of the ethical elements and motives when we conceive of the state not as an association but as an ethical kingdom, is the most elevated priority of the constitution (§. 38).

Political freedom in the strict sense consists in the actual, well-ordered participation of the people in the exercise of public power, and is therefore distinct from *civic* freedom, i.e., the protection of the citizen in the sphere of individual life and in individual entitlement. Civic freedom is an absolute requirement on the constitution, while political freedom is a privilege. For this reason, the estate-based monarchy, for example, is a higher form of constitution than the simple, and the estate-based form of the recent state-legal character is in turn a higher form than the earlier one of private-legal character. On the other hand, it is erroneous to maintain that political freedom, in particular in a definite, namely the highest, measure, and in a definite form, is an absolute requirement, although a certain level of it in one form or another is in fact indispensable to secure civic freedom. Political freedom has its true realization only where it naturally has the protection of civic freedom and the legal condition as its root and motive, not where it is introduced simply for itself. For the people has the injunction to ensure its rights and its ethical order, not the entitlement to appropriate the government as government to itself, not to rule for the sake of ruling. Political freedom has its specific content and <157> purpose in the former case; it is abstract in the latter. The true "manly liberty" (Burke) which commands respect and participation, which poetry has celebrated in all ages, therefore consists in the defense of the real goods of life, property, the sanctity of family and home, settled religious faith, settled received mores and laws, which are objects of devotion; it consists in resistance to arbitrariness in the administration of criminal justice, taxation, to intervention in family bonds, to suppression of belief, to the abolition of existing laws and arrangements which are dear to the nation. By contrast, an idle and empty sense of freedom seeks mere freedom as such, seeks the rule of its will (or the popular will, as the case may be) as such, or the protection of religious, indeed, anti-religious convictions which could arise as a result, and laws which have not even been issued, for which there cannot yet be any love. In this respect our age also deceives itself with an alleged spiritualistic sense of freedom, supposedly directed to the spiritual goods of thought and speech and governing as such, but which in fact is only an abstract sense of freedom (I. [*Philosophical Foundations*], §. 4).

§. 68. The Mixed Constitution

The result of these principles for the external form of the state is in general the preference for the *mixed constitution* (understanding this concept in the proper, albeit not in the strictest sense, §. 64), or, more descriptively expressed, the *richly structured* [reichgegliederten] *constitution*. It incorporates most of the various elements and ideas of the state, protects the various conditions and interests, invigorates the various ethical motives. This insight has always filled the more thorough appraisers of the body politic. Remarkably, the totality of the ancient world's wisdom regarding the state declares itself against its democracy – democracy which later became the object of admiration and, in part, the desire of the Germanic peoples – and praises the mixed constitution. Leaving aside Plato's monarchic-aristocratic state ideal, Aristotle characterizes the most perfect constitution as the "polity" in opposition to "democracy," i.e., as he himself explains it, where the collective is to rule and **<158>** actually does rule, as opposed to democracy, where the collective rules only in name, the majority of the poor rule in fact. His idea is thus, that *all classes* [Lagen] *and interests* should have enough influence on public rule to protect themselves. This idea certainly needs a broader application than Aristotle makes of it, in that it is not merely differences in wealth which ground differing interests, but also differences in rank, life activity, education, religion; and, in that it is not merely differing human conditions which are to find their development and their protection, but also various elements of the state structure; but still, it is the same idea that we have here expressed.

Likewise the *manner in which* the constitution is to be mixed is quite incompletely grasped by Aristotle, for the mixture which he proposes in his *Politics* is much more a middle-of-the-road between the two opposites of aristocracy and democracy than an organic connection of them. To wit, e.g., a *middling* income is to be associated with entry into the popular assembly, the magistracies are to be appointed neither according to wealth, nor according to lot, but according to election; the wealthy are to receive a fine for failing to appear at the assembly, while the poor are to receive a cash reward for appearing, so that both turn up in numbers. Hereby an element is intended as the decisive power in the state which is neither aristocratic nor democratic but a cross between the two, while the true mixed constitution consists in strengthening each of the various elements in itself (and indeed, in our case, kingship, landed aristocracy, citizenry, etc.) while mutually conditioning each in their activity. Cicero, who, like Aristotle, declared the mixed constitution to be the best one, already conceives it in this more proper significance, finding it in an appropriate combination, as separate independent elements, of democracy, aristocracy, and even monarchical elements; the perspective of Roman conditions led him to this conclusion. It is natural that the entirety of medieval literature, in line with Aristotle's authority, decided in favor of the mixed constitution. In accordance with this authority, it praises the polity without always understanding it in Aristotle's specific sense; thus, e.g., it is obviously no precise application of this concept when Fortescue declares the **<159>** English constitution to be a polity.

The most extreme contrast to our preference for the mixed, i.e., richly structured constitution is the doctrine of Rousseau and Sieyès. Their supreme postulate of the constitution is precisely *absolute simplicity*, i.e., only one element through and through, protecting only one and the same equal condition of all, developing only one ethical and political motive; their constitutional ideal is thus indiscriminate chaotic democracy. If there really were no various human life occupations according to wealth, kind of wealth, activity of rank – if kingship really were not an eternal idea of the state, but merely a misunderstanding of the mechanical requirement for a bearer of the executive power – if only one motive really filled men, devotion to the numerically mediated will of the majority of fellow citizens, and not a corporative, not an ecclesiastical, not a love for the entirely specific arrangements for the sake of their excellent content rather than for the sake of their majority sanction, not a personal dependence and piety regarding the ruling authority – if all of this really were so, then the absolute simple constitution, as taught by Rousseau and Sieyès, would be the proper one and the purpose of humanity, which, then, would be quite easy of attainment. If, however, those various conditions, interests, and elements are grounded in the essence of the nation and the state, then such a constitution produces a disturbance of the public condition. It ought not be disconcerting that such a single simple ethical-political motive, the motive of knowing oneself as one and equal – the truth of which by no means can be denied in its sphere – when emphasized with the elimination of all other motives and elements and made into the impulse of the public condition, works wonders of enthusiasm for the short period in which it gets to know itself in its full force and intensity and becomes roused to overcome resistance. But in itself it has no formative power, and over the long run, when enthusiasm cools along with the consumed material, it is nothing else than an impoverishment of life.

Chapter 3: Kingship

§. 69. Kingship as the Supreme Form of Rule

<161> It lies in the essence of the state as ethical kingdom that an ethical power be established in it, over the people, with inherent regard, and that this power be self-conscious, self-powerful, personal. This is the *purpose* (τέλος) *of hereditary monarchy*. It is established in order that there exist a rule over men, personal, united in itself, grounded in itself, not given by them, therefore elevated and majestic over them, powerful to keep them in order and to lead them, holy to fill them with awe. The rule of the state, thus the *state* itself, *becomes personal in the king*.

The monarchy, therefore, above all has the advantage of *unity* and *personality of rule*, which concentrates itself in one man continuously able to act, and which cannot disintegrate, from which stems agreement and mutual adjustment in arrangement and energy in implementation.

It has the still much more significant advantage of *originality* and *elevation of rule*, whereby the ruler in no respect is a subject [Unterthan] or dependent upon subjects, but stands always and everywhere over them, that his power is not derived from the subjects but exists in itself; this yields the absoluteness of regard and of respect, and freedom from the interests which divide and prejudice the subjects.

The advantage of the unity of power was already brought out by ancient writers with regard to monarchy, they grounding it on the one hand on divine rule, on the other on the examples of nature in bees and birds.[92] Yet the other

---

[92] Thus Thomas Aquinas both in the *Summa Theol.* and in his book *de reg. princip.* Then Salmasius against Milton, Mariana, et al.: it runs through everything. Otherwise in Dante (*de Monarch.* l. 1). According to him, the human race is best off "quando, secundum quod potest, Deo assimilatur. Sed genus humanum maxime Deo assimilatur, quando maxime est unum" [when, as far as it can, it becomes like unto God. But the human race is most like unto God when it is most one]. "Unum" however is usually when it is subject to a single prince. Here, thus, the idea that the people (with regard to the universal emperorship, the human race) not only be ruled in a unified manner, but that it itself attain unity and a certain degree of personality.

advantage of monarchy, that of the <162> exaltedness of power, they overlook, and therefore usually declare themselves (e.g., Aquinas) for elective monarchy, to which the example of the Christian-German emperorship induces them.

These features are the general requirement of all forms of state. Even in the republic, the unity of rule is pursued through voting and the establishment of independently acting magistracies, and a form of dignity rests on the particular bearers of public power and on the popular representation. But the various votes of an assembly do not yield coherence as do the various decisions of a man, and the magistrates, who in turn are also subjects, do not have the dignity of a king. In the former, the features are realized in an artificial manner, in the latter in a more natural, living, and therefore also more forceful manner.

§. 70. Hereditary Monarchy

In terms of its essence, therefore, monarchy is *hereditary*. The power of the king must be self-contained (*aseitas*), with no assistance from subjects, no election, no recognition through ancestors, no lot. The king must be king of himself, through his existence, his birth. The royal quality must lie inseparably in the person of the king. This is why he inherits the throne and leaves it to his heirs. The dynasty is then an uninterrupted and interminable unity. "The king does not die!" In this manner, he is the power in the state, without cause, without beginning, without end. The first accession to the throne by the dynasty was of course an act of time; but once having attained the throne, the significance attends it of having always been there and in future always being there. Only because the king is there of himself, through his birth, and the line of princes extending <163> themselves from themselves, is the princely power absolutely elevated over the subjects, and only in the prince does the state thereby also attain personality, for it belongs to the concept of personality to exist in itself, originally and unceasingly. The indivisibility and lawful ordinance of succession to the throne is, however, necessary for two reasons: to give to royal power the state character, and to secure and independently entitle the particular ruler.

As this all follows from the deeper ethical significance of kingship, so is it also confirmed in the outcome. Only kingship through the right of succession grants the independence and impartiality simply to attend to the interests of the state, and to be at the beck and call of no one, whether one who raised the king to the throne, or who will raise his descendants to it; only kingship through the right of succession has the regard which one obeys as necessarily existing without choice, without doubt, without repentance; only kingship through the right of succession has the peace which accompanies it irrevocably; only it hinders the struggle for the throne which must arise when the throne is given through election, or where it is disputed among the scions of the dynasty. With elective monarchy, the subjects are the origin of the king's power who in them has someone higher over himself, and the state has no uninterrupted bearer of its personality, and thus no true personification. The advantage that, with elective monarchy, the most capable can be chosen, is not decisive; for the main aspect of the monarchy is not the capability of the prince – other organs and arrangements exist for this – but the elevation of his position, and the strength of his regard.

§. 71. The Personality of the Prince and of the State

The prince has his power as the *sovereign of the state,* in that he represents it, i.e., *he identifies himself with it,* he is *its personification.* It is therefore a *right of the prince,* although nevertheless a *public power.* For, in order for this identification to be perfected and thereby for the state truly to become personal in the prince, the power and majesty of the **<164>** state must be vested in the prince or [bez.] the dynasty as an original right and an indestructible (indefeasible) quality inherent in his person. The prince, therefore, does not have a mere office, function, or service on behalf of the state, standing opposite the state as another subject, but the innermost self-possession of power and majesty, like the state itself. Kingship and priesthood can be distinguished in this, that the priesthood does not entail an identification with the church and therefore ever only remains a service for the church. Even the popes never describe the church, like the kings do the state, as *their* kingdom (or their church).

But on the other hand, by virtue of this identification with the state, the power of the prince is absolutely fixed according to the principles of the state. He does not possess it for his private purposes and interests and cannot use them according to his private will. For this reason, the entire arrangement of princely power, bequeathal, extent, and content of authorizations, measure and limits and manner of their use and their disposability, is directed to his legal duties in terms of the requirement of the state, not according to personal entitlement. It is not that a human personality is to rule over the state in the person of the prince (see above, note 69), but that the state become personal in the prince.[93] God did not hand over humanity to be ruled by individual persons who are only accountable beyond the grave, but He set up an order and institution, and individual men as chiefs therein. This distinguishes the true state-oriented monarchy from the patrimonial, which is only the undeveloped beginning thereof. In particular, however, the public character of the princely power lies in the possibility, in fact the necessity, of its restriction. The statement of Louis XIV, "l'état c'est moi," expresses this identification of state and prince, and in itself it is completely true. But Louis XIV intended it falsely: he only sees the one line of consequences from it, that the state is subsumed in the person of the king, and not the other, that the king is sub- **<165>** sumed in the institution of the state.

Accordingly, if the king rules as sovereign of the state, so is his rule yet likewise *paternal.* The born ruler, whose person is invested with regard and power over subjects and the obligation to care for their good, has a paternal position and vocation.[94] The public-legal aspect of institution does not rule out the personal aspect of conviction. The king accordingly is obligated to love and take an interest in his people, and the subjects are obligated not merely to obedience but also to personal faithfulness and piety, and patriotism includes not merely devotion to and self-sacrifice for the state but also to and for the princely house and the person of the king. For this reason, kingship as a rule only bears its best fruit where the hereditary king reigns.

§. 72. Kingship and Sovereignty

The *content* of princely power, accordingly, is *sovereignty,* as discussed above (§. 55). The king is sovereign – that is his concept – and a king who is not sovereign is an absurdity.[95] All rule and all law, accordingly, proceeds from the king and exists by his regard; he appoints to offices, he unites the various branches of

---

[93] Schubarth, *Ueber die Unvereinbarkeit der Hegel'schen Staatslehre mit dem obersten Lebens- und Entwickelungsprinzip des preußischen Staats* [Regarding the Irreconcilability of the Hegelian Doctrine of State with the Supreme Life and Development Principle of the Prussian State] confuses this in that he declares the Prussian state to be based on the personality of the princely dynasty and seeks to find the Protestant principle here.

[94] "L'autorité royale est paternelle, et son propre caractère c'est la bonté" [Royal authority is paternal, and its own character is kindness] (Bossuet).

[95] Compare below, §. 145.

power in himself, and everything is allowed to him which at all lies in the sphere of state power, to the degree that it is not especially withdrawn from him through the constitution (*in dubio pro rege* [in doubt, reserved to the king]). He himself, however, cannot be coerced into anything, and no power and no court of justice exists over him, either over his person or over his royal right.[96]

The *power of prevention*, unconditional prevention (veto) to be **<166>** exact, is the absolute indispensable attribute of the king, apart from which the concept of sovereignty, and thus also of the king, ceases. The sovereign can be limited, but he cannot be coerced. The king must be an elevated and independent power over the nation, and, as such, must be able to reject every positive act contradicting his convictions, even against the nation's most determined will, its most agitated onslaught. The modern view cannot understand this. Is the will of one man to have as much value as the will of 25 million men? That contradicts the ABC! Thus Sieyès: his political insight never got beyond the ABC. It is not one man against 20 million here, but a position, an institution: the position of an impartial ruler over all subject-interests, a central and unitary point in the nation; the institution established precisely in order that men have a higher regard over them than their own wills. This position and institution is of no less importance than 20 million individuals. To be king and to have no veto would also be the ethical destruction of personality, such as is not found anywhere else in the human condition. The civil servant forced into a positive act against his ethical conviction can resign his office; but kingship is not calculated for incessant abdication, whereby the king lays down his crown as a minister does his portfolio. In terms of the constitution, the king's veto therefore must be without limit, otherwise he is no longer king; factually, there is always a limit in the necessity of things, in the irresistible power of historical progress.[97] But the king must also

---

[96] It therefore makes no sense to add up the royal authorizations, for the king possesses the entire state power; it would be adding up the activity of the state. The form of their expression as well as their restriction to the various spheres of the state (e.g., regarding the popular representation, administration of criminal justice, the civil service, the church, etc.) first arises with these spheres.

[97] Regarding the power of delay [suspensive Veto], compare the relevant discussion in my book, *Die Revolution und die constitutionelle Monarchie: eine Reihe ineinander-*

possess a *power of positive rule* within the restrictions of the law and the cooperation of the appointed ministries. It is a false pursuit which, in order for the state not to depend on the arbitrary character of the king, attempts to exclude the influence of his personality, and restricts him to the confirmation of **<167>** that which others have decided, to "dot the 'i,'" so that he, himself without a will, his unremovable existence providing the most minimal support, like a mere post upon which the state is fastened. This too is contrary to the meaning and foundation of kingship. If the king is to impart the advantage of personality to the rule of the state, he must then also be able to use it as a person, i.e., in his freedom. Certainly, a considerable part of the fortunes of the people is thereby put in the hands of a man. But this is not some sort of curse of monarchy as compared to other constitutions, but the general curse of temporal existence in opposition to eternal, it being the case that humanity is not in God and ruled by Him. As long as this lasts, men must rule over men; it is and must be a good thing when a noble and wise regent holds the scepter, and a bad thing when an incapable or unworthy regent does. Should one in this manner make the king into a mere shadow king, then the regard and living respect which of necessity belong to kingship vanish. This does not give power to law or true wisdom in time, as one perhaps misleads himself, but only to other personalities, individuals or multitudes, and moreover, that which one continues to expect from kingship – the preservation of peace and order and unity – is no longer attained.[98] **<168>**

---

greifende Abhandlungen [The Revolution and Constitutional Monarchy: A Series of Interconnecting Essays]. In spite of all its mastery, Mirabeau's renowned speech in favor of the royal veto itself rests on the mechanical conception of the king as executive power and therefore neither contains decisive arguments nor yields a satisfactory result.

[98] Hegel himself first expressed the thought that the prince is "the subjectivity" or the "personality of the state" (*Grundlinien der Philosophie des Rechts* [Baselines of the Philosophy of Law], §. 279), which would lead one to expect a worthy and free position for princes from his doctrine. But for him personality in general is the *empty I,* which obtains its content from something else, from the Idea, of which this I is set up as one of its aspects (*Philosophie des Rechts,* §. 5 and §. 13); it is thus only the "abstract and to that degree groundless self-determination of the will, in which lies the final element of

---

decision [in welcher das Letzte der Entscheidung liegt]" (see also I. [*Philosophical Foundations*], §. 5, p. 19). From this follows that oft-mentioned, doubtless authentic statement (*Philosophie des Rechts,* §. 280): "he only has to say Yes and dot the 'i'," and "the objective side alone befits the law, to which the monarch has to add his subjective 'I wish' [Ich will]." For, according to Hegel's basic view, the prince, precisely because he is the personality (not the substance) of the state, must be without influence on the content of the state; instead, the latter is to arise out of the substantial impersonal aspect of the law, and the meaning of his personal strength is not breakdown, composition, and penetration in unity, but simply the "formal points of decision," "the final thing which the consideration of grounds and counter grounds, between which it ever swings back and forth, breaks off, and through the 'I will' decides."

While, according to Hegel, the impersonal world-Idea drops the aspect of personality in order to return to itself as substance, we recognize personality as the alpha and omega, as the primeval being which includes substance within itself, and refers everything which it unleashes back to itself, the person, as that in which and through which is all content. Now it is correct that "the personality of the state" is not of the sort of personality of men or of God, that here the unshakeable substantial basis is not to lie in the person, the prince himself, but in legal institutions outside of him. Precisely because of this, we do not, as does Hegel, hold the state to be the "perfect concrete objectivity of will"; this we find only in the kingdom of God, the personality, subjectivity of which, God, is as such also the objectivity and substance as well. But regardless of this, the production of content, material determination and not mere formal decision, lies *ineradicably* in the essence of personality, so much so that it must also accrue to the prince in the state in broad extent.

Enough, then, of Hegel's philosophical conception of kingship.

Considered purely as political result, Hegel's statement is indisputable that as the state becomes more highly developed, the existing law and the ordered course of administration occupy a larger sphere, for which reason princely individuality will shed its earlier significance, as it ought to (see below, §. 77 at the close). But this complete absorption of its significance is a fundamental error. The personality of the prince is and everywhere remains a most essential factor, likewise regarding content, not merely there where the monarchical principle is conserved – and the assumption that all constitutions must be made equal to the English is false – but even in the English constitution.

Such rule of the king rests on his own personal regard, not, as far as content goes, in its being merely the enforcement of law. There are, as explained above (§. 53), two authorities in the state, the personal authority of state power, which is in the monarchy of the king, and the impersonal authority of the law. These are indissolubly connected but nevertheless have independent validity, each in its own power. It is therefore necessary that the law also be a power in the state which the king does not suppress, from which he cannot **<169>** be separated, although the law cannot and ought not be the sole authority. This is the point of the basic principle of the constitution of 1791: "The king rules only through the law and can demand obedience only in the name of the law." But the king is no less an authority, and he rules by virtue of this authority, not in the name of the law; the subjects owe obedience not only to the law, but also to the personal will of the king as such (within the bounds of the law). They are to obey him, not because he commands and executes what is prescribed by the law, but because he is the king; and the law is valid by virtue of the king in no less degree than that the regard of the king is based on the law.

The concept of *sovereignty,* in the specific significance which it obtained in France, and which in Germany, upon the dissolution of the Empire, came in place of *territorial supremacy* [Landeshoheit], is certainly the true expression of royal power. It signifies that royal power is grounded not in a property right but in the ethical order and therefore has its content only through that ethical order, and not through coincidental events and grounds of acquisition. It establishes the indivisibility of state power, which, not being an epitome of chance acquisition of authorizations, for that reason cannot as branches (e.g., the administration of justice, rights of taxation or safe conduct) be entrusted to foreign rulers or subjects for their proprietary [eigenberechtigter] administration. It also comprises the full elevation of princes over subjects, whereby the latter cannot prosecute him with regard to actions of government, or ultimately, as in earlier times, look to their rights with force of arms. On the other hand, by no means does it

---

Even here, the mentality and capability of the king is of great influence on the progress of the constitution as well as the national destiny, and what it loses in influence accrues not only to the laws but also in turn to other personalities, ministers, popular leaders, etc. Never does the state so become constitution and course of administration (substance) that its history ceases; history is made by personalities.

abolish restriction on princely power through law and constitution, and through estates and acquired rights. Publicists of the Rhine Confederation characterized sovereignty as an unrestricted power (*potestas legibus haud restricta*), and the princes factually exercised it thusly, albeit wrongfully. German sovereigns certainly could maintain, and with justice, that the extraordinary power [Ausnahmsgewalt] of the state (*potestas eminens*) which until then was accorded to the Empire over the territorial constitutions, and often exercised by it (e.g., the prohibition on unauthorized assembly of the estates and armed resistance, the command to allow the prince to examine the estates' tax <170> office, etc., by which all received constitutional rights of the estates were broken), had been transferred to them, and which, in the great catastrophe of the present, had to be exercised by them in a manner incomparably expanded. Even so, this does not go as far as the fundamental non-recognition of all acquired rights, which characterized the period of the Rhine Confederation.

§. 73. The Natural Base of Kingship: Power

The king's power has its *natural base* primarily in *command of the army.* Although an ethical-legal power, kingship still rests on this factual power. The king is the first warrior in the country; he is the supreme general. The protection of the people, the strength to provide them that protection domestically and abroad, is the natural origin of the right to rule them. Princely power was formed in history from the position of being the first in battle, leader (duke, dux), and it cannot be separated from this root. Even though other tasks than military protection predominantly comprise the royal vocation, it still is the essential condition of all the others. In this, kingship has just the same natural foundation as the nobility. It is not natural when, in certain oriental states (e.g., Egypt), by way of exception to the rule, the king belongs to the priestly rather than the warrior caste. The one who protects the people on Earth, not the one who teaches them about Heaven, is the born ruler regarding the earthly condition. Only where God Himself in an earthly manner protects the people, in direct theocratic fashion, by means of miracle, there the protector, the governor, are the instruments of His extraordinary influence and rightly so. It is precisely power which everywhere appoints to rule, be it natural, be it supernatural. Thus we find among the Jewish people during the period of the Judges that God alternately chose as His instruments warriors then prophets, leaders of the sword and then proclaimers of His Word, Gideon then Samuel. When, however, the

Jewish people got its wish and entered into the general natural condition of states, obtaining a king "like all the nations" in renunciation of God's immediate rule, then it had to be a warrior – Saul, **<171>** David.

It is therefore unnatural when, in theory, the royal vocation is conceived merely as a regency, the king as the supreme civil servant, as if advanced civilization were only a matter of reasonable government and no longer of power. The king is above all the supreme lord protector of the state, not merely the "supreme servant of the state." Frederick II may have defined the king in that manner, but in his person he was the most glorious refutation of his own definition. The president of a republic certainly is not necessarily a soldier, but neither is he sovereign; he does not bear the ground of state power in himself. This is not to say that the king must have the personal gift of a general; he does not require the gift of civil government either, for that is a matter of heredity. But he must be educated militarily and must see himself as the head of the army, as a soldier. It is one of the most obvious indications of the untenability of the constitutional theory that, according to its view of ministerial responsibility, it must exclude the personal waging of war by the king. Since George II's victory at Dettingen (1743), thus as long as this ministerial accountability has been in full force in England, no king has commanded his troops.

The other natural base of royal power is (again, in analogy to the nobility) landed property, *large-scale landholding in the country*. Not that the right to territory is the legal ground of princely power. For the property of the prince in all the land and soil of the country never existed in the larger states of Europe, nor in those of Germany, and the actual territorial right (which is not property but a political power over the soil, see §. 44) is not the ground of the power of the ruling authority but much rather the product of it. But sizeable truly private landed property within the country is a factual base for the vocation of princely power. For it also preserves, similarly to command of the army, a factual power as support to the legal-ethical power of the ruling authority. This as well, therefore, was historically an essential moment for the origin of the princely houses in Europe, and especially in Germany, and it is natural that it always remain their base. The dynasty should belong to the ancient leading lineages of manorial lords [Grundherren]; in fact it **<172>** should be one which throughout history granted the country wherewithal from its own wealth, and the king is always to remain the owner of his domains, always the disbursor to the state, not the recipient from it.

In this manner, the earlier stages of state rule – patriarchal family power (§. 71), the power of vassals, the manorial nobility – are preserved in the higher, the actual state power, in a manner corresponding to nature's laws of formation, while in the republican constitution they disappear from it.

§. 74. Divine Right and Legitimacy

The power of the king is "by the grace of God," it is a "divine right." This is in fact true for all state power, including the republic (§. 48). But the divine regard and the majesty of state power proves to be more visible and vital in a personal bearer who in no way is a subject; and with hereditary monarchy, what is additional is that the possessor of state power has that possession apart from human interference, through *divine providence* [göttliche Fügung], to which men are to subject themselves in reverence. Here therefore rests the regard of the ruler, not merely on a general command and order of God, as with all ruling authority, but likewise additionally on a special (although in no way immediately personal, intervening in nature) arrangement of God. This is the *principle of legitimacy* such as is peculiar to hereditary monarchy. It has not merely the juridical meaning of lawful succession as against usurpation, but also the religious one of recognition of the divine sanction and awe (*sacrosanctitas*) for the one appointed to the throne by God's providence.

This distinguishes the persons separated from God from those bound to Him. The former wish only to recognize that which was accomplished by their own act, the latter holds to be most holy precisely that which apart from his aid has come about through a higher power. It is therefore a characteristic trait of the times that the form of the state appears that much higher and satisfactory to the degree that the ruling authority is established by the choice of the subjects, to the degree that power lies in such hands as those one has chosen, in the delegate, as op- <173> posed to the hereditary king. It is the same characteristic trait which considers the kingship to be a mere *social,* and not a *legitimate,* institution, i.e., merely an institution [Anstalt] which men (namely the bourgeoisie) have set over themselves out of rational adjudication of their interests and for the sake of expediency, not an institution which has its regard through a superhuman power and which is to uphold an inherently sacred order. From thence comes assent to every humiliation of the kingship, from thence the set conception that the king ought not resist the will of the people and the opinion of the people. *Divine right* (full authority [Vollmacht]) and *legitimacy* are therefore different, albeit related, concepts, the former signifying that the authority by virtue of which the king rules is from God, the latter, that his accession to the throne is from God. *These are the Christian principle of the state.* As such, they are universal-historically opposed to the principle of the Revolution, of popular sovereignty. They give to state rule its specific steadfastness and elevation, and that supra-earthly consecration, such as is only found in the monarchy. This principle first proves itself in its truth and purity when the patrimonial character has been overcome, when the prince possesses and bequeaths power no longer as his human property, and therefore arbitrarily, but as his divine mission, and therefore according to the necessity of the state.[99] **<175>**

---

[99] Zachariä in his *Deutsches Staats- und Bundesrecht* [German State and Confederal Law], 1st ed., vol. II, p. 73, declares the principle of legitimacy to be "just as dreadful and irrational as its extreme [opposite]: the principle of popular sovereignty," and my "attempt to justify it as something characteristic of hereditary monarchy, and to advance it with 'divine right' as the 'Christian principle of the state,' to be unsuccessful." His evidence is the rational one that "Christianity knows nothing of a hereditary kingship privileged in this fashion," and that "human legal consciousness, which by its very nature is mutable, in no way puts on a straitjacket," and the historical one that the "German emperor, although appointed by election, nevertheless was considered to be the most legitimate monarch by the grace of God according to the law of the Middle Ages." Now precisely in these sections contested by Zachariä, I began by saying that the "power of God's grace and the divine right of all state power also holds in the republic," and similarly in an earlier place (§. 66) I vindicate freedom for all forms of state and their individual worth against any kind of order of precedence; in fact, I apply the principle of legitimacy in a universal sense to the republic as well (see my piece, *Die Revolution und die constitutionelle Monarchie* [The Revolution and the Constitutional Monarchy], p. 20). There was therefore no reason for this retort of "privileged hereditary monarchy" and "straitjacket." But the above statement only says that Christianity's revealed commandment to obey the ruling authority *as ordained by God*, albeit valid for all forms of state, is demonstrated in hereditary monarchy in eminent manner, as here the vocation of a specific person to the office of ruling authority rests likewise on the divine decree,

---

and the principle of legitimacy, which factually as a matter of history is virtually solely asserted by hereditary monarchy, signifies nothing other than this devotion to the lawful prince as the God-ordained and decreed ruling authority. When however Zachariä declares my description of legitimacy – "the right of the divine decree as opposed to the human act, the given authority as opposed to made authority" – to be a "*vacuous play with words,*" in that "an act of election rests as much on God's decree as does an act of procreation" – while everything *in itself* does rest on God's decree, not just an act of procreation or election but also a successful revolt or murder, *with regard to the participating persons* the act of election by which the specific king is set up is their act, and the act of procreation which provided them with this king is a pure decree over them.

But as far as playing with words goes, the matter can no longer be dismissed as such given the catastrophe following 1848. For in what else did the opposition between the proponents of the legitimate sovereigns in Germany and the unwavering proponents of the "*conclusively* decided German imperial constitution" consist than in this, that the former obeyed the constitution and the ruling authority with joy, while the latter would only obey that constitution and ruling authority which they had set up by their act, in accordance with their wisdom; that the former adhered to the "given authority," the latter the "made authority"; was this opposition which moved the world an empty playing with words? When I, as I did above, describe clearly and distinctly the catastrophe which manifested itself in Germany in universal-historical terms, ought not my opponents respond to it, at least after that catastrophe has occurred? The appeal to the German emperor already demonstrates nothing, in that the election of the emperor was not in the least, either directly or indirectly, based on popular election, it being conducted through hereditary princes and archbishops. But it is fully refuted by the idea of the German (more appropriately, Roman) emperorship. This cannot be put on a line with other states, for it was no national kingdom but a Christian world empire, and as such set much more in analogy to the spiritual kingdom of the church. Accordingly, one considered the imperial status, similar to the papal, as an office, and only thereby were the Pope and the German princes able to transform it from its original hereditary character into the electoral character. For this reason, precisely in accordance with the viewpoint of the period, from which comes the regard of the emperor as "the most legitimate monarch by the grace of God," the imperial status was not acquired directly through election, but first through the confirmation and coronation by the Pope as earthly vicar of

Nemesis in history interrupts legitimacy, punishing injustice with injustice, so that what is human and temporal stops considering itself self-empowered and unending. In this way, the illegitimately arisen dynasty becomes legitimate, during the course of time, with the passing of generations. For it befits the current generation not to drag before its judgment seat that which God, apart from its assistance, has allowed and through the ages has upheld; not to efface the course of events to begin decision anew. When this holy force of time enters, there is no rule regarding it, as little as there is with the degree to which obedience is owed to the unlawful but already securely ordered rule, or with the degree to which defection from such rule in favor of the lawful, exiled king is called for. Such depends on the particular condition of things, and the particular calls [Aufforderungen] of individuals, each according to their position. This constitutes no contradiction of the principle of legitimacy per se, as little as does the conflict of duties form a conflict with the ethical commandment. All of the casuistry by which the impossibility of consistently carrying out a principle is demonstrated does not prove the principle to be incorrect, but only that earthly existence is imperfect. The principle of legitimacy itself, however, delineates nothing other than the right of the divine decree as opposed to the human act, the given authority as opposed to made authority.

§. 75. The Limitations on Monarchy

If then the originality and independence of power <176> lies in the essence of kingship, this is by no means true of *unlimitedness*. Unlimited royal power would be against the order of nature; for among similar beings, the one cannot rule over the other on the basis of personal right, but only by virtue of a vocation in an institution, and then precisely only up to the limits which this vocation entails. It would be contrary to the essence of the state, which of necessity contains within itself both a general lawfulness and a secure activity of manifold organs. It would even be contrary to the consecration of kingship itself, for

---

Christ. In fact, Zachariä's polemic is not so much directed against the assumed privilege of hereditary monarchy as against the divine right of the ruling authority in general, against the "theory by the grace of God" (pp. 57–59). The so esteemed and leading exponent of state law, since he just as decisively rejects the doctrine of contract and popular sovereignty, takes his position regarding the final ground of the state equally between heaven and earth, on the neutral ground of the air (compare note to §. 52).

kingship demands an ethical basis for power in the same way that personality and the freedom of men requires an ethical basis of the will (I. [*Philosophical Foundations*], §. 40), and this it has precisely in the laws (the ethos) of the state. The limits of royal power by no means contain a contradiction with divine right and legitimacy. Because the king has his authorization [Vollmacht] *from God,* it does not necessarily follow that he has this authoritization *over everything.* If it were said (in theocratic manner) that the king is the viceroy of God, the same obedience would be owed to him as to God, and certainly his power would be without limit. But what is being said here is that his possession of royal power, as well as the rights constitutionally contained in it, are based in God's decree and divine order, not on the will of the people, and what follows from this is only that this power cannot be taken away from him by the people and need not be used in accordance with the will of the people, not that it has no limit or requires submission outside of its bounds.

There has therefore never been an entirely unlimited monarchy (as form of constitution). Even in the allegedly arbitrary despotisms of the orient, there exists an infinitely strong and extended limit in the basic concepts and arrangements of religion, which the ruler dare not overstep, which he cannot overstep without the power serving him being turned against him. The character of European monarchy, however, consists in the prince being limited by the rights of subjects and the people, and it is precisely in this manner that monarchy is distinguished from despotism. Here, the limit on princely power is generally and of necessity the law and the independent judge; with a higher level of constitutional development, there come public offices as necessary intermediate organs, and finally the territorial representation. By means of these <177> elements, the princely power is supplemented into a complete state organization, and all supplementation is likewise limitation; for only the complete is unlimited. One therefore should not disregard the positive meaning of such a constitution, the supplementation, and one may with the same right label it the developed, the cultivated monarchy as the limited. Neither is limitation as such a lesser purpose, for it withdraws a temptation from human (sinful) personality so that the entire institution is kept from its caprice.

Accordingly, the law is not to be a mere internal order of the king's conscience, as the absolutists would have it, but an external state-legal limit. To this end it is characterized by its specific development and consistent exercise, the violation of a certain and continuously observed law requires rare impudence, by the oath of the king to uphold it, by the obligation and responsibility of the highest civil servants, by censure and impeachment [Anklage] by the estates, each according to the constitution. Should the king nevertheless exceed the lawful bounds, should he pursue the overthrow of the constitution, still his rule ought not be taken from him, there is no court over him: but his command will find no execution. For while the subject ought not to judge over his regents, he ought and must judge over his own conscience, and there must be found some boundary of obedience and compliance. This is also found in the unlimited monarchy where the order of the king runs against God's commandment or against the general sense of law and honor. If, however, the law is developed and recognized as a limit on the king, then its positive regulations and the existing constitution become an affair of conscience, the overthrow of which no well-meaning person ought to get involved with.

All of this is of course no complete external guarantee, for enough instruments might be found who would obey regardless; hence, the limit on the king in the final analysis rests only on the ethical power of the public mind and the strength it lends to institutions. This is also sufficient. Fear of the categorically evil and the judgment of impartial persons is the most basic foundation of all **<178>** social arrangements, and despite everything, in the final analysis one must repose in the faith that he who has power will not attempt the extreme, and that, should he do so, he will not be able to break the resistance of public sentiment. The constitution must ensure that the king cannot exceed the law without this coming to the decisive awareness and public pronouncement of himself and the people. This will restrain him and will weaken his power in other cases. On the other hand, an institution [Einrichtung] which mechanically makes his infringement impossible, which thus inserts a power that immediately shows him the boundary by force, or in the end dethrones him, cannot and ought not to exist. Such a power would in turn require a higher one watching over its proper use, and so on into infinity.[100] There must be an authority beyond

---

[100] Initially it was considered sufficient for the charter to be set under the guarantee of the chambers. What happens then when the chambers themselves help the king to violate it? For this reason it is to be set under the guarantee of the National Guard against

which none exists, *prima sedes a nemine judicatur* [the first seat is judged by no one].

In the monarchy thus formed, the king does not appear as a ruler *over the state,* like God over His kingdom, but as a *ruler within the state.* If he were a ruler over the state, he would not need the state for his power, and his power would be unrestricted. But because he is a ruler within the state, his power is limited by the state as a whole. He has power through the state, power which he can use only within the bounds of the state. The king is placed above the state in the way that the head is above the body, and vice versa, the state is above the king in the way that the whole body and its law are above the head. It is the structure of the body into which he is inserted like the other members, from which he cannot step out, which he cannot dissolve. Thus the king relates to the state; but the people are in every respect under the king.

Even in the limited monarchy – commensurate with the concept of sovereignty – no power is set up which coerces the king, but only a power which the king cannot coerce. Therefore, the boundaries extend only to the particular law, within which, however, his rule must remain free. Where the law no longer commands, and only persons can judge with their personal judgment, there the king must command, not other persons (minister, estates). The civil servants who hereby serve for the implementation of his orders, if monarchy is to exist at all, ought not be accountable for those orders, otherwise the royal power, rather than being limited, would be subjected to a higher power which judges over its use (positively) and calls it to account. On the other hand, by no means does limited monarchy mean that the king has discharged his duty simply by adhering to the law. The external limit on his power only extends to the law, but the inward demand of vocational faithfulness and conscientiousness **<179>** permeates his entire royal office. It is the honor of the king that all law manifests its validity by proceeding from him through his regard, just as does the image of the state, which inheres in him and unfolds out of him into outward form. For the mentality which engendered the law also to be the driving force of his government, even in those things which are not determined by the law, answers to

---

the king and chambers! But we must press our questioning further: "if the National Guard is also found faithless," as the "real" men of the July Revolution actually were reproached with?

the obligation that the king also preserve the living source of law in himself. This is the divine law of his mission, for which no accountability and no restricting power exists on Earth, yet for which the judgment of the world and of posterity, and the results of government, already form an ethical court.

§. 76. The Significance of Kingship

In this way the king is the personal center of all power. He is the born ruler with inherent majesty. He is in need of nothing, has received nothing from the subjects and need receive nothing; he is simply there, and merely has to vouchsafe to them that, in his position, he has no occasion for jealousy and envy and ill will towards others, in that he has everything in sufficiency. He is the personal representative of the care of the state, the vessel which is to take up in itself the divine care which founds the state and reveal it with his own conviction. Here is the dome of the earthly building, and a reflection from above rests on it. It becomes glory when the personality of the monarch meets it receptively. A God-fearing and God-illuminated king is the most glorious thing that can exist on Earth.

This is the significance of kingship. It is one of the sacred age-old foundations of human existence, as is landholding, as is marriage. As they have, so it has existed from the beginning, since the peoples have led an ordered existence of peace and culture in enduring habitations, hailed as an arrangement of the Godhead, as a good deed of the human race, and it will always exist, as will they, as long as states exist, as long as history endures, until God once again receives mankind under His own rule, and the heavenly kingdom steps into the place of the earthly.

The liberal rationalistic doctrine of state lacks the concept of <180> the king. This is one of the clearest proofs of its paltriness. At best it possesses "an individual who holds the executive power," a hereditary supreme civil servant. But the originality and fullness of power, the inherent majesty, the authorization [Vollmacht] of something higher, invisible, in short, everything specific to kingship, simply cannot be integrated into its standpoint.

No arrangement, however, is good for itself alone; none fulfills its purpose for itself alone. It can do that only when men understand it and comply with it. In fact, apart from this proper appreciation, it is no longer the same arrangement. Even marriage is a miserable institution which scarcely deserves the name marriage when spouses view it merely as a means to the ordered gratification of the sex drive rather than at the same time as the bond of ethical and religious life-community. In the same way, kingship does not fulfill its purpose when, in accordance with the sense of more recent cultured opinion, mere mechanical guarantee is sought in it. The king then believes he has done enough when he keeps the law; the people, when it does not rise up and use force. Soon, however, kingship appears to be a necessary evil to most, a superfluous burden to the short-sighted. Even here where the spirit has gone from it, monarchy, through the unity and strength of its rule, surpasses the other forms of state; even here, it preserves itself as the basic pillar of public order, outside of which there is no other.

§. 77. The Assimilation of Kingship to the State

Germanic kingship originally had more the character of voluntary subjection, the king having more the position of a first among equals. In this spirit arose the feudal monarchy, as a bond of reciprocal faithfulness of private-legal sort, as a gradation of similar rulers. The Germanic mixture of hereditary and elective monarchy, the entitlement of descendants, and yet the requirement of free recognition and devotion, is of the same spirit. By contrast, actual kingship was formed from the Roman concepts of power and majesty of the state, together with the Christian recognition of ruling authority set up by God as a **<181>** public power absolutely elevated above the subjects. The two opposing elements filled history continually. One was able to apply Daniel's prophecy of the kingdom mixed of clay and ore, for the Germanic is an element of softness and flexibility, while the Roman lends the state iron firmness. To the degree that the private- and feudal-legal character held, the king essentially, and in terms of form, was no different from the nobility. Every great man ruled on his land and soil like a king. To the degree, however, that the concept of true royal power was effective, the nobility had to relate to him as subjects to the ruler. Here arose the struggle of the kingship with the aristocracy which runs through the Middle Ages, the former driven by the consciousness of lawful supreme power, the latter by the consciousness of lawful equality and independence. Kingship arose triumphant from the struggle. The rule of the state, which, plant-like, had arisen from the ground in innumerable manorial estates, now received, as if an animal body, the unity of the head (§. 10). Finally, in the 18th century the last remainder of aristocratic power was broken and kingship rose to hitherto unknown heights. The German territorial powers, after gradually having attained independence, immediately discovered their example in European kingships. No less did the state-oriented character develop more and more in the inner arrangement of princely power: ordered succession, indivisibility and inalienability of the land, centralization of government. But with the collapse of the feudal nobility, the only power facing the princes had fallen; thus did monarchy everywhere become, if not legally, still factually unlimited.

It is against this that the political aspiration of the present is directed. Now there is to be a state-oriented power, the inner necessity of the community, to mitigate or even to determine the princely power through relevant organs and based on public national valuation, as once was done with the more arbitrary power of individual estates and their rights. This aspiration must be purified of the erroneous admixture of popular sovereignty, democracy, mechanical division of power, etc., but by no means is it to be rejected, especially not to restore the private-legal <182> character once held by princely power, by stifling the germs of state formation already contained in it and now unfolding.

Just as the power of the king in those times was unlimited, so was the veneration of it unpurified. It surpassed the human measure, the king being considered not an authorized representative [Bevollmächtigter] but a viceroy or symbol of God. Not only was veneration extended to the private life of the king, which it certainly ought to, but also to the meaningless, often even to the unworthy aspects of this private life, to coming and going, to getting up and laying down, to play and hunting, even to devotion to immoral inclinations. His favor held as the highest happiness and first honor, his judgment the standard, his pleasure the purpose even for all intellectual endeavors in art and science and mores. Thus was he more than a mere head of state, but head and center of all of life, that of which the state itself should be nothing more than the mere upholder.

We should willingly consign to extinction this exaggeration and impurity, the dross of monarchy. Kingship thus purified does not accord less with the pious and holy conception, but more. It ever remains a God-established authority, ruling in His name, and responsible to Him; it ever remains a personal majesty, a personal power to be used in accordance with freedom. But if the majesty appears more as an emanation of the divine office than of its human bearer, the people are not thereby drawn away from the holiness of kingship but are only pointed from the man who receives this holiness to the one from whom it emanates. And when the king no longer sets his foot over the state, as if an earthly god, but has become one with it, as a member, as the chosen head, then human greatness does not to exceed its measure and the wisdom of God is made clear, who rules men by such a wonderfully structured institution, instead of assigning it to a few persons to rule as they see fit.

Progress in the spirit of the Reformation, the realization of its principles in the area of politics, causes mere human-personal and thus arbitrary rule to give place, and human common life directly to come under an ethical and so divine order which is also inscribed in the <183> consciousness of the nation (the political community). This is something entirely different from the will of the nation being the source of royal power and the guideline of its use; the latter is not the principle of the Reformation but of rationalism and the Revolution. The spirit of the Reformation would have the king be a *state king,* not a *citizen king.*[101]

§. 78. Of the Right of Succession

In terms of the essence of hereditary monarchy and, in particular, the principle of legitimacy, the right of succession of the dynasty (of the agnates) cannot be withdrawn; it cannot validly be rescinded by the king, either alone or together with the estates, through an act of sovereignty or a law – of course, excluding the case of incapacity to rule. For this right is no right that stands *under* state power, thus inferior to its supreme power (omnipotence of Parliament), as with the rights of subjects, corporations, privileged classes; it is a moment that *helps to constitute* state power itself, in analogy to the right of the sovereign itself. When, thus, the rescinding of acquired rights of subjects, of the nobility, etc., can be only (materially) unjustified, not (formally) unlawful (§. 41), so is the rescinding of the agnatic right of succession to the throne unlawful and legally invalid, similar to the dethroning of a king, and should the current sovereign pass away, the excluded person still becomes the sovereign *ipso jure;* and should he dispute the crown, it is not for that reason an uprising but assertion of that royal right.[102]

---

[101] [A reference to Louis Philippe I (1773–1850).]

[102] It is adduced against this that the agnates have no *jus quaesitum* [right to recover] up until the moment the throne devolves, but that the existing succession ordinance only allows them the mere possibility of a future right which, according to known legal

Only under the validity of this principle is the king truly king by birth (§. 70) and is the personal state power an independent power and authority alongside <184> the laws, although, conversely, the law of succession is the expression of the right of descent. Self-evidently, another principle can hold in the positive constitution, according to law or custom, the consequence either of the more despotic principle, whereby the particular regent has no limits to his power, as for example in the Russian and oriental kingdoms, or the more republican principle, that the law, as it arises through the prince and estates, absorbs the independent personal entitlement. But the principle of hereditary monarchy, in terms of its full concept, requires the right of lineage to be as inviolable as the right of the ruling king.

In England, during the renowned debate in the House of Lords regarding the Bill of Exclusion, the principle of the inviolability of the right of lineage was solemnly declared, and the Act of Settlement did not revoke it; for even if that act really infringed better claims than those of the House of Hanover, in particular of Savoy, nevertheless it did not decide the issue but only continued in the line of the dethronement of James II, and rests on the same motive – the safeguarding of Protestantism – as the Bill of Exclusion, an act which the English themselves consider to be a revolution, albeit a lawful one. This principle did receive a shock from the law under Queen Anne, which, in support of the Act of Settlement, declared as high treason any assertion that the king and Parliament have no power to make laws concerning the succession to the throne. In Spain, the matter is highly complicated by the fact that the current rescinding of the Salic law likewise is grounded on the view that significant (material and formal) doubts underlay the lawfulness of the introduction of this law by the first Bourbon king. For Germany, however, the inviolability of the agnatic law must be maintained, and therefore among us the house law [Hausgesetz] is always to be kept separate from the constitution, even when it is a supplementary portion of the latter, in that the prince cannot change it apart from the estates,

---

principles, can be withdrawn by a new law. But this would only be true if it had to do with Roman civil succession, not however with a *successio ex pacto et providentia majorum* [succession by agreement and providence of ancestors], which succession to the throne indisputably still is, and least of all is applicable in the case of succession based on the grounds enumerated above.

but neither with the estates apart from consent of the agnates. Often this is manifested in the form whereby the house law is promulgated apart from the constitution and is only confirmed and guaranteed in it.

Accordingly, while in actual hereditary monarchy the agnates **<185>** have an indefeasible right to the succession, they have no such right to the unalterable preservation of existing constitutional and other state relations. In hereditary monarchy, the acquisition of the crown is a personal (private patrimonial) right of the dynasty, but the government of the country is a public affair which only came into its own under the apprenticeship of primogeniture and sovereignty. For this reason, the acts of the national government, their legal validity and legal obligation, cannot depend on the consent of the agnates. But the national government not only is charged with the conferral of rights upon individuals (conferment of privileges, of irrevocable offices, contracting of public debt), but also the conferral of rights to land and people, the granting of new territorial rights [Landesfreiheiten], the introduction of a new constitution. In all of this, as it belongs to the concept of the ship of state, the sovereign has complete power and is not bound to the will of successors. A limit only consists in the essential rights of the princely power not being curtailed, for this would deprive it of the *object* of the right of lineage, thus, in terms of consequence, even thwart it. Without the consent of the agnates, therefore, the sovereign may as little give up such rights as he, without that consent, should introduce a republican constitution. In concrete cases, these limits may be difficult to ascertain, for which reason it is advisable to obtain the consent of the agnates; in Germany, its establishment is eased by the development of the criteria of the monarchical principle. One cannot say of a constitution which does not violate the monarchical principle, that it deprives the agnates of the object of the right of lineage. This right may apply differently in accordance with positive law and custom, but in such a case sovereignty and full primogeniture do not exist. The requirement of the consent of the agnates to the conferral of territorial rights or the introduction of new constitutions, even in terms of the monarchical principle, is the true expression of the patrimonial principle, according to which the national government with its emoluments and amenities is the private right of the prince and the dynasty; for this reason, like a feudal or trust holding, it ought not be encumbered apart from the consent of the agnates; therefore agnatic consent is required not merely for **<186>** a new national constitution but also for the conferral of definite state offices, for the contracting of state debt.[103] On the other hand, that the right of succession of the agnates cannot be rescinded apart from their consent is not an expression of the patrimonial principle but of hereditary monarchy as such. The former contradicts the essence of sovereignty and the state-oriented character, the latter does not.

Acts taken by the prince as prince, i.e., on behalf of the state, bind the successor, be he an agnate, a cognate, or a complete stranger. This follows from the unity and uninterruptedness of the state as a public order and institution, and from the unity and uninterruptedness of the princely power, the entire entitlement and activity of which is based on this institution. It is for this reason that the successor is the representative of his predecessor in his princely position; in this respect, he is one and the same subject with him, to wit, the supreme state authority, which ever remains the same even though its holders change. But this assumes, as is self-evident, that the act was binding also on the author of it; orders which he himself might rescind can of necessity also be rescinded by his successor, precisely because of the unity of both. Likewise, it is assumed that the act did not deprive the successor of an indefeasible right without his consent. In terms of the above, this would include the case in which the right of succession is curtailed, but not that in which a new constitution is introduced.

§. 79. Financing the Princely House

It is required for the dignity of the princely position that the income for the sustenance of the king as well as for the maintenance of the luster of the crown be the proper right of the king, not a grant, certainly not an arbitrary grant of the people. The <187> *ancient institution of the princely demesne* [Kammergutes] settled this, albeit in patrimonial fashion. The prince maintained the state through the demesne as if from his own private property, and by his own private discretion determined what to apply to the territorial government and what to his own personal use, and he could freely alienate it as well. Purposes of a state-

---

[103] Thus it was actually found in earlier times, that e.g. in Lippe the descendants co-occupied the offices, that in Anhalt the *primogenitus* ruled only *commissorio nomine* for the entire house, merely for the greater luster of the family; on the other hand, Moser (*Familien-Staats-Recht derer teutschen Reichsstände* [Familial State Law of the German Imperial Estates], I, p. 463) already noted that one should introduce primogeniture either properly or not at all.

oriented character, namely those which distinguish it from patrimonial holding [Chatoullgut], were already to be found in the princely demesne in its original form, and were expanded over the course of time. Thus, the administration by public officials apart from the patrimonial holding, the inseparable annexation to state succession, and, later, the frequent requirement of partly agnatic, partly territorial estates-oriented consent for alienation.

The *English institution of the Civil List*, by contrast, stands purely on state-oriented ground, but only by yielding up the true monarchical position. There the king receives his income like an official, and with every case of succession, the Parliament has it in its power to reduce the king's income, to put him on a lower salary. Thus, there is the necessitous, the receiving rather than the granting – thus, the absence of the necessary royal dignity – whereby the king is abandoned at the start of his government to the will of those who are to stand below him, and the same thing happens later to his heirs to the throne, where such is the case. In England, this is historically justified since the kings squandered the royal demesne, and to a degree it is moderated in that the Civil List is considered to be the property of the king up until a certain amount, to wit, to the level of the dedicated crown revenues, which are revertible in case the Civil List is refused. In France, however, given the transformation of the received royal demesne into national property, it is completely established on principle that the income of the king is to consist, not in crown holdings, but only in the Civil List.

The institution of the Civil List which has been introduced by the *recent German constitutions* is of a fundamentally different character than the English. Here, the crown estates are considered to be the property of the crown as they were before; they or their revenues, as the case may be, are remitted to the state, and in exchange the prince <188> is paid annually his regular sum, ever as replacement and reimbursement of his original claim to the crown estates. This is the notion that in the most manifold forms always comes out the same, whether the Civil List is "permanent" (or what amounts to the same thing: "not to be reduced without the consent of the prince") and additionally rooted in the estate or property reserved to the estate of the prince, or it is declared that the estate belongs to the prince but the yield is applied to his court only up to a determinate amount with the remainder going to the public treasury, or that the prince reserves the recovery of the estate in the event that the Civil List is reduced (Bavaria, Baden, Electoral Hesse, Saxony, etc.). This indeed is nothing other than the ancient institution of the princely demesne purified in a state-oriented character appropriate to the times. In this manner is effectuated, firstly, the inalienability of the princely demesne, secondly, the legally established distinction of so much going to the state, so much to the expenses of the princely household and court. This and only this is the distinction between the current constitutional German state law and the ancient right of the princely demesne. By contrast, the notion of receiving from and granting by the people or the estates, and the possibility of refusal, of a reduction, which is the characteristic of the English Civil List, has no application in the German constitutional states. It therefore answers fully to the German constitutional principle, namely the full sovereignty of the prince, his independent elevated position, together with state-oriented necessity and order.

Chapter 4: The Basic Law of the State

§. 80. The Basic Law of the State: Foundational Rules

<189> The regulations [Ordnungen] regarding the essential parts of the constitution – form of government, succession to the throne, rights of regents, of estates, of municipalities, citizens, state religion – are by definition separated from the other regulations in that they contain the foundations of the entire state, the condition of all government, the dearest rights of the nation. They, first and foremost, are what limit the prince. The epitome of these regulations is the *basic law* [Grundgesetz] *of the state.* This has a special venerableness and, where possible, special guarantees. In more recent times, it is usually labeled, in accordance with its content, *constitution* [Konstitution], *law of constitution* [Verfassungsgesetz], *constitution* [Verfassung]. In a stricter, and nowadays common, signification, one understands by *basic law* or constitution those regulations only to the degree that they are put down in written law, chartered documentarily.[104]

§. 81. From Isolated Privileges to Coherent Constitution

In earlier times, the basic law consisted mainly in individual (private) rights, namely *princely house law* [fürstlichen Hausgesetz], which as a rule depended merely on the agreement of the agnates, **<190>** and *territorial freedoms,* the chief portion of which were concessions to the individual estates, over which, each for itself, they could dispose, i.e., negotiate with the prince. In more recent times, by contrast, the basic law, in line with the idea of the state, has been formed into a whole. In none of its components can it be changed merely by the participant (succession to the throne merely by the members of the princely house, privileges of nobility merely through renunciation by the noble estate, etc.) but

---

[104] Hereby arises a *formal* concept of the constitution, which one ought not confuse with its *material* concept. It signifies the laws included in the document or, even without a document, which are held to be steadfast rights of the land [des Landes], and which, where special guarantees are given, are ranged thereunder. There can be much here which does not belong to the constitution in a material sense. The opposite of the formal concept of the constitution, then, is not the administration but the common laws [die gemeinen Gesetze] (*leges fundamentales* and *civiles*).

everywhere only through the joint power of the state, through the princes and the entire territorial representation taken together. This is the concept of the *constitution,* in accordance with its true conception. It contrasts with the older form of constitutional laws, the "territorial freedoms," "territorial privileges," but no less so with the constitution which is not fixed in specific legal rules [Rechtssätzen], nor represented by bodies of the estates, which therefore is indeterminate and, within extreme limits, placed at the discretion of the prince.[105] In contrast to all of this, putting down the entirety of state law in a document, or above all reshaping it at one point in time while nullifying everything that came before, is by no means a part of the concept of the constitution but only describes a form thereof, and precisely the misguided one. Our interpretation of this concept confirms its universal-historical origin, the English constitution, in which, undeniably, only the former and not the latter character is found.

The otherwise well-intentioned resistance to fixed or, above all, written constitutions has its basis in the false concept of the constitution. Otherwise, it is a denial precisely of historical development. Even in ancient times, official relations were not without any constitution, i.e., not without law or the representation of it over against territorial lords. Only in those days, **<191>** it was those isolated and, in terms of content, chance privileges of the estates which formed the constitution. As the territorial supremacy developed into one true kingship from the aggregate of royal authorizations, so also did those immunities have to join with each other into a whole, and that which inwardly corresponded to the relation everywhere drove out that which had come about by chance. It is not that limited rule stepped in the place of unlimited, but rather that the order of the structured state came in place of the incoherent privileges of the estates. *Sovereignty* thus necessarily corresponds to the *constitution,* as territorial supremacy does to the freedoms of the estates. Because the supreme power was the first to receive a state-oriented character, a transition period was needed in which, for lack of significant territorial representation, constitutional law also lacked firmness and steadfastness, and custom and the praxis of government compensated

---

[105] One cannot say, e.g., that Austria (1856) is without a constitution, that the princely power of taxation is without limit there, but only that this limit is unexpressed, is not represented by the estates, for which reason the prince has to determine it and is in his right as long as he does not extend it to ridiculous lengths.

for this lack or rendered it unnoticeable. Even so, it is against the law of natural development for a condition of uncertainty, an order merely factually preserved by custom, to continue to exist forever; it had to come to either actual despotism, as with Louis XIV, or to a much more certain legal character.

§. 82. Conditions for a Written Constitution

The constitution, like all law, was not preceded by intention and reflection but was given with the state from the beginning. The proper and natural thing now is for it *further to develop as a given thing,* i.e., that it be further developed out of its already existing elements, and only in those parts where a need for change clearly arises as a result of events or changed appreciation. It is grounded in individual acts from various times and captured in individual documents which accompanied them. Such are the *historical constitutions*, to which in particular belongs the English.

The extreme opposite to this are the *revolutionary* or *constituting* [konstituirenden] *constitutions* (France, Spain, Portugal, etc.) which nullify the entire received constitutional condition, even the supreme authority, in order newly to erect the constitution, and thus the state, **<192>** from that point on, from elements which have no connection with those of the previous constitution. These are outrageous and absurd.

Between these stand the *considered* [reflektirten] *constitutions,* which are based on the given constitutional condition but which carry out deep restructuring reforms (materially) in the existing elements, and thereupon (formally) put these down in a main document covering the entire public-legal condition. Such are advisable where deep changes have proceeded in life itself, the old relations in many cases have broken up, died off, or become unstable, and new conditions and demands have matured. Their justification and benefit depend on whether they are given and understood in the manner and sense of the historical and not the revolutionary, as enhancement of, and not as opposition to, historical advance. To wit:

1. They must proceed from the *existing authority* in the state, whether the prince issues them merely from his own absolute power – *decreed* [oktroyirte] *constitutions* – or consent is obtained either from the existing territorial representation or one specially formed to this end – *ratified* [paciscirte] *constitutions.* In the latter case, by no means is the existing constitution suspended until the new one is established contractually; rather, the existing constitution, thus the

princely power in its position up to that point, continues, should agreement not be reached. The decreed constitutions and the ratified, only in this permissible sense, together form the opposite of the *constituting* constitutions. Of course, whether the decision to grant the constitution came through the prince's own inward motive, the pressure of public opinion, or popular unrest and commotion, is not here under consideration; the point is not factual motives but legal valuation.

2. They ought not annul the existing legal condition but, to the degree that they have not altered that condition, leave it in force and conserve the content of the existing elements and rights, reconciling those with the new principles rather than demolishing them (II. [*Principles of Law*], §. 21). Thus, in Germany in particular, the norms regarding political and ecclesiastical relations stemming from former times, when recognized as binding by the government, are certainly just as good a guar- **<193>** antee of rights and freedom as in the case where the government promises to subject itself in future to new, just-issued laws, while disregarding those which did not require introduction. For this reason, it is a great lack in German constitutions that the following concession is not expressly included: in everything which new laws or the changed condition have not provided for, the former principles of state and ecclesiastical law will retain their steadfast validity.[106] It cannot be foreseen how many of the most important relations for individuals and corporations may yet be brought into question when it depends upon whether the old guarantees are valid or whether nothing is valid which is not contained in the charter. Even the new basic laws first gain their proper confirmation and confidence when one considers them in connection with the old, as expansion and development and not as an entirely new construction.

3. The constitution ought not make the claim that it, as such, is the ground of all rights and the source of sanctity; the legal and ethical bonds which the constitution has as content are this. Kingship, acquired rights, rights of confession, have independent validity and are sacred in themselves; they lend the constitution its sanctity rather than receive that sanctity from it. Particularly

---

[106] Since then the Prussian constitutional charter has made a laudable exception to this. In Article 109 it actually contains the regulation I had found lacking in the others. Admittedly, it also has a systematically exhaustive character.

questionable are those clauses in the constitution which give the appearance that the supreme authority in the state, and the supreme legal truths, are first established by the constitution, are only valid by virtue of the constitution, and therefore can be repealed and amended.[107] **<194>**

4. Therefore, the constitution, the written law, should not be regarded as the center of life. Its authority over the course of time is to recede behind prescriptive usage [verjährten Uebung]. This can already be said today of individual principles of public law, e.g., of the independence of the administration of justice, regarding which no one who expresses it thinks of the relevant articles in the constitution. In this manner, the law appears as something higher over man, not as his own work; as an inner rule of relations, not as a norm laid upon them from outside; and it is accompanied by the consciousness of necessity, which gives it strength, and of long application, which gives it clarity. On the other hand, written constitutions are accompanied by continual reflection, whether it could be better otherwise and, as a result, whether it should be otherwise, and are of doubtful interpretation, in that the act, the praxis, is indisputably clear, not the word. Such a prescriptive praxis supported by written law is the true restraint of princely power. The latter is not to be restrained by the opinion of the houses of the representative body, or the ministers, or the newspapers, or by a suddenly issued dead letter of a law, but by the entire ship of state maintaining an ordered, consistent course confirmed by history and tradition, thus, that the

---

[107] Conservatives therefore have taken especial offense precisely to the clauses which have the appearance of favoring kingship, e.g., "the king is the head of state, his person is sanctified and inviolable." On the other hand, these clauses are also defended from the monarchical standpoint (v. Radowitz), whereby one places the kingship under the protection of the power which the trend of the times esteems, the constitution. Now it cannot be denied that the right of the king, as far as it is contested, can be guaranteed and confirmed anew in the constitution just as well as can that of the subject. Thus, e.g., the clause: "the king unites in himself all the rights of state power," disposes of the entire doctrine of the separation of powers. The point is whether, in terms of the approach of the constitution in general and in terms of the content and wording [Fassung] of the clauses concerned, it manifests itself as a defense against challenge or as a new institution of kingship and an exhaustive list of the rights thereof.

basic principles are determined of their own accord by law and custom, independently both of the prince and of these other elements.

5. The constitution is not to have a *systematically exhaustive form,* which only allows an exception here and there as something unexpected, for which then at best (such as according to Article 109 of the Prussian constitutional charter) the former laws are **<195>** to remain in force. It may extend itself to all relations of public law, and make new and important regulations for each of them; but it ought never take the position that it must newly set up the concerned relation, or determine it in its totality, but instead that it everywhere assumes this legal order as existing, historically given, which it amends or reconfirms only in the points concerned. A new register of public law, as complete as possible, can be a requirement. But this requirement would be much more fruitfully satisfied by a scientific work (e.g., Gratian's *Decretum*) or by an officially arranged register not invested with the dignity of law. For, in that case, praxis can lean upon such a register without being bound to it; neither is that which is not included annulled, nor is that which is included made into the register's own creation.

6. Beyond this, it would usually be the natural course of development for such considered constitutions that they be formed not by one legislative act or one document but by a *series of continuous acts*, so that, in this manner as well, they approximate the historical constitutions. Thus, where a need to change the constitution into the new type has been recognized, the first act has been to form a territorial representation and establish its authorizations. Only then might stipulations regarding expanded freedom of the press, the right to religious associations, the administration of justice regarding gaps in the law [über Justizverfassung in Zwischenräumen] follow for each, according to requirement and mature preparation.[108] With the contrary procedure, such as has been followed in Germany since 1817 – apart from all other aforementioned disadvantages –the entire public legal condition is hastily locked in, and without sufficient circumspection, which only with difficulty can be amended.

---

[108] As is self-evident, this advice (given by me in *The Monarchical Principle* in 1845 [see ch. 12 below]), cannot be followed factually when the new constitution is brought about through popular uprising, which cannot wait patiently but uses its present superiority to force the concession of all its demands once and for all.

Accordingly, the character which is to be avoided, even in **<196>** constitutions drafted in a document is, in a word, *codification* (II. [*Principles of Law*], §. 21). This does not excuse, e.g., a delay in the granting of the constitution – the justification the constitutional party tends to make in response to objection to their charter – for apart from the fact that the demand for a constitution as *they* made it can rightfully be refused, even the necessity suddenly to give a comprehensive and essentially rearranged constitution does not yet entail the necessity to give it in the form of codification.

§. 83. Vague Principle to be Excluded from the Constitution

Apart from the general evils of codification, the newer constitutions for the most part have a special one which is not even essential to codification. This is the inclusion of regulations in the constitutional charter which are not laws, but mere political pronouncements or theoretical statements.

This includes *general principles, tendencies,* in fact often mere *aphorisms.* (For example: "science and its teaching is free"; "the privileges of the estates are abolished"; "all Germans are equal before the law.") Often they are completely empty, but even when they say something, they do so in such generality that they are incapable of any legal application, as little as is so-called natural law (II. [*Principles of Law*], §. 12, note). Here also belong the *announcements and promises of future laws.* (For example: "one and the same civil and criminal code is to exist for the entire kingdom"; "the minister is accountable, the cases of accountability and their punishment will be more closely determined in a law.") These promises are not amenable to legal application and have no binding force. They cannot, as is self-evident, bind either subjects, judges, or officials to obedience because in terms of content they are not current law but only express the object of a future law. Nor can they bind the legislator (government and territorial representation) to provide the promised law, and this on two grounds. *Firstly,* the legislator cannot be bound by a law at all. As the author of the law, he always stands over the law and can even remove the announcement from the constitu- **<197>** tional charter; and with regard to the law in question, it is in his power at any time to issue it or not to issue it, and if he issues it, that is his act and his responsibility anew. He cannot be considered to be the mere executor of a (constitutional) law presented to him. Government and chambers therefore in conscience ought not to pass a promised law, which, at the moment it is to be passed, they recognize to be ruinous.[109] *Secondly,* such announcements or promises do not contain the detail, in fact usually not even the conditions, of the law to be enacted, and therefore cannot oblige the enactment of a *specific,* i.e., precisely *this or that particular* law. King or houses may, even when they consider themselves bound to the promise at all and sincerely wish to fulfill it, nevertheless refuse the specific proposal in question (e.g., the promised general civil code, the promised law regarding ministerial accountability), and can do the same with every future proposal, thus rendering the promise itself factually ineffective, without any conflicting aim.[110] The only legal effect such promises can have is that no new law may be issued which contradicts them. But even this effect can only take place where the principle applies that the constitutional charter may not be indirectly amended by deviating laws, and it is not of great concern, because if the legislative power decides on such a law, it also decides on the necessary amendment of the constitution. In this manner, such promises and announcements in fact are without legal consequence, and therefore scarcely anything other than **<198>** "monologues of the legislator" (v. Gerlach).

The inclusion of such theoretical statements and political announcements in the constitutional charter therefore runs contrary to the *dignity of the basic law,* for what above all befits that law is that its rules bind securely and steadfastly. But it also leads to *legal uncertainty,* since the boundary is often difficult to find, to what extent it (especially if it merely consists in repeal) really and immediate-

---

[109] This is not to say that the prince is not afterward bound by promises he makes in difficult times to the people, in order to calm or inspire them. Only this, that such promises only ground a moral duty, one of honor, against which, in extreme cases, the other moral duty, not to watch the state plunge into the abyss, ever retains some importance; and the inclusion of such a promise in the constitutional charter lends it no other legal character. At any rate, this promise can neither morally nor legally bind the members of the chambers, who themselves represent the people, and thus are the recipients of the promise.

[110] For this reason, such promises themselves do not bind the legislative assembly, if one, in accordance with the Revolution doctrine, considers the constitution as the work of the sovereign people and the constituting assembly, and the legislative only to be the executor of it (see next chapter).

ly gives or does not give a binding law.[111] No less does it bring about *political dissatisfaction,* since expectations are placed in these aphorisms and promises to the people, and differently for different parties, which are not fulfilled; and the false impression they give, even though inherent in the necessity of the matter, is charged to the dishonesty of the government.

Prior to a century ago, it was still something unknown for the principles and resolutions of legislation themselves to be promulgated as laws. That this has now become general custom has its ground not least in the viewpoint according to which the state is built not on positive historical right, but on reason and the particular rational conception, in terms of which it is to be ruled less according to specific laws than according to political tendencies. The constitution of 1791 with which this custom began makes this, its deepest origin, abundantly clear.

Now it is not to be denied that basic laws, which in this matter are to be distinguished from other laws, also have the task of *moral reinforcement and assurance.* Therefore, inclusion in the basic law or in the category of basic laws is not to be directed purely in terms of scientific demarcation – thus, which objects pertain to the constitution, and which to the civil law, criminal law, etc. – but instead in terms of what has been the subject of challenge, abuse, political struggle. For this reason, oftentimes only **<199>** the institution as a whole is to be guaranteed in the basic law, while its implementation falls to the other forms of legislation. Therefore, the basic law often contains provisions which only inculcate, guarantee, confirm by oath as it were, already existing law. Even so, in all of this the basic law can never be lacking in the essential characteristics of law: *certain content* and *binding force.* Hence, these reproaches against the errors of written charters are not to undermine the true nature of the basic law. Institutions which contain a guarantee of freedom and law are not to be relegated to mere special legislation and deprived of the solemn guarantee of the basic law. There is not even to be any sifting and weeding, motivated by doctrinaire nervousness, should here and there a statement be found in the constitution which sounds more like a moral sanction than a law. But the guarantee of specific institutions

[111] So for example the uncertainty as to whether "equality before the law" and "abolition of estate privileges" have any influence on the legal relations of the mediatized estates, and, if so, what? Or whether the "abolition of the death penalty" comes into effect immediately, or only when a law puts another penalty in the place of it.

is something other than the guarantee of mere commonplaces; the confirmation of existing laws is something other than the promise and announcement of future laws; political pronouncements as isolated exceptions are something other than general characteristics of the constitution. Finally, all of this, of course, only concerns the *form* of the legal condition and, therefore, in importance stands far behind its *content,* the actual regulations and legal principles. But the *revolutionary and doctrinaire* form is a great evil, for which time and insight must bring recovery.[112]

[112] It has in particular been Herr von Gerlach who in the Prussian chamber from the beginning of the revision of the constitution onward has continually led the struggle against codification: see his speech of September 8th, 1849, and many later.

Chapter 5: Regarding the Distinction Between Constitutional and Other Laws

§. 84. The Proper Import of the Distinction

<201> The distinction between basic laws (*lois fondamentales*) or constitutional laws and other laws, as has been explained, is grounded in the nature of the matter and therefore has been in use in science for some time; among others, it was used by the great exponents of the state law of the German Empire.[113] In terms of sanctity, many other laws are the equal of basic laws, as for example the law regarding monogamy, children's right of succession. But the basic laws are also the precondition and the guarantee of all others, and they exist in the character not merely of laws but of national entitlement. For this reason there is due them a special guarantee and honor, and a special constancy. This is the purpose of the distinction.

But the most profitable condition is for this distinction to assert itself only in the general legal consciousness and in living valuation, not in a different manner of legal treatment; for it is the case both that the border between fundamental and other laws is fluid, and that among fundamental laws themselves there is not a slight gradation in importance and dignity. This is the older manner. So stood matters in the German Empire, so they stand in England. In England there is legally no distinction between constitutional and other laws. Law is law. The laws of all sorts fall under the same conditions of amendment, and the king swears not to the constitution but to the laws of the kingdom. But in the legal consciousness of the nation, there is an <202> essential distinction. The stipulations of Magna Charta, the Declaration of Rights, the right of representation of the various counties and cities, etc., are certainly not viewed as being as easily amended as a regular civil law or a law regulating the public welfare. And this distinct valuation in the legal consciousness achieves the same thing as the formal complication of the amendment process, and it achieves it more naturally,

---

[113] J. J. Moser, *Teutsches Staatsrecht* [German State Law], I, p. 51; Puetter, *inst. jur. publ.* cap. 5.

in that it dovetails with the degree of dignity of the law concerned.[114] In the older German territorial state law, there is most certainly the legal distinction between laws concerning territorial freedoms, which are subject to the consent of the estates, and other laws which are only subject to their advice. But this distinction in its demarcation and consequences is connected not so much with the notions of the basic law as with the notions of the special privileges (*jura singulorum*) of the estates, and at any rate has no place where the other laws require the consent of the territorial representation.

§. 85. How to Apply the Distinction, and How Not to

The constitutions given in Germany since 1817, on the other hand, usually decree a distinction in the formal legal treatment between constitutional and other laws. The same holds true, as is self-evident, not merely of the initially given constitutional charter, but also of all later laws on which, upon enactment, the <203> character of constitutional law is conferred. The most common such regulations are the following: that only the constitution is sworn to, not the other laws – that amendment of the constitution is subject to greater difficulty (two-thirds vote or repeated votes are required, a proposal can only proceed from the crown, etc.) – that no other law should be given that conflicts with, partially repeals, or indirectly changes the constitution. The purpose of these regulations is the guarantee, venerableness, and continuity of the constitution. The natural constitutions carry these in themselves; the newly fashioned have them provided by law, or at least the attempt is made to do so. There is therefore in itself and in general nothing to argue against their appropriateness. But under the

[114] English state law [Staatsrecht] does contain complications to the amendment process. So, e.g., according to resolutions of the House of Commons, in matters of religion or trade or taxation, a bill cannot be brought before the House before the motion has been examined and approved by a committee of the entire house. Kingship and peerage are so guaranteed by a law of Charles II that the mere assertion of that law's dispensability is a capital crime. But the complications hold, as this makes clear, only for a few especially designated objects, and do not at all follow from the demarcation of constitutional from other laws. Even the Roman *leges sacratae,* which both the solemn oath sworn by all citizens to them and the outlaw status set for their infringement, distinguished them from other laws, were entirely specific stipulations, not a category of laws, and, in particular, not the epitome of basic laws.

given conditions or in this manner of implementation, they are subject to reservations.

Firstly, complication of the amendment process is only fruitful when the constitution, as it stands, merits preservation; but precisely with these new constitutions, which have arisen in doctrinaire or even revolutionary manner, amendment should instead be made easier, in order to be able to eliminate the many inappropriate, even ruinous things that they contain – "the broad stamp of their origin" – before the damage is done. Complication was arranged on good grounds in the period of 1817, in order to set a limit to the urge to progress of the political movement; now, though, the opposite holds true, a curative reaction should be allowed free rein. Secondly, the formal distinction of both categories ever assumes a constitutional charter, in that, outside of such a charter, complete uncertainty exists as to what is constitutional law and what is not; it therefore locks public law in the form of codification for all time, and contains from the beginning a disparagement of tradition, even when the most important constitutional principles rest thereupon, as against written laws. These reservations are disposed of when the complication of amendment is pronounced not only for "constitutional laws" as a category but for specific laws or specifically indicated objects (e.g., laws concerning the rights of the crown and chambers or the church, etc.), for which England already provides an example (note 114 above). Beyond this, not much is achieved. One may decree constitutions, but **<204>** one cannot decree venerableness and continuity for those constitutions. This can be done only through their content, and the preservation thereof in life, for which reason constitutions variously maintain themselves in accordance with their regulations. So, e.g., in Prussia, a petition to abolish hereditary monarchy would founder not on the requirement of a two-thirds vote but on the immediate outburst of indignation; by contrast, the petition to abolish the entire constitutional charter was debated in 1852 and 1853 in all calm and circumspection. One might still legally treat the constitution as a "mere number in the law gazette," but for those who truly are concerned with the respect and devotion of the nation, its honor will nevertheless be maintained, and for the rest, all such provisos are in vain.

As for the provision that no other law may nullify [derogiren] the constitutional charter, it runs contrary to the living mutual effect of laws which is grounded in nature, according to which the new law has innumerable relations to the most varied other laws, partly touching them, restricting them, otherwise taking after them. It therefore on the one hand faces the legislator with the awkward task of having to formulate ahead of time and artificially the relation of the new law to the relevant law in the constitutional charter, a relation which would naturally arise in its application, and on the other hand forms a restriction for laws, the necessity for which one recognizes the urgency but which cannot easily be brought into systematic unity with the stipulations, especially clauses, of the constitutional charter.[115] Beyond this, in this procedure one is **<205>** usually led

[115] The matter concerned here is this: The constitutional charter states e.g. that "the municipalities have *elected* ruling authorities." Now then, in a law concerning the municipal ordinance for certain areas the office of *hereditary* sheriff is restored. This law would then be considered not to be an (indirect) alteration and restriction of that rule in the constitutional charter, but a contradiction of it, and therefore could not be passed, not even under the terms of a constitutional amendment (two-thirds vote or repeated vote). Rather, in order to pass it, one would have to change the constitution in that point in order to remove the contradiction. Hereby one runs into difficulties which at times are virtually insoluble (for example: "municipalities and provinces are to have *elected* ruling authorities, excluding hereditary sheriffs in certain areas of Province X and the municipalities consisting in day laborers and excluding the independent part of the manorial lords in the district assemblies"), or one resorts to the time-honored proviso by which the ordinance is made colorless ("the municipalities have *elected* ruling authorities. *The law determines exceptions.*"). By contrast, in England there is no objection to, e.g., a new law in certain cases disposing of trial by jury without thereby altering the general assurance of trial by jury in Magna Charta and the Declaration of Rights.

I myself was the first to express the principle of the inadmissibility of indirect amendment of the Prussian constitutional charter, prior to any amendment being proposed (session of the first chamber, January 29th, 1850), not on the basis of a political principle, but in terms of the Prussian constitutional charter. I have explained the treatment technique required for this in the report on the law on ministerial accountability (session of April 9th, 1851). One and the same vote must decide upon both the provision of the new law that is against the constitution and the amendment of the constitution – that is, at the same time. But the constitutional party goes much further (session of February 23rd, 1852). It demanded (in express opposition to my assertion of simultane-

by the intention of maintaining the constitution as something unhistorical, timeless, self-contained, while the other laws develop further in a living, changing manner, according to which one enacts alterations in the constitutional charter, not as a new constitutional law, as a constitutional novel, but retroactively corrects it in the constitutional charter itself: "Sections 23–25 of the constitutional charter are abolished; *the following stipulations take their place.*"

§. 86. The Distinction Falsely Understood

Something entirely other than the distinction between constitutional and other laws in the sense described here is that which the Revolution has brought about. Here the constitution is considered to be the primeval act by which the people first establish the state itself and institute its ruling authorities and powers, while the other laws proceed from these ruling authorities and powers. In this way, then, constitution does not mean fundamental law, constitutional law, but *constituting,* i.e., *state-establishing* law. In this sense, one therefore also sets

---

ity) that the amendment to the constitution must precede any debate of a law contrary to it. It remained unclear whether this preceding amendment should be understood as an act of legislative power or only as a resolution of the chamber concerned. The former alone is the logical consequence. Because as long as the constitution is in force, it would be an act of treason [Attentat] to pass, or even to discuss, a law that contradicts it. But in both cases the demand is unworkable, because it would risk voting to amend the constitution without the law being adopted, the purpose for which and in the assumption of which it is being voted for. I have demonstrated this in the report with an example. Incidentally, it goes without saying that if a later law not only amends a provision of the constitution but also renders the relevant relationship unregulated, a regulation must be provided for this at the same time. If, for example, the constitution says, "The Chamber shall consist of ninety members, namely the mayors of the twenty cities, etc.," and under the new municipal ordinance five cities are to lose their municipal rights and their mayors, then at the same time an order must also be issued regarding the members of the Chamber. But this would have to occur even if that provision were not in the constitution but in a mere electoral ordinance; this follows generally from the mutual relationship of the laws, not only from the relationship between constitutional and other laws. The impossibility of a prior amendment of the constitution, when it is still uncertain whether the municipal ordinance will be adopted afterward, is also evident from this example.

constituting (i.e., state-establishing) assemblies against legislative assemblies. This is the implementation of the natural-law theory regarding the establishment of the state: entry into the civil condition from the state of nature by a contract of all with all. According to this distinction, the constitution rests on an *entirely* <206> *different authority* than the other laws, the latter on the authority of the existing state power (king, national representation), the former on the authority of the masses, which themselves first set up the latter. The aim of the distinction therefore is also entirely different: not to endow the constitutional law with greater dignity and continuity, but to ensure the subjects, the people, to whom alone is due the erection of the state and establishment of the constitution, their rights. It also yields entirely different consequences than those mere difficulties of amendment. To wit, the constitution is not to be amended by the existing state power, king and territorial representation, but only by the people, either through direct vote in the primeval assembly, or (through diluted implementation of principles) by means of representatives for which they give instructions or at least are elected precisely for this purpose.[116] In like manner came the demand in the instruction [cahier] of Paris in 1789, as also in the later sessions of the National Assembly; indeed, even the royalists resorted to these principles, in order thereby to thwart the decisions of the National Assembly (Maurice). And vice versa, for the amendment, or at least the establishment, of the constitution, the people is not to be bound to the consent or opposition of the existing state power, as Mirabeau clearly stated in his speech regarding the veto; the veto is due the king only for legislation, while the constitution, which in concept the people gives to itself, cannot, as is self-evident, be subject to a veto. The same standpoint as Mirabeau was taken by the constitutional party in the German National Assembly. It intended to grant veto power to the Kaiser regarding future legislation, but would recognize no monarchical veto for the constituting of Germany.

---

[116] So for example according to the constitution of Belgium, the legislative power (the king and both houses) cannot decide on any changes in the constitution but only declare that one of its provisions needs revision. Once that is declared, both houses are *ipso jure* (*de plein droit*) dissolved, and only the newly elected representatives (thus ad hoc mandated by the voters) together with the king may pass the proposed amendment, by two-thirds vote in each chamber.

<207> The distinction of constitutional and other laws in this sense, as stands to reason, is nothing other than the application of the doctrine of popular sovereignty. Consistently implemented, it is the dissolution of the state; even in weakened implementation, such as in Belgium, it is always a proclamation of false principles and therefore a corruption of public sentiment when the subjects of the state view themselves as the state-constituting power. The agitation of the people during elections to constituting assemblies (among which are also numbered those called for the revision or amendment of the constitution) was demonstrated to us in Germany by the most recent experience.

When the distinction between constitutional and other laws usual in the German constitutions is fully separated from the revolutionary distinction, it is still not entirely free of those influences. The indignation regarding amendment, and the so highly elevated requirement that the fundamental law must be changed *before* a deviating law may be approved, is still consciously or unconsciously determined partly by the theory that the constitution erects the state and therefore is of an entirely different sort than other laws. Here is the true relation: the state is an original and self-contained institution over the people, and state power, as one and the same authority based solely on itself, gives all laws, those over the other conditions as well as those over the constitution, i.e., even over itself.

§. 87. The Distinction is Fundamental to Federalism

For *a union of states* [Staatenverein] (confederation, federation) the distinction between constituting and other laws, constituting and legislative assemblies, is entirely apropos and historically also first arose in them (in America).

The union of states is built by states originally sovereign, and even afterward to a certain degree sovereign, thus not subjected to federal power. It is therefore not, like the simple state, an original and self-existing whole; it actually is first established through contractual convening (of course, not of individuals but of states) and <208> through the federal law (act of union). With the union of states, therefore, it is actually another subject upon whose authority the federal constitution rests and upon whose authority the laws which proceed from it are based, the former on the authority of the sovereign states, the latter on the authority of the federal power. For this reason, in terms of law and the nature of the case, the federal constitution cannot be amended by the federal power, but only through the independent states which erected it. In particular, the federal power cannot possibly be entitled to make amendments by which the federal power is extended further, and the independence of the individual states is restricted further, than the limits consented to at the establishment of the federation. For the union of states, it is therefore appropriate and in fact necessary that amendments of the federal constitution be given only through consent of all participating states, thus in *constituting* and not legislative manner.[117] The distinction between constituting and other laws, constituting and legislative assemblies, is therefore only valid for international relations. Its application in France to the internal state constitution has made every Frenchman into a sovereign state and made France into an international-legal union of these twenty million Frenchmen.

---

[117] So, for example, in Germany the federal assembly, where it treats of fundamental laws, *jura singulorum* [particular rights or special privileges], affairs of religion, organic federal institutions and ordinances of common utility (as through which likewise a new restriction of sovereignty manifests itself) decides (decided) in constituting fashion, i.e., only with the unanimity of all states, while over all other matters it does so in legislative fashion, i.e., through procedural majority vote. In North America, where the union of states had more of an impulse toward unity, the principle was maintained, albeit in somewhat moderated fashion. For amendments to the union constitution, the proposal had to proceed from two-thirds of the votes in both houses of Congress, or from two-thirds of the legislative bodies of the states, and for it to become law, it required the approval of three-fourths of the states (in their legislative bodies, or assemblies especially called to that end). But the equal voting rights of the states in the Senate are entirely off-limits to the federal power [i.e., cannot be removed via amendment].

Chapter 6: The Oath to the Constitution and the Cure of Destructive Constitutions

§. 88. The Significance of the Oath

<209> A guarantee of the legal order in the state, especially from those upon whom its maintenance depends, is a natural necessity and therefore has always existed. To this pertain the documentary confirmations of territorial freedoms in accessions to government, the assurance on princely word and honor. Now the oath is the acme of these guarantees. To swear this oath specifically to the fundamental law is certainly the most harmless of all the distinctions attributed to it above other laws. For indirectly this implies the observance of all other laws, and everywhere in life the meaning arises that, above all, one does not wish to violate the order of the authorities from whom the laws emanate, and consequently also the laws emanating from them. This is indisputably the meaning of the oath sworn to *the laws in their entirety* in England, in that the king swears "to govern the people of this Kingdom according to the statutes *in Parliament agreed on,* and the laws and customs of the same." And, certainly, in the German states according to the most recent constitutions, the oath sworn to the *constitution alone* had no other significance than this. Even the question as to whether one swore to the constitutional *charter* or to the *constitution* is of no interest in terms of legal consequence, when otherwise the constitutional charter recognizes the older law as continuing, insofar as it is not specifically repealed. For the relationship of this document to the other parts of the constitution is necessarily determined in both cases by the constitution itself as the supreme or at least the most recent law. To swear to the constitution in its entirety, and not merely to the charter alone, has the interest of leaving no room for the misconception that the law exists <210> only in and by virtue of the charter.[118] With

---

[118] As is well known, this was a matter of party strife in Prussia in 1849. On the one hand, it was emphatically asserted that it is not the constitutional charter that is being invoked, but the entire constitution (i.e. including older estates' rights, etc.), while the other (liberal) side objected to this with the same degree of emphasis. I stated at the very beginning of the dispute that it did not have the significance that is attributed to it, and

the older type, the prince swears an oath to the constitution while the country swears allegiance and obedience to the prince. The state here manifests itself as a bond of mutual personal rights; hence, the country guarantees the prince his supremacy, while the prince guarantees the country its rights. In this manner, in the German Empire only the emperor swore allegiance to the electoral charter [Wahlkapitulation] and the rights of the empire, while the estates of the empire,

---

that the reason why the conservatives can take the oath of allegiance to the constitution with a clear conscience and without contradicting their political creed is not because one swears by the whole constitution and not merely the document, but rather that one swears only by the laws of the constitution, not by its real or supposed tendencies and motives (meeting of the First Chamber, 17 Dec. 1849 and 29 Jan. 1850). It seems to me that this was confirmed by the outcome. When the legality of the restoration of the district and provincial assemblies, something that the charter does not mention, was later (1850) debated, the question of application would have arisen whether or not the same were included in the sworn constitution. Regardless, that debate was not influenced by this. Rather, the decision could be based on and was also sought by both parties only on whether the 1850 charter had repealed the earlier provincial statutes or not. In the former case, it did not help that it was also invoked as part of the Prussian constitution, because the 1850 constitution always remained the newer and stronger law; in the latter case, it existed by right, even if only the charter had been invoked, precisely according to the charter itself, since it confirmed the older laws (Art. 109). The situation would have been different only if one of the parties had asserted that the document of 1850 itself – whether in its entirety or in some of its points – should not have been issued because of the conflicting right of the provincial assemblies, i.e., that it had in fact repealed them, or should not have repealed them. But then it would not have been enough to extend the oath of allegiance to the entire constitution, even outside the document; rather, the oath to the document of 1850 itself, as an unlawfully issued document, should not have been taken at all. But where a state's charter declares all public law to be repealed except for the charter itself, there is indeed a diametrical contradiction between swearing an oath to the entire (historically inherited) constitution and swearing an oath to the charter. In this case, it is not possible to swear an oath to the charter as part of the constitution, but one either swears an oath to the whole historically inherited constitution with the exclusion of the charter, or to the charter with the exclusion of this constitution.

and only those with an imperial fief, swore the oath of allegiance to him. Therefore, in the German territories only the prince confirmed the constitution (territorial freedoms) while the country swore fealty. In precisely this sense, in England still today the constitution (the laws) is sworn to by the king, not by subjects, officials, members of parliament. The latter rather swear the oath of allegiance.

Yet, as it is true progress for the state to be recognized as a common higher order and task over prince and people, so is it appropriate that now as well territorial representatives, officials, subjects promise observance of the constitution alongside allegiance and obedience to the prince.[119] This oath to the constitution by all means contains a restriction of the oath of fealty – which is why those in military service are not to take it – yet in no less degree than the old oath of fealty in the German territories (and still in England), through the connection which fealty has to the territorial sovereign confirmation of freedoms. For this reason, those who take the oath stand in no other relation to the constitution than that which is entailed in their vocation anyway; thus, in particular, the oath does not give officials the right to judge the constitutionality of the prince or their superiors (see the following chapter). **<211>**

§. 89. The Imprudence of Oaths to Flawed Constitutions

When, accordingly, the oath to the constitution in general is justified, the oath to any particular constitution may not be so, in particular not to the kind of constitutions being issued in recent times. When formerly the prince swore to the territorial freedoms, either ancient or consented to for the first time, it was beyond any suspicion. He could infallibly keep his oath if only he wished to do so conscientiously. The same is not true with constitutions which all at once give the state an entirely new form according to a new doctrine and give overwhelming power to a hitherto unknown and unproven element. It is a mere experiment which no one knows will work. In particular, this holds true for constitutions

---

[119] That the imperial chamber court members swore *"to judge"* according to imperial laws as well as relevant territorial ordinances lies in the nature of the judges' oath; by contrast, it can be seen as a transition to the new constitutional oath on the part of officials that the imperial privy counselors swore "… *to heed* … the imperial electoral charter besides the common written laws … and as best and most usefully *to counsel* His Majesty."

which include one-man, one-vote elections, annual tax and budget refusal by the houses, unlimited right of association and assembly, and the like. There is no assurance that a body politic can be joined with a radical popular representation and unlimited individual freedom, but rather the opposite. But it is contrary to piety to call upon God as witness and avenger for a commitment regarding which, at the moment of acceptance, one has doubts as to whether it can be fulfilled. The lesser the guarantee a constitution provides for order and ruling authority, the greater the presumption in swearing an oath to it. The most reasonable and ethical thing to occur from the Revolution of 1789 up to now is that no one swore an oath to the constitution of 1848 – excepting the president of the republic. What a plethora of oath-breaking was thereby spared!

§. 90. A Sworn Oath is a Binding Oath

But if such a constitution is sworn to, then it also stands under the sanctity of the oath, like any other. The poor condition of a constitution does not make it invalid, and the oath sworn to it non-binding. When it otherwise rightfully exists, it cannot, even if not sworn to, be overthrown without violating law, and beyond that, where it is sworn to, not without oath-breaking. It is **<212>** erroneous doctrine which has it that the oath to such constitutions as were engendered in the year 1848 should be non-binding because it conflicts with God's command and order ("the duties to God"). For there is no immediate and unconditional command of God regarding forms of constitution. Although political truths are grounded in God's command and order and their violation in the year of the Revolution sprang from ungodly [gottwidrigen] sentiments – unbelief, unwillingness respecting obedience, discipline, and subordination – this knowledge is nevertheless ever mediated by human opinion, and its application is conditioned by the character of the situation. It is not written in the same way: "thou shalt not have one-man-one-vote, annual refusal to consent to taxes, separation of the legislative and executive power," as it is written, "thou shalt not have false gods, shalt not commit murder, adultery," etc.; and the same political establishment can be lawful and good in America, but rebellious and destructive in Europe. For this reason, it is sin to implement such a constitution but not sin to live under it, and while a duty exists to work to amend it with all appropriate means, a competence to dispose of it contrary to law and oath does not. The vocation of the ruling authority extends no farther than its right, its legal power. Moreover, under that doctrine there would be no limit to the extent to which a constitution would be in accordance with God's command and therefore binding. One-man-one-vote, Prussian property classes, semi-estates constitution [halbständische Verfassung] prior to 1848, the Haller-Gentz estates system – likewise rights of the chambers in English-Belgian manner, in the manner of the German constitution of 1817, mere advisory chambers, or in fact no chambers – where is, where begins, the godliness here? If one constitution cannot generally be prescribed as dogma, then another cannot be declared non-binding because unconditionally heretical. In the most extreme cases, because the constitution has led to anarchy, to the impossibility of all government, to the danger of collapse outwardly or inwardly, the prince, according to the most supreme law of self-preservation of the state, may be forced unilaterally to abolish it, in which case it at least was preceded by the breach of oath or fealty from the other side. But this occurs only because of the constitution's actually manifested result, not because of a judgment regarding its character and according to mere political doctrine, be it ever so trenchant; and it occurs as an emergency, and never without wounding the conscience, not as the application of a straightforward ethical principle.[120]

---

[120] Compensating for the violation of an oath in abolishing a constitution by having the prince first perform an act of public penance [Bußakt] for the sin of having allowed such a constitution in the first place, is no way out of the problem. Misgivings should already be aroused by the fact that such is not a means to which one may resort as a matter of personal discretion in order to dissolve well-founded obligations. But in itself the means is based on an insufficient conception of penance. Penance [Buße] is not the mere confession of a committed sin, but also the inward permeation of this realization and thereby the determination voluntarily to bear the consequences of this sin for oneself and to remedy them in the world through endeavor and self-sacrifice. A prince who has sworn to a radical constitution and truly does penance for it should not enact such penance through a public spectacle but, in the way of loyalty in steadfast composure under inward prayer, to apply all his actions and aspirations to the gradual remediation of the damage of the constitution. Through the example of irreproachable conduct and conscientious fulfillment of the duties of rulership, through the testing of a mind bound to God without regard for human applause, through reflection and scrupulousness in measures and choice of servants, to struggle in such laborious work undaunted by diffi-

§. 91. The Remedy for Flawed Constitutions: Amendment

The damage from constitutions stemming from the Revolution therefore can only be remedied *by due process of law* through *amendment* (or *repeal*).

This has – even with sworn constitutions – no hindrance and no limits. It does not violate the *assumed obligation and the oath sworn to it.* For it is not against the constitution, but in accordance with the constitution, and where everyone with a right to determine the constitution of the country (king and both chambers) is in agreement, no obligation can be violated.

It does not violate *piety to the constitution as such.* For piety is owed only to legal relations and ethical bonds, not to a charter. As it <214> itself is only something externally juridical, it stands only under external juridical considerations. In terms of content, however, a constitution the essence of which is totally to reorder the state in terms of the momentary plans of men, apart from any consideration of what already exists and the venerability thereof – one which is totally constructed on impiety – cannot be the object of piety.

Neither does lawful amendment violate *faithfulness to the people;* for the constitution is not a promise to the people outside of its legal representation, and faithfulness to the people calls for the remedy, not the maintenance, of injurious institutions.

Finally, just because it accords with an intention contrary to that which prevailed at the introduction, it does not violate *fairness to the party loyal to the constitution.* For the constitution is a law, not a peace treaty of parties regarding intentions to be observed; fairness therefore only obligates to its ordinances, not its intentions, and the same freedom which the then-dominant party had, to follow its intention regarding the constitution when it was introduced, is enjoyed by the other party now in power, to follow its own, contrary, intention to amend it.

Accordingly, just as the lawful amendment of the constitution violates no consideration of duty, so does it also by no means infringe *political wisdom* which holds that one should avoid shocks to the public legal consciousness and "allow the young tender plant first to take root." For a shock to the legal consciousness is only effected by the amendment of historically constructed, time-

---

culties and hindrances – that would be true penance. It is not true penance to remove a sworn constitution as easily as it was given: by the stroke of a pen.

tested order, not the amendment of a new artificial constituting of the state, and least of all when it concerns the restoration of the old natural historical order. Knocking out natural teeth gives a shock; removing artificial teeth does not. Neither will such a new constitution take root over time, as did the one it displaced. It is not the distinction between young and old, but the distinction between natural-historical and manufactured. A palisade can stand for a long time, yet for all that it will not become a forest.

The only real restrictions on amendment are the *acquired rights* founded by the new constitution. Yet one ought not to consider freedoms and capacities ordered merely in the character of public institutions and political principles, without specific guarantee to **<215>** specific participants, to be acquired rights. Thus, in particular, it is an erroneous viewpoint to hold that general suffrage and, above all, the equal voting right of all independent inhabitants of the country, as an acquired right cannot be abolished.

The resistance to any amendment out of pure reverence to the constitution, as was the peculiar characteristic of the Feuillants (*amis de la constitution,* 1791), rests on the erroneous ethical viewpoint of holding the humanly constructed charter as such to be sacred, rather than the bonds grounded in nature, and on the erroneous political viewpoint, that what matters is only having any sort of legal order, as opposed to the arbitrary power of the prince, and, finally, on the factual delusion that one can keep a constitution of whatever sort, as long as one wishes to do so. The latter delusion was natural with the initial attempt in 1791, and the reverence for the constitution on the part of the Feuillants was certainly meant uprightly. They defended the constitution against all parties. Currently, the program of a sacred unchangeable constitution is usually only a pretext to protect the liberal achievement against the monarchical-conservative movement, and the adherents thereof willingly lend a hand when amendments to the constitution implement liberal principles.

The lawful amendment offers various methods: *complete abolition* of the constitution (by due process of law) is, of course, called for where the constitution has entirely fallen under revolutionary principles. So, e.g., with the constitution of 1791, where nothing else could be done with it. Apart from this, though, the question is whether in general to forswear the territorial representation and the guarantees put under its protection, which is a question that falls under the judgment regarding absolute monarchy (see ch. 14 below). The *revision* of the constitution, i.e., repeated discussion of the collective articles with an eye to recovery or improvement, is a *counter-codification,* and therefore is as unadvisable as was the initial codification. Precisely to this category belongs the plan to transform the constitution, via a legislative act, into individual assurances (territorial freedoms). The proper manner of recovery is therefore the *amendment in details* where the need makes itself felt, and among these in partic- **<216>** ular the "*occasional amendment*," i.e., that which is brought about in order to be able to enact a special law recognized as necessary.

Chapter 7: Public Offices

§. 92. Public Officials as Supplementary to the Prince

<217> To the prince, public offices [Staatsämter] are partly advisory, partly means of implementation with regard to the maintenance of public conditions under him; and they are so, not as mere personal aides to him ("in partem sollicitudinis ejus vocati"), but as the institutional members of the state, the supreme ruling member of which is the prince. For the prince as sovereign guarantees the power of supreme decision, the innermost personality of the state, while the officials guarantee the forces of insight and expertise, themselves developed as organs in the polity, in order to arrive at the proper decision and bring it to special realization, in order for the various relations to receive their necessary and regulated care. As such, they supplement the princes to form complete state rule, but not in separated manner, with the prince affording only regard and sanction, the officials affording intelligence and thus content to rule, but in the extension of his intelligence in organic permeation; for without his own insight, the sovereign cannot evaluate the advice of the officials so as to decide for himself. For this reason, the prince and his officials together form one undivided "government" [Regierung] (*Gouvernement*). The prince is the supreme ruling will in the state, while the officials (excluding judges) can only act in accordance with his commands and must obey them if they wish to remain in their offices. But just as expansion through officials lies in the organic construction of the state, so is the prince for his part bound to their mediation. In the developed constitution, he cannot rule otherwise than by taking on the advice of officials (ministers, council of state), and through the medium thereof, i.e., by issuing an order to the appropriate office; he can do this precisely as sovereign, not as private lord. Thus, in particular, the <218> principle of the necessary ministerial countersignature has the significance not merely of guarding against violation of the constitution, but also no less of guarding against unadvised decisions of the prince and against disorder in the use of administrative organs (direct princely command to a subordinate official). Because of this latter significance, the countersignature has become a legal form even in non-constitutional states.

The offices, therefore, stand in a hierarchy of super- and subordination and in a distribution in terms of districts, departments and branches of activity, as a mutually intertwined structure, the supreme ruling unity of which is the prince.

§. 93. Nevertheless They are Servants of the State

The officials therefore are *princely servants,* for they are simple organs of the sovereign will and are obligated to personal obedience and faithfulness to the prince. But they are not personal servants; rather, they are servants of him as sovereign, thus to the degree that he is identical to the state (§. 71), and thus *state servants.* This is what Haller and his school dispute. According to their conception, the officials are *mere* princely servants, and thus to be distinguished from court servants or private servants of the prince, only because the one is given one job, the other another (the former the care for the common welfare, etc., the latter for the stable, the kitchen, festivities), similar to the coachman and the bookkeeper in the house of a banker. There can therefore be no question of another obligation than the will of the prince, and the law can have no other meaning for them than an instruction of service given them by the prince. In reality, however, the officials serve the prince as organic members of the polity, in accordance with its laws. Just as the will of the sovereign and the law together form the supreme power in the state (§. 53), so, and in the same manner, are the officials serviceable to both together. In particular, they must both apply the law, apart from specific princely command, directly across a broad range of **<219>** their official activity, and plead for it against princely command, through remonstration, refusal, resignation, in accordance with their position. For the individual subordinate official is of course in the end obligated to adhere to the principle of subordination, but the organism of officials as a whole, thus in their supreme members, as being a supplementation of the sovereign, must have a (negative) independence against him, a duty of refusal, where law and right are violated. Such a duty of officials to the law exists everywhere as a matter of course.[121] Peculiar to the contemporary (constitutionalist [konstitutionellen])

---

[121] "What, then, if a territorial lord commands a committee [Kollegio], council, official, officer, etc., to do something which one knows to be contrary to the territorial constitution? He who fears God more than man, or is otherwise an honorable man, refuses with humility and does not do it but rather suffers under that which he cannot change.

development of the constitution – apart from the greater extension of the law – is the express oath of officials to the law and constitution, and their accountability to the estates. This oath does not abolish the relation of subordination among the officials with the consequences thereof. However, that relation only entails obedience in the case of infringing the law in particulars, not regarding the abrogation of the constitution as a whole. Certainly, in constitutional charters the oath is everywhere intended to be a guarantee against this.

§. 94. Proper Arrangements for the Tenure of Officials

Officials are to be appointed in terms of *capacity,* the decisive factor for public office being insight and expertise, just as, for the throne, it is strength and loftiness of regard. As little, then, as the prince is to be appointed in terms of capacity (§. 70), just as little are officials to be appointed according to birth. But at the level closest to <220> immediate implementation, the office quite appropriately combines affinity to the conditions to be addressed with an objective orientation.

Should accession to office be considered a civic duty, then it should affect all equally, and thus only temporarily be assumed, and so it usually is in republics, in that here the magistracy, as co-bearer of sovereignty, cannot without danger be made permanent. Should, on the contrary, the office exist as enduring life vocation, as estate, then accession must be a matter of free will. In monarchical states, this must be the rule. The same continuity of government which characterizes monarchy also requires continuity of public office. Periodic appointment of the same is therefore contrary to the essence of monarchy and is a lower stage of political institutions generally.

Appointment to and dismissal from public office must accrue to the sovereign by virtue of the unity (personality) of state power. On that basis, public officials cannot have an irrevocable right (*jus quaesitum*) to the office itself, i.e.,

---

But because few think in this manner, which is the way things are [so geht es halt wie es geht], at the great Day of Judgment it will go the way it goes [wird es ... gehen wie es gehen wird] for the one who commanded and for the one who obeyed." Johann Jacob Moser, *Von der teutschen Reichs-Stände Länden* [Of the German Imperial Estates Territories], p. 1157.

its functions.[122] An irrevocable right to the allocated salary, entirely or in part, and to the rank, i.e., the recognition of capacity for the office, is due him, which straightaway becomes a part of his personal quality, and protects him from being demoted to a lesser category of service. This is the principle of the *irremovability* [Unentfernbarkeit] *of officials.* It is imperative both by the consideration of officials, who have devoted their education and life-activity to the state with the relinquishment of other income, and by the consideration of the public well-being, that officials maintain their independence through a secure position, both from below against bribery, and from above against unlawful commands. Self-sufficiency [Nichtsbedürftigkeit], independence, form part of the vocation of ruler. As this is valid in supreme degree for the prince, so it is also in lesser degree for officials. Nor does the estates-oriented constitution exclude this principle, if the monarchical prin- **<221>** ciple rules in it. But this must have a limit (always excluding judges), even in a monarchy without estates. Otherwise the unity and energy of the government is threatened from the other side. The sovereign must have unfettered power to transfer officials, to relieve them of their office, to put them in retirement, in fact, even to withdraw a certain portion of income in this case. I cannot but praise the Bavarian distinction between an estates salary and a civil service salary (even if the latter, as opposed to the former, is excessive) as a happy medium.

Should irremovability exist to the extent that officials cannot be transferred apart from fault and judicial sentence, cannot be removed from activities, cannot lose any portion of their income, then there is no remedy for incapacity or mediocrity, then the middling and lower ranks are always in a position to thwart the intentions of the central government, even if only through lackluster fulfillment, for how can proceedings be conducted against this, even if only disciplinary? Then every office is an impregnable castle to defy the sovereign, similarly to vassals of yore. A civil service arrangement of this sort has not yet existed in history until this point. In terms of the older German establishment, offices could be granted subject to notice [auf Kündigung] or permanently, according to what the prince agrees to do, but even with permanent grant of office, the officials only have a right against removal of salary and dishonorable discharge,

---

[122] In many German states, even the judges have no right to their functions, but simply to rank and salary. It is otherwise regarding English chief justices.

not against dismissal at pleasure in general; this is indubitably in accordance with supreme-court findings [reichsgerichtlichen Erkenntnissen].[123] In terms of the French establishment (in certain degree the English as well), the offices are entirely dismissible at will.

Finally, it is a political monstrosity likewise to ensure access to the chambers to such absolutely irremovable officials. That is to erect in the administration itself an opposition to the adminis- **<222>** tration, which neutralizes it and restores in another, much more dubious manner the rule of the bureaucrats [Beamtenherrschaft] which one wished to mitigate by means of the estates system.

The principle of irremovability lends to the civil service a *private-legal aspect.* But it is by no means a mere contractual relationship (*locatio operarum*)[124]; rather, it is originally and as a whole a public relationship, hence not only the way the office is administered, but also the claims of the official are governed by public laws that do not allow for contractual changes, e.g. the principle of irremovability itself, from which no waiver is possible. The private-legal aspect is only expressed in the fact that the acquired rights of the civil servant have the character of private law, which cannot be waived, and that private stipulations between the government and civil servants are permissible within the basic constitutional provisions.

§. 95. The Personality of the Prince and of the State

Sovereignty (unity and concentration) is first realized through the organism of state offices; for only through it is the entire administration serviceable to the supreme single will. On the other hand, the public character of the state, the guarantee of it as institution, rests no less on it, so that the objective intelligence and objective motive, the requirement and necessity of the matter everywhere determine the government of the state. Hereby, then, is the personality of the government of the state completed. The prince rules as personal supreme will,

---

[123] Johann Jacob Moser, *Von der Landeshoheit im Weltlichen* [Regarding Territorial Supremacy in Temporal Affairs], p. 129; Cramer, *Wetzlarische Nebenstunden* [Wetzlar After-Hours], Vol. 38, p. 81.

[124] This was the older conception, according to which irremovability was viewed simply as an affair of agreement, and debate only concerned whether, in the case of doubt, notice or permanence should be assumed in the contract (Moser, Cramer, Strube, et al.).

but on the basis of law as the ethos of the state, and through the medium of public offices as bearers of the powers of judgment and needs resting in the constitution itself, in accordance with their spheres [Sphären]. The personality of the prince thereby becomes <223> an objective personality, the personality of the state.[125] The element of the constitution which now is formed by public offices was fulfilled, in the time of feudalism, by the manorial lords (vassals). Accordingly, the care for the public condition under the princes was an appendage of landed property, and a consequence of a personal power over the inhabitants of the soil, thus a private entitlement of its bearers, irremovable, under mere private obligation to the prince. This establishment did have the advantage that the ruler (the manorial lord) had an interest in the welfare of the underlings, which is of course a guarantee only as far as this community of interest reaches. Against this, it suffered from the deep flaw that *the public power was not attended to according to public determining principles* (thus also, no division according to activities, but only according to districts, and no integrating organs in terms of expertise, for the consulted advisers and the like are only personal assistants); the *unity and certainty of rule* is lacking (ordinances from the prince encounter poor observance, when not in fact disobedience and resistance); the *subjects,* being subjected to a bare personal private-legal power, want for *right and dignity.*

The civil service is therefore a great advance in the development of states. Through it, the government is everywhere planned, deliberate, intelligent, adequate to the task at hand. The furtherance of the civil service at the expense of

---

[125] When, in accordance with this, personality emerges as a type [Typus] of the state (Book I [*Philosophical Foundations*], §. 6), something Plato recognized in his putting the just state in parallel with the just man, so with Hegel according to his standpoint of the syllogism, or the dialectical law: generality, particularity, and the union of both. From this resulted for him the legislative power, which establishes the general (prince and estates), government power, which applies the law to particular spheres (subsumption), and the princely power (conclusion and unity of both). Now the government power is the significance of public officials. But Hegel's construct does not hit the mark, because officials as a rule do not have to apply the law but execute the free commands and ordinances of the prince; thus they do not so much have as task the application of the general to the particular, but rather execution from the center to the periphery, and, beyond this, they form the prince's council.

the nobility, as lay in the devel- <224> opment of sovereignty, is for that reason everywhere endorsed.[126]

But on the other hand, it entails the danger that the activity of the government becomes severed from actual conditions and popular elements, that is, the exercisers of these offices do not share the same standpoint, do not personally share the interests (they own no landed property, they do not engage in business and trade). Hereby easily emerges a formalism of action and a mechanism contrary to actual interests, so that the service itself becomes the goal rather than the matter which is to be served, and compliance with the ordered conduct of business, closing the file, is considered more important than real assistance. Beyond this, a caste spirit develops within the civil service, and the labored operation of the machine represented by the civil service becomes an insurmountable wall of separation and an inhibition between prince and people. This is not remedied by estates-oriented representation alone, which only incidentally breaks through the mechanism of action without transforming it in its entirety. But this can often be effected by involving the bearers of interests themselves directly in the administration, such that the immediate provision comes partly or entirely to them, while the supreme guidance remains in the hands of the princely officials. In this manner, representation in the government is likewise shifted, in organic permeation. This can occur in manifold ways according to the conditions of the specific country. To this pertains self-governance of local communities and corporations, the consultation of estates delegates in the government (Mecklenburg district administator [Landräthe]), the formation of governing councils from estates members under the leadership of the princely Gouverneur (Belgian provincial administration), the transfer of administrative activities of the province or the district to respected landowners (English Lord Lieutenant, sheriff, Prussian district administrator), the manorial and communal concern for the welfare of the inhabitants [Polizey]. The attending to public business by an estate which stands impartially <225> above the conflicts of interests and has, as its motive, simple truth, justice [Recht], the common welfare, answers to the German condition and German sensibilities; but the moderation of the civil

---

[126] In France, the breakthrough of the feudal power by the civil service did not benefit the condition of the nation, in that the offices were vendible and heritable, and a caste developed around them (*noblesse de robe*).

service through connection with such estates-oriented elements is also beneficial to Germany (§. 31).

The same principle of bare mechanical action from which springs the elimination of all estates-oriented elements from the administration also suits the exaggerated fondness for the *collegial constitution* [kollegiale Verfassung] of offices. Personality is more energetic, more creative, and, by virtue of undivided responsibility, provides in a certain respect even greater guarantee than the college [Kollegium] or much more than the impersonal nature of collegial voting. Where the concern merely is legally to apply established principles, the application of which the one personality must judge no differently from another, then collegial voting is appropriate, thus for higher courts. Likewise is collegial advice appropriate where standing principles are to be established for the future. Apart from this, however, the individual official is everywhere of higher value. This holds true throughout for the administration, and no less so for the lowest courts, which not only must pass sentence, but also give instructions regarding procedures, and engage with the parties.

Chapter 8: The Constitution of the Estates of the Realm

§. 96. The Estates of the Realm as Embodiment of Freedom

<227> The purpose (τέλος) of the constitution of the estates of the realm [der reichsständischen Verfassung] is *political freedom.*

If it lies in the nature of the state, it being an ethical kingdom, to have its power established over the subjects as absolutely exalted, as is achieved most decisively in monarchy, it is on the other hand no less the case that obedience to this power be free, independent, inward, as answering to personal ethical essence. This, and nothing else, is the innermost significance of political freedom. Political freedom therefore does not consist in the people having sovereign power, or they ruling themselves (popular sovereignty, democracy), but in the people being ruled in accordance with *their rights,* i.e., in the recognition of specific competencies and a specific sphere of independence for individuals and for the whole; and that they be ruled on the *basis* of *their own life valuation* (ethos), i.e., that the laws or the supreme principles of government remain connected to this, in their development in the same way as when they originally arose. Nevertheless, the greatest elevation of this freedom, and its most developed guarantee, is for the people *themselves* to have the right and the power of *representing* this through their own act (personally) vis-à-vis the government. Such representation, then, becomes necessary to participation and cooperation in the exercise of state power.

The general law of the ethical world is that obedience is to become internalized, that the moral law is to determine people primarily as the will of God but subsequently no less as their own innermost being and will (I. [*Philosophical Foundations*], §. 32). Just so is the law of the state to exist both as a power *over* the people, as a command proceeding <228> from a higher authority (king), and as a power *in* the people, as a postulate of their own will and acknowledgment.

The organ with the vocation to this representation and cooperation is the *estates of the realm* [Reichsstände]. For as the assembly of the select (the elite) from all estates, they are the *true* and *pure expression* (representation) of the people in accordance with their complete essence, according to all their rights, interests, and wealth [Vermögen], the *true witnesses* of national life valuation, and, as well, the concentration of the people into a single acting subject capable of self-understanding and conscious decision, and, therefore, in control of itself. One might say that in them the innermost idea (proto-image) of the popular existence, the prototype which underlies it in its most widespread extension, has become animatedly personal. Hereby they are a power and authority over the entire people, and nevertheless at the same time one with them, in which they only recognize themselves, and thus are called to act in their name.[127] With that, a bond is created between government and people. For the prince, as simple elevated power over the people, does not share their condition. He may recognize it from sympathy and concern, but it is not his own, he does not recognize it from his own experience; here there is a gap between him and the people. A power of assistance is vouchsafed to the estates which, it belonging to the people themselves, carries their entire interest within it. The estates unite both conditions: that of the subjects, in that they experience the consequence of all public measures along with them, and that of **<229>** the government, in that they participate in the establishment of these measures.[128] They therefore have their own

---

[127] Where there is real representation, power is also due. I have authority to act and to arrange on behalf of the one whose essence (qualities and interests) I carry in myself in full elevated manner. The relation between prince and estates therefore rests on the divergent manner in which they represent the nation. The prince represents the state, the ethical order, which is to exist over persons, thus the nation in its vocation to maintain such an order. The estates represent the people, i.e., the nation in its vocation to obey this order, the persons in their manifold social stations as they are subject to the leading of the state [Staatslenkung] and experience that leading as either beneficial or disadvantageous over them. They therefore do not represent those classes [Klassen] which are themselves organs of this leading (the army and the civil service).

[128] "Therefore in well order'd Commonwealths, where the good of the whole is so considered, as it ought, the *Legislative* Power is put into the hands of divers Persons who duly Assembled, have by themselves, or jointly with others, a Power to make Laws, which when they have done, being separated again, they are themselves subject to the Laws, they have made; which is a new and near tie upon them...." Locke, *Second Treatise of Civil Government,* §. 143. "Being of a middle nature between subject and government." Burke, *Thoughts on the Cause of the Present Discontent.* "Considered as *mediating*

interest and the means to represent the people, and yet, in that they themselves are put in the position of the ruling power and share its demands, likewise the interest and understanding for the decisive considerations of the government. They make it possible for the government to put itself in the condition of the people, and for the people to put themselves in the condition of the government. Through them, therefore, the gap is filled and the people fraternize with the same rulership which they are to obey with reverence.

The institution of the estates of the realm is therefore the extension of monarchy. It confirms the personality (concentration) of royal rule over against the personality (freedom, inwardness, self-action) of obedience, and the elevation of royal power over against a connection of living permeation and union between government and people. Through it, therefore, the idea of an ethical kingdom, a thoroughly personal rule (§. 36), as far as form is concerned, is realized absolutely and in the highest fashion. Political freedom, namely in this subordination and attachment to higher royal authority, is an outflow of the Christian principle no less than is the divine right of kings and legitimacy, the former however only as goal or good, the latter as basic principle and command.

The significance of the estates of the realm, then, is an *agency* [Vertretung] *of the people,* in the sense that they guard over the <230> rights and interests of the people, not in the sense that they as proxy exercise a power originally and actually due the people themselves; and a *representation* [Repräsentation] of the people, in the sense that they livingly manifest the true essence, the idea of the popular existence, not that they manifest the people, i.e., the mass of individual persons of which it exists. The popular representation [Volksvertretung] is thus, in terms of its true significance, anything but a consequence of the notion of popular sovereignty. On the contrary, it is precisely opposed to it, in that it presupposes the people as the obeying part, requiring a protection from the sovereign prince. As little are the estates of the realm, in terms of their significance, mandataries of the people, bound to the will of their principal, be it the classes

---

organ, the estates stand between the government in general on the one hand and the people dispersed in particular spheres and individuals on the other. Their purpose demands of them as much the sense and sentiment of the state and the government as the interests of the particular spheres and individuals." Hegel, *Grundlinien der Philosophie des Rechts* [Baselines of the Philosophy of Law], §. 302.

and districts out of which they are sent, or the entire nation which they represent as a whole; rather, they are a higher power over the entire people; their judgment is valid as the most high and most real judgment of the people, for which reason their actions bind the people. Having said that, in terms of their person and sentiment they are to possess the confidence of the people and therefore, in by far the greater part, to be characterized by their confidence, although their actions and decisions ought not to be characterized by the will of the people, but by their own independent higher judgment. Election of person and commission to actions are by all means to be distinguished. By virtue of this understanding of the estates of the realm, the objection is removed that it could not matter to each individual person whether he has the millionth portion, and indirectly at that, of influence on legislation or not (Vollgraff). The point here is not to bestow this influence on individual persons but on the people as a spiritual whole. Or, in other words, persons are to participate in the rule of the state not according to their sensate empirical existence (*homo phaenomenon*) but according to their ethical spiritual existence, and from this point of view they are one whole, who have their expression and action only in a structured arrangement and not in the sum of individuals. It is therefore not the mechanical rationale of difficult implementation for which reason a representative body, and not the entire people, participate in legislation, but the ethical political rationale that it is not the <231> mass, but only the elected of the people, who are to determine the public condition.

As the legal relation of the estates of the realm, it follows that: vis-à-vis the king, they are subjects, not merely as individuals but also as an assembly, although they do have rights and legal recourse against him; and vis-à-vis the people, they are office, regard, ruling authority, but only under the king and through him.

§. 97. Composition of the Estates

The *constituting* of the assembly of the estates of the realm, accordingly, rests on the notion of a *representation* [Repräsentation] of the *true popular existence.*

In terms of its true existence, the people is an articulation of estates, and has for its substrate the land and soil of the country. "Estate" in its political significance is the life-vocation only to the degree that it also effects a unity of political interests and political position, and thus only in the characteristic large groups (agriculture – commerce and trade – cure of souls), and only in connection with local and governing [obrigkeitlichen] associations. The large governing associations, which are founded in locality and vocational community, and which fall immediately under the highest territorial supremacy, are the estates in the political sense. There are therefore the following: landed aristocracy, cities, rural communities, and, in accordance with the specific constitution, the clergy of the national church. On the other hand, merchants, bakers, butchers, and the like, as such constitute civil but not political estates. These estates in their diversity, and landownership in general, therefore form the foundation for the true constituting of all territorial representation [Landesvertretung]. The people is not an amorphous mass, a collection of individuals; the sentiment of the people, therefore, only rarely consists in the equal sentiment of individuals; but rather for most things develops differently in terms of those differing life situations, and therefore as a totality only has its seat in the entire structure. In that the people are represented, it is not mere persons that are repre- **<232>** sented but also, and above all, things, i.e., objective conditions and institutions [Anstalten], human life positions; and the aim (τέλος) of representation is not to assert the will of individual persons in the state, but the inherent interest of those estates and vocational positions, and the single joint sentiment arising from them.

The territorial representation, therefore, is not to proceed from the undistinguished mass of the people but from those specific distinguished estates; and, likewise, it should be aimed at maintaining the specific significance and advantage of each of these, in correspondence with the whole. To leave an estate unprotected because it is of lesser numbers than the others, thus to sacrifice it to the majority precisely because it is a minority, is most certainly an injustice. When an estate is to be refused an equal weighting in representation with the others, the demonstration that fewer persons are resident in it, which is how Sieyès thought to dismiss as absurd the separate representation of the nobility and the clergy, is not enough to do that, but only the demonstration that the estate has no special material, political, or ethical significance worth maintaining. Sieyès' reasoning against the nobility and clergy, that 200,000 people cannot have the same power of representation (veto) that 20,000,000 have, would therefore lead to independent property-owners not being able to have an equal representation with proletarians, day laborers, journeymen, beggars, etc., these being the majority. Accordingly, the manner of representation of necessity is arranged according to the given condition of the estates, for it is to display the elements extant in the people in terms of their existing relations and bring these to effectiveness. Although landed property must never form the only aspect of representation, it is for all that the most significant one; its estate being the precondition of all other estates, it is the key element upon which the public welfare depends, and the constant aspect of the public condition.

Furthermore, men are not to take part in representation simply as men, but only to the degree that they have an estate-oriented quality [eine ständische Qualität], taking this in the broadest sense, i.e., a significance for the common condition and a fixed position in <233> its organism, thus only to the degree that they can identify with the material interests and professional branches in which the life of the nation unfolds. It is therefore unjust to demand a part in representation for the so-called intellectual leaders [Kapacitäten]; for these, when they do not invest a public office (e.g., members of universities and academies), are not co-bearers of the popular existence, but mere particular livelihoods.[129] The same holds true for the proletarian; for though his labor certainly is an integrating aspect in the organism of the national economy, personally he has no determinate, secure, equally crucial position in it. The same is true for the bare capitalists, for their interest is not bound to the land, which is why their person is not identified with the things which are to be represented. In everything, a certain independence and a participation in the maintenance of the public order generally is required for the right of representation, it being participation in rule. Persons who are absolutely dependent upon other citizens or who do not share an interest in the continuation of secure property and trade relations, but whose interest rather opposes them, have no vocation to issue laws and to participate in government.

Property [Der Besitz] therefore is in a dual respect the regular qualification for the territorial representation; for one thing, because it connects one to a specific estate or corporation (landed property, municipal association) each according to its manner, and for another, because it guarantees independence and general interest in the existing order. The contrary doctrine, requiring universal suffrage without regard to estate and possession (Chartism), rests on the notion

---

[129] Something else again are the provisions for intellectual leaders [Intelligenzen] in the organic popular estates themselves, such that, e.g., a class is able to elect its representative from another class or another district.

that the meaning of popular representation is to assert the will of individual persons. The consequence of this notion would not, however, be universal suffrage, but the immediate exercise of legislative power by the collective, as Rousseau more observantly demands; for my will in no way comes to expression through my subordinating <234> myself, by means of the right to vote, to someone over whom I thereafter no longer can exercise any influence. Or it is based on the view of favoring the people forming the numerically larger class, the poor, at the expense of the security of the legal condition.

Universal suffrage cannot by any means be grounded in legal principles, the alleged primeval right of men, since participation in representation in general, like all participation in rule and governing power, is not a right of the person (primeval right) but a right of vocation, and since, in particular, it is a protection or right gained through inward acquisition, not for people as individuals but for people as a whole, for which reason one may only lay a claim to participation in it to the degree that one has a significance for the whole and safeguards it.

But on the other hand the people is still a national and civil unity, regardless of its arrangement in terms of estates. For this reason, the territorial representation is to embrace the entire nation. The upper classes [die höheren Stände] are not to be separated from the remainder of the people to form the representation, nor are the leading elements of individual estates to be separated from their other members to do so. The estates, as soon as they themselves cease to be enclosed bodies under autocratic ruling authorities like unto the state itself, are no longer to be represented exclusively by those authorities. A degree of influence should also be open to personal trust, to a greater or lesser degree, but always within the bounds of the necessary guarantees for objective standards.

Furthermore, the territorial representation, although based on differentiated estates, nevertheless is always to act as a whole. Whether divided into several departments (curiae, chambers) or forming a single college, whether its decisions arise through majority vote [Ueberstimmung] (either according to curiae or head count) or through reciprocal veto, it must always stand opposite the government as one indivisible body which takes only collective decisions.

Finally, the territorial representation as the actual representation of the nation is to be a higher power over the nation, independent in its decisions, adverting only to its own judgment.

This distinguishes true *territorial representation* [Landesvertretung] (or *popular represent-* <235> *tation* [Volksvertretung] in a more justified sense than what has hitherto been usual) from mere *estates-oriented representation* [ständischer Vertretung]. Accordingly, it is not merely the members [Gliedmaaßen] of the people's existence that are represented but the unity, not merely objective conditions and interests but the people in whom those conditions and interests are found. By contrast, the system of the Revolution, which is what one usually understands by "representative system," represents the unity of the people apart from the foundation of its arrangement in estates, and people apart from the foundation of their objective conditions. This is no longer territorial representation, nor even actual popular representation, but mere *persons' representation* [Menschenvertretung].

The principle of organic representation by estates is that which first arises in history, because it is the first, the imperative in terms of the matter at hand. The same holds true for all times and under all conditions. A condition in which people form a mere spiritual community without material foundation and various material occupations and purposes, corresponding therefore to the undistinguished representation of the people as mere embodiment of personalities, can factually never arise. Progress in history does not consist in the casting aside of estate-oriented principles but in bare estate-oriented representation becoming likewise national-uniform representation, and it consists in the estates of the realm going from being mere mandataries of their electoral districts to being a higher decisive power over the entire people, to being the true center (in a certain sense, personality) of it, in which the nation recognizes itself as one. All of this is an advance toward higher unity and spiritual community and to greater consciousness and self-activity of the nation, thus to higher realization of the idea of the ethical kingdom. While the material organic coherence of popular life, to which the estate-oriented structure gives form, is to ascend to higher spiritual unity, it must not vanish; it cannot cease to be the foundation for that unity. <236>

§. 98. The Role and Proper Evolution of the Estates

In terms of the significance elucidated above (§. 96), the activity of the estates has a dual purpose: *protection of rights,* and the *assessment of new laws* in terms of the *conviction of the people,* or, extending this farther, the assurance that the government in general is based on the conviction of the people. This is why there exist, on the one hand, the right of grant of supply [Steuerbewilligung] (that is, the budget and oversight thereof), grievances [Beschwerde], impeachments [Anklage], and on the other, the right of advice and consent regarding laws, petitioning, requests [Desiderien], discussion of government measures.

As the institution of *representation,* the estates only have their power through and in the prince, from whom alone, as sovereign, all power and all regard in the state can proceed. They have no direct power over the people or over the civil service, they can give no one instructions, can subpoena no one; that which they achieve, they achieve only through the prince. Even their own activity is of necessity based on the authorization of the prince; they are called, assembled, dismissed by him. Likewise, their power consists not in themselves looking after conditions, but, in that the government looks after this, in asserting the rights and mentality of the people to the government; and, accordingly, it extends only as far as hindering the prince regarding something and submitting something to him with the emphasis of their moral influence to take it into consideration, not, however, positively prescribing something to him. Their power is everywhere only impediment and suggestion, not positive arrangement and formation. In particular, the legislative power by no means pertains to them, contrary to the common theory that they are either the primary subject of this power or that they share it equally with the prince; the prince as sovereign has the legislative power and thus the sanction, the proclamation, and, regularly as well, the drafting (initiative) of laws, while the estates have only advice, consent, petition.

Accordingly, their position with regard to public affairs is entirely different from that of the government. The government is the ruling and formative principle in the state, the territorial representa- <237> tion is the protective and proposing one. The former therefore gives to the arrangement the specific developed shape, the latter is only entitled to the general sketch; the affair of the government is the plan and coherence of the whole of the ship of state, while the affair of the territorial representation is mainly the result of individual resolutions for specific rights and for the national condition. This is the normal situation. A shading of the activity of the estates into the actual sphere of the government, in accordance with the individuality of the constitution, as takes place in particular in England, is therefore neither ruled out nor a refutation of the actual concept of the constitution of the estates of the realm. The more this is the case, the more the estates-oriented constitution tends toward the republican. If transitions exist everywhere, why should there not be an estates-oriented constitution gravitating toward the republican?

This position of the territorial representation vis-à-vis the king lies inalterably in the concept of the constitution of the estates of the realm. Here as well, therefore, desirable progress in history is not that whereby royal sovereignty is overpowered, but only that whereby state power becomes more concentrated. The right of the territorial representation metamorphoses from the arbitrary disposal over a separate private sphere into ordered concurrence regarding public leadership itself, bound to legal restrictions (state-legal character). Of necessity, the territorial representation thereby becomes an integrating, continuously active element of state rule, and vice versa, the latter obtains through it the guarantee of its inner necessity and lawfulness. The entire public condition, which to that point had stood under two separate acting subjects, thereby comes under one undivided acting power. Just as, therefore, historical progress in relation to the development of the assembly of the estates of the realm pursues the undivided unity of the nation in its representation, so, too, in relation to the rights of the nation, it pursues the undivided unity and reciprocal adjustment of the ship of state. It is the self-same idea of the ethical kingdom which is manifested in both.

Of this historical progression the following chapter will deal in greater detail. **<238>**

§. 99. The Essential Nature of Estates Representation

This is the basic idea of the constitution of the estates of the realm. It allows the most manifold ways of implementation. The activity of the territorial representation can vary according to manner and extent, from the assertion of a few determinate and even extremely restricted rights to the full permeation of the royal power, and, thereby, co-determination of the entire public condition (England). All of these stages are right and good according to time, country, and the lawfulness of their emergence. But the significance of basic elements cannot be eliminated; the power of representation cannot itself be elevated to the supreme (sovereign) power (as with the revolutionary constitutions), otherwise the constitution will collapse; nor should it be reduced to a silhouette, otherwise its life will end. In the same manner, the formation of the territorial representation can be manifold, the one estate or the other may preponderate, this or that estate may be lacking, e.g., the clergy, universities; voting may have a greater or a more restricted role, electability may, along with the greater extension of suffrage, be restricted to the higher estates (England), territorial representation can be arranged in curiae, chambers, in the most manifold manner, the course of business may take place in this or that manner. But the basic principles must be maintained. It must not lack the main elements of national existence, it must not be a mere aggregate without a corporative basis, nor, conversely, disintegrate into separate corporative groups and lose the character of a single popular representation.

§. 100. Popular Sovereignty and Representation

The *liberal-constitutional theory* (Locke, Blackstone, Montesquieu, Delolme, Rousseau, Aretin, Rotteck, etc.) is based on the principle of popular sovereignty (Rousseau), i.e., that the entirety of individuals is entitled to the supreme power, and is modified only in part (depending upon the political wing) by the constitutional principle, i.e., the postulate of a mechanical balance of powers (Montesquieu). In ac- **<239>** cordance therewith, the representing assembly is a popular representation [Volksvertretung] in the sense of proxy [Stellvertretung], i.e., exercising the rights to which, strictly speaking, the collective mass is entitled; therefore, it is formed from the undistinguished collective mass, all citizens have the same voting right and the same electability, with voting being conducted according to mere numerical departments, without consideration of estate-classes [Standesklassen], and the elected are joined in an assembly which votes by head count. For all that, the right to which the collective mass is entitled and which this representation therefore exercises is nothing less than sovereignty itself. It therefore has the legislative power as the highest exercise of state power, the prince being only the executive, and this only in its service. Such is the consequence stemming from the principle of popular sovereignty.

The theory receives modifications from the constitutional principle, principally two: the veto of the king, be it absolute or provisional, and the division into two chambers, though not different estates, and with an inner divergence of elements, but only externally, to obtain a mechanical counterweight, an equilibrium. This theory is not a constitution of the state but its dissolution, for it destroys that which makes the state the state, the higher authority over individuals and the mass. As this occurs already in terms of ideas and principle, so must it also follow everywhere in implementation, and history has confirmed this.

When Cazalès once expressively depicted the germ of self-destruction inherent in the republican constitution, someone cried out to him, "Even in the representative constitution?" See how one deceives himself! A true republic always has an element of given unity and authority, which this constitution entirely lacks.

The theory propounded in opposition to this by Haller's school[130] is based on a complete private-legal conception of the state. <240> Accordingly, the prince is the holder of the territorial government as his private property, for which reason he exercises it unrestrictedly, apart from any influence or involvement of the territorial estates. The latter, for their part, have private entitlements which the prince cannot infringe, and the purpose of the assembled estates is to represent these private entitlements against him or to come to terms with him with regard to them. These rights consist primarily in freedom of property from fiscal burdens and in such things as particular acquired privileges. Rights of the people as a whole, especially their rights to be ruled according to their traditional laws and mores, is not what this is about. It is for this reason that each estate represents its right for itself, in curiae which deal with the prince entirely independently one from another, only uniting for the purpose of strengthening their position.

This theory destroys all unity, as it does all higher order and necessity in the state; it makes of it an aggregate of isolated coexisting absolute private rights. It is irreconcilable with the present-day regulated working of administration and the requirements imposed on it. For instance, the rights to which it entitles the estates, such as unconditional refusal to consent to taxes [Steuerverweigerung], are no longer possible, and the rights that it would have to grant them, namely, cooperation for the public condition, it denies them; its real consequence would therefore be the destruction of the institution of the estates, regardless of whether the estates, which it presupposes, any longer exist or any longer possess the natural power upon which their activity formerly rested. This theory is a

[130] Vollgraff, *Die Täuschungen des Repräsentatif-Systems* [The Delusions of the Representative System]; Jarcke, *Die ständische Verfassung und die deutschen Constitutionen* [The Estates-Oriented Constitution and the German Constitutions]; in general, the Berliner *Politische Wochenblatt* [Political Weekly].

distortion of the German constitution of territorial estates in the same way that the constitutional theory is a distortion of the English constitution.

Both theories, then, are incapable of capturing reality; both must reject as rash or as bare abuse a broad class of constitutional forms which have maintained themselves in life and in history. The liberal theory cannot recognize the older estates-oriented constitution as real; in fact, at bottom it cannot do so regarding any truly existing constitution, for in none of these is the consequence of its **<241>** principle realized, nor could it be. And except for the older German territorial estates, the Hallerian theory cannot recognize any constitution as real; in particular, the English constitution is to it a mere corruption of the estates-oriented constitution.[131]

---

[131] Hegel's conception of the "constitutional monarchy" contains the essential advance on Montesquieu et al., in conceiving the unity of state power (sovereignty) in the prince ("princely power") and the sphere of the estates in cooperation, in particular in (subjective) appropriation of (objective) laws proceeding from the government, and in illuminating this with pertinent arguments. Because Hegel develops the entire institution not from the real relation of kingship to people but from the abstract concepts of power and its functions, his conception has a formalistic character, in its results as well. To wit, in the significance of the estates he only conceives of the one side, the assessment of laws, while ignoring the other, the protection and assertion of rights; accordingly, grievances, impeachments, petition, even the approval of taxes and oversight of the budget, in the manner in which the legislative (rule-issuing) power is entitled to these merely integrating aspects, cannot be understood. To consider such a protection necessarily to be maintained vis-à-vis the government is to him "the attitude of the rabble," and even the assessment of laws is to him less an essential influence on them than an establishment merely to enable the subjective aspect to come into existence, that the will already existing "in itself" in the measures of the government also become "for itself," similar to, e.g., where, according to German principles, lawfully necessary taxes must yet always be consented to. Accordingly, therefore, just as he restricts the significance of the prince to mere formal authorization (§. 280), he restricts the significance of the popular representative to mere formal appropriation (§. 301), and one must ask, from whom then does the law – the higher regard over both being something we also recognize – receive the further development of its content, and from whom do the decisive acts of the

moment proceed? Perhaps from the concepts which lend themselves reality? This notwithstanding, Hegel performed the great service of being the first to have stated the true relation between prince and estates in general and in essence.

Chapter 9: The Older and the Newer Estates

§. 101. The Older and the Newer Estates Systems

<243> The institution of estates of the realm [reichsständische Institution] had a different basic character in more ancient than in recent times, which makes vain the effort to stand on the ground of the older estates-system by holding fast to its principle while allowing for differing applications of it in accordance with changed relations. Every more recent constitution must be established in terms of the newer principle and must be understood and maintained in terms of it. This distinction between older and newer estates can be characterized as the distinction between the patrimonial-estates principle and the nation-state-oriented principle. The first shaped the character of the European assemblies of the realm [Reichsversammlungen], most strongly those of the German lands [Landschaft], up until the time of the French Revolution; the latter was first realized in the constitution of the English parliament. Both basic characters will be set over against each other and brought to clarity.

In the German states, the older constitution of estates of the realm is monarchical-aristocratical, that is, feudal. The great (immediate) vassals of the king comprised his council, certainly as the representatives of the regions they headed or which belonged to them, not in the modern sense, to assert the will of the population of these regions, but in the sense by which a prince represents his domain. The high clergy joined itself to this, in part due to the regard of the ecclesiastical office, in part due to their being enfeoffed with landholdings. Cities were later brought in throughout the kingdoms of Europe, albeit with a subordinate status, which only gradually grew to equality, often in the character of a vassal of the <244> crown. These are the feudal estates.

The task of these estates of the realm is advice and aid (*conseil et aide*). That which initially manifested itself as an advantage to the king and as assistance and goodwill on the part of the estates – after all, independence and absence of obligation formed the rule and went without saying – in later times, after imposition and obligation became more common, came to manifest itself as protection for the estates and restriction on the king, as the right of consent or denial. Even so, with regard to both advice and aid the relation between king and estates lacked precise establishment, was vague, was determined more by prevailing factual superior force than sure legal principles; and even where it was more precisely determined, it was, for both sides, more of the nature of personal (private) entitlement and power than institutional ordinance and necessity.

This private-legal character came most to the fore in the German territorial estates, modeled on the European imperial diets, on entirely natural grounds. At that time, German territorial supremacy by no means had the character of full ruling power; instead, it consisted in certain ruling powers which had been acquired in patrimonial fashion from the actual ruling authority, the Emperor, and therefore had an admixture of a private-legal, partisan position vis-à-vis the subjects. This alone explains the fact that armed resistance against the territorial lord was not entirely forbidden, either in the eyes of the territory or in his own, while that exercised against the actual ruling authority, i.e., against the Emperor, was then, as it is now, considered to be as good as insurrection. For example, the League of the Lion [Löwenbund] joined forces for armed protection against anyone (i.e., even the territorial rulers) with the exception of the Emperor and the Pope. In particular, however, the emergence of the territorial estates was based purely on the motivation of such a private-legal partisan protection. The unifications out of which the territorial estates arose formed themselves to maintain their independence and their privileges against interventions of the territorial rulers, in particular against taxation, which is why this also became their enduring character. While the European assemblies of the realm and **<245>** the earlier *placita* of the German territories predominantly had the significance of *councils* for the imperial or territorial government, the territorial estates predominantly had the significance of safeguarding their rights, of defense against the princes. Their position resembles, to draw a parallel, not so much that of the parliaments in the old sense, i.e., the Lords and bishops, as rather that of the House of Commons at the time of its emergence. Hence the private-legal model makes its appearance here as nowhere else. Here the power of the prince and the rights of the estates, and that of each estate for itself, manifest themselves rather as special entitlements which have arisen accidentally, are entitled to arbitrary separate disposition, and which aim at the personal interest of the territorial prince and the concerned estates, respectively, without being related to the public condition as a higher unity, to that degree being likewise determined by a higher necessity.

§. 102. The Private-Legal Character of the Older Estates

Accordingly, the older territorial representation had a *feudalistic* character. Just as the entire edifice of the state is a gradation of legally entitled ruling authorities between the supreme lord and the population, just so did the territorial representation consist purely in such ruling authorities which protect themselves and their subjects against the supreme lord. The highest ruling authority of the land discusses and comes to terms with the lower authorities (*superioritas subordinata*): this is the significance of the older territorial estates. Thus, in particular, the knights sat in the German territorial estates as legally entitled ruling authorities, as patrimonial lords of the land, the magistrates sat as legally entitled ruling authorities in the cities, based on their own co-optation. The members of the territorial assembly [Landtag] thus represented the population not so much as estate and associates than as subjects and masters, similar to the way the estates of the realm represented their territory [Territorium] at the imperial diet.

The older territorial representation also had a *private-legal* character, in particular in the German territories. This is demon- <246> strated firstly in the *constituting* of the territory.

Those who had a seat and a voice in it (knights, prelates) defended only themselves or their inferiors (tenants [Hintersassen]) merely for their own interests; the direct tenants of the prince were therefore entirely unrepresented. It was no exception where delegates of corporations had seats in the territory (mayors, delegates from the knighthood [ritterschaftliche Deputirte]); for, in point of fact, these likewise defended and represented the corporations themselves, in that the delegates could only vote as they were mandated. By virtue of these mandates, the cities (municipal authorities), etc., actually had a seat in the territorial assembly, and not the mayor. Furthermore, each estate formed its own council [Kurie] and therefore could not be simply outvoted by the others, which is entirely proper, but more than that, it could also negotiate with, consent to, come to terms with, the prince for itself alone, without approval of the others. The salient character of the older constitution is not what the Hallerian School indicates it to be, that no estate might dispose over the purse of another, but instead the reverse, that each estate might dispose over its own purse apart from the others.[132] Finally, the prince could, at his pleasure, call the estates or leave off

[132] Confirmed by no less than an imperial court finding [reichsgerichtliches Erkenntniß] regarding Mecklenburg.

of doing so according to his own need and advantage, and conversely the estates could assemble on their own apart from any appointment from the prince.

The private-legal character is also manifest in its activity, whereby the state is divided into a sphere of princely and a sphere of estate discretion, apart from any higher unity and necessity. The prince has demesnes and regalia (later on, in many countries also indirect taxes) as if it were his own property apart from any say or oversight on the part of the estates, whereas the estates, apart from the exceptions of a few legally necessary taxes, could arbitrarily renege on taxes, or link them to arbitrary conditions, in the same way that private individuals settle their affairs with each other. For their part, the estates took care of the raising, the adminis- <247> tration, often even the expenditure of the taxes they consented to. The princes were not even entitled to inspection and supervision of the estates' fiscal policy, and only later were they able to assert this right, in which they were also supported by the imperial courts. In this manner, each side had its part purely for itself, and the peculiar character of the German estates system proved to be that the state budget was borne by two subjects: the territorial prince's treasury [Kammerkasse] and the estates' tax collector's office [Steuerkasse]. Each of these was in itself a legal person, and might settle affairs with each other, pursue lawsuits, each contribute to this or that territorial need in accordance with its receipts, and the obligations vis-à-vis the state (salaries, loans, etc.) had either the one or the other as debtor, and the debt of the one had no effect on the other. In the same spirit, consent to the laws was, at least in later times,[133] quite commonly restricted to the *jura singulorum,* i.e., the special acquired rights of a private-legal character of the concerned estates, together or separately. If these were rights of one single estate, it could effectively consent, renounce, apart from the others. Even the alienation of the territory at first was only gradually, and by no means generally, bound to their consent, and that of the demesnes only occasionally. On the other hand, the territorial estates were

---

[133] When in earlier times the estates often gave consent to all laws, this was not based upon a state-legal principle, such as, e.g., in England or in our contemporary constitution, but merely on the fact that the territorial supremacy did not include the right of legislation, and thus the territorial lord could only exercise that right in the path of free agreement. Since then, however, legislation being viewed as an essential part of the territorial supremacy, usually the right of consent on the part of the estates vanishes as long as their *jura singulorum* are not concerned.

not a mere *institution* [Institution], that is, a supplementary member of state power, so having public functions with reference to the state in the way the English parliament is such an institution; they were a *corporation* [Korporation], a *community* [Kommune], that is, a subject entirely separate from the state, with purposes, activities, and capacities to which they were entitled in their distinction from the state, which thus could be resolved or asserted, as the case may **<248>** be, purely by themselves, without concurrence of the prince; they had the rights of a moral (i.e., thus private) person: separate property, capacity to pursue lawsuits, both financial, as the representative of the state separated from the Treasury and in fact opposing it, and political. The *"territory"* was absolutely a separate legal subject over against the *prince,* and the courts, imperial or territorial as the case might be, comprised the higher power over both.[134] For this reason, the territorial estates were likewise an ever-existing legal subject, while nowadays, following the dissolution of the chamber or even the close of the territorial diet, no subject any longer exists which is legitimized as territorial representation.

That is how deeply, thoroughly ingrained the private-legal type of the older constitution of the territorial estates was. Nevertheless, this by no means exhausted its essence. An effect with regard to the public was so deeply grounded in this institution that it never could be lacking. Even in those days, the common interest of the territory was guarded by the estates, and common rights of the territory existed, albeit making up a far more restricted sphere; thus, e.g., in the defense against interference in religion, against division and alienation and the like, the estates truly represented the people. It was precisely the innermost tendency of historical progress to shuffle off this type, which the Haller School views as the only true one. Thus, for example, are to be found partly in general, in fact by imperial law, partly at least in several territories, the abolition of unauthorized assemblies, the restriction of separate settlements of individual

---

[134] This is most evident, as has just been shown, with regard to the financial budget, but it applies to all legal relationships. So e.g. the electoral Saxon estates acted as principal intervening parties towards the electoral prince and the count of Schwarzburg in the Imperial Chamber Court [R. C. G.] regarding the subordination of the latter, in order to overrule an agreement reached between the two. In those days the estates also sent deputations not merely to the Emperor and Empire but also to other princes (e.g., if one was oppressing the territory).

estates with princes, periodic mandatory assembly, contributions from princely demesnes balanced with estates' revenues; and those constitutions which most partook of <249> this public-legal correction, in particular the Mecklenburg constitution, were precisely the ones which maintained their significance for the longest time.

Since the end of the 16th century, however, an essential change has taken place in this respect. Of these elements, each of which supplied the state from private means and in certain degree for their private ends, it was the princely power which at this time gained more and more of the state-legal character. From that time onward, it was regarded as the power to provide for the state and the public welfare, while the estates continued to retain their character as private classes having certain rights to their separate advantage. In this manner, the prince became identified in public opinion with the state, precisely as the reverse is now true, people and state are often considered to be one and the same, and with just as little justification. In this manner there arose that *territorial lordship* (*territorialism*) which Thomasius in the starkest manner advocates against the estates just as much as against the church. In consequence of this, it was a simple matter for the princes, especially those of the larger territories, to crush the rights of the estates as being irreconcilable with the higher considerations of the state; in this they had opinion and the trend of the times on their side. Taking shape at this time were the civil service, which drew the administration to itself, and the standing army, which on the one hand shifted factual power from the knighthood and thence the territorial estates to the princes, and on the other contained a demand, yea a necessity, on the princes not to abide by a refusal of taxes by the estates, this core of the private-legal estates-system. The situation was approaching whereby the rapid growth of that sovereignty would break all estate-oriented rights as on a brass rock ("rocher de bronze"). Indeed, a constitution of estates of this aged character could not maintain itself as soon as the notion of the state as one undivided public institution arose. Nothing else than this, however, is the development of territorial supremacy to sovereignty. The point in time at which sovereignty had matured and, shedding along with the dissolution of the Empire the last husks which had covered it, stood complete and prominent, of necessity was likewise the point in time at which, formally and legally, the old German territorial estates ceased. <250>

§. 103. The Development of State-Oriented Representation

The antitype of this private-legal type, which characterized the German territorial estates and likewise, albeit in lesser degree, all European assemblies of the realm prior to the Revolution, is provided us by the constitution of the English estates. There, on the basis of a predisposition tending from the start in that direction, that constitution gained a state-legal, public character – the mature stage of the institution – in part through violent overthrow, in part through an imperceptibly progressing restructuring, and indeed without giving up its uninterrupted historical unity. We might also characterize this as the *constitutional* character, taking this concept in a different sense than currently is usual, namely, the division of state power and restriction of the king to the mere executive. In this, England is the bearer of a universal-historical advance, for which reason in what follows we will describe the outlines of such a state-legal constitution of the estates of the realm according to the English example.

The state-oriented constitutional character of the English constitution consists, as far as the development and position of the parliament is concerned, in its being a *national representation,* not a *private, estate-oriented* one. Not that its estate-oriented members were dissolved into a mere aggregate – the Lords, prelates, landowners, cities, the latter as closed corporations, are represented – but that this representation, composed of estates and corporations, nevertheless together forms a single complete and undivided national representation.

To be precise, the collective population, all classes of the people, i.e., all those joined to the territory through some material interest, some possession, have a share in it. Those not competent to be elected to Parliament at least participate in elections for it. Furthermore, the representation of the collective estates forms a whole that only acts as a unity, in that no house can act for itself apart from the other, in particular to consent to something; and, finally, as national representation, it stands both over the entirety of the people and over the districts [Kreisen] from which they proceeded, in that their <251> members are bound to no mandate, but only vote according to their own conviction. This latter fundamental principle, already recognized under Queen Elizabeth, first bestowed the true state-oriented character on the assembly of the realm. With the mandates of the older establishment, the assembly stands under the will of separate estates and aristocratically-ruled corporations [Körperschaften]; with the mandates mutually agreed upon during the Revolution, it stands under the will of the collected individuals in terms of numerical divisions, although because of the above-mentioned principle, it is an institutional [anstaltliche] power, as such over the joint mass as well as the individual estates, portraying the nation as one spiritual entirety, which is the state-oriented principle, in contradiction to both the private-legal and the popular-rule principle. Herewith, of necessity, the assembly of the realm, or the uniform nation represented by it, is the sole and complete disposer over all political rights. With the consent of the king, it can dispose over the rights of each and every estate, each and every corporation, in the formal sense unrestrictedly, in the material sense having to recognize limits (omnipotence of Parliament), and vice versa, no estate, class, city can dispose over its political rights apart from the assembly's will. The old territorial estates to a certain degree were only a kind of political stock exchange, where every estate separately concluded its business with the prince or other estates; Parliament is a higher national uniform institution, through which the nation determines its condition in its entirety as well as for its individual classes.

The institution of both houses (two-chamber system) is likewise an advance toward state-oriented character. According to the curial system, the estates stand facing each other as private-legal corporations, having to protect their particular interest against each other[135]; with the system of Parliament, the two houses face each other as political institutions, calculated to represent their public importance; the House of Lords appears as **<252>** that which represents the position of hereditary lords, and thereby in particular the aspect of historical cohesion of the nation and the (objective) foundations of the state, against the subjective and momentary interests of the great popular majority in the lower house. For this reason, in the curial system several estates cannot be easily melded into one curia, while in both houses, various estates are joined which have that public significance in common with each other, thus especially in the upper house the high nobility, the highest dignitaries in the church, and, following an expansion already possible in England and more developed elsewhere, the notables of the army and of the civil service. Likewise, part of this system necessarily entails that an aristocratic element be represented in the lower house

---

[135] Where this is not the case, as in the German imperial assembly, there they appear as powers, to a degree as subjects at international law.

(gentry). Curia as estate-oriented bodies are sharply distinguished, while houses as political bodies require transitions and mediations.

The English upper house is often considered to be a leftover of medieval feudalism, but in connection with the other house as system of both houses, it is instead the breakthrough of more recent times, the transformation of the private-legal curial system into the state-oriented form [Gestalt]. From this point on, therefore, the system of two houses forms the rule in the larger kingdoms of Europe, just as the system of three curia did before. When at first glance it seems to be more organic when the specific estates (nobility, clergy, citizens [Bürger], farmers) face each other as separate bodies, with a radical constitutional separation it is the general political interest which separates them into the two divisions, not the specific estate interest. Just as the republican constitution separates the state government into the two chief opposites, aristocracy and democracy c.q. citizenry [Bürgerthum], the constitution of the estates of the realm separates the territorial representation. Theoretically it cannot be denied that in this system, voting by head count, such as takes place in the lower house, can lead to an estate being infringed in its essential interest by a majority of the others. Practically, however, such outcomes are limited, **<253>** first, by the manifold interweaving of interests among several estates, then treatment from the motivation of mutuality, and finally the impartial protection of the prince. By contrast, negotiations between estates today so predominantly concern general national affairs (in particular legislation) that a separation of city and country and clergy is unnatural, a reciprocal veto impossible. For this reason, the curial constitution is gradually vanishing entirely from the times, and even where it is maintained, as for example in Sweden, there the curial principle, at least, is given up; for so, at any rate, must one view the reciprocal veto, although according to the Swedish constitution, agreement occurs either through the majority of three curia against the fourth or, where two stand against two, by means of the meeting of committees, which gives the decision. Incidentally, a right of protest on the part of individual estates, for certain specific rights having this effect legally ascribed to them, is compatible with the new estates system under all forms.[136]

---

[136] A characteristic expression of such a national representation in distinction to the older particularism of estates is the oath to the national welfare [Nationalwohl], which

With this uniform national representation, then, the old feudal characteristic of the representation of the country through autonomous ruling authorities ceased. It is no longer the gentry with right of jurisdiction who are the exclusive representatives of the entire rural populace, nor the mayor and aldermen of a magistracy made independent of the city by means of co-optation who are the exclusive representatives of the municipal populace. In England, the last remaining vestige of such a character <254> in municipal representation (the four systems) was abolished by the Reform Bill. Hereby of necessity appeared a new aspect in representation: *deputation, periodic election.* The establishment of periodic election embodies the idea of a further development of the institution of territorial representation. Hereby, then, it becomes representation of associates by associates [Genossen durch Genossen], of the actual class of subjects [der eigentlichen Unterthanenlage], built no longer on mere material community of interests and vocation but likewise on personal shared confidence, in which the entire population actively participates. But it is also scarcely avoidable, given the greater extent of contemporary states and the entry of numerous estates of farmers in the representation, while not all of them, not even all the sheriffs, can have seats in the chamber, and farmers' delegates with lifetime positions gained by cooptation, as in Tyrol, have lost their luster. Even in the older constitution, though, there was deputation and election where the peasantry was represented (e.g., East Frisia, Württemberg). As a result, however, deputation through election undeniably has its great dangers: agitation, intrigues, insurrection against the ruling authority. Even so, the institution of election cannot be wanting if territorial representation is to exist at all in more recent times; yet it requires securities and moderations: longer terms of office, public balloting, stable

---

the new constitutions occasionally stipulate to representatives. This by no means restricts their assertion of the particular rights and interests of their estate; on the contrary, it is for this reason that they are elected from the various estates, but it is only to supersede the earlier adversarial position, by which each estate cared only for its own interests and not at the same time for the interests of others, even in the consciousness of their deleteriousness to the whole. The national welfare is not an abstract welfare outside of the various classes of the nation; it is nothing other than the harmonious welfare of the classes taken together, each according to its special needs. The oath to the national welfare thus includes, not excludes, the welfare of the estate.

electoral bodies, bestowal of a portion of voting rights to designated positions [gegebene Stellungen]. Such moderations exist in England, in part legally and in part factually, and existed in yet more abundant measure prior to the Reform Bill. This makes the institution of election possible in England.

Another means of moderation was introduced in France: the *mediated* (indirect) *election.* In itself, this is unnatural. A mediated election through a multiplicity of levels of representation (district, provincial, and territorial representation) is natural; a mediated election merely through several votes is not. Now then, the objection to such a double vote is somewhat alleviated when one proceeds from the notion that it is not the individual person that is to be represented, his will to be asserted, but that of the people as a spiritual unity. For even if, in the case of indirect elections, the final **<255>** result, considered individually, is often one that the first voters did not intend, on the whole it will still be based on their sentiments. "Public opinion ever remains the Great Elector," and the authenticity and popular character of representation ought not be sought in the mechanics of voting, but instead in the public morality. For this reason, indirect elections are not in principle reprehensible, and even though the simple election, such as it exists in England, is most certainly sounder and worthier, it can scarcely be attempted on the continent. But one ought, as is self-evident, only view this indirect election among us as an indispensable protection against the most extreme shock and dissolution, not as a positive or even a sufficient safeguard for the territorial representation.

The strongest objection to the newer sort of representation is *systematic corruption,* which tends to accompany it. As long as the country's corporations made their own decisions, there could be no question of bribery; but now that a few people decide for the entire country, one bribes them and arbitrarily rules the country through them. Now, one must pose the question regarding the older estates-system, whether it was something other than today's bribery that princes (for example, in Saxony) maintained the tax exemption for the knights even after knight service was discontinued, this against the well-founded claims of the cities, in order for them to be willing to allow their tenants [Hintersassen] to be taxed; or whether similar means may not have been applied by influential mayors, aldermen (in that they and not the entire community decided), members of territorial councils, at that time? For this reason, then, the current estates-system does not of necessity carry that system of corruption within itself.

As far as England is concerned, one can hardly label it bribery that the party which gains power mans the offices (and usually only the highest ones in the state) with its own, the more so that there everyone stands and falls with his party. In France, though, corruption seems to be an inescapable evil. For there, the ministers are not leaders of a parliamentary party, which in fact rule and administer, but directors of an independent administration, separate from the chamber, albeit entirely dependent upon the vote of the delegates. In Germany, on the other hand, where the monarchical principle other- **<256>** wise rules in the constitution (ch. 12), the government does need a party: that is, men who are in general conservative, loyal, disposed in favor of the existing order, not such as consent to all of the government's impositions and proposals. When here a system of corruption is established, it is only the fault of the persons, not of the institution.

The transition also extends to the forms of conducting business. As long as the represented themselves had a seat in the assembly [Landschaft], the guarantee of their rights lay in secrecy, in them conferring only amongst themselves regarding their interest, in the measures they took and the originators thereof not being made public, in particular in them not becoming known to the prince. But in the territorial assembly, those who used to represent themselves no longer do so, but represent the entire population, and they do so on their own account, not as mandataries. In this case, the security of the entitled parties (precisely this population) now lies in publicity; for this affords, on the one hand, a moral impulse to the representatives for their manner of action, and, on the other, a guideline to the voters for their future voting. Essentially, then, the newer form of territorial representation is that in which the decisions and votes of individual members are made public. A system whereby the constituents receive no knowledge of the conduct of elected representatives is deficient. **<257>** On the other hand, publicity through the swift simultaneous pressure of negotiations and the presence of spectators in the galleries, although certainly belonging to a lively, developed territorial representation, cannot be viewed as an essential requirement and therefore may only arise fully as the result of lengthy activity of the estates of the realm, the political and moral strengthening of character, and the steadiness of constitutional legal concepts and forms. Publicity, especially the immediate bodily presence of spectators, also harbors its great dangers; nowadays, it requires less courage and self-denial to act against the government than against the tyranny of public opinion. Even in England, the latter sort of publicity is newer and is a mere privilege of those houses, in that each house may at any moment withdraw for a specific hearing, or even forever, through simple "resolutions," whenever it wishes. On the other hand, given the state-oriented character of the territorial assembly, the presence and share in decisions of royal officials (ministers) is necessary in one form or another. It was in earlier times connected with the secrecy of hearings that the estates in every case informed the prince in memoranda not merely of their decisions but also their motives, while, in accordance with the English method, these motives become clear through the debates. Only for extraordinary occasions can memoranda ("addresses") yet still be needed. In these points, the newer estates-system requires newer forms of doing business, but outside of that there is no reason to exchange the older German estates-oriented form of business for the English or French.

§. 104. Institutions of the Modern Estates

The rights which, according to the English state-oriented character, accrue to the estates of the realm are of the sort that provide a legal order and public necessity to the governance of the state as a whole. For here, the estates of the realm are not guardians of their particular rights but an integrating element of state power itself, and, therefore, everywhere have a regular and necessary concurrence with the king; for this reason they have no rights and activity for themselves alone, as is the case with communes or corporations. As a result, in no sphere is the state left to princes or estates for their own private ends and will; instead it is maintained inseparably by both, according to the purposes inhering in it, as state, standing under one indivisible rule, regardless of whether or not the estates are an entitled power alongside the prince.

This transition manifests itself, in terms of form, in the regular periodic election to, and the regular periodic calling of, the estates. It manifests itself even more significantly in the thing itself.

In this spirit, the basic law [Grundgesetz] is already a public regulation which comprises the collective constitutional condition as one indivisible whole, one right of the collective nation, so that succession to the throne and the house law of the dynastic family cannot be modified apart from the parliament, and the constitutional position of this or that estate **<258>** cannot be modified apart from the prince and the assembled parliament.

In the same spirit, however, the collective legal condition, even apart from the basic law, is placed under the protection of the territorial assembly; namely, it has a deciding, i.e., a preventing vote not only regarding particular rights (*jura singulorum*) but also regarding all laws. In England, this right of consent to laws is included in a yet more significant one whereby all laws must be proposed by Parliament (initiative); but the general feature of the newer national representation is precisely that no law can be issued apart from the will of the latter. A condition in which the government consults the estates only when it considers it appropriate can hardly be considered an estates-oriented constitution; estates of this sort are much rather mere distinguished personages. It is more significant when every law must be submitted to the estates for consideration, as is the case, e.g., in Mecklenburg with regard to the "indifferent laws."[137] But an estates-oriented constitution of the realm of the newer state-oriented character includes the right to veto by the estates of the realm. That is precisely its principle and its innermost meaning: that the nation has a right to its existing order and does not need to accept any arbitrary innovation in the foundations of its state, that the state cannot be changed at the discretion of the ruler. Precisely this right of consent makes a conservative power of the territorial assembly. By its nature, the representation is predominantly conservative, and all conservation is truly representative and protective. As little as the room afforded the territorial assembly to challenge the existing order is to be expanded, that much is its power to be established where it is effective in protecting the existing order from the government.

The spirit of the newer estates system evinces itself most decisively in the sphere of public finance in the institution of the *budget* [Budgets]. Rather than the estates' granting individual taxes and overseeing the application of these

---

[137] ["The estates are granted the right to deliberate on matters of indifference, and the right to grant approval on the others, so that in such cases, the law only becomes valid when the prince and the estates agree. From this it follows that the estates, even if they wanted to, are not allowed to concern themselves with the general welfare of the state at all, but only to defend their privileges. The consequence of this was the well-known backwardness of Mecklenburg in cultural and political matters." Herman Brunswig, "Die mecklenburgische Verfassungsfrage" [The Mecklenburg Constitution Question] *Zeitschrift für Politik,* Vol. 2 (1909), pp. 107–118; citation, p. 109.]

taxes, here the grant of supply is based on an appraisal of all income and outlays of the state; it is enacted as a supplementary element of a law for the state finances for the upcoming period, and **<259>** the entire application, the observance of this law, is subject to the oversight of the estates. Total state finances hereby manifest themselves as a systematic-uniform, lawfully ordered whole, no longer financed from two generically different sources, in a manner of speaking, two different legal subjects (demesne, tax office); instead, demesne and taxes fall under the shared higher concept of public funds, and have only one subject which disposes over them, the state power.

As a result, the concept of the budget of necessity includes *specification* [Specialität], i.e., that the government comply with the main positions included in the budget. An estimate merely to get an idea of the total sum of the state's financial requirement without any binding effect is in itself worthless. For when it does not everywhere have to be complied with, then the precondition is lacking under which any estimate has to be made at all. When, for example, the government in the budget assesses the requirement for schools at 100,000 Reichsthaler but turns around and uses these revenues not for schools but for the army, then the budget in this case indeed was no estimate. It is even more difficult to monitor the legal use of funds when the use of the funds is not governed by any law at all. But the most important significance of this institution lies precisely in the fact that it is no longer the territorial assembly that protects the people from certain levies and burdens in the state budget, but rather that the state budget itself is subject to a legal necessity guaranteed by the territorial assembly.

The institution of the budget and its specification being preeminent expressions of the state-oriented character, they are even more unpopular among the proponents of the old private-legal character than are other aspects of that character. The objection that the estates themselves determine the state budget, in this taking the place of the government, does not touch on the institution itself but on the individual form given it in England, and even then not absolutely. For such an objection is only valid when the specification (this restriction on the government) extends into detail, and when the estates arbitrarily revise the budget and through **<260>** these revisions can stipulate taxes. That this does not of necessity belong to the institution of the budget will be shown below (ch. 12), and it is certainly a different question whether the estates have a right to make the budget or the right to make the government comply with the given budget.

The institution of the budget must displace the venerable right of *arbitrary refusal to consent to taxes.* Budget and unconditional refusal to consent to taxes belong to two entirely different principles and systems, the former the state-oriented, the latter the private-oriented. Should the contributions of subjects be considered a matter of their mere caprice and absolute disposition, then the public income (demesne, regalia) must likewise be considered a matter of princely caprice and absolute free princely application. If, however, the state budget is subject to a legally ordered course of business, which is the point of the budget, then the territorial assembly must just as necessarily cover its requirement as the government must comply with it. It used to be the interest of the people to pay nothing more than it wished, and this accorded with the unconditional refusal to consent to taxes; now it is in the interest of the people to have a guarantee that the joint public means be applied to the public purpose, which reflects concurrence in administering the state budget, consent on the basis of the budget, and assessment of the total expenditure. In that case, both are achieved: arbitrariness is denied to the government and the estates, and the state and its requirement are established as a higher power over them both.

Unconditional refusal to consent to taxes is thus, in itself and in terms of the matter concerned, in contradiction with the new institution of the budget. The "constitutional theory" which adheres to it as a fundamental rule is unable to provide any reason for it derived from the nature of the state budget; but that theory considers it, and avowedly so, to be merely an external means for an end lying outside the state budget, namely, as a means for the power of the territorial assembly against the government. Such treatment of a matter according to a consideration lying entirely outside of it is in itself inappropriate and superficial, but beyond this, the territorial assembly hereby receives not a mere power **<261>** of protection against the government but a power of absolute rule; the balance is not thereby restored but abolished, for the government has no similar means to use against the territorial assembly, such as the latter has against the government with the refusal to consent to taxes. Therefore, refusal to consent to taxes has everywhere been the grounds for revolutions in more recent times. In England, the connection of the budget and the refusal to consent to taxes was created apart from theory, through the unintentional course of history, and we will return to the effect of this; the use of the right of refusal to consent to taxes as a means for other goals is held today, by both parties in England, to be unseemly and revolutionary. As an aside, it is remarkable that in the instructions (*cahiers*) given to the delegates for the general estates in 1789, the old right to consent to or deny taxes as private contributions (*aides*) to the royal revenue, and the principle of popular sovereignty, in accordance with which all public income and outlays must lawfully be grounded only on the will and decision of the people, were intermingled as if they were one and the same.

This transformation of the consent to individual taxes into involvement in the entirety of state finances has a redounding effect on the entire external estates institution, by external necessity furnishing it with the form which, as already noted, it needs to have for internal reasons, in terms of the newer character. Therefore, regular assemblies of the estates are necessary; the separated session of the curial system is no longer capable of being implemented; the mandates are no longer possible.

This, then, constitutes the character of the newer estate system: representation of all classes in the nation, the greater portion through delegation; uniform treatment of assemblies of the estates of the realm, and independence from their constituents; regular appointment, indivisibility of the organic law, consent by the estates to all laws, budget and assessment of state finances. The completeness and unity of popular representation and the unity and legal arrangement of the ship of state mutually condition each other and together form the expression of the idea of the state as a public-necessary order overarching prince and people, which carries in itself its laws and its bases of determination. This character of the constitution of **<262>** the estates of the realm is that which through its development has made England into the bearer of a world-historical advance and a classic example for Europe. It did not, however, develop from the start on the basis of a mere principle, but in the formation and thus conservation of given elements, and in this as well, in this spirit of conservative-historical development, it is no less the classic example. On the other hand, the individuality of the English constitution is in no way the object of imitation. This individuality in fact also includes the supremacy of Parliament over the king, of which we will treat more extensively in its own chapter.

Chapter 10: The Constitutions of the French Revolution

§. 105. Total Break with the Estates-Oriented Constitution

<263> If, then, an inner development of the constitution of the estates of the realm as one and the same institution manifests itself in history, and the English constitution is the one in which this development occurred, the constitutional effort of the French Revolution stands entirely outside the ranks of this institution, it being not a species of constitution of the estates of the realm but precisely the opposite.

In France, after the old constitution of the estates of the realm was quashed by the king, the Revolution of 1789 engendered a new one, entirely breaking with everything in existence (*a priori*). This constitution, therefore, did not have, as did the English, historical bases and elements but was exclusively the consequence of the dominant theory and dominant sentiment of that moment. The political, or better, state-legal viewpoint which filled the times was preeminently the doctrine of Rousseau, i.e., the doctrine of the sovereignty of the people and the conception of the people as an undistinguished mass in terms of mere numerical relations. To this was added Montesquieu's constitutional theory, the doctrine of the separation of powers and establishment of a mechanical equilibrium. These theories, even though they contradict each other, had run together in the public mind, just as is the case currently amongst ourselves, although the former dominated. Still, the sentiment which filled the minds was a well-founded, albeit passionate, embitterment against the long-exercised despotism of the kings, and even more against the outrageous haughtiness of the nobility. All of this found its deepest **<264>** foundation in the collapse of mores and faith, in the reigning materialism. There was not, as was the case in the time of the first English revolution, a consciousness among the people that it was called *by God* to be the bearer of power, and that it therefore had to conduct itself according to His ordinance, but, rather, that it itself was the absolute ethical power on earth, and owed account of its will to no one; there was not, as in the English Revolution, indignation regarding the loose morals of the preeminent, but only regarding their higher position; there was no intention for man to answer to his eternal and temporal purpose, but only to assert his rights. In this manner arose the constitution of 1791; how was it to be made into a secure construction of freedom and order?

The Revolution was already complete in the national consciousness when King Louis XVI called the estates of the realm. The mandates of the electoral bodies to their delegates (*cahiers*) were largely worded as follows: with regard to the new constitution, the people is sovereign, but Louis XVI would remain hereditary monarch. Monarchy was therefore no longer considered to be an existing authority but something about which one might decide whether to establish or not. How was a settlement possible where the king was of the opinion that he could call the estates of the realm by virtue of his royal power, while the people from their own sovereignty sent representatives to him, who would themselves first establish him as king, of course under the conditions that they themselves set? That nevertheless a doctrine which completely filled the national consciousness would gain the victory, and that the nation would be given an organ and central focus to express itself and to assemble, was part of the necessary course of events. In the struggle over the mandates, the basic principle materialized that the people is an undistinguished mass, while in the opposition to royal dissolution of the assembly, the principle was realized that the people is a higher power over the constitution and constitutional authority. The question was whether the military power, which the king possessed as a remnant of the older political viewpoint, would prevail against the changed viewpoint. Severed from its root, even it did not follow through, leaving the king no other choice than to bow **<265>** before the newly formed power.

The question as to whether the Revolution could have been avoided is not an idle one, although scarcely answerable. In any case, the king would have had to issue a constitution prior to calling the estates of the realm, a constitution rich in concessions but with precise establishment regarding the composition and rights of the estates of the realm.

§. 106. The Absolute Sovereign Assembly

The principles which brought about the Revolution likewise fill the constitution which proceeded from it.

Hence, the composition of the National Assembly, entirely lacking in observance either of rank and corporate community or of landholding, was based entirely on numerical division. Representatives were first apportioned according to considerations of surface area, level of taxation, and head count; they were later merely head count, elected according to a completely trivial property qualification for the franchise and electoral eligibility, and then joined in one single undivided corporation [Kollegium], in which majority voting held. It is no longer territorial representation at all, and therefore in truth no longer popular representation, but rather mere persons-representation [Menschen-vertretung].

Officially, the national representative assembly had the legislative power; factually, it had the sovereign power. It stood and acted on its own authority, assembled, constituted, disbanded itself, determined the order of its sessions, all apart from empowerment by the king; it could not be dissolved, and was permanent. It had the complete legislative power, to wit, the power to draft and to decree legislation, while the king only had the power to publish, not sanction, laws, only the power to suggest laws (proposal), not draft them (proposition), and the king's right of hindrance was only provisional. It established the budget alone and without restriction, it decided over war and peace, the former together with the king, the latter on its own. The king was a mere executive power, not as an independent power in the state but merely as a menial instrument of the **<266>** National Assembly.

Therefore, unaccountability, which in terms of its nature only attends actual sovereignty, could not be attributed to the king. The unaccountability which the constitution of 1791 did attach to the king was only apparent, since after his abdication he was to remain accountable for his royal acts and, at the same time, it identified the transgressions for which his abdication was legally approved. Add to this the sophistical distinctions whereby the king only possessed an administrative and not an absolute unaccountability, that he was only unaccountable as king and not as man (Brissot), or that he was tried not as king but as enemy (Robespierre, St. Just). The constitution of 1791 essentially realized the doctrine of Rousseau. Apart from a few minor deviations, it only fell short of this prototype in that the people did not issue laws immediately itself in its collective mass, as Rousseau absolutely required, but through representatives. Yet even this was added to the constitution of 1793, in that it allowed the original assemblies [Urversammlungen] to vote, though only nominally, since such could not be made reality.

§. 107. Its Positive Contribution

Obviously, this constitution is not a species or genus of institution of the estates of the realm, as are the older or newer German constitutions, or the English, but is rather the complete opposite. As the term already indicates, it does not form part of the concept of constitution of the estates of the realm because it takes as its basis a people not composed of various estates; and the innermost character of the same is lacking in it, the representation of the people to the prince as sovereign, in that it makes the people, c.q. the representative assembly, itself into the sovereign. The only monarchical trait which it allows to exist, heritability, has no justification within it; for heritability demands the elevated position of the ruling authority, of the sovereign (§. 70), not mere executive power. Even in itself, though, it is, in terms of its basic principle, without possibility of **<267>** existence. In terms of its principle, the king has no power vis-à-vis the national representation, but according to the same principle the latter likewise has no power over against the popular mass; in fact, even the law itself is subordinate to the latter, as its own work. While in this manner it elevates the popular caprice to the supreme power, it effectuated a permanence of the Revolution in the continuing overthrow of constitutions until the despotism of the Napoleonic Empire, which in the end was followed not by internal development but by the external power of the restoration of the old monarchy. The great sign and judgment over this revolution theory is that its constitutions not merely have no duration, but that hardly any could even come to realization. To use the celebrated expression, no constitution of France ever became a reality.

That which shines as truth out of all that error and destruction, however, is the recognition of human rights (Book III [*Private Law*], §. 19), the uniformity [Einheitlichkeit] of the people, and the dignity which it possesses in this unity [Einheit] vis-à-vis the king. All of this first came to conscious and energetic power here. In England, the right of the citizens is more positive-legal; in France, it is the absolute entitlement of persons as an eternal ordinance of things. In England, the estates-oriented organization gradually developed into a balanced and conjoined unity, while in France, the uniformity of the nation and its representation manifested itself as independent first principle (albeit falsely, as sole principle). That the people as such, the personalities and not merely the material conditions, were to be represented, was achieved in England by way of approximation, and in part unintentionally, while in the latter, it was the decisive viewpoint. The dignity of the nation in England exists factually, while in the latter it is the most pronounced principle. This truth is, of course, only a ghastly aberration, when, as in this case, it is separated from the higher, fully harmonic whole to which it belongs, as a right of man without connection to divine and human-historical order, as unity of the nation without estates-oriented organization, as dignity without higher regard over it. But it is an achievement when it is integrated as a member in the totality of the ethical order. In such an integration, it ensures that that which in England exists historically and **<268>** positive-legally likewise obtains its deeper ethical, and thus enduring significance, and that that which there is wavering, is decisively and immutably determined.

Chapter 11: Estates-Oriented vs. Representative Constitution

§. 108. A False Opposition

<269> It was in opposition to these French constitutions, to the overthrow of the monarchy and the overthrow of the constitution of the estates of the realm, that the reactionary theory we sketched above was developed in Germany. Therefore, from this school stems the opposition between the estates-oriented and the representative constitution which nowadays in Germany is counted among the rallying cries of the political parties. It was Genz who first, at the Carlsbad conferences [of 1819], endeavored to secure the promise of territorial estates-oriented constitutions in the Act of Confederation as against the imbroglio of the representative constitution, and occasioned the official pronouncements in this sense. Later, in consequence of movements after the July Revolution, Vollgraff and Jarcke furnished a complete scientific implementation of this opposition, making it the school's confession.

To the degree that this doctrine is aimed at keeping us from the representative constitution in the sense of the French Revolution, one must extend to it the most enthusiastic gratitude. In itself, however, that *contradiction* is as little *logical* as it is *historical;* because by "representative," it understands the principle and the constitution of the Revolution, while by "estates-oriented," it understands the old German territorial estates-oriented constitution, and by means of these two contrary but not contradictory concepts, it aims to order and so to pass judgment upon all possible forms of constitution. But between a representation of the people as bare mass of men with sovereign power on the one hand, and a representation of isolated estates for the sake of their private rights on the other, there is a <270> significant third alternative for which absolutely no place is found here. Above all, the English constitution belongs in such a category, and one certainly cannot deny its historical existence or, without superficiality, its logical idea. At the least, one does not do it justice when one characterizes this unique, self-contained constitution, which has surpassed all German territorial estates-oriented constitutions in inner coherence as well as durability and sustainability, as a mere "corruption of the estates-oriented constitution." By posing such a dilemma, this doctrine embraces one constitution which is objectionable and another which is impossible, thereby ruling out the truly fruitful one which the times demand.

Genz had already characterized the estates-oriented constitution so particularly in terms of the ancient example that a transformation into the new character no longer had any place. He discovers the representative constitution everywhere that representation does not take place exclusively "through self-existing corporations," where the representative does not "exclusively" represent the rights and interests of *individual* estates, where *popular election* exists, and thus characterizes the English constitution as a representative constitution without further ado; this is even more the case with his followers, Jarcke and his adherents. A constitution is representative in their sense, i.e., French-Revolutionary, when it merely deviates from the type of the old German territory in any manner. Where elected delegates attend the territorial assembly rather than the heads of the corporations as their born representatives, where there are two chambers instead of three curiae with their separate resolutions, where no mandates exist, where the sessions are open to the public, where the estates consent to taxes not individually but on the basis of the budget, where they have approbation of laws which do not concern their *jura singulorum* – there reigns the representative principle, which must be eradicated. In this manner, Jarcke in particular runs through the German constitutions and characterizes them in terms of the only true system of the old German territorial constitution, whereby that which agrees is orthodox, that which disagrees is heretical.

This is a manner of procedure entirely of the same sort as the **<271>** constitutionalists, who likewise propound a certain special constitution (two chambers with legislative power, the royal veto, ministerial accountability, royal non-interference, separation of justice and administration, freedom of the press with trial by jury, etc.) as the only reasonable state law, and, in terms of this, praise or reject every constitution in its individual parts, according to their agreement with this absolute standard. It is difficult to say what is more reasonable, the only admissible constitution as they derive it from logical principles, or the only admissible constitution as they take it from a period of history and from a specific country, a country that at the time of this constitution was not even a state in the fullest sense of the word, the territorial representation of which was not an imperial but, in a sense, only a provincial representation.

When Jarcke finds that the German constitutions yet contain significant estates-oriented character traits, and that one needs to purify them from admixture of the representative system (which sums up the entire agenda), one may object that even those states which, with awareness and intent, pursue such a pure estates-oriented constitution, nevertheless are incapable of withstanding what he calls the representative system. Compare, for example, the composition of the estates assembly according to the Bavarian constitution of 1817, which in essentials was to be representative, with that according to the Prussian edict regarding provincial estates, which was to be in the historical estates-oriented spirit, and therefore was greeted by Haller with praise, and one must raise the question, by what right is the one seen in the one light, the other in the other? Election and delegation are in both, as is the differentiated vote [die abgestufte Wahl]. The rural delegates required three votes in the Prussian provinces, the urban delegates usually two (according to Vollgraff, distilled through three retorts), just as in Bavaria. In no less degree do the smaller cities in Austria elect common delegates by means of the previous election of simple electors. Both here and there, the balloting takes place by head count, and the aid of a separate vote for an estate disadvantaged by the majority, which has no **<272>** effect other than the mere possibility of royal consideration, is attained in Bavaria through an address from the delegates of this estate, with the same result. That here eligibility for election in the urban and rural classes depends not merely on urban or rural possessions but also on urban and rural occupation is certainly of an estates character; but should one attend to the result, then the mayor, who as such is eligible for election in Prussia, is scarcely a different element than a landowning or home-owning lawyer and civil servant, who are eligible for election in Bavaria. Therefore, in representative Bavaria a nobility is represented, while in Prussia only a landholding gentry is. This parallel should entail neither praise nor reproach, but merely guard from imaginations and classifications which have no corresponding object in reality.

§. 109. Both Estates Organization and National Unity

Actually, the mixture of both characters found everywhere nowadays in the new estates-oriented institutions, which precipitated the Haller school's bestowal of praise or rejection, is precisely the irrefutable postulate of the times, even if the manner of mixture is here better, there worse, and perhaps not yet everywhere sufficiently resolved. As far as the *rights* of the estates are concerned, this mixture is unavoidable because the contemporary constitution of the estates of the realm must share the state-oriented character with the representative system while sharing the character of protection of the people and popular participation with the old territorial estates system, rather than popular sovereignty. As far as the *composition* of the estates of the realm is concerned, this mixture is unavoidable because the contemporary constitution of the estates of the realm must share with the French representative system national unity, with the old territorial estates system the organization from estates. This union of both characters will be extensively discussed in the following chapter in connection with the rights of the estates of the realm. But its composition, which here occupies us, must now of necessity rest on two principles which permeate everything: the distinction of estates and the unity of the nation, the representation of material con- <273> ditions and occupations and the representation of the people in them. What that school therefore designates as an emanation of the French representative principle would be so only if it stood alone. In this interpenetration, however, it is rather only an emanation of the national or state-civic principle in contrast to the estates-oriented principle, and is thus only one of two equally essential sides of national existence.

To call it French (revolutionary) representative in this interpenetration is therefore completely untrue. It simply exhibits highly significant traits which of necessity must be valid for the national or civil principle, and others which must be so for the estates principle. So, for example, as a necessary consequence of the national principle, we recognize the abolition of curial separatism, the mandates, etc., while we recognize, as the necessary consequence of the estates principle, election according to specific different estates. But within these fixed determinate boundaries, there is yet a broader space for the necessary expression of the one and the other principle, for which the one or the other may predominate; and it cannot be said how wide this or that may go, or which is the better one. So, for example, whether mere rural or urban property, or whether, in addition, rural or urban occupation should be a requirement for eligibility for election in these classes; or whether candidates must be taken from the same district; or whether an estate should be able to elect its representative from some other estate representable in the territorial assembly; or whether the cities only as corporations, and then only a few of them, should send representatives, as is the case in England, or whether the urban population, hence with the participation of all the cities, should send representatives, as is everywhere the case on the Continent. In this full range, there is no judgment that the one is clearly the true one or the one appropriate to the times, while the other is to be rejected. It is only a mutual more-or-less of two equally necessary aspects. In general, therefore, what is appropriate here is a tempered attitude (*juste milieu*), such as Aristotle commonly put forward as a guideline.

In particular, considerations have to be decided upon which are not of a <274> principled sort, but rather are derived from the circumstances: whether, for example, sufficient intelligence is to be found among men of an occupation joined in an estate, etc. Beyond this, the historical progression which one can trace is, in the natural course of things, from the estates organization to national unity, and not the reverse; the former can be enlarged in ever greater degree, but one cannot go from the latter back to the former after having given up on it. The general goal however, in accordance with the entire discussion, is that national unity does not arise merely as *external result* from the representation of the joint estates, without determining the position and the consciousness of those individual estates, but that it be the *inwardly determining principle* of the entire estates institution, that, upon its basis, the estates first separate, in order then to unite together; this is the immediate gain of the world-historical events in France.

When, accordingly, we reject the doctrine which anxiously and one-sidedly holds fast to the old-school principle of estates isolation, even so we recognize its well-founded motive, which is that public opinion is largely filled with the manner of thinking of the French Revolution, according to which national unity and equality is sought not in the full representation of all classes, but in the undistinguished commingling of all people, in classlessness [Klassenlosigkeit].

Chapter 12: The Monarchical Principle[138]

§. 110. The English Parliamentary Principle

<275> The German Confederation established as the supreme rule of the German estates system the maintenance of the monarchical principle. And when compared with constitutions of foreign states, current German constitutions have more or less a certain common character which cannot but be considered the expression of this principle. But a clear and comprehensive discussion of what is to be understood by the monarchical principle and what it entails has not yet been provided, either ex officio or scientifically. Concept and content of the monarchical principle would most securely be clarified, then, by firstly seeking out and examining its opposite.

Such is, initially, the principle of popular sovereignty and the principle of the separation of powers with the restriction of the king to the executive, as these principles of the French Revolution have been realized in their various phases. In opposition to this, the Charter of 1814 states that all official order stems from the king in whom the collective state power is united, and following this example, the German constitutions have included most of the princi- <276> ples expressed therein. But in all of this, we find monarchical sovereignty rather than the monarchical principle, for monarchical sovereignty excludes popular sovereignty and the separation of powers. If this were all there was to it, then the monarchical principle would not have to be emphasized. But that this is not all there is to it is demonstrated by the fact that partly the Confederation, partly

[138] This exposition of the monarchical principle first appeared in 1845 as a special pamphlet with a preface, and was then included as a chapter in the second edition of the *Doctrine of State* (the first edition already contained the ideas, but only scattered and less forcefully expressed). Therefore, to understand it one must take into account the *condition of all the states at that time.* It is supplemented by my later exposition, *Die Revolution und die constitutionelle Monarchie: eine Reihe ineinandergreifende Abhandlungen* [The Revolution and Constitutional Monarchy: A Series of Interconnecting Essays] (Autumn 1848); by my speech of October 16th, 1849; and by the introduction to my collected speeches (see now also Stahl, *Die gegenwärtigen Parteien in Staat und Kirche* [The Current Parties in State and Church], 1868).

the constitutions exclude a series of institutions which conflict not with princely sovereignty but only with the monarchical principle.

The actual and specific opposition to the monarchical principle is therefore the *parliamentary principle* as we will call it, i.e., the predominant position of the parliament vis-à-vis the king, as developed in England and, of course, as sought in the constitutions based in popular sovereignty in greater, not lesser, degree. The investigation of this position of the English parliament will therefore prepare us for the certain understanding of the monarchical principle.

To begin at the beginning, it consists in the parliament *legally* having a form of *joint sovereignty* with the king; this legal position of Parliament's is *factually,* i.e., in terms of result, beyond all comparison the *decisive* power for the public condition. Partly it is grounded in legally established rights, partly in mere custom and the predominating viewpoint, which however, as will be shown, inevitably proceed from those rights. They are the following:

Regarding legislation, Parliament not only has the right of petition but also the *initiative* (bill), i.e., the drafting of laws, the detailed statement of proposed laws, while the king has the right merely to consent to or reject the drafts presented to him. The crown as such presents no draft legislation. Instead of the king being the legislator, such as is entailed in the age-old concept of kingship, with the estates agreeing, refusing, suggesting, the reverse is the case here, the parliament is the legislator, i.e., it is the form-giving power on behalf of the legal condition, the king merely confirming or refusing. In terms of its innermost essence, the petition is only the expression of the popular desire vis-à-vis a higher authority, while the proposition (initiative) is the activity of a legislative authority. But even the royal right of hin- <277> drance (veto) will in fact be considerably undermined by the initiative of Parliament. The mere petition for a bill may be freely rejected, but if Parliament has spent its sittings in drawing up a bill which has been carried into effect, perhaps for months riveting the attention of the country upon it, it will be difficult for the crown to say no to it, and indeed, no use has been made of the royal veto in England since Queen Anne.

Add to this *the enormous scope which the concept of law has in England,* and thus parliamentary consent and initiative. All general regulations, even public welfare and administrative, have the validity of laws, so that, apart from the mere execution of these laws, only a few scanty regulations for the sphere of "proclamation" (*ordonnance*), i.e., the royal enactment apart from Parliament, remain.

In fact, even disposition on behalf of specific relations, which on the Continent is everywhere allotted to the administration, such as, e.g., consent to a monopoly for an inventor, a street for a community or county, authorization to dissolve the bond of marriage, dispositions regarding encumbered property and the like, fall within the sphere of law under the title of *private bills* (derived from the position of Parliament as court of law), and therefore are looked after by Parliament, subject to the bare consent or refusal of the king.

It is, therefore, in connection with these rights of Parliament, extending even unto the drafting and administration of laws, that detailed inquiries are everywhere required, that subjects and officials also can independently subpoena and examine, apart from the mediation of the crown.

Regarding the state budget, Parliament has the right of *unconditional refusal to consent to taxes.* This old medieval, private-legal, arbitrary capacity, in connection with the more recent institution of the budget (through which the right of refusal extends to the entirety of the state budget as one indivisible whole), has indirectly the result that, with every serious fracture between king and Parliament, the king necessarily yields, that he therefore cannot deny demands which Parliament states categorically, particularly the lower house with its consent to funding, even if he wishes to. Certainly public **<278>** opinion and political custom now discourage the right of refusal to consent to taxes, viewing this as a revolutionary measure, but this is only because public opinion and political custom have already decided that the king cannot refuse anything to Parliament and in particular the lower house, and (we shall have to return to this) that he cannot follow any other system of government than that which the House of Commons specifies to him.

Apart from this indirect result, brought about by the connection of the unconditional refusal to consent to taxes and the budget, there is already the direct one, that Parliament establishes the state budget. The specification of the budget has no limits, and the lower house can reduce outlays not only in their entirety, but can also decide on reductions in every item, and in fact can determine their form and object in detail; the crown must consent to all of it, since apart from it, it can levy no taxes.[139]

---

[139] The earmarking of perpetual (mandatory) taxes in such large sums has its ground not in consideration of the crown but in consideration of the holders of public debt;

A no less effective authorization than the consent to the budget is the consent to the Mutiny Act. The law of subordination, apart from which no army can exist and which elsewhere is taken for granted, in England expires yearly, and when it is not renewed by Parliament the army ceases to exist and the soldiers are released from all military duties. The way this institution of necessity keeps the king from opposing any resistance to Parliament in extreme conflict is quite plain. In itself, however, it is a consequence of the co-sovereignty of Parliament, for it does not include a joint command of the army (wherein Parliament appoints the leader who must follow its commands, as the Long Parliament sought regarding the militia), although it does include a joint authorization for that.

The position of Parliament vis-à-vis the high-court judges is **<279>** similar. By the Act of Settlement, these are secure in their positions as long as they continue in good behavior (*Quamdiu se bene gesserint*); therefore, they cannot be removed by the king on his own, but they can at the request of Parliament.[140]

The competence of each house to punish slander inflicted either on its own members or on anyone else on behalf of its own members lends Parliament a form of sovereign position.

Finally, Parliament legally has a power over the *person of the minister*, and thereby factually over *state government in its entirety,* which is virtually without limit. Because Parliament in both its houses joins the roles of prosecutor and judge over the ministers; because its punishment is capital; because crimes for which an official can be condemned are not legally restricted; rather, anything can be characterized as a crime through the broad proviso in the law of high treason of Edward III; and because of the exorbitant institution of the bill of attainder; all of this taken together puts the ministers in an unconditional dependence upon Parliament, while having hardly anything to fear from the king. For his part, the king cannot make the slightest disposition, not even the slightest expression, without a countersignature of such ministers, themselves totally dependent upon Parliament.

---

likewise, the restriction which the House of Commons sets on its own request for taxes and outlays is based on consideration for the taxpayers.

[140] "But upon the address of both houses of parliament it may be lawful to remove them." Hallam, *Const. His.* III, p. 262.

From this unconditional dependence of ministers on Parliament, in particular in connection with Parliament's other rights, emerges by factual necessity that which is customarily known as *parliamentary government.* It consists in nothing other than ministers having the entire government put into their hands apart from any consideration of the will of the king and conducted with unconditional consideration for the will of Parliament. Above all, it is a political maxim that ministers suffer no interference from the king either in details or in principle, and, therefore, it is another political maxim that ministers no longer remain in office if they lose the confidence of Parliament, especially the lower house, either through an express <280> vote or by failing to attain the requisite majority for their proposals. Thereby, the factual condition is for Parliament to be split into two large political parties, each of which has its own determinate leaders designated by its own acknowledgment. The king therefore can do nothing other than make ministers of the leaders of the house majority party and can do nothing other than leave the government to them. His conviction, his will, does not come into consideration; Parliament of itself produces the ministers, and they rule on the basis of parliamentary sentiment as the chosen leaders of Parliament, not as servants of the king, or, in other words, the majority party in Parliament always rules the kingdom by means of its leaders.

Therefore, one can hardly raise an objection to our discussion to this point, to the effect that the king likewise has a means against Parliament in the right to dissolve the lower house, just as Parliament has against him ministerial accountability and the right to refuse to consent to taxation; for the result of these means lies entirely outside his power. The political party which prevails through its "connexions" confronts him again with a commanding majority. It is a general, natural demand that the ministers, as adepts of the administration, essentially be left independent regarding the overall scheme thereof; this holds true even of absolute monarchy, and even Parliament restrains itself vis-à-vis its leaders regarding individual questions, and waives its own judgment when they demand it. But the characteristic thing regarding the English establishment is that the king has no decisive part in the whole direction of the government, that he is excluded not only from the administration but also from the government. The king can certainly exercise some influence: because the predominant party is not always as closely united and certain of its triumph, and within it, in turn, the leaders are not so exactly designated, and finally, individual questions are not always the logical expression of a principle – for these reasons, both the parties and the ministers have some ground to maintain contact with the king, which lends some weight to his own will. Yet it is the rule that the king must allow unpopular ministers and an unpopular manner of government to fall without his own influence, and in any case he can gain some influence only through chance circumstances and the pru- **<281>** dent utilization thereof, or through the particular steadfastness of his character; he has no influence of himself and everywhere, by virtue of his royal position.

In England, one speaks of the prerogatives of the crown. Such a prerogative of the crown, apart from the appointment of top officials, is, in particular, representation outward, thus the position of the nation in the great international relations. Legally this matter is also plainly subordinate to the crown. But if one investigates the matter more closely to see in which hand this prerogative factually lies and must lie, then here again it is with the ministers and thus those whom the ministers designate and who are dependent upon the ministers. Yes, even the selection of persons for legations becomes a matter of discussion in the house and thus a matter of moral necessity, and it happens that the ministers fill the offices at court against the king's will.

Thus it stands in the closest relation and correspondence to this that no act of government can be attributed to the king, but instead to the countersigning minister. Even the King's Speech, spoken by his own mouth, is considered to be given him by the ministers, and naming the king in Parliament in any way is strictly prohibited, apparently out of reverence for the king but in fact out of zeal for the total power of the houses, which makes room for the king's personal unaccountability but allows no step by the government to be withdrawn from its judgment, the demand of its sovereign accountability. The fiction "the king can do no wrong" sounds like a thoroughly monarchical principle, but he can do no wrong because he cannot do anything at all. The elevation here provided him is only the elevation of the knob atop a church steeple, about which no one cares. All of this has now been developed much further in theory, especially in France, by which a so-called "constitutional state law" has been developed requiring the "absolute neutrality" of the king. It is viewed as a violation hereof that, for instance, Louis Philippe indicated his joy at a vote which accorded with the sentiment of his ministry. The king is not only to have no power, he is not even to have a will, a conviction, an inclination in political matters.

This entire system, which one calls parliamentary government, **<282>** developed completely beginning with the rulers from the house of Hanover, and rests immediately on custom, maxims, an image of statesmanlike honor, not on law, and precisely because of this, because it does not rest on law, the king may still exercise a degree of influence on it. But it is nevertheless an inevitable consequence, according to the laws of nature, of the rights that Parliament has according to the law, and through which it has supreme power over the king. Where, in the case of extreme opposition, Parliament *legally* possesses the means to force the king unconditionally to yield, to subordinate himself to it – the unconditional refusal to consent to taxes, refusal to fund the military, unconditional ministerial accountability – there it is legally, i.e., not according to the letter but rather the inevitable effect of the law, the supreme power in the state, and it is as necessary that the entire government be directed in accordance with its will, and not the king's, as a stone falling down rather than up.

In summary, the current English constitution can be characterized herein: by law, the king is sovereign in that he has the power of absolute veto, cannot be coerced into anything, imparts to all laws their sanction, is elevated and unaccountable; but, already legally, Parliament has co-sovereignty, since with its rights it not only permeates the entire sphere of the government but in many parts even participates in the authorization thereof. This is in accordance with the current manner of speaking, by which Parliament is characterized as the king and both houses as one undivided, undifferentiated power, as the one supreme state authority, as with the German imperial constitution a similar relation is depicted with the similar expression, "emperor and empire." Even more so in terms of factual consequence, the king is not the decisive and form-giving power for the entire ship of state (legislation, administration, state budget), Parliament is. The nation in its parliamentary representation rules itself, and the king only stands over it, while he (formally) imparts the sanction to the government and, as the case may be, moderates it to the degree that circumstances support him. This is what we call the *parliamentary principle.* It unmistakably gravitates toward the republic. For every state must be a republic in the broad sense, i.e., a legally ordered commonwealth existing in accordance with its own **<283>** requirements and goals, but the republic in the strict sense consists in the self-rule of the nation which forms the state, the way the local community does, and has no independent power decisive to the public condition over it, for such a power is the concept of the king.[141]

§. 111. The Monarchical Principle

In distinction to this, we must discover the *monarchical principle* in the princely power which in terms of law stands over the popular representation, impervious, and which in terms of fact is the center of gravity of the constitution, remaining the positive formative power in the state, the leader of development. This demonstrates that the monarchical principle is something other, in fact something greater than the sovereignty of the king. In England there is the sovereignty of the king in contrast to popular sovereignty and the separation of powers, but not the monarchical principle. Vice versa, in the German territories during the time of the imperial association, no princely sovereignty existed, not even inwardly, for the prince vis-à-vis his subjects had to submit to the legal proceedings of higher courts for his governing actions; but the monarchical principle did exist in the prince, in his being the center of gravity of the constitution and in the estates not having any co-supremacy. The sovereignty of the king is a

[141] As far as the institutions are concerned, the position of the king in France is not much different from that in England, but he does have much freer scope. He proposes laws together with the chambers, he has a wider scope of administration without the involvement of the chambers, and in a centralized state the army is not authorized annually for him and the accountability of his ministers is not so unlimited. But here the king and his entire constitution stand on the crater of popular sovereignty, and even if it is easier in good times to bring a sovereign people under one's thumb than a semi-sovereign parliament, it is still not permissible – excepting in times of threats to the existing order – for the king to have a will, even according to the French constitutional principle. In England, the king is subject to the will of the people as a result of those institutions; in France, he is supposed to be subject to it as a direct ethical and political principle. Nevertheless, the King of the French has a will and a powerful one. Yet this is not based on the constitution, but rather (apart from the well-known constitutional means) on the personality of the king, on the inexperience of the parties and coteries and, above all, on the fear of new upheavals, the present basic motive of the well-to-do, who do not find the same guarantees in the French chambers as they do in the English Parliament and therefore, according to the eternal law of nature, gather around the protective banner of the monarch.

pure and direct legal concept, while the monarchical principle characterizes a factual position, which yet is the consequence, the effect, of rights. This, then, is the concept of the monarchical principle.

In the old German territorial constitution, in which the estates only exercised certain private-legal privileges in a sphere separated from the collective guidance of the state, the monarchical principle went without saying and maintained itself without further ado, and underwent no challenge, for the estates had little significance for the state as such. Currently, however, the difficulty <284> and problem for Germany is for the monarchical power to maintain itself as such, given the state-oriented character of the estates system which includes a concurrence of the estates for essential spheres of the state, and as integrating element of the public constitution. It definitely would seem that the adoption of such a state-oriented (constitutional) character of the estates system, as developed in England, would of necessity and inexorably lead to the adoption of the predominant position of the parliament and that the German princes would find themselves faced with the alternative either of rejecting or impeding the recent development of the estates system or of relinquishing their truly monarchical position and climbing down to the subordinate level at which the king of England undeniably finds himself. Yet this is not the case: the state-oriented (constitutional) character of the estates constitution, which is a necessary requirement of the times, and the parliamentary principle are by no means incapable of separation, and it is by no means necessary to restrict the estates to isolated rights (consent to certain taxes, consent in the interference with *jura singulorum*) or to exclude them from any cooperation for the joint guidance of the state in order to maintain the monarchical principle. Precisely the institution upon which the supremacy of Parliament in England rests as upon its foundations also shows us, by way of contrast, the institution upon which the monarchical principle is based, and it is to be emphasized that such can be maintained without yielding the state-oriented character.

§. 112. The Estates' Consent to Laws

In terms of the monarchical principle, the prince not only is vested with the execution of the laws and regulations necessary to this end, to which constitutionalism restricts him, but also the *entire sphere of administration,* which is his alone. Regulations for the public welfare and the like, which do not establish the legal condition or, moreover, administrative dispositions and decisions in individual cases (private dossiers), therefore cannot be subject to the consent of the estates. Similarly, in terms of the monarchical principle, the drafting of laws (initiative, proposition) ac- **<285>** crues to the princes while the petition accrues to the estates. None of this stands in contradiction to the estates-oriented right of consent to the laws drafted by the princes, which is an outflow of the constitutional principle.

In this regard, one of the most significant tasks of German constitutional state law is the sphere of estates-oriented rights of consent regarding legislation, or, in other words, to determine more closely the boundaries of *law* and of *decree* [Verordnung]. Most of the German constitutional charters designate the sphere of estates-oriented consent (in Prussia, the estates-oriented advisory council) as the laws which "*concern freedom or property of state members.*" This is an extremely flimsy regulation. If one understands by this all regulations *restricting the freedom* of subjects, then the entire administration falls under the estates. How few administrative decrees there are which do not restrict freedom! That subjects are not to travel without passes, that laborers are not to visit this or that country, property owners are not to build in such and such a manner, that plans entailing fire hazard or danger to health are prohibited, likewise dance parties on certain days or for certain ages, etc., all of this restricts, and so in this sense concerns, freedom. Should one instead understand such regulation to pertain only to laws which *abolish* freedom in the strict sense, i.e., *freedom of spatial movement* (*vis locomotiva,* in English legal terminology), then the right of consent by the estates only extends to penal and public-welfare punishments, while a divorce law, laws regarding the appointment and custody of a guardian and the like, are withdrawn from them, which in turn is unnatural.

The thought underlying this regulation is certainly none other than: the laws which affect the *legal sphere of the individual* shall require the consent of the estates. This has a twofold significance. Firstly, it embraces the entire *private-legal condition,* a concept which is something else entirely than that of the older *jura singulorum,* as it includes not merely laws which take away the object of an already acquired right, but also those regarding the future acquisition, content, and loss of private rights, and personal integrity, thus not merely laws which pronounce expropriations, the abolition of privileges, **<286>** etc., but also the entire civil- and criminal legislation, and the procedural norms in both dimensions as their appendix. Secondly, the legal sphere of the individual also includes his *freedom vis-à-vis state power,* to the degree that this exists *as a legal relation.* In this respect, all norms which *put burdens on subjects,* such as laws regarding military service obligation, billeting obligation, compulsory school attendance, jury duty, and the like, require estates' consent. This can also be extended to mere *restriction* of subjects where such, as far as form is concerned, until that point had neither legally nor customarily existed, in particular in their employment, e.g., a new prohibition on peddling. By contrast, regulations regarding health, construction, security policy and the like are not laws, for they do not put positive burdens on subjects which they as individuals have to bear, but only restrictions in consequence of public establishment, and in a sphere in which the competence of public regulation, and thereby restriction of individual freedom, in itself already is established legally. Thus, although they factually restrict freedom, they do not do so as legal relation. Therefore, the measure and limit of punishment for the violation of public welfare ordinances [Polizeystrafen] is an affair of law, while public welfare prohibitions [Polizeystrafverbote] within traditional spheres of activity (games of chance, secret societies) are not everywhere of necessity laws.

Apart from these laws regarding the legal sphere of the individual, there is another class of regulations accruing to the estates, i.e., the laws *regarding the constitution itself,* the *constitutional laws.* This is the sphere in the present day corresponding to the ancient sphere of the *jura singulorum.* As a rule, estates' consent was not then required (only advice) for laws pertaining to the private legal condition, for instance, a new civil code; these were the "indifferent laws," as is still the case in Mecklenburg.[142] By contrast, to remove or to change noble jurisdiction or privileges of the cities or immunities of the clergy did require their consent. The *jura singulorum* therefore did not include the civil condition, but rather the constitution of the country. This is now otherwise. The constitution as embodiment of public, systematically connected principles has now arisen in place of such *jura singulorum.* In German constitutional charters, therefore, amendments of **<287>** the constitution, the constitutional laws, are subject to consent in addition to the laws concerning freedom and property.

Accordingly, the following in general is established: In terms of German constitutional state law, firstly *norms concerning the public legal formation of the state,*

---

[142] [See footnote 137 above.]

i.e., the constitutional laws, are subject to estates' consent; secondly, norms which concern the *legal sphere of individuals* (i.e., judicial sentencing, private-legal relations, legal relations of subjects' freedom vis-à-vis state power). By contrast, administrative norms, i.e., norms of *public functioning* in the sphere of public welfare, finances, the military, etc., are not subject to it. These together form the field of regulations, which according to English and French state law require consent for the most part. In terms of German state law, therefore, consent is required only for norms of legislation which ground an actual legal relation (private or public), not those which merely ground a legal regulation of government action. That beyond this, even in the field of law the instructions for implementation can be issued as regulations, is self-evident. Notwithstanding variations in implementation, one will find these principles confirmed in essentials by the practice of German states, even in the case of dissimilar expression in constitutional charters.

§. 113. The Estates' Control of the Budget

According to the monarchical principle, an unconditional *refusal to consent to taxes* which puts the government itself in question, which compels the prince to obey the estates in everything, cannot be allowed. Furthermore, according to the monarchical principle the state budget itself must be set by the *prince,* and not the estates. None of this stands in contradiction to the constitutional institution of the *budget and its specification.* The monarchical principle requires here above all that specification does not descend into the details, so that, for example, it is agreed with the estates in the budget which building is to be paid for from the rural building budget, how much of the military budget is to be used for infantry, **<288>** cavalry, etc. That is administration. This does not, however, rule out the main positions being set – whether more or less is, of course, not based on principle – so that, lawfully, they cannot be exceeded.[143]

Secondly, the monarchical principle requires that the estates not be able to modify the proposed budget at will by erasures on the one hand and additions on the other, so that the prince, just as with a bill, either accepts the amendments or must abandon the entire law for the state budget, thus including all taxes.

---

[143] Presentation of details as record and basis for estimates, and presentation of the same as legally unalterable items, are of course two different things. Only the latter, not the former, is to be ruled out.

Such a dictatorship of the estates over the state budget is simply in contradiction to the monarchical principle.

Nevertheless the estates, even though they may not dictate, yet may have an influence on the state budget, and that not merely in terms of quantity, the level of public outlays, but partly also quality, the objects of expenditure. This can be arranged in many different ways. Estates can have the right of reduction regarding individual specific items, in order to direct a tax reduction, the ancient right of the estates, to a specific object. The increase of revenues or the increase of outlays can be subject to their right of consent. A distinction can be made between necessary and voluntary outlays. It would also answer to the state-oriented character of modern times if the collective budget, in the manner in which it traditionally developed, in terms of a certain inner necessity, would be maintained as a legal basis in revenues and outlays that the estates in no way can modify, but whereby the prince likewise could do nothing without the consent of the estates: that every amendment in both revenues and outlays, but only the amendment, is the object of their influence, their hindrance. Of course, this cannot be implemented, or is of no use, where specificity of the budget descends into details, for in details the state budget is changing constantly. These arrangements necessarily mutually condition each other, as they are the consequence of a principle.

If the estates are jointly to administer the state budget, which is what **<289>** specification usually involves, they cannot be hindered from dictating it as well. But specification can be implemented where it is restricted to main items. Here remains a broad basis of regularity, amendments are only gradual, needed now for this item, now for that one. The outcome of this arrangement is that the estates will not be able to dictate the state budget or any other wishes to the government by not approving the taxes or the budget, because the prince can continue to govern even if he is not granted the amendment that has just been requested, or the sum that has just been omitted is not replaced; but on the other hand, taxes are not demanded of the estates for a system of outlays which the government always sets by virtue of plenitude of power, apart from their consent; and by means of the financial budget they maintain an equilibrium, not a dictatorship, regarding their other wishes, in that it is in the government's interest to stay in their good graces, precisely regarding these individual amendments.

This, then, is the proper constitution of the estates of the realm: the prince does not have to obey the will of the estates, but neither is he so positioned as to be entirely independent of the will of the estates. Where a constitution is being introduced, such safeguarding institutions are therefore possible in a variety of ways. In terms of existing constitutional state law, by contrast, the estates have the right to renew consent to taxes in each fiscal period and, to the degree that necessary taxes are not involved, to refuse them, and this right does not contradict the monarchical principle. In case of doubt it must be assumed that the estates consent not to the expenditure but rather the taxes upon demonstration of the necessity of the expenditure. Therefore, if the necessity is not demonstrated, they may refuse the required sum to be taxed and may also designate the budget [Etat] that will be cut on that account, e.g., the agriculture budget, religious affairs budget [Kultusetat], since the need for such an expenditure was not shown for these. Even so, they cannot designate the *specific item of outlay* of the budget to be omitted, e.g., this or that building on the agriculture budget, the costs of a seminary on the religious affairs <290> budget. Rather, the government has the choice of which of the non-legally necessary expenditures it wants to drop if its budget is reduced.

This is the juridical consequence of the historical right to consent to taxes of the German territorial estates, in application to the new institution of the budget (fiscal administration [Etatwirthschaft]) which came in place of individual objects of application. The distinction between budget and specific object designates the transition from the ancient state law to the modern one and is the most significant both for the consent to taxes and for the assessment of application (compliance with items). It needs to be considered more in this sweeping effect than hitherto has occurred. In any case, in terms of the monarchical principle, the estates do not have to consent to the budget but only to consent to the taxes on the basis of the budget, or to consent, for instance, to the amendments to a budget held to be traditional.

It also answers to the monarchical principle that the budget be set for a longer period, as arranged in the German constitutions, instead of yearly, as in England. In general, the intervals of the assembly of the estates essentially correspond with the specific underlying principle. If the popular representative assembly is sovereign, the actual lawgiver as in 1791, then it must be permanent. If the king is sovereign but the assembly is the preponderant power in the state, determining the details of administration, as in England, then it cannot be permanent, but must be convened within the shortest interval. If the king truly rules, and if the assembly, as its concept states, is only the territorial representation, only jointly determining the laws, etc., then it requires convocations only between longer intervals. But when it has no official significance, only assisting the princely patrimonial power in the protection of estates' special privileges, then its convocation is not periodic, legal, but dependent upon the caprice and need of the prince.

§. 114. Ministerial Accountability and the Monarchical Principle

<291> Finally, the monarchical principle above all requires and above all consists in this, that *the prince has the right and power to govern independently.*

This rules out accountability of a minister in the manner and extent as it exists in England. Ministerial accountability in the German constitutional states, therefore, is of an entirely different character. Jurisdiction is not entrusted to the estates but, upon a joint impeachment on their part [gemeinsame Anklage], is transferred to a court of law external to them (the supreme territorial court or their own state court); punishments are not capital, and impeachments are restricted to violation, in fact often intentional violation, of the constitution. Furthermore, with the current individual proceedings for a ministerial impeachment in Germany, the principle has been settled that the minister remains in office rather than relinquishing it merely upon impeachment by the estates (prior to verdict), as long as he retains the confidence of the prince. All of this is not merely an incomparably more restricted power on the part of the estates over the minister, but an institution of an entirely different principle. Here, ministerial accountability merely serves the goal of *constitutionality,* not, as in England, the goal of *parliamentary government.* This means that it exists to ensure that every measure is in accordance with the constitution, not to ensure that every measure is in accordance with the will of the estates and receives the subsequent consent of the estates. The minister is liable for inefficient administration, for damages he does to the country, only not to the estates but to the prince. Therefore, no minister can refuse a royal order on the ground that he bears responsibility to the estates, unless the order runs contrary to the constitution.

Accordingly, the German constitutions impart to the estates, in addition to impeachment, usually the *right of appeal* [Recht der Beschwerde]. Such has no application in the English system. Where the entire government is subject to the accountability of the estates and its judgment, what meaning would such an appeal to the king have? If Parliament is dissatisfied with something, it can itself obtain redress and retribution without opposition; it does not need the king <292> for this. By contrast, if the impeachment is restricted to mere constitutional violations, even intentional ones, then a broad sphere is left in which the help of the prince can be invited. The appeal presupposes the prince to be a higher, more powerful, freely acting party. Where it ceases to apply, it is a sign that the monarchical principle has ceased.

Even with this restriction, it cannot be maintained that ministerial impeachment runs contrary to the monarchical principle. No co-sovereignty is entailed in it, the prince is not positively compelled to do anything; even the (negative) prevention of repetition of the measure which gave rise to the impeachment is only indirect. By it, the estates do not necessarily become overmighty, for the ministers, apart from violations of the constitution, always have more reason to attach themselves to the prince than to the estates. On the other hand, even in this form one cannot pass off ministerial impeachment as *everywhere essential* in the development of the estates system, and, above all, not at the beginning.

In general, the point is to inaugurate the influence of the estates and to put the legal order under their control; but regarding the most extreme protection of the constitution, one naturally sees to it only when the need has been shown for it. This protection in the final analysis resides in the power of sentiment, for what happens when the prince, contrary to the constitution, refuses to allow his ministers to be tried? Similarly, many gradations are possible here; the right of the estates simply to petition the prince to bring ministers to trial is an age-old one, it was exercised by the old French estates general, it is perhaps the origin and the earliest form of the English bill of attainder, since no competence for actual impeachment yet existed; in this manner, then, conditions can be set, and set in many ways, for which alone the petition of impeachment has to be followed up. Additionally, the protection sought in ministerial impeachment can in many cases be vouchsafed in another manner: regarding financial conflicts, through court decision or arbitration[144]; regarding undertakings against the

[144] The decisions of 1834 rejected the practice of the estates in the constitutional states whereby sums spent unlawfully were held to be still in the treasury, and so were

constitution, through **<293>** court decision or mediation by the German Confederation. The extreme measure of asserting the estates' rights is the most difficult point, it is the knife-edge upon which the constitution stands, and upon which it cannot maintain itself without falling to one side or the other. If this measure is sufficient with entire certainty, then even in the case of its abuse it is necessarily so powerful, and therefore absolutely threatening, that the princely power can be broken by it; if there is no such measure, then the danger is that the estates' rights will be rendered nugatory. A detailed development of the various manners for the various forms of violation could lead to an approximate solution to the problem. In case of doubt, however, the decisive consideration in terms of the monarchical principle, in particular in a large kingdom, must be the maintenance of the royal regard, and precisely the more so if the estates likewise with less sufficient legal competencies still always have a security of incalculable strength in their moral effect, while the prince finds his power merely in law and right. Did not, for example, the Prussian provincial estates, which in terms of law only had an advisory voice, not have a much more effective veto than the king of England, to whom a hindering voice is granted by law?

In the same way that in terms of the **<294>** monarchical principle ministerial impeachment cannot extend farther than violation of the constitution, the countersignature does not extend farther than regulations and decrees, thus not to royal declarations. These, oral or written, public or private, cannot be subject to any restriction. He who would and should rule must be able to express the

---

included in scheduled taxes (which is only a complement), as if such was not more loyal and old-territorial-estates-oriented than the impeachment of the minister of finance. This is the simple consequence: if account must be rendered to the estates, they have the right to refuse to recognize non-budgetary outlays and thus to view such outlays as if account thereof had not been rendered to them. The rest will take care of itself or remain undecided. What the estates, in particular of Bavaria, to which this applies, thus wanted was nothing other than not to have to submit a complaint to the officials (council of state) but, when it concerns their own purse, to have only their own judgment count (or that of a court of law). One wonders what would happen if the sum has been spent? Court decision or arbitration would establish whether, according to the object concerned, it would be charged against the Civil List or, in other cases, whether it would be saved from the specific post that the estates request or the government proposes.

sentiment by which he rules and with which he takes every individual measure.[145]

The right of princes to govern independently, which entails these legal restrictions on ministerial accountability and countersignature, finds no less expression in relation to mores and maxims of statesmanship.

According to the parliamentary principle, it is taboo to name the king in proceedings and so to attribute an act to him; therefore vice versa, according to the monarchical principle it must be taboo to characterize acts of government as issuing merely from the ministers instead of the king, where this does not lie particularly in the nature of the case. This does not rule out bold opposition to governmental acts. In earlier European assemblies of the realm and in the German territories, the prince was certainly as highly honored as the king of England is today; nevertheless, there was no fiction either that the prince could do no wrong, or that everything was done by his ministers, and yet reproach and rejection of propositions, appeals against measures and the spirit of the government without any restriction, was not any less allowable and common. **<295>** Even the personal actions of the prince could be disputed without infringing his regard, when the estates did not stand over the government as an authority, but rather as subjects seeking redress. The prohibition against naming the prince, which has also made its way into German assembly procedural regulations, is an atrophy of the monarchical principle. In terms of appearance, it serves to secure his elevation, but in fact it serves to eliminate it. Hereby I only controvert the

---

[145] A German sovereign found himself induced to make the announcement that the dissolution of the chamber was not, as the opposition supposed, the abetting of his minister, but his own will. This announcement was disputed by the opposition because it appeared without a countersignature. In the specific case, this conflict reminds one of the Biblical saying: "we piped for you" etc.; for when the opposition prodded the prince to hear his own sentiment, how can it complain when he makes it known to them? Yet in general and everywhere, such a declaration, which itself is not a decree, requires no countersignature and involves no ministerial accountability in terms of German state law. The minister he defended appealed to the fact that, in Germany, matters are different than in England, for the "sovereignty of princes" was still valid here, to which he received the reply, whether the king of England was not sovereign? He should much rather have objected that in Germany the *monarchical principle* is valid constitutionally; for then the true ground would have been disclosed.

absolute exclusion of the royal name. As a rule, it is most convenient that "the government" be named, prince and minister together, for this answers to the reality, and where it has to do with violation of law and with fault, naturally the minister alone. But regarding measures which are not disputed in terms of legality, it must also be possible to declare a royal will, which then can only be treated as royal. Certainly it is of the utmost benefit that majesty stands above the actions of the government, that initially everything manifest itself as issuing from the ministers or on the advice of the ministers, that thereby animosity only fall upon their heads, and that redress is expected from the impartial royal decision. But this means that the monarch must have the opportunity to decide for himself, even if in reality he does not do so at first, that the final decision must really come from him personally. This is not now the case in England and is ruled out by the taboo on the royal name. In any case, there the hatred is visited on the head of the minister, yet redress is not sought from the king, who does not act; rather, Parliament itself obtains redress.

Likewise in terms of the monarchical principle it cannot be allowable that the estates hold a vote of no confidence in the minister; likewise not that the minister resigns his office when he gets outvoted in the chamber. Even with impeachment by the estates, a German minister, as mentioned, has no obligation of honor to resign prior to the court's decision.

Here we arrive at the decisive point of the modern estates system and the German constitutional future. The question is whether the prince will rule, or the chamber majorities? One could easily imagine that the English custom, according to which the minister resigns after a so-called defeat, is only the necessary consequence of all developed **<296>** constitutions of the estates of the realm, for if the estates have the capacity to hinder laws, then it is a simple matter to not pass any laws when the majority of the estates opposes the minister, and so prevent the minister from governing. But this only holds true under the supposition that the estates, apart from this right of hindrance against new laws, possess yet other means to afford the government embarrassments, in particular regarding finances. If the estates refuse taxes, secret funds, and the like, then, of course, governing cannot continue, and the king must take the ministers that the estates want. By contrast, if the state budget is secure in its present form, independent of the caprice of the estates, then the mere rejection of the minister's legislative proposals cannot force his retirement. For governance can continue along the lines of the existing laws apart from any new ones, and the question then is whether the nation has a greater interest in the new law or in the government; as a result, the chamber opposition is forced to give in. Yet precisely because of this, it will not occur to the estates to use the rejection of laws as a means to the removal of the minister. In every constitution of the estates of the realm, the prince must take consideration of the estates. He is not to rule with ministers who form the most extreme opposition to the popular sentiment, in fact to the spirit of the constitution, and yet he is not to be determined in the choice of his minister by this or that political party, and even less by this or that shade thereof, by this or that coterie, and above all by this or that individual; by his regard he will be able to uphold the principles of the minority and moderate those of the majority, without having to put the government in its hands. He will be able to oppose the paroxysms of the time with the unwavering resistance of his better judgment and, if it only truly satisfies the deeper interests, to bring an independent plan to fulfillment in spite of all challenges. With all true constitutions of the estates of the realm, the prince is required to take consideration of the estates, but they are no less required to do so of the prince; these are two subjects of independent, albeit diverse power. Under the parliamentary principle, the prince ceases to be such.

The phenomenon of the English constitution, whereby **<297>** the minister and the government system are determined by the majority of the lower house rather than by the king, is therefore not the naturally necessary consequence of the estates-oriented right of consent to laws and the budget but only the naturally necessary consequence of the estates-oriented dictatorship over the state budget, over the persons of the ministers, and similar determinations; therefore, it does not pertain to the constitution of the estates of the realm, nor the constitutional constitution [konstitutionellen Verfassung] in general, but only the specific institutions of the parliamentary principle.

§. 115. True Constitutional Monarchy

Summarizing all of this once more, the monarchical principle is based on the prince alone having the drafting of laws (initiative), the estates only consent and petition; he alone possessing the administration: administrative regulations are not valid as laws and so subject to the consent of the estates, and administrative decrees (private bills) even less so; that he has both his own princely income and the means of the state budget independent of the will of the estates, only requiring the estates for optional outlays or for increases or amendments within the received traditional system of the state budget; finally, that all these rights are really, not apparently, exercised, and to this end the countersignature and responsibility of the minister, or other means of estates' protection, extend no farther than what is in keeping with the constitution. These institutions are, as is everywhere to be seen, very well reconcilable with the development of the estates system in the new state-oriented (constitutional) character; they require neither a weakened assembly of the realm nor one established in terms of the private-legal type. In consequence of this, the estates are by no means restricted to asserting isolated competencies; rather, the great, powerful significance remains to them of protection of the joint, public, legal condition; they are the guardians and guarantors for the maintenance of observance of the laws, for order and lawful expenditure in the state budget; and they exercise a moral power of sugges- **<298>** tion and further development. While according to the English principle they themselves determine the collective ship of state, here they are restricted to the maintenance or co-determination of the legal fundamentals by which the ship of state proceeds. This and only this is their lesser position.

By contrast, the question presses as to whether these institutions are also suitable actually to maintain the monarchical power. Would not this combined power of popular council and popular movements in short order overpower these bulwarks of monarchy, especially in a time in which public opinion is absolutely more in favor of the opposition than the authority? Does not the first step here lead, as if on a slippery slope, from the peak downward unstoppably to the depths? Historical experience provides nothing to go by here. The failed enterprise of the Restoration to unite the constitutional constitution and the monarchical principle is no proof against the possibility, because the Restoration infringed everything we are discussing here, and juxtaposed the most contradictory institutions: exclusion of estates-oriented initiative and unconditional refusal to consent to taxes, enormous property qualification and mere numerical system of representation, recklessness in the election of ministers and unrestricted freedom of the press, political emancipation without freedom of worship. But the German constitutional states are no more proof of the possibility of such a union, since here the monarchical power gained a support from the non-constitutional great powers of Germany. The danger that, regardless of all those securities, the monarchical power will be overpowered by the estates of the realm, cannot be denied. A constitution of the estates of the realm which renders impossible the mastering of the monarchy, simply does not exist. As it is now, a security for the monarchy under all conditions, thus regardless of what kind of government, is scarcely possible any longer; even the unrestricted monarchy can succumb, through blunders by the government, to the same power which one fears in the estates.

Security is therefore to be found not merely in the constitution but likewise in the manner of governing. If the manner of governing is not strong, energetic, resting on firm albeit moderate prin- **<299>** ciples, then to that degree, factually contrary to the constitution, power will accrue to the estates and will become parliamentary, especially when the constitution is first introduced and thus lacks the secure basis of prescriptive usage. It follows the natural law of the strong over the weak. The constitution cannot achieve more than keep the monarchy from being overthrown of itself and in an orderly manner, such as is established in the institutions of Western states by necessity. It can only ensure that the monarchy will not have to resort to a special ploy (neutralizing the institutions) to maintain its strength, that it is only necessary for the monarchy to maintain its position, not first win it from the estates in a fortuitous eventuality.

This cannot be emphasized strongly enough; it is the central issue when treating of the final decision. Without being prepared, without a closed system of administration secure in ends as well as means, a government cannot confront a newly called assembly of estates of the realm if it does not wish to gamble on its existence. We maintain that one need not fear the sea when one confronts it with a well-masted ship rather than with a small boat (which is what the English and French constitutions are as far as monarchy is concerned). But we do not maintain that with a good ship it will go at sea as on land, or that the only thing needed is a properly constructed ship, and not also proper piloting.

This is the outline of the fundamental thought of the existing German constitutional monarchy. It is a constitution of the estates of the realm in *state-oriented* (public) character under the *monarchical principle.*

Where the German constitutions already contain something deviating from this, they should not be dumped for that reason. The steadfastness of existing law should not be affected by any reasoning or political conviction. But in cases where positive determinations are lacking, this principle should be applied in German constitutions, and where a new introduction or future development is concerned, it is the guideline. Hereby it is self-evident, and has already been suggested throughout, that the monarchical principle not only can be realized in various ways but that it also, in <300> greater or lesser degree, can determine the constitution. The sphere of laws and thus of estates' consent can be more or less expanded, as can the estates' right of consent and share in decisions for the state budget; the specification of the budget can be conducted in more or less detail; the accountability of the minister can be more or less severe, more or less dependent upon the will of the prince. When the estates have real rights, then in return for them their right of petition and their consultative vote (debate [Diskussion]) can be restricted. The forms of conducting business can elevate or diminish the effect of estates' debates, etc.

§. 116. Power of Advice versus Power of Consent by the Estates

A yet stronger security for the monarchical principle is now being found in the restriction of the estates to a mere *advisory capacity* rather than consent. Especially for *Prussia,* the constitution intended – unwaveringly – by Friedrich Wilhelm III was none other than: in formation [Bildung] and efficacy, estates of the *modern type,* but with *a mere advisory voice.* Already in the edict of October 27th, 1810, at the time of the greatest tribulation of the war, nothing else was promised than

> to give the nation a suitably established representation, both in the provinces and for the whole, the advice of which we will gladly make use, and through which we will continually give to our faithful subjects the conviction, in accordance with our conviction as father of the country, that the condition of the state and the finances is improving.

Just as certain was the tone of the famed and decisive decree of May 22nd, 1815:

> §. 4. The efficacy of the territorial representation extends to *advice* regarding all objects of *legislation* which concern the personal and property rights of the citizens *inclusive* <301> *of taxation.*

Likewise, all letters patent connected with acquired territory, as well as all of Hardenberg's declarations, without exception speak of nothing but advising estates, and Prussia's draft to the Vienna conference to establish the German Confederation essentially corresponded to this. It was therefore everywhere only *advice* which was intended for the estates of the realm. This notwithstanding, a soundly ordered constitution [Verfassung] and "charter," a *constitution* [Konstitution], was intended which, accordingly, set the government under public civil principles, and ensured to the estates an ongoing and full insight into the state budget and advice for all laws regarding the civil legal condition, not merely those concerning the *jura singulorum.*

Nowadays, therefore, it is the opinion of many, among whom the most highly esteemed, that in Prussia in the event of the convening of the estates of the realm, that these should only provide advice, while the contrary would threaten the continuing existence of the monarchy. It seems that advisory estates leave power undiminished in the hands of the king, providing no hindrance to energy and agreement in all legislative and administrative measures. Beyond this, they have the advantage of making possible a freer valuation of the views brought forward, instead of, for the sake of strictness of form, abandoning a bill for the lack of a few votes, which perhaps was more plausibly and in a livelier fashion defended than attacked. We do not deny the weight of this viewpoint, and, assuming that mere advisory estates truly provide a greater degree of security for the monarchy, we could even agree with it. That this is a yet more decisive consideration than that of elevating the activity of the estates, is the viewpoint from which we also begin. But we still have to question that premise. If the government is in secure possession of financial means and in secure possession of (even if constitutionally restricted) public welfare administration [Polizeigewalt], as we require, if it is not dependent upon the estates for the necessary taxes, not dependent on "laws" against political associations and the like, then the estates' right of consent cannot really threaten the <302> monarchy. Only the moral effectiveness of the estates' petition, and popular agitation, would form a threat, and this is no less the case with advisory estates than with consenting estates.

On the other hand, we have grave misgivings regarding advisory estates for every large monarchy (and therefore Prussia as well), and in fact – entirely apart from the fact that, to us, consent seems to be the natural position for the estates – precisely in the interest of monarchy:

1) The institution of advisory estates is an instigation to continuous constitutional struggle. The granting of advice contains no recognition of entitlement, the estates have no awareness that they accomplish something, are useful for something, and therefore have an aspiration to expand their rights, and yet advice gives them a factual power in the moral efficacy of the expression of the estates' opinion, which supports that aspiration. It may therefore everywhere be better advised to entrust the estates with certain rights than give them a position in which they attempt to win rights for themselves. In that case they could come away with more booty than they would originally have been satisfied with. In fact, in itself and immediately, the estates' advice, precisely through the contradiction between legal insignificance and factual importance, is often a greater restriction than is consent. So, for example, with the refusal of consent one may repeat the proposal in the following assembly or dissolve the house; all of this would make no sense with an estates' vote which one did not have to follow, and yet one often cannot disregard it.

2) The institution of advisory estates puts the government in moral embarrassment. By that institution, it often finds itself in the predicament of either embittering the country by not taking the estates' vote into consideration or of giving a sign of weakness by doing so. So in particular, with laws which in terms of their nature are proposed with the announcement of a principled, even ethical necessity, the government facing consenting estates can by virtue of legal necessity allow the law to fall with honor, while when facing advisory estates, in the case of the law's dis- <303> pleasing them, it can neither follow through without losing popularity nor give up without losing regard.

3) The institution of advisory estates leads to continual tumult in the country. To wit, in that they have no legal power to hinder displeasing laws and demands, they by the necessity of the matter are relegated to hindering them by the exertion of moral power. If they have the power of consent, the estates know that their mere "no!", be it ever so quiet, is sufficient; if they only have advice, they can promise nothing through their mere "no!", but merely from the energy of this "no" they must show the government how strongly they are violated by the proposition; they must call upon the sentiment of the people for assistance, day in and day out they must huff and puff with moral effect; in fact, they must

continually maintain the storm they engender, for if it is stilled, then the government's view threatens to become fulfilled.[146] So, for example, in Bavaria in 1837, a law to introduce corporal punishment was taken up by the estates with great displeasure and then immediately rejected, but the matter was dismissed without consequence; in the Prussian Rhine province regarding a similar law, the entire population was brought into uproar and kept there.

Admittedly, the estates must everywhere, at least in terms of the monarchical principle, in the final analysis be based on moral power, but that moral power should only guarantee their recognized rights, not come in their place.

4) Advisory estates have a greater temptation to reject good but unpopular laws, since their "no" does not bind the government, and therefore their responsibility seems lesser. Vice versa, <304> when they reject bad but popular laws, it does not work disfavor against the government because the government can still enact them. They therefore do not, as do consenting estates, gain strength from government restriction.

5) Finally, in terms of their essence, advisory estates are unnatural. The king demands good advice from his officials, his ministers, his council of state, or from notables. A territorial representation is only possible on the ground of recognition that the country has certain rights, in particular a right to the existing legal condition, of which it cannot be divested without its consent. A periodic delegation from the entire country, and periodic convocation of larger estates of the realm merely for the goal of moral demonstrations therefore factually yields an imbalance between the strength of promise and the insignificance of its object, between effort and result. In the end, however, the disadvantage is on the side of the government, in that with actual greater restriction it gives the impression of unrestrictedness. It is like a costly yet shabby-looking gift. The

---

[146] One could argue that this and the previous evil apply just as well in the case of consenting states with regard to petitions. But not to grant a petition is never regarded as oppression, as is the introduction of a new law against the public opinion; therefore, it takes exceptional strength on the part of the government to accomplish the latter but very little for the former, and with the usual state of the government, the estates can hope to use agitation to avert the introduction of a law but not to obtain the granting of a petition. It is only with regard to complaints about violated rights that a similar relationship exists.

solution to the problem cannot under any circumstance be sought in the advisory estates. For everything which with us makes the territorial representation problematic – the lack of a historically generated representation rooted in the consciousness of the nation, civil servants as delegates standing in opposition to the government, the attempt of the government to corrupt them and the other members of the house – all of this is found just as well with advisory estates, when they are not entirely lacking in significance, in which case they are better off being absent altogether.

Of course one gets beyond all of this when a government, as many would like, has so much energy that in everything it only follows its own insight, and pays no further regard to the voice of the estates than when it itself is convinced by them. We certainly wish the government steadiness and energy, but such a lack of consideration, even when power is given to that end, does not accord with the significance of the estates, not even the of merely advisory sort; through it, public opinion in itself and as such will maintain <305> some influence with the government. Opinions and wishes can, if need be, also be ascertained in other ways, in any case without such an ordered institution, and it would hardly be wise to call for the will of the nation to be made manifest by means of a regulated institution when all the while one does not wish to be bound by it.

In this regard, then, there are only two forms of institution which beyond doubt are in themselves in agreement and enduring. The first is the purely monarchical one, in which all final decisions rest with the prince; it does not require the consent of the estates, nor does it need a regularly required appeal and consultation with them. How could a monarch who recognizes no legal resistance to his legislative power develop and sanction an element that would offer him, albeit without legal right, resistance often virtually insurmountable! The other institution is the estates-oriented or constitutional, by which the estates are recognized as supplementary element of the government, essential to which is their right of consent. By contrast, for estates of regular necessary convocation and inquiry, but with mere advice, it is, at least in a larger independent monarchy, doubtful whether it can be a viable institution, i.e., one which can exist over the long term, whether this institution must not rather pass into either the impotence or the supremacy of the estates.

Such an institution cannot be compared with the position the estates often had in former times. This was a chiaroscuro of advice and consent (not the decisiveness of the former); it presumed no regular necessary convocation and was maintained in a harmless, legally indefinite time. Even in later times, such a regularly ordered assembly with mere advice would have been possible (although none actually did exist), as long, namely, as the absolute power of the monarch was the ruling opinion and moral power in the people. At that time, all estates-oriented discussion automatically was directed, as it were, to the prince, to convince him and to move him (as with the English House of Commons, discussion is always directed to the Speaker); today, by contrast, it is everywhere directed to the people, in order to harness public opinion. This is a fact, and besides, the full-blown <306> development of the activity of the estates of the realm is scarcely capable of implementation apart from a right thereto under the consistent absolute arbitration of the prince.

We therefore seek the protection of the monarchy not in the diminished weight of estates activity but in its position. We seek it in the proper interleaving of government power and estates' entitlement, whereby the government alone determines the course of the whole, while the estates only join in deciding certain questions, the former acting entirely freely on the basis of the existing legal order, the latter having the right to maintain the existing legal order; whereby the paths of the movement of the government (public welfare regulation, determination of the state budget, etc.) and the paths of the movement of subjects (property, freedom against penal power, taxes, maintenance of the constitution) are separated, the former reserved to the government, the latter conceded to the estates.[147]

---

[147] In the second edition, there followed here a statement, "that in the case of a constitution of the estates of the realm, Prussia had to maintain the monarchical principle in an incomparably higher measure than the smaller German states, for the unity of its provinces and for its position outward"; "no parity [Gleichstellung] with the current German constitutions ought to be claimed for Prussia"; and it was proposed, "instead of excluding all estates' competencies of consent and authorization" that such be granted, but with the proviso "that the king remain the supreme judge over conflicts regarding the application of the constitution," thus that the "ever doubtful boundaries" be determined by him. The detailed depiction and justification given there, however, holds no interest now. The text under nos. 4 and 5 on pp. 303ff. above was added to the third edition.

§. 117. The Monarchical Principle as Cornerstone of the Estates-Oriented Polity

The monarchical principle as here depicted – we repeat – is the *foundation of German state law and German state wisdom.*

It cannot be denied that the English constitution is an example for the European future, but only in the aspect of its state-oriented character, not in its parliamentary supremacy. The latter is a consequence not merely of special historical events but also special <307> ongoing conditions: two revolutions, repeated accessions to the throne of foreign dynasties without any root in the country, the consolidation and power of both political parties, the dissipation of crown demesnes. It therefore pertains to the deepest individuality of the English constitution, and for that reason is lawful, excellent, beneficent for England, but neither comparable to nor capable of imitation by other states. And even for England, it is not certain whether, with the continuing diminution in the significance of the upper house and the advancement of the lower classes, the time will yet come in which the requirement of a strong monarchy will be generally perceived.

It cannot be maintained that this parliamentary supremacy in itself is the higher constitutional condition, as little as it is the lower, just as no general preference between monarchy and the republic can be determined. The question between the monarchical and the parliamentary principle at bottom is only the repetition, in a narrower sphere, of the question between monarchy and the republic. In every age, various forms of government have been extant for the various states; with this or that people, the monarchical, the aristocratic, or the democratic element has been predominant; each could in its fashion and for its conditions be excellent, and this manifoldness and individuality ought to and must also be valid for the future: nothing general and uniform can be hoped for in this. Therefore, within the sphere of the constitution of the estates of the realm, the preponderance of the parliament over the king, thus the republican element over the monarchical, cannot be the general task; such can only consist in the establishment of that which should stand over all those elements: inner necessity and lawfulness in the institution of the state. Only here and no further is there a general measure of the constitution in our time. The spirit and will of the nation cannot rule, it not being a personality; therefore, rule will always be conducted either by kings, or by ministers, or by a powerful or energetic party, and there is no universal verdict as to whether this or that is the better. The spirit and will of the nation can, however, support the lawful order of the state, and form the basis for the government, and this can be achieved just as well under the monarchical principle as under the <308> parliamentary. If instead of inner lawfulness and necessity, the greatest possible expansion of estates' power and suppression of the monarchy were a great good and a general task, then the English would have to do away with their constitution and take on the North American one. When the parliamentary principle is considered not as an English peculiarity but as a general constitutional goal, in the manner that the state-oriented character of the English constitution truly is such a general goal, it leads inevitably to the constitution of North America; and that the latter is more fruitful, satisfactory, and excellent than the English or ours, no impartial person would maintain.

This, then, must be made clear: if one wishes for the parliamentary principle where it does not already exist historically, then one wishes for nothing other than the republic, regardless of monarchical trappings. By contrast, as a rule and under normal relations the monarchical principle is the normal, i.e., the proper and appropriate one, even if it is not absolutely better or higher. Just as according to the testimony of all ages, monarchy is the normal constitution of the state and the republic is only an individual vocation of certain states, so within the estates constitution is the relation between the monarchical and the parliamentary principle. In case of doubt, the strength of the central power in the state is the first, the indispensable, the more excellent, over against the strength of the periphery, and for the latter to develop to the place appropriate to it, through the steady growth of its activity rather than all at once, is the healthy manner of progress. It is therefore a deception to say that the interest of the people is promoted in proportion to the rights of the estates of the realm. On the contrary, a certain measure of estates' rights, whereby the government retains its independence and elevation, does the most to ensure that interest; for when the government is robbed of this position, it is put in the necessity of corrupting the estates. One is then free of the power of the prince but falls into the power of the leading men of state, who, in order to maintain a ministry, bestow the means and offices of the country on delegates, and streets, bridges, and the like, on electoral districts. One is ruled by parties rather than the impartial <309> power of the prince.

Just as no general requirement exists for the parliamentary principle, so is there likewise no general aptitude for it. The English certainly do not merely possess special political gifts: the sense of independence, common activity, and, at the same time, of existing (not merely self-made) laws and acquired rights – gifts, which certainly every people, when treating simply of themselves, would rightly or wrongly attribute to themselves in the same degree; they also possess the habituation to, and exercise of, rule, which they have acquired gradually over the centuries, and, what is much more, which build a dam against their own infringement, and which apparently no people can give to itself. To this is added another decisive circumstance. In England, it is the two political parties which, both through great linkages ("connexions") of leading families and through their organization as a party, possess factual power, to which the legal power of the king must be subordinated. In truth, it is not so much the power of Parliament which displaces it as the power of the two federations in the country. Precisely this factually extant element, which weakens the monarchy, also provides a guarantee of order which instead allows monarchy to be missed. These alliances, namely, are themselves a power of unity and order in the manner of higher regard, to which individuals and coteries with their viewpoints and ambition have to subordinate themselves; if some authority and power exists other than the king, with the same energy, then the latter will not be so much missed.

Such a situation can however neither be found nor produced elsewhere; and so, when elsewhere the unifying point of the crown gives way, the nation, which was only unified in opposition, splits up into a plethora of parties and connections which reciprocally frustrate each other in their enterprises. Thus, in France we continually witness the phenomenon by which a large majority is found in order to cause a ministry to fall, but then, without royal influence, there is none to maintain another ministry; that the minister who suffers a defeat in the house nevertheless must remain in office, since every possible ministry following it will find even less support. There is therefore nothing more unnatural than the requirement of the <310> French opposition, that the king not govern (*gouverner*), but follow England's example and allow the house majorities to govern. In England, it is an existing power that wrested the scepter from the king; in France, one demands that the scepter be abandoned so that perhaps a power, no trace of which has yet been seen, will take it up. If it had not been France's fortune to have as king a head of state who in all of Europe was the most capable of governing, then one would have seen to what lengths parliamentary government would lead. This king had the enormous task not merely of having to govern despite resistance, but also of having to maintain the appearance of not governing.

In Germany in particular, the monarchical principle is legally grounded, for the prince always abided in this right, and the recent expansions of the estates system were not wrung from him but freely conceded. It is, however, also the most beneficial for Germany. For apart from the confusion which always and everywhere threatens from its diminution, this is to be added in Germany, that with the entirely chance fragmentation and conglomeration of territories into states entirely lacking in tribal and historical community, the center of gravity of the constitution and the spirit of governing must have its seat in the prince and not in the estates assembly, if otherwise unity and coherence is to be preserved and energy projected.

In Germany there are, furthermore, other guarantees beyond the influence of the estates which one ought not count as lesser than that, and which can only continue to exist with the maintenance of the monarchical principle. To this above all belongs the *intelligent, honorable, and irremovable German civil service.* The irremovability of officials has been declared by esteemed and upright liberal politicians to be irreconcilable with a constitutional constitution [konstitutioneller Verfassung]. But one must make a distinction: it is irreconcilable with the estates-oriented constitution in terms of the parliamentary principle, but not the estates-oriented constitution in terms of the monarchical principle, i.e., it is irreconcilable with ministers whom Parliament can ruin whenever it wishes, and who for the positive value of their administration are subjected to the judgment of Par- **<311>** liament in all measures; but it is quite reconcilable with ministers subject only to the prince for the administration, and answerable to the estates only regarding observance of the constitution.

In Germany as everywhere, consciously or unconsciously, the prevailing oppositional course of the times is turned precisely against the monarchical principle. It is filled with imagery that, as with England, the entire administration, even the position outward, should be determined by the nation, i.e., the house majorities and in any case the press, and by the axiom that this is the only reasonable condition. To this is attributable the dissatisfaction with all concessions, in that they cannot possibly go that far, as well as the transfer of English parliamentary customs and maxims to German constitutions in the estates assemblies, as if their validity was self-evident. A predominantly aristocratic parliament, as in England, is of course not what is wanted; one combines two things which hitherto never existed in combination, a predominantly democratically-composed estates assembly, as does not exist in England, and the parliamentary principle, which exists only in England and nowhere else – and this is the ideal. Beyond this, in England in terms of its medieval character, the relation between king, ministers, and Parliament is without precise legal stipulation, factually unstable, floating, while on the Continent it is formulated in modern mathematical precision. An English king of personal energy could in an emergency maintain a ministry against the majority, while here from the start this is an apodictic violation of "constitutional state law." Conceived in this manner, there remains no other function to princes than mere vote-counting, to draw the resultant conclusion as to which system is to be asserted and which leader is immediately to enter into the ministry, a function which properly could be handled without a king, by the director of the house, perhaps even its clerk. Clearly stated, what is expected of the king from this side is therefore nothing other than the abdication of the crown. Behind all appearance – that the king holds the veto, that he chooses ministers, that he can rule the more forcefully with a parliament – there is no other result in the matter than this. As long, however, as **<312>** the world stands, no prince, no aristocratic body, no popular assembly ever committed political suicide, ever took a step without having to, which not only restricts but abolishes its power. The peoples have no right to demand such a revolution of the existing constitution, and the princes have no right to allow it. They must not allow the power entrusted them by God to slip from their hand in favor of an unknown and untested power which is first to arise only in the future. In fact, they above all are no less responsible to the people for maintaining the most secure guarantee of its welfare and its rights, which is the monarchy, than they are to grant it a secure public legal condition and a broad sphere of its own cooperation and public activity.

This widely-held manner of thinking and political orientation is, therefore, precisely one of the serious problems which stand in the way of the invigoration of estates-oriented institutions.

On the other side, one appeals to the conscientiousness of the princes and the duty of trust in order to reject estates' rights and state-legal guarantees. This argumentation holds no weight. It could be opposed with the same right by an appeal to the loyalty of the people and the presumption of confidence in them, in order to reject the guarantees of the monarchical principle. The confidence both of princes in the people and of the people in princes is ever indispensable for the public prosperity; and with bad will or misunderstanding, or with distrust, all mechanical protection is in vain. This does not, however, rule out the safeguarding by a legally unswerving order of the position of both parts in their essential features. One has more confidence when in his entire situation he is not dependent upon others, and it is no unfair demand that that which he has coming to him not be dependent upon the goodwill of another, but upon his own right and power.

A much more significant argument against state-legal guarantees than the appeal to the personal conscientiousness of the prince is the appeal to the traditional manner of governing. Custom and practice are everywhere better and firmer than written law. Thus, <313> when in a royal lineage it is a tested tradition to govern not according to caprice but according to principles of state, and to recognize in the laws and the regulated course of administration a restriction which is the true principle of governing even more than is the will of the people, then the jump from such an existing guarantee of civil order and freedom to have a go with a new, generically different one, seems an ungrounded, hazardous undertaking. But something other than this jump is the development and confirmation of an element which to this point had been neglected, while preserving existing guarantees, therefore precisely in terms of the degree of that element's preservability.

With this political confession of faith, we therefore again tread on the soil of impartiality and serious willingness for political freedom, on which the German sovereigns found themselves in the wake of the war of liberation, when they consulted regarding the future constitution of the confederation. The guarantee of a secure legal condition of subjects through a territorial estates' constitution was then the enlightened viewpoint, not in terms of the old restriction to privileged estates but in the manner "that all classes of citizen might participate therein." By contrast, both with the establishment of Article 13 of the Confederation Charter and the negotiations preceding it, a removal of the monarchical principle was not in anyone's mind. The rights which were to be assured as a minimum to the estates were those which, in accordance with the drafts proposed to that end, were of the form that do not diminish what is yet allowable according to the monarchical principle. The Austro-Prussian drafts allow the estates only advice, and consent only for *new* taxes, while beyond that the memorandum from the Hanoverian envoys of October 21st, 1814 and that of the 29 smaller sovereignties dated November 16th, allowed consent to laws and, in the case of malversation by servants of state, appeals to princes.

Therefore, when the German princes beginning in 1819 set themselves the task of upholding the monarchical principle as their most urgent duty, since foreign events and domestic moods seemed threatening, it was no contradiction to their original intention. They wished, **<314>** first, to support the rights of subjects against the territorial despotism of the Rhine Confederation, then the stability of the monarchy against that unrestrained movement of the people, and this is entirely consistent. The contradiction, or at least a noteworthy divergence from the originally pursued course, lies in the fact that with the newly added task the older receded, that, although the previous intentions were not legally withdrawn, still the energy of implementation from that moment merely went into hindering the popular movement, not in establishing a public legal condition; only a maximum of estates' rights was established, leaving undone the establishment of a minimum of estates' rights, which was the original intention, whereby every institution to which the sovereign gave the name territorial estates was judged to be in accordance with Article 13. An impartial judgment would nevertheless not leave the level of political culture [Bildung] at the time out of consideration. The "constitutional state law" drawn up by a confederation assembly envoy can be considered the general creed [Symbolum] of this. According to it, it holds as an accepted fact that the successor to the throne has to be brought up, not by his royal father, but constitutionally by a commission of the popular assembly. Where would one have ended up if under the rule of this doctrine Austria and Prussia had introduced "constitutions"? May the point in time arrive that energy toward both sides is possible, that a clear and full consciousness develops, and, thereby, a guarantee everywhere to defend the one bravely without overstepping the other! May the popular-rule party and the royal party be subsumed into a higher view of the state as the ethical intellectual kingdom, in which the ethical authority elevated over the people, which is the king, and the people itself as ethical community, take up their necessary and firmly delimited position.

Chapter 13: Territorial Representation after 1848

§. 118. The Changed Situation

In the previous chapters, which are reprinted almost unchanged from the second edition (1846), the development of the institution of territorial representation is presented according to its various stages and the principles and issues taken from them – private and state, estates-oriented and representative, monarchical and parliamentary.

Since then, the catastrophe of 1848 took place. It was a world-historical judgment, first on liberal constitutionalism, and then on democracy. In France, the one collapsed after the other, and absolute power was established. But it was precisely through this catastrophe leading to absolutism in France, that Prussia joined the ranks of the "constitutional states," i.e., the states with territorial representation and with guaranteed rights for their subjects, and it fell to it to establish the institution in a sustainable way which to that point had been untenable. Prussia now sets the example of a large realm, independent, without foreign support, with a newer form of territorial representation in which exists the monarchical principle, i.e., monarchy maintains the free and powerful position as described in the previous chapter.

Here as well, the parties of the revolution surged confusedly first in the chaos of the summer of 1848. Democratic constitutionalism after 1791 and liberal constitutionalism after 1830 which, it was thought, could only be made the "truth" by completely excluding all royal influence, struggled for dominance. Even there, however, decidedly monarchical sentiment arose, at least in the press, since it was virtually excluded from the representative bodies. But with the "saving act" of the adjournment of the National Assembly (November 9th, 1848), the monarchy was restored to its power; it triumphed over both contradictions in rapid progression, by the power of thought as well as of arms, not only regarding the measures of the moment but likewise lasting principles and institutions.

First of all, democracy was overcome by the imposition of the constitution through royal authority, the abolition of the army's oath to the constitution,[148] the abolition of the citizen militia, the laws on the press, associations, the state of siege, and the introduction of the three property classes instead of equal suffrage. But the sting was also taken out of liberal constitutionalism. The decisive blow came with the parrying of the constitutional right to refuse taxes in the First Chamber (October 16th–19th, 1849).[149] This broke the omnipotence which had formerly been exercised by constitutional doctrine in chambers and public opinion, the belief in its scientific indisputability. Other positions that had been considered insurmountable also fell in rapid succession. The continuation of the payment of existing expenses until a new agreement is reached was not established by law but by the process of 1850–1851.[150] The law on the impeachment of ministers, introduced by the government itself and fought against in vain by a minority in the Second Chamber, was rejected in the First Chamber.[151]

In addition to these decisive features of the monarchical principle, another was added: the recognition of an area in which the king exercises his power alone, without the legal and even without the moral influence of the territorial representation, thus the opposite of 1640. One such is the relation to the established Protestant Church. While in England the king must also exercise his supreme-episcopal right through responsible ministers, and it is exercised according to the mindset of these ministers and their party, the King of Prussia exercises it independently of chambers and ministers, legally and morally. The selection of proposals from the provincial parliament, which, since it only has an advisory role, receives its final decision from the king, can also be counted as such.

---

[148] Article 108 of the Prussian Constitution of 1850: "The army is not sworn to the constitution." Cf. Count Arnim-Boitzenburg: "On the swearing of the army to the constitution, written in August 1849."

[149] Article 109 of the Prussian Constitution: "The existing taxes and duties will continue to be levied... until they are changed by law." Cf. my speech of Oct. 16th, 1849, First Chamber (see appendix).

[150] Regarding the proposal to legally establish an ordinary budget which can only be amended by law, and an extraordinary budget which has not yet received the approval of the Second Chamber, see the proceedings of the First Chamber, February 14th, 1852.

[151] See my report on behalf of the commission, and the proceedings of the First Chamber of 1851.

Through all these things, regardless of their relative importance, the king retains a power of personal will, and the entire constitutional way of thinking by which the king only orders what the ministers decide, can get no foothold.

The expressions of 1848 that remained in the Prussian constitution are by no means matters of indifference. Likewise, questionable institutions remain. For example, a narrower restriction for the sphere of law is lacking such as would keep all general ordinances, including the merely administrative, from falling under it. The authority to provisionally impose actual laws ahead of their approval by the chambers is, on the one hand, no substitute for this and, on the other, an irregularity in itself which can only be consented to in an emergency. Nevertheless, the overall result is that the king really "has the right and power to govern independently" (§. 114). He really chooses his ministers freely, and it no longer occurs to anyone to resign if they have the chambers against them. He really determines the system of government; his will decides on domestic and foreign policy, on the appointment of all officials. The speech from the throne really is his speech, the expression of his sentiments, not those of his ministers.

Nevertheless, there is a territorial representation with a newer public-state-oriented character and with a decisive vote, and which is not powerless. How many a law, how many a tax, and of opposing party colors, has been defeated by it, and how many things have been made possible by it that would not have been presumed without its support. Whatever name one wants to give to this present constitution of Prussia, if one avoids the term "constitutional monarchy" because of its misinterpretation, the fact remains: it is a *restricted* kingship, but not a weakened one, not a mere *sham, nominal* kingship; it is a subspecies of the *monarchy*, and not, as according to constitutional doctrine, a subspecies of the *republic*. The king does not, as in the latter case, have the mere *right* of sovereignty without the *exercise* thereof (similar to the *nudum jus quiritium*); he also has the full independent exercise thereof. And yet it is not a restricted kingship in the old-established sense, where the public authority was merely that of the sovereign, and the estates only represented special rights; the king's right and the right of territorial representation permeate one another in one and the same public profession. In essence, according to the Final Act of the Congress of Vienna in 1820, "all state authority is united in the head of the state, and the sovereign is bound to the co-operation of the estates only in the exercise of certain rights"; but these certain rights are precisely of such a nature that they determine the state of the polity, that it is a co-operation of two powers for the state. This is the state of the law as I formulated it in 1845 and posited its possibility (see above, §§. 100 and 104). It is the actual refutation of the view of Haller and Genz, that there is no national representation of a monarchical character except that of the old estates. It is no less an actual refutation of Macaulay's view that to move from the medieval constitution (the corporative kingdom) there are only two ways, either to absolute monarchy (Louis XIV) or to the present English, that is, to the subjugated monarchy.

It is true that some of the power that the king maintains under the current constitution can be attributed to the reactionary current of opinion which has arisen in the wake of the Revolution, and in this respect the current state of Prussia only proves that such power is possible under such a constitution, but not that it is permanent. The main thing, however, is that the king's power rests not on mere sentiment but on those institutions, and if they did not exist, that power would have been broken by the opposition. A large part of the people, unbound by unshakable conviction or given to uncertainty, swings to where the power is. If the final outcome were to be expected on the side of the opposition, it might perhaps have the majority, as the king mostly has it now. But precisely for that reason, in a more revolutionary and agitated time, those institutions will be a sufficiently strong bulwark to assert the power of the crown; indeed, they are of such a nature that in an extreme clash, the outcome must rather be the dissolution of the territorial representation than the undermining of the monarchy. If it turns out differently, it is not due to the institutions but to mistakes, through which even the most absolute monarchy can be overthrown, or to world-historical currents that no constitution can stop.

A far greater difficulty than finding the right relationship between the king and the territorial representation is the appropriate shape to give to the territorial representation, for on this depends its continued existence. For this problem, which has yet to be solved, a significant insight can be gained from the experience since 1848, which, however, must be re-established upon first principles.

§. 119. The Upper House – Valuation

If one asks which system is currently appropriate for the representation of a country, particularly in Germany, then the establishment of *two chambers* or *houses* is beyond doubt. The institution of the three curiae belongs to the older system of estates, that of the single chamber to the Revolution. Since the medieval curia system was broken in England and the territorial representation of the new state was established, the institution of the two chambers is also practiced by all states of the civilized world, insofar as they have a territorial representation. All the constitutional monarchies of Europe have adopted it in one form or another, and those that have not do not come into consideration; for the French constitution of 1791 and the Spanish constitution of 1820 had only an ephemeral existence, and the German states which are too small to sustain the heavy political apparatus of the two chambers have nevertheless introduced the elements of an upper house, hereditary individual votes, in their one chamber. But even republican North America has followed the English example in its own way. Both the constitution of the United States and that of each individual state have a senate in addition to a house of representatives.[152] This form of national representation undoubtedly has an inner law and a general necessity for our time.

Just as the territorial representation is no longer intended to safeguard the special rights of the various estates but to fulfill a public function for the whole of the state, it is also of necessity no longer divided into the three or four *bodies of estates*, but into the two *political institutions*: the upper and lower houses. They are based, historically as well as essentially, on the contrast between the *ruling* and the *common* (i.e., non-ruling) position. The upper house was originally formed by the actual *nobility*, the bearers of independent and comprehensive authority over a fiefdom, the barons, and, because of similar rights, the prelates. With the development of the state, authority other than that of the sovereign was almost entirely eliminated, and the nobility was thus diminished in number and influence; therefore, other prominent existences whose significance lies in their actual power needed to join it. But it is always the great figures of the country that the upper house represents, and the secure seat in the house, independent of changing elections, itself grants a kind of ruling position even after

---

[152] In Pennsylvania, only one chamber was initially set up, prompted by Franklin's rather misleading mockery that the two-chamber system was like hitching a horse to the front of a cart and another one to the back, causing them to go in opposite directions. But here, as in some other states that tried the same, they soon found themselves compelled to introduce a senate.

personal authority outside of it has ceased. These positions, the prominent position of power and the position of the general population, are the two poles around which the political as opposed to the estate-oriented life of the people revolves, and the essence of the two chambers is to bring both to effectiveness and influence, especially the former, which represents the nation in its unity in an eminent sense, and which would otherwise disappear without effect, overwhelmed by the majority. This completeness and thus well-being of the country's representation is the justification and the true significance of the "two-chamber system."

The value of the upper house, then, is above all the prestige and the natural and moral power that the consent of such an assembly lends to laws and measures, the sounding-out against the sentiments of the country which this provides. On the other hand, its value is proportional to the influence on laws and measures that it affords to the gifts, views and motivations of the higher positions in life. This provides a power of preservation and continuity, of historical sense, of higher, freer, calmer judgment, of natural preference for all authority. The upper house thus forms a dam against the rush for popular rule, equality, dissolution; for even though it is erroneous to think that such a rush lies in the nature or even the vocation of the lower house, that house, being of the populace, cannot offer the same resistance, given its dependency on the votes of the masses. Then again, when it fulfills its task, it itself provides the impetus for increases and new creations in the sense of organic bonds, discipline and unification for great patriotic purposes. In particular, the upper house still has the value of mediation between the crown and the lower house. The similarity of position and interests brings it closer to the crown; the aspect of an advisor to the crown predominates, while in the lower house it is the aspect of a protector of the population's interests that predominates. Therefore, it strengthens the moral power of the lower house vis-à-vis the crown, since in the event of crown resistance to the lower house, it deflects disfavor. Along with this effect for the public interest, which is its most essential character, it also always secures the rights and interests of the classes it comprises, especially this political vocation of theirs, which is itself their supreme right. That is the organic and legal significance of the upper house. Besides, it has the mechanical effect of promoting the maturity of the deliberation by means of the counterweight of the two chambers.

From this importance of the upper house it also follows that the granting of seats must depend to a large extent on the king. For in a monarchical state, a position of authority can only come from the prince, and therefore an appointment by the king is absolutely necessary for hereditary and lifelong participation in the representation of the country, just as it is absolutely inadmissible for temporary participation. In particular, however, the task of mediation requires the king to have a strong influence, and for this reason his right of appointment should be unrestricted for the hereditary members, and possibly also for lifelong members in terms of number.

The essence of the upper house, then, does not consist in securing the special rights of the members appointed to it but in securing their effectiveness for their public office. The latter has reason and justification only in the former. The mere protection of rights and interests belongs to the curial system, and there, as a rule, different classes with different rights and interests could not be represented in one curia, as in the upper house. Indeed, the upper house fulfills its task all the better the less the aristocratic classes of which it consists also enjoy legal privileges, for which Sieyès praises the English House of Lords.

Likewise, the essence of the upper house does not consist in the mere mechanical counterweight of the two chambers, but in their inner content, in the development of the power of the higher elements of the nation. The mechanical result, the protection against rashness and precipitation, is only a secondary effect, just as in the human body the well-ordered organic limbs simultaneously support each other mechanically, and the mechanical support also ceases as soon as an organic function is disturbed. The superficiality of the doctrine of the Revolution is to seek in this the essence of the "two-chamber system." Only this was therefore asserted in the constituent assemblies of North America, France, and Belgium as the reason and advantage of it.[153] Consequently, in the end, the

---

[153] During the French Revolution, it was agreed that the constituent assembly should be a single chamber, because the aim was to abolish abuses without delay. But an important faction strove to establish two chambers at a later date. The rapporteur, the Archbishop of Bordeaux (July 27th, 1789) cites the following as a motive for this: "pour prévenir toute surprise et toute précipitation, pour assurer la maturité des délibérations" [to prevent surprise and haste, to ensure mature deliberations]; and also: "que

emphasis was placed solely on the duality of the chambers without any regard to their nature, and especially the aristocratic components of the upper house, and therefore to form both chambers from the same fabric of the general popular vote, as in France, under the constitution of 1795, the Council of Elders, while the Lag-Ding under the Norwegian constitution are formed solely from the homogeneous mass of deputies for the duration of the Rikdagen. But in this way even that mechanical result is not attained; for two chambers composed of the same popular element, of the same party, will do little to hinder each other from rushing into precipitate action. In particular, the protection of the crown can be expected only from a chamber the members of which are attached to their own position in life, and not from the mere establishment of two chambers.[154]

---

l'intervention du roi dans la législation serait vaine, illusoire et sans force contre la masse irrésistible des volontés nationales, portées par une seule chambre" [that the king's intervention in legislation would be vain, illusory and without force against the irresistible mass of national wills, carried by a single chamber]. However, it is emphasized that the division of the legislative body into two chambers "doit être sans égard aux distinctions d'ordre" [should not regard distinctions of rank]. Mounier, on the other hand, at least recognizes "que les sénateurs et les représentants devraient être dans une position différente afin de n'être pas animés des mêmes passions" [that senators and representatives should be in a different position so as not to be driven by the same passions]. Similarly Lally-Tolendal. Longevity or longer duration is to make the difference. All this presupposes an aggregational representation of the people.

[154] Incidentally, it is a fallacy that if a true and efficient upper house exists, the rights and prerogatives of the crown may be diminished. The best-organized upper house cannot form a bulwark against onslaught if the crown is not already strong and independent in itself. In the present situation, any aristocratic element must be overwhelmed by the majority, but the monarchy is capable at all times of asserting a power in opinion, and it alone is then able to support the peerage, just as it is supported by it. In England, the point of no return has already been reached: the House of Lords is the weaker link in Parliament, and it is clear that the disproportion will continue to increase; and the fact that there is no remedy for this is simply due to the limited power of the English monarchy. As long as the upper house is the center of gravity of the constitution, the unlim-

§. 120. The Upper House – Composition

That is the significance of an upper house. From this we can derive a standard for its formation: the material of an upper house is the *elements of power in the land.* It has to embrace the outstanding existences, the great men of the country, everything that is distinguished as an individual existence or as a small circle or as an institution of power and prestige. In this element of power, what is at the top is what is the origin of the whole institution, the old aristocracy and the houses elevated to its position by this – the *hereditary peerage.* From time immemorial, the highest dignitaries of the church and, in more recent times, since the civil service is undeniably a power, the dignitaries of the civil service, appointed by the king for life, have been ranked with them. The hereditary peerage has irreplaceable advantages: the family prestige handed down from history, the security of one's own position and thus independence up and down, the sons' education for a certain future career, the similarity to the royal position and thus the special ability to mediate between throne and people.

Nevertheless, it is no longer appropriate for the hereditary peerage to be the sole, or even the main, component of the upper house. For it is no longer the main element of power in the country. At present, there no longer exist any individual houses that, like those of the former nobility, would, at the head of numerous vassals and subjects, command a power over the entire population and would thus be suited to form a house in relation to the lower house. In England, the House of Lords has traditionally enjoyed prestige from the times of the Norman barons, and even there it is becoming more and more powerless in the face of the House of Commons. But where a new upper house is formed from scratch, the current hereditary peers, who represent nothing but their own family with a small entourage, are not remotely capable of balancing the general chamber of the people. Furthermore, precisely because of their powerlessness,

---

ited royal right to create peers grants the crown significant power. But if the lower house has become the center of gravity, then this right is just one more tool in the lower house's power kit, making it omnipotent through the instrument of the crown. In this case, restricting the right of creation increases royal power, for then the king can withdraw behind the aristocracy against the pressure of the lower house. For this reason among others, the bill to restrict the royal right of peer nomination under George I failed in the lower house.

such high-ranking individuals often face temptation from the fear of losing their popularity. The former members of the imperial estates, in particular, are mostly newcomers at the territorial level [im Lande]. Finally, it is a bad state of affairs when all members of the upper house are appointed by the current government; this undermines independence, and the recognition of independence, which is a major advantage of this institution.

There is an increasing tendency to adopt the Montesquieuian theory, derived from England, that the essence of the upper house is hereditary peerage, and in this respect the upper house is thought to be conservative at the highest level, although this institution is already in decline in England and has been abandoned everywhere else. But what the hereditary peerage lacks in strength cannot possibly be made up by those life-long members. Therefore, at present, other elements of power must enter the upper house. This is mainly the basic aristocracy in a broader sense – the *knighthood*, and, as inseparable from the knighthood everywhere, the most important *cities*. These broader elements cannot, of course, take their seats in the upper house in person, but only through representation, either through periodic delegation or through presentation for the free royal appointment for life. It is the knighthood that now really constitutes the aristocratic power almost everywhere in Germany and especially in Prussia; as a collective body it owns a large part of the land; it has many dependents and many supporters; it is closely interwoven, is intertwined with the history of the country, includes the distinguished names in war and peace, and the consciousness of its own power and its own history also gives it a spirit of independence and resistance to the times. Therefore, in the upper house the knighthood must now take a strong and, if it does not form the center of gravity in the lower house, the predominant position. A larger measure of ownership or special properties of the same (age, entailed position [fideikommissarischer Verband]) can always be made a requirement. But no separate estate shall be formed above the knighthood, nor shall the upper house be separated from the body of the knighthood. Likewise the most important cities as representing the interests of the entirety of the urban communities in the land form an element of power, and if the upper house passes from the estate of the lords to the knighthood, these cannot be excluded since they are not overshadowed as much by the latter as by the former. Their right of deputation or presentation must then be exercised either by the magistrates or by an urban aristocracy of wealth and commercial power.

In this manner the two ways oppose each other: the first chamber, according to the previous conservative theory and the example of the restoration, from hereditary peers and personal notables appointed by the king for life, versus the first chamber with a composition of the estates, mainly an important aristocratic component in addition to the hereditary peerage, elected or presented by the estate itself. The former is based on the power of a few families and on royal appointment, while the latter is rooted in the most powerful elements in the country. The latter alone therefore yet guarantees what the former guaranteed in ancient times but is no longer capable of: a strong conservative power and a strong support for the crown. In addition, it is these elements (the knighthood and the cities) and not a newly created higher nobility that are the historically legitimate estates for representation in our German states, and so, from a legal point of view, their political vocation, which was taken from them in the old form, must be preserved for them in the new.

There is no objection from the fact that the knighthood and the cities have their natural seat in the lower house; for, apart from the fact that this is no longer the case (especially for the knighthood), it is precisely in the institution of the two houses, in contrast to the curiae, that the same class can be represented in different ways in both. Lifelong tenure, presentation, and the higher requirements of the knighthood estate or the municipal position mean that the representation of these estates in the upper house always constitutes a different element than in the lower house. Only the degree of representation, especially of the knighthood, must naturally be smaller in the upper house the more strongly it is represented in the lower house, and vice versa.

Nor does this constitute a violation of the royal right of appointment. The right of presentation as a sort of expert opinion of the estate does not in any way diminish it. But even the addition of a freely elected element alongside the king's appointment does not annul the decisive royal influence which is an essential feature of the upper house, and it is fully justified in the face of a lower house that entirely lacks an estate orientation, and especially for the initial establishment of the upper house, in order not to confer the lifelong seat without any period of probation. In that case, the oligarchic electors rather than the deputies would take a dominant position. Finally, there is also concern that such a chamber, through the weight of the knighthood, would become an unassailable aristocratic power against the crown. In our time, both the power of the citizenry and its movement and the dependence of the aristocracy on the crown are too great for that. Moreover, the aristocratic power always finds its correction in the other elements and in the unlimited royal right of free appointment.[155]

But the political task is to give the upper house moral superiority over the lower. According to the liberal system, the gradation goes from bottom to top: the lower house is supposed to have the greatest power, the upper house the lesser, the king the least. The correct relationship is the exact opposite. The king is supposed to be the supreme power, with the upper house after him. This is not at all conceivable in the case of an upper house according to the usual doctrine, which is based solely on royal appointment; on the other hand, it can be achieved through an upper house that is also based on the powerful classes of the country, if it also has the intellectuals (of both parties). In addition, the number of members must be in a corresponding proportion to the other chamber, which, after all, is important for prestige and a solemn impression.[156]

---

[155] The Prussian First Chamber from November 1852 to May 1854 was based to an unprecedented extent on the representation of the knighthood, and yet the government managed to push through two laws that were most contrary to the interests thereof, on the new formation of the First Chamber and on the mash tax.

[156] Compare my speeches in the First Chamber of 22 November 1849 and 5 March 1852 (see *Siebzehn parlamentarische Reden und drei Vorträge* [Seventeen Parliamentary Speeches and Three Lectures], pp. 53ff.). Our proposal of 22 November 1849 for the revision of the constitution included as a main element, in addition to the hereditary members, 60 deputies from the large landowners and 40 from the larger merchants and manufacturers. The motion was defeated. But a similar composition was later enforced by royal decree: in addition to the hereditary and a very limited number of life-long members, 90 deputies from the highest taxpayers (in fact, the landowners), 30 from the municipal councils of the larger cities. That is the nature of Article 65 of the Constitution. When in 1852, the formation of the upper house by royal appointment of hereditary and life-long members was proposed instead (by Heffter-Koppe, which reportedly was favored by the government itself), we opposed it but declared our agreement with the universal quality of heredity or life tenure and universal royal appointment, if the

§. 121. The Lower House – Valuation and Composition

The lower house represents the population at large. The principle governing the formation of the lower house, as indeed of the entire current territorial representation, is *unified national representation*, but on an *estates basis*. The estates, however, always remain the same: the basic aristocracy, where such exists, urban communities, rural communities (§. 97).

Any formation of the lower house without this estate-based foundation is a corruption and therefore an evil, be it based on *universal suffrage*, mere *property qualification*, or so-called *representation of interests*. Universal suffrage, the real hallmark of the Revolution, unsettles the state in its depths and turns its fortress into a storm-tossed sea. The mere property qualification is a means of countering the influence of the masses, a surrogate for true representation, but it nevertheless lacks the levers of estate-based thinking, of organic and moral motives. The representation of interests – that farmers, tailors, bakers, factory owners, large and small merchants, doctors, scholars, artists, each of these classes delegates their special representatives – is a notion that only emerged in 1848. People sensed the perniciousness of atomistic elections and yet recoiled from estate representation as from criminal reaction. It is wrong in principle because these occupations have no distinct political significance and no political power, and in the process of execution it leads to infinite complication and to completely random and arbitrary grouping.

But neither can a lower house prove itself in the present if the elements of the estates within it do not unite for the sake of national unity. The fact that separate deliberation and voting by the estates – the curia system – is no longer permissible lies in the very concept of the lower house. But even what is now exclusively understood to be the *estates structure* – that the representatives of

---

latter was to a considerable extent based on the presentation of the classes concerned, as well as our agreement that the standard of taxpaying should be replaced by the standard of certain qualities, "old and established property," and finally with the king's unlimited right to appoint life-long members without qualification (proposal by Count von Alvensleben, Dr. Stahl, Baron von Gasfron). The current formation of the upper house in accordance with the decree of 12October 1854 therefore essentially corresponds to the principles we advocated at the time and explained in the cited speech of March 5.

each of the three estates, knighthood, cities, and rural communities, are delegated *especially* (usually in equal parts) and *from their own midst*, even if they subsequently vote together by head in the chamber itself – may not suffice for the current task, especially in larger kingdoms. The system of estates in this sense is still to be recommended for the representation of smaller districts (circles, provinces), which really only concern estate affairs (e.g. road construction, poorhouses, fire insurance, etc.) and the estates coming to an agreement regarding those affairs, but it is not equally recommended for the representation of the entire territory. For here it is throughout a matter of general political questions (civil and criminal legislation, the press, the relationship to the church, etc.), and for these the consciousness of the *national* community should fundamentally prevail over that of the *estate*, and *principles* over *interests*. But the sharp juxtaposition of the estates is an obstacle to this. It is particularly disadvantageous that the knighthood, as a separate estate, arouses the jealousy of the others and yet has no power of resistance against their majority. There is also the questionability as to the ability of the peasant representatives to address these issues. This may have existed to some extent in several German states before 1848. However, the chambers of that time were not exactly characterized by conservative power.

The principle of the lower house is not its own estates structure, but its structure based on the structure of estates in the country, thus on elements of the estates, and the motivation here is not to secure the estates as such but to extract the conservative attitude and power from the population by virtue of the elements of the estates. The best composition of the lower house in our time is therefore: *a predominantly aristocratic chamber which nevertheless is closely connected to the entire population by the form of delegation*. By aristocracy, I do not mean birthright aristocracy but the landed aristocracy and the leaders of all classes who by their distinction have the interest of preservation, and this aristocracy should not have any importance on its own but only in its integration with the population as a whole. A majority of the knighthood separated from the other estates, with an independent right, does not correspond to the essence of the lower house nor to the real power relations of the estates in the present. That is the problem.[157] A safe and satisfactory solution to this problem has yet to be found, and it can only be found according to the particular circumstances of the

[157] The institutions for this can be of many kinds. I emphasize some features as particularly useful, not as absolutely necessary:

1) *Joint representation of the entire rural population*, with the knighthood and rural communities delegating jointly, and then by law providing the vast majority of representatives vis-à-vis the urban population (regularly two-thirds).

2) *Greater voting power for the upper classes in the electoral assembly.* The landed proprietors should (in accordance with 1) be mixed with the others already at the election of delegates, not first in the chamber, but they should nevertheless have a higher right to vote, in that in themselves they are (born) electors, while the rural communities send electors; these then together form an electoral assembly to choose delegates for the chamber. This will bear its full fruit as jealousy between these two classes fades away over time. The execution is most properly done in an organic way whereby the mayors of a complex of rural communities come together and choose the electors for the electoral assembly from among themselves. Then the numerical ratio between the representation of the knighthood and the rural communities can be determined in proportion to their share of the land; but it can also be done in the manner that is currently practiced, through the voting rights of individuals. In that case, the day laborers who depend on the knighthood must also be granted their share of the vote as citizens. In both cases, it is appropriate to also give the clergy of the public church (Protestant and Catholic) a special right to vote and to participate in the electoral assembly. They would, in particular, provide a moral mediation in the rural electoral assembly and possibly even a numerical decision between the knighthood and the peasantry. One may consider the eligibility for election to be inappropriate for the clergy's vocation, but not the right to vote, and if one misses a special place for the intellectual leaders [die Kapacitäten] among the classes represented, then it is precisely the clergy to whom this place in particular belongs, since they represent the spiritual and moral principle above all else. Even the Prussian system of the three property classes, as little as it is correct in principle and guaranteed in success, is based on that idea, in that it gives the landed aristocracy, in addition to their own direct voting rights in the first class, a share in the third class by means of their power over the day laborers. It is only because of this that it has succeeded to this point, so that it cannot be abandoned without a secure replacement.

---

3) Formation of an aristocratic electoral element in the cities. This is afforded either by lifelong magistracy or by the outstanding members of the commercial and industrial classes, or by both together. Here, too, the rest of the population or the guilds can participate through deputations, and here, too, the participation of the clergy and, if necessary, of other notabilities (directors of grammar schools, heads of municipal agencies [Behördenvorstände]) is appropriate.
4) Restriction of eligibility to the upper classes. This could be done in such a way that only a landowner is eligible to be a representative of the rural population (knight), and only a magistrate or a great tradesman for the urban population. However, this would push the civic concept of representation too far into the background behind the class concept, and, touching the main issue, it would overly restrict the election of qualified persons. It would therefore be better to raise the property qualification, and best of all, if the country is rich enough to afford it, to attain this indirectly through the *abolition of parliamentary remuneration*. This may appear at first to be a mere mechanical expedient, but in reality it is also the expression of the old Germanic principle that the entire population may take their representatives only from the upper classes, and that a main lever of the change party [Bewegungspartei] may lie in parliamentary remuneration, as is already shown by the impetuous demand for its introduction on the part of the English Chartists. But if the abolition of remuneration is to prevent an excess of electors from the inhabitants of the city where a court is held, it is necessary to restrict the deputies (all or some) to those from the province. These two factors, the preponderance of the rural population over the cities and the exclusive eligibility of the upper classes are the decisive ones for success. This is proven by the fact of our earlier provisional first chamber. It was elected by the entire population, and therefore with the actual preponderance of the rural population. The low property qualification of 500 thalers of income was a condition of the right to vote, and the deputies received no allowances. It was a decidedly conservative chamber, a true representation of the Prussian state, containing the intelligentsia of all parties.
5) *Public voice voting*, as the only way in which the upper classes can influence the lower.
6) *Formation of provincial electoral colleges above the district colleges*. In France, there were electoral colleges of the arrondissements (or cantons) and the departments. However, the arrangement was that the voters of the departments together with the electors elected by the cantons chose the deputies. But the district electoral colleges and the

---

provincial electoral colleges could also send their deputies separately. The latter could consist of the most highly taxed landowners in the province, the mayors of the cities, the highest clergy, the presidents of the colleges, etc. My proposal of 1852–1853 also falls into this category. The government wanted to get rid of the electoral elements for the first chamber according to article 65 (90 elected by the large landowners, 30 by the first cities). I therefore proposed that they be transferred to the second chamber, leaving the system of three property classes for half of the current number, and adding those 120 in place of the other half. These two elements would have behaved like district and provincial deputies. The proposal was in line with what already existed, and even if it was not as precise as it could have been, it would have achieved the main goal of securing conservative power in the second chamber, which no other plan has promised so far. It had to be dropped because the government opposed it.

I am only giving these suggestions as a contribution to the appropriate formation of a lower house. However, completely different methods could also be tried (e.g., election by the district assemblies).

The electoral system of the Restoration also sought to create an aristocratic chamber on a general civic basis. The 1814 charter requires a direct tax of 300 francs for the electors and 1,000 francs for the deputies. But it makes no distinction between the city and the countryside. The government's 1815 project was to ensure that the ministry had influence over the elections. At the first level of voting (canton), the 60 highest taxpayers and a large number of intellectual leaders and functionaries (priests, justices of the peace, presidents of colleges) were appointed as born electors (électeur à droit); at the second level of voting (department), the 60 highest direct taxpayers of the department, 10 most highly taxed merchants and higher functionaries (bishops, presidents of higher colleges, general procurators) were added to the candidates from the cantons. The *chambre introuvable* was outraged by this electoral law as an undertaking to destroy parliamentary independence and free popular representation and to bring administrative liberalism to power. In opposition to this, it proposed a project under the leadership of Billele which eliminated all these functions and all born voters, and included in the lowest electoral level all those who paid a direct tax of 80 francs. The latter was intended to include the rural population, which in many provinces was royalist and loyal to the nobility. In its fundamental opposition to all ministerial influence and to all électeurs à droit, it was wrong. Government influence as such, regardless of its principles, is a

country, and therefore only on the basis of a precise knowledge of it. But the problem itself is not in doubt: a predominantly aristocratic chamber on a democratic (i.e., general citizenship) basis. The fact that this is the true type of the new national representation is confirmed by the example of England. Only in this way has the House of Commons proved itself for so long. It does not itself consist of estates, but it is based on estates: town and country, freeholders and feudal tenants. The aristocracy has no separate delegation, and one cannot say of any member of the House, "You sit here for the aristocracy." Nevertheless, only men from the upper classes sit in the House, and the aristocracy, especially the landed aristocracy, has the predominant influence on the delegation. The condition of eligibility in the countryside (knightly ownership, later, however, only a large land income, and finally a mere property qualification) and the voting rights of the rotten boroughs secure him, and the more they are abolished, which is the current trend, the more impossible landed representation becomes in England as well. These special institutions of England are not the subject of imitation, but their result shows what the general problem is. At least for larger kingdoms it is not right to seek the remedy and the correction of the revolutionary representative system in the restoration of the strict three-way division of the estates rather than in the preponderance of the aristocratic and, with it, the conservative element; it is not right to counter the power of circumstances by indicating that the representation of the country should be based simply on estate interests; it should instead be led away from false principles to true political and religious principles.

---

necessity in our time. On the other hand, it may have been right to resist the 60 most heavily taxed. The lesser rural population, allied as they are with the aristocracy, are the conservative force, and the middle class, which was then the ministerial party against the royalists, is the liberal opposition to the ministry under all other circumstances.

The English electoral system before the Reform Act was admittedly irregular and in need of expansion. But it seems absurd and unlawful only according to the principle of equal rights to representation. Russell's latest draft, which was temporarily withdrawn due to the war, no longer falls short of the doctrinarism of the liberals on the Continent but combines it with the most detailed calculation of electoral success in favor of the Whigs. If reform really does go that far and that fast, it is very doubtful whether parliamentarism will last much longer in England.

§. 122. The Lower House – Length of Sessions

The longer the term, the more beneficial the influence on the second chamber. This lessens the agitation and conceit of popular rule, gives the representatives greater independence from their constituents and from the daily press, and gives the government the power to keep a loyal chamber for a long time, without hindering it from dissolving a disloyal one. It is therefore advisable to dissolve the parliament before the legal term of expiration, even in peaceful times, so that there is no appearance of a conflict with the chamber and an appeal to the people, but a simple administrative measure and prerogative of the crown, as indeed it originally was in England and nothing more before the party struggles led the king to set a limit for the duration of parliament. Lengthy periods of deliberation are not advisable. They are certainly conducive to saving time and energy, but perhaps disadvantageous for the importance of the territorial representation and its integration into the state organism (§. 123). For that purpose, it is much more desirable to strive for *shorter sessions*. There are two means to this end: setting aside a permanent portion in the budget that is not repeatedly discussed, and presentation by the government only of individual laws, not codifications. Both are also necessary for other reasons.[158]

§. 123. Integration of the Representative Body in the State

It is unmistakably a weakness and deficiency of the newer form of territorial representation that it does not engage in the functions of the state organism as a complementary link. It is merely a control vis-à-vis the state, never itself their bearer or organ. Therefore, if it is eliminated, legally or illegally, no gap is created; the state machine continues to run as before, the subjects are not affected. All that is needed for this is the (negative) order for its abolition, not the (positive) order for a replacement.

---

[158] The waste of time caused by an excessive number of amendments can be prevented, on the one hand, by internal chamber and party discipline, and on the other by the government making sure that unnecessary amendments lead to the withdrawal of the law under consideration. On the other hand, to legally deprive the chamber of the right to amend and to limit it to acceptance or rejection impairs the dignity of the territorial representation, and not only cuts off real improvement but also the beneficial influence of free deliberation (cf. Montalembert June 22, 1852).

The situation is quite different with the older territorial representation. It had indispensable functions itself; if it ceased, they would come to a standstill. Thus, in Prussia, the district assemblies resisted the revolution of 1848 by virtue of this older type. There was no other organ than they to take care of the district's property, fire protection, etc. But even in England, if Parliament were abolished, untold confusion would immediately ensue. There would be no body for divorce proceedings, the granting of commercial monopolies, the building of roads, for investigations and surveys of the most diverse kind, and even for a large part of supreme court decisions. This weakness of the newer territorial representation is essentially based on the overall type of our institutions, the sharp, abstract division of all functions. But if for that reason it is not possible to enhance the representative body immediately and as a whole, still a significant advance towards the organic permeation of positions, towards the involvement of the territorial representation in administrative functions, is possible. This is not against its nature as representation (§. 98), as long as these functions are not thereby severed from the king. For example, the council of state could be brought into an organic connection with the territorial representation, and mainly with first chamber so as to increase its prestige, whereby the king would only appoint members of the first chamber to the same (similarly to his only appointing members of parliament as ministers), and only a small number as the actual council of state, always appointing the others in turn and especially for certain deliberations from the chamber, and likewise taking the authority for deciding conflicts of jurisdiction only from its members. In this case, the chamber, or even both chambers, could be granted the right to present a certain number of these members. These and similar institutions, which decidedly strengthen the institution of territorial representation, are only to be found in places where the safeguards for its formation have been found, so that its continued existence is guaranteed as possible and beneficial.

§. 124. The Representative Body as Conservative Bulwark

This doctrine of the rights and the formation of the territorial representation is not intended to render it harmless. The intention is nothing less than to transform it from a force of subversion into a force of preservation, from an institution of rebellion against the royal regard into an institution to strengthen the royal regard; that it represent the historical state, as it once did revolutionary progress, and provide a guarantee of continuity; that it be the loyal guardian of the rights of the crown as it once was the rival of the crown, and that it thereby also call forth a conservative party in the country and serve as its center and guide. Such a monarchical-conservative national representation would be no less a protection for general civil rights and freedoms than the liberal one, and would be even more powerful precisely because of the weight that this attitude gives it. It would maintain the same, and even greater, independence from the crown, and would by no means sink to the level of a mere mindless tool of the crown. Its resistance could only be directed against the measures of the crown, never the power thereof. But above all the statesmanlike conscientiousness and honor of not remaining in the highest offices while denying one's own convictions and publicly represented character – this moral truth gained in England, which could be described as the "mainspring" (in the Montesquieuian sense) of the new state (constitutional) monarchy – must never be lost by such monarchical-conservative representation of the country. However, it will necessarily only extend to the principles; it will extend to measures only in cases of high evidence and heavy responsibility; it will never extend to personnel and coterie issues (including retaining friends as colleagues in office). As a result, the king may well be compelled to renounce the service of a man whose ability he would like to use, and may also be compelled to give in to his minister in this and that; such is appropriate and not unmonarchical, but he will never be compelled to follow principles which he does not recognize as the right ones, or to entrust men in whom he has no confidence. The king's business is both to rule and to govern, but not simply to give orders. The ministers together and individually represent the necessity of the matter, and are therefore not mindless tools for the execution of his will, but his organic complement, and he should therefore find in them a limit. That is the right relationship. The English one, on the other hand, is not that they be a limit to the king, as tools which can only be used in a certain course, but that they are the self-determining power of the government.

That is the constitutional monarchy and territorial representation of which I said: "It should be the natural maturity of the constitution of Germanic states, therefore the completion of the old imperial monarchy, not its abolition." The prerequisite for this, of course, is for loyalty, as is the natural sense of the population everywhere, not to be completely destroyed by doctrine or events. If rationalism and liberalism run rampant among the people, then no other constitution is possible than absolutism, whether it occurs immediately, or follows the intermediate stage of a revolutionary phase.

Chapter 14: Absolute Monarchy

§. 125. Absolute Monarchy Defined

<317> By *absolute monarchy*, as a technical concept, one currently understands a form of government in which the public order (legislation and state finances) is determined solely by princes, without the restriction and guarantee of a territorial representation, in consequence of which the constitution is not as developed and formally determined, yet in which strict observance of promulgated laws, independence of the judiciary, and secure rights of subjects do exist. Absolute monarchy therefore is entirely different from *despotism.* In the latter, the prince in person is the judge, lord of the lives and property of subjects, owner of the lands, thus unrestricted possessor not merely of the legislative but also of the judicial power, not mere orderer of the public but also lord over the private sphere, although there as well, most traditional laws and mores, especially religion and the clergy, to some degree order and temper his power. Despotism rests on a servile spirit of subjection, corresponding to the spirit of pre-Christian religion. It still has its ambit in the Orient. In Christian Europe, it is not despotism but absolute monarchy which is found as a form of state. Here, however, there are two phases to be distinguished: absolute monarchy on the basis of legitimacy – *absolute monarchy in the strict sense;* and absolute monarchy based on the Revolution – *imperialism* [i.e., Bonapartism].

Absolute monarchy such as is based on legitimacy characterizes the progression from the Middle Ages into the modern world epoch; its foundation occurred in the time shortly before the Reformation and afterwards until the Peace of Westphalia. It is chiefly represented in the Hispano-Austrian, the old French, the Danish, and the Prussian monarchy. It being the outcome of injustice on the part of the estates and injustice on the part of the king, it nevertheless had as its <318> world-historical motivation the transformation of the kingdom from the patrimonial and feudal into the state-oriented form, from dispersed, autonomous into uniform, centralized rule. Its essence therefore is the supreme power of the king over the estates-oriented elements, in particular the aristocratic, the power of incisive transformation in the historical legal condition, the unfolding of the mechanistic means for the concentration and energy of the state government – the standing army and the civil service.

Absolute monarchy such as is based on the Revolution arose through the world-historical catastrophe in France as a remedy for its consequences, yet still upon the same principles. The essence thereof is *the foundation of the entire state order on mechanistic rather than organic and ethical forces.* The supreme authority itself is not, as in the other case, erected upon the ethical basis, law and divine sanction, but ostensibly on the popular will, in fact upon power and acquiescence in the inevitable. The old estates elements and their autonomy, and the historical law, are not, as in the other case, subordinated to the sovereign, but destroyed at the root and absolutely. It recognizes no in-itself-immutable law at all. The considerations of state power supersede all law. The church is tended to as mere means, and merely according to the measure of political goals. The civil service serves less to maintain the conditions than merely to fortify the supreme power; it does not form an estate of independent spirit and honor; rather than an obstruction to absolutism, then, it is precisely absolutism's instrument.[159]

---

[159] The character trait of mechanism runs through the entire constitution of the consular and imperial [Napoleonic] regimes. It is the work of Sieyès and Bonaparte together. From the very beginning of the republic, Sieyès advocated the mechanical alongside the popular-rule view, and his other illusions being dispelled by ten years of experience, this was the only one left he held onto. He no longer seeks freedom in the rule of the will of the people, but, given the extreme opposition to such rule, he seeks it in the separation and neutralization of power. In his draft, on which the constitution of the year 8 is based, he now pushes this separation, which he always pursued, to the extreme. It not only divides the legislative and executive powers among different organs, but divides these two powers within themselves, giving the legislature the power to make the laws without the power to debate them, the tribunal the power to discuss them without resolving them, to the great electors the power to appoint the highest officials for the state government without any part of their own in the state government, to the preserving senate the power to repeal laws for unconstitutionality and to assimilate persons without the power to legislate or administer. It is the delusion that a state authority the organs of which are all either powerless or completely dependent can, taken together, function as a real state authority. Even without a Buonaparte, this constitution would have immediately annulled itself according to a natural law, namely, either the executive officials would have had to eliminate the great elector and the absorbent senate, or one

---

of them would have had to usurp the executive functions. But even the formation of the organs for those various functions is purely mechanical, solved as much by the will of the people as by all the estates and corporative underpinnings. The representative bodies are first made by the Provisional Government (and all from the same material), and then maintain and create themselves, similar to a spiral staircase. In particular, this kind of aristocratic chamber, which is sought in the Senate of Preservation, is formed purely mechanically, without any basis in birth or property or other official position. This was Sieyès' plan.

Buonaparte also sought to base the state on mechanics, only his mechanics have a different goal. Through them, Sieyès strives for freedom and thus for the mutual paralysis, the powerlessness of power; Buonaparte, conversely, for the omnipotence of power. He therefore immediately rejected any division of the executive and replaced the great electors, consuls and absorptive power with the first consul, then the hereditary emperor with full executive power, and later strengthened this truly monarchical power even further through the influence of the emperor on the formation of the other organs, namely the Senate, and the powers which he gave this dependent Senate the right to declare and amend the constitution, to dissolve the legislative body, etc., and by the abolition of the tribunes. On the other hand, he was quite willing to tolerate the reciprocal pulverization of the representative bodies, because it served his omnipotence when the popular representation, of which, according to the views of the time, he could not do without, was annihilated within itself. But he also retained this formation of the people's representation by mechanical means. The later transformation of the lists of notables into the candidate proposals of the electoral colleges changes little in this character. Yes, just as Sieyès had undertaken to form an aristocracy by mechanical means at his Constituent Senate, so Napoleon made a similar attempt in his Legion of Honor. Precisely as a counterweight to the natural bond, which rested on class or traditional sentiment or party conviction, he wanted to found a bond on this order that would make and manage the government arbitrarily, in that all to whom it was awarded – general, private, scholar and merchant, former Jacobin and royalist – should know themselves as one body and be inspired by one corporate spirit. But Napoleon's organization of the internal administration, the prefect, sub-prefect, and mayor, who are appointed by the emperor and govern unrestrictedly through the law and representation of the provinces and municipalities, is ultimately merely a mechanism of governmental

§. 126. Imperialism as Mechanism Devoid of Virtue

Despotism had its justification in a certain cultural stage of peoples, and thus had a future ahead of it, of development into higher culture and a higher form of state.

Imperialism, in the manner **<319>** in which it was brought about – through the nation's heavy burden of guilt and resulting severe calamity – had in this circumstance just as much justification for the times and exceptional conditions as it had untenability in terms of principle and as a general enduring order. It is the rescue of the society from anarchy and the destruction of democratic fanaticism, the restoration of external mechanical order; it protects the primary indispensable goods: life, property, family; it maintains freedom of conscience in the spirit of the Revolution, allows the administration of justice in general and in principle to exist, even though, e.g., the sovereign interferes in it in individual cases for his political goals. This gives it a claim to gratitude on the part of society, and a title of power, one that, although not the right of the old dynasty, yet is valid vis-à-vis the evanescent will of the people.

But under imperialism, public political life has lost its ethical goods and ethical motives. In the imperial regime, there are not the traits of monarchical virtue, of zeal and strict observance of duty regarding the immutable law or the immutable right of the people. Even if the nation's moral inclinations, especially honor and patriotism in France, continue to have an effect over a long period of time, and even if the war hero also ignites a sense of glory and devotion out of admiration for him, the ethically binding powers have disappeared from the body politic. It now rests only on need, utility, and ambition. What above all constitutes the principled and permanent disavowal of the highest ethical ground of the state order is the confession of revolution, in particular the proclamation of popular sovereignty, which itself derives the supreme power from

---

omnipotence. Even in legislation for the most intimate private legal relationships, this displacement of moral considerations by mechanical ones is evident. Thus, for example, divorce by mutual consent is permitted in violation of the moral principle, but it is so encumbered with difficulties and chicanery that in practice divorce is largely prevented. Similarly, the child's claim to maintenance is denied even when paternity is proven out of wedlock, precisely in order to deter the female sex from such liaisons. But in such mechanical matters the imperial institutions are indisputably the masters.

universal suffrage. But a kingdom of mere mechanical power and entitlement without ethically binding forces is incapable of maintaining an enduring body politic, and finally, in this form, must succumb to its own inner contradiction: the proclamation of the sovereign popular will, and the sole validity of the imperial will; the celebration of the Revolution which planted individual freedom as its banner, and the total constriction of individual freedom. State power thus itself sanctions the principle in accordance with which it lawfully may be discarded in the event of dissatisfaction, and even sanctions the standard by which it becomes invalid **<320>** from dissatisfaction. In a political piece published in 1852, the spirited argument was made that France's greatness and well-being has always rested on absolute monarchy and could only rest on it; but it was silent as to how the old absolute monarchy, which in fact alone enduringly grounded that greatness and well-being, was of such an entirely different form than that of the Empire.

Imperialism, even though in itself scarcely capable of an enduring existence, nevertheless forms a great danger to Europe. Absolute monarchy on the basis of the Revolution provides as little security for the historical legal condition among the peoples as does the republic on the basis of the Revolution; for this reason the glistening mechanical result is a great temptation for legitimate absolute monarchies, to give themselves over to a similar spirit of institution and government, to break with everything which yet was of estates-oriented and corporate independence and which is of historical law in their territories, and to establish governmental omnipotence.[160] Bonapartism had this effect in the states of the Rhine Confederation, and the indignation or remorse regarding it was manifested at the negotiations of the Vienna Congress. The danger is now that something like a more powerful state than those will follow this example, since the recent defeat of a terrible revolution apparently offers a similar set of circumstances. The legitimate absolute monarchies, to the degree that they imitate imperialism, do not take into account that they, in favor of momentary results, thereby undermine the principles upon which they themselves rest, and assert a power which, with equal right, could at some point be turned against them.

---

[160] See my speech of April 24th, 1855 (*Parlamentarische Reden* [Parliamentary Speeches], pp. 39ff.).

§. 127. Validity of Absolute Monarchy Dependent upon Circumstances

Absolute monarchy in the true sense of the word is a generally natural, and therefore satisfactory, constitution, no less than is estates-oriented monarchy. It is not restricted to a lower level of <321> culture, as is despotism; peoples of the highest spiritual and ethical stage might yet exist in it. Nor is it a mere state of emergency as is imperialism; its essence is to rest absolutely upon ethical foundations and motives. It is put in the shadow by monarchy with territorial representation, by virtue of the lesser degree of political freedom, but it does not need to be entirely lacking in this freedom, and in place thereof it can afford other advantages, particularly more energetic government. In itself, therefore, the estates-oriented constitution is the richer, the more complete; but in each individual case it depends on the whole individuality of its condition and its history whether the monarchy, with or without territorial representation, is appropriate for it, and in any case whether the monarchy is better without territorial representation than with one that, by its institution or spirit, endangers more than furthers the highest aims of the state.

The liberal constitutional theory fundamentally and radically combats absolute monarchy. Constitutions and territorial representation, the latter clothed with extensive power, are the unconditional demand of law and reason, which once put forward by the people cannot be refused. Thus until 1848 it was the usual viewpoint among us, and such is still widespread, that absolute monarchy is an unlawful, unsatisfactory, in the long run unendurable form of state which at best had a world-historical vocation as a transition to break the power of the old feudal estates but which, having fulfilled that vocation, has lost its justification. With such a fundamental rejection of absolute monarchy, most of the evils that one may encounter in the civil condition are simply attributed to it, while their cure is expected from the constitution and the popular representation. This viewpoint is unfounded and rejected by experience. Absolute monarchy is neither contrary to legal principles, nor does it withhold the rights of the people, nor is it lacking in general necessary perfection. The ruinous despotism of a single ruler (Louis XIV) is not its concept, and the dreadful state of affairs that a period endures because of that (petticoat government, sale of subjects into foreign military service) does not belong so much to the form of absolute monarchy as to the spirit of the age and the other aspects of public <322> institutions.

By contrast, prosperity, culture, mores everywhere likewise thrived under absolute monarchy, and the power of the state, apart from the island country [England], arose under the absolute royal power. The great powers of the Continent – France, Austria, Prussia, Russia – became such only through the unity and energy which this form of state provides.[161]

On the other hand, at various times in history when it triumphantly put down the old estates power or defeated the Revolution, absolute monarchy has received a sort of scientific representation which saw the declaration reflected in world events that it was the only allowable form of state, or at least claimed the inadmissibility of any legal restriction of the prince. Thus, the expositions of Filmer, Bossuet, Wandelin.[162] This viewpoint also had proponents among us shortly before and after 1848, and, accordingly, there exists a doctrine of the unconditional necessity of absolute monarchy, just as there exists a doctrine of the unconditional necessity of constitutional monarchy. It is rooted partly in religious reasons, that the king as the ruling authority established by God cannot be legally restricted by the subjects, and partly on political reasons, that the state cannot bear a dualism of power. Advisory territorial representation is therefore the most that it recognizes as being compatible with monarchy.

This doctrine is likewise unfounded. Unrestricted royal power does not follow from its divine sanction (§. 75) and it is one thing for the subjects not to exercise their right by force against the highest ruling authority, something else altogether for them not to have a right of cooperation and hindrance vis-à-vis the highest ruling authority. In particular, there is no divine command regarding who is to be the ruling authority, whether a prince or a senate or comitia, a prince alone **<323>** or jointly with a cooperating consenting parliament. Just as the republic is a form of state compatible with religion, just so is a restricted

---

[161] Montalembert was justified in not finding in imperialism any guarantee of Catholic interests; but one cannot agree with him when he does find such guarantee in French parliamentarianism, control of powers, territorial representation, such as they are.

[162] Filmer, *Patriarcha or the natural power of kings*; Joannes Wandelini, *Juris regii* ἀνυπευθύνου *et solutissimi cum potestate summa nulli nisi deo obnoxia* etc.; Bossuet, *Politique tirée des propres paroles de la sainte écriture.*

monarchy. The error lies in conceiving the prince to be God's vicar.[163] God's power certainly cannot depend upon human consent. The ruling authority has its power from God, but this does not in any way make it God's vicar, and even if it did, it would be so only as the entire ruling authority and as the ruling authority ordered within itself, thus the prince in his constitutional supplementation.

But a dualism of power is not effected if, under the sovereign and by virtue of his authority, other organs participate in the exercise of power, when he otherwise is not positively coerced, but only restrained, conditioned in his activity. Reductions, even inappropriate inhibitions of power, are not yet the destruction of their unity. Such dualism runs through all of nature: in all organic bodies, manifold forces function apart from the supreme central force, members have

---

[163] Thus Bossuet, livre IV, art. 1 prop. 1. 2: "l'autorité Royale est absolue .... Les jugements souverains sont attribués à Dieu même, ... Ne jugez point contre le juge .... Il faut donc obéir aux Princes comme à la justice même ... ils sont des Dieux et participent en quelque façon à l'indépendance divine" [Royal authority is absolute .... Sovereign judgments are attributed to God himself .... Do not judge against the judge .... It is therefore necessary to obey the Princes as if it were justice itself .... they are Gods and in some way participate in divine independence]. Then liv. 5 art. 4 prop. 1: „la majesté est l'image de la grandeur de Dieu dans le Prince. La puissance de Dieu se fait sentir en un instant de l'extrémité du monde à l'autre, la puissance royale agit en même temps dans tout le Royaume: elle tient tout le Royaume en état, comme Dieu y tient tout le monde. Considérez le prince dans son cabinet. De là partent les ordres qui font aller de concert les magistrats et les capitaines, les citoyens etc. C'est l'image de Dieu, qui assis dans son trône au plus haut des cieux fait aller toute la nature!" [Majesty is the image of God's greatness in the Prince. The power of God is felt in an instant from one end of the world to the other, the royal power acts at the same time throughout the Kingdom: it keeps the whole Kingdom in order, as God keeps the whole world in order. Consider the prince in his study. From there come the orders that make the magistrates and captains, the citizens, etc. work together. It is the image of God, who, seated on his throne at the highest point in the heavens, makes all of nature work together!]. Bossuet only overlooks the fact that God accomplishes all this in person, while the king accomplishes it with the help of this great state organism, which consists of many other personalities and is based on laws that, in any case, were not given by the present king.

not only remonstration but also resistance, and, in fact, the higher the organism the more so, and such resistance in the state serves precisely its maintenance and continuity. The accusation of dualism of state power, by which it cancels itself out, does not even apply to the English constitution, in that, despite the theory of division of powers, it is in fact based on one sole power, that of the lower house, which is only restrained by the upper house and the king. France in its constitutional constitution [konstitutionellen Verfassung] certainly offered the spectacle of a not yet defeated monarchy and a statutorily established opposition in the houses struggling with each other over the supreme power and pursuing contradictory goals in opposition to each other. But this is not based on the essence of a territorial representation and its right to consent or refusal, but on the false institutions which give the houses supremacy over the king, and on the false doctrine of the age, which sets this supremacy up as a command to them, and in all respects drives them toward goals which every government as such must combat. **<324>**

On the other hand, when the complete hopelessness of wresting power from the king is established in the institutions, the territorial representation surely becomes a cooperating restricting organ, not a second opposed power; and the more the axioms of liberalism yield to sound doctrine, or the houses include conservative elements, the more a uniform course between government and houses will come about for individual measures as well. If the right of consent of the houses truly embodied a violation either of the divine sanction of monarchy or the unity of state power, then such was also of necessity contained in the legal independence of the judiciary, in the legal inviolability of life, property, and the freedom of subjects; then here as well, the will of the king ought not be restricted farther than through advice and presentation.

For this reason, a fundamental objection to territorial representation has as little merit as it has against absolute monarchy. For the continental realms, doubts regarding them can only be derived from the given conditions. To wit, with the advanced, even forced dismemberment of society, it is difficult to find a true representation of the country, and it is that much more difficult with the ruling animosity toward that aristocratic preponderance in the territorial representation, apart from which it could not even exist. Furthermore, it contains the most severe flaw that the territorial representation, however one wishes to arrange it, is without historical duration, is something newly made, and thus neither in itself is a binding and position-preserving tradition, nor has a consciousness of its necessity in the country. Finally, in the wake of the erosive measures in which one got lost over a long period of time, and most starkly in 1848, there is often a powerful, considered restoration; but the territorial representation can become a restriction to this restoration in the same way that it, by virtue of its right of consent, acts as a restriction on innovation and thus functions as a power of maintenance.

This is the true state of affairs, for which reason the decision between absolute monarchy and monarchy with territorial representation cannot be made according to political doctrine but only according to a **<325>** more proper evaluation of specific conditions in each state.

§. 128. Gradual Development of Estates

No impartial observer will deny that Austria as a collective realm can have no other constitution than absolute monarchy.

The combination of various peoples, and the inferior development of many of them, render a common assembly of the estates of the realm simply impossible. Freedom for Austria consists not in the general assembly of the realm, but in the preservation of national rights and mores for the various crown lands. In this as well, the right of the estates, if not cast down in imperialistic fashion, must be moderated in accordance with the considerations of military and political unity. The emperor must be strong, especially in the German lands, if he is to rule the non-German ones. For this reason, as follows from our exposition, Austria need not take second place to other states in dignity, civility, and satisfaction.

In Prussia as well, there are weighty reasons for absolute monarchy. A third can be added to the above-mentioned general considerations: that the Prussian state does not have its origin and unity through nationality, as do England and France, but through the crown; that the entire patriotic tradition and the entire memory of glory belongs to the absolute monarchy; and that the external power position of Prussia is difficult as it is, and must not be made more difficult by weakening the government in any way. Notwithstanding this, abolition of the territorial representation, even when attainable by legal process, is inadvisable.

The Prussian people has a degree of cultivation [Bildung] and spiritual agitation sufficient to make its participation in the body politic, and an ordered organ for such participation, entirely appropriate. The other defects of the constitutional constitution [konstitutioneller Verfassung] have been essentially weeded out (§. 118). There is no example of such a position of the crown as now exists in Prussia in any of the states the fate of which stands as a refutation of the "constitutional monarchy." The influence of the chambers has not as yet **<326>** manifested itself as being destructive. On the contrary, under the chambers the Prussian legislation predominantly was restored, while before that, without the chambers, it was often revolutionized. As long as that is the case, there is likewise no danger that its existence will gradually sap the loyalty of the population. Individual abuses proceeding from the clauses of the constitutional charter or their improper application, e.g., the exploitation of equality, the denial of protection to the Christian church against the encroachment of the sects, form no evidence against the entire type, and in any case testify more against the charter than against the territorial representation. What problem situations are found in the public condition – proletariat, conflicts in areas of religion, difficulties with the daily press – find their grounds as little in the chambers as hitherto in absolute monarchy, and will not therefore be removed by their elimination. The chambers form no hindrance to that which the country yearns for in the wake of the disappointment of the constitutional system – simple strong government directed to real goods. The government which takes this road with clarity, will have in them a devoted following. In order to keep the destructive opposition powerless, it is only required that the government itself be uniformly conservative.

On the other hand, it is no good to underestimate an institution once it has come into existence that was overestimated prior to its coming into existence. The territorial representation is the natural organ for preserving the legal order, for assessing the government in terms of the public ethical-rational judgment, and a certain satisfaction, a self-assurance on the part of the nation, is undeniably gained through it. That however is only a moral strengthening for the government, which can risk laws and measures supported by the chambers which, given the predominant prejudice, it perhaps would have second thoughts presenting to the country on its own. In particular, where public opinion is developed and taken into account by the government, as was the case in Prussia long before the constitution, it is a relief to have in the territorial representation a uniform, legitimate, and ordered organ of that opinion, instead of a confused enunciation through the unauthorized, unaccountable voices of the daily press, so that it does not go about like a phantom <327> threatening everywhere without being in some way tangible. For many measures (e.g., suppression of dissidents' assemblies, Austria's march to Holstein) which the press hitherto exploited to generate unremitting excitement, investigation and voting in the house calms public opinion. In fact, the entire aura of liberal doctrine, which in the sphere of the daily press maintains itself by the predominance of its papers and by ignoring and shouting down everything else, has diminished in the sphere of the chambers since having to engage the conservative side in equal battle, man to man. Where territorial representation is supplemented with estates-oriented and aristocratic elements, as in Prussia, it has the advantage of providing a significant tempering of and correction to the bureaucratic direction of the government. Prussia's vocation for Germany is not to give the example of energy grounded in ruthless power; it is the ethical powers of law, of culture, of honor and freedom upon which it depends, and for that, it is to be the model and support of the smaller German states.

For this reason, the constitution and territorial representation should not be abolished but should continue their development in the trodden path. The higher political wisdom is not merely negatively to defeat them but to bend to advantage institutions in which the flow of the times is running, to make them serviceable for the goods which, in terms of their nature, they should promote, and which form a threat only through degeneration and false form. It remains to be seen whether this will be successful; what is required is not to turn back from the way already embarked upon, because of the danger of having to attempt it again. It is highhandedness [Eigenmacht] to make a constitutional monarchy from an absolute one, and an absolute monarchy from a constitutional one, and it is a sign of incapacity always to shift the terrain to solve the problem rather than to take the given terrain and utilize and give shape to its conditions. *Hic Rhodus hic salta.*[164] **<328>** Such things as the current mind-set running contrary to the chambers, should be the last thing to induce this. The slightest thing turns it, or even nothing at all. What therefore would bring the greatest blessing would be to do the right thing in the condition in which one finds oneself, as something providentially given, unless it be evil pure and simple.

---

164 [The punch line of one of Aesop's fables – "here is Rhodes, jump here!" – where someone claiming some great achievement is challenged to repeat it then and there.]

Should the effort to construct a salutary element from the chambers not work out, then for this eventuality we keep open, in the inviolate right of the crown, the power of aid and recovery.[165]

§. 129. Absolute Monarchy Rightly Ordered

If, accordingly, absolute monarchy is a legally grounded state, often the sole possible form of state, the equal of any other, then the conditions of its well-orderedness are no less an object of the doctrine of state than are those of constitutional monarchy. They are as follows:

Absolute monarchy must afford the guarantee for law and liberty, through uniform observance and traditional manner of government, which in constitutional monarchy is expected from the territorial representation. To this belong particularly: prompt independent administration of justice, legal restrictions and forms on government action in favor of the public welfare [Polizey], ordered process for all administration, the reverse of *tel est nostre plaisir* [such is our pleasure], the recognition of personality, its independence and its honor in subjects, consideration of the grounded public judgment, immutability of all law. In particular, absolute monarchy must champion historical conditions and historical law, in that the kingdom itself rests on them. Likewise, absolute monarchy is required to progress from **<329>** arbitrary character to the character of legal order.[166]

Absolute monarchy, having arisen by triumphing over the estates-oriented and aristocratic elements, gains strength and completion by preserving these elements and subsuming them in its own organization of power. The nobility are not to be preferred, but are to be won over to the public service; the urban magistracy is to be utilized as a government organ while preserving municipal autonomy. It is a great advantage of the Prussian monarchy that the nobility has

---

[165] Compare in this regard my speeches in the First Chamber of January 26th, 1852, and February 24th, 1853 (*Siebzehn parlamentarische Reden und drei Vorträge* [Seventeen Parliamentary Speeches and Three Lectures], pp. 17, 27). In essence, I stated this viewpoint regarding the position of Prussia in the first edition of this volume, 1837, pp. 302–303.

[166] Only in such a traditional manner of government, not in the mere conscience of the king, can Bossuet's distinction between *gouvernement absolu* and *gouvernement arbitraire* be founded.

for a long while participated in government service and even more in the army. The earlier vassal relation thus naturally was transferred to the officer and civil service corps, through which, apart from its own ethical traits, an ethic of feudal devotion and troth mingled together with feudal independence and honor. To this we add the equal opportunity for careers to all capable persons. The lack thereof was the tragedy of France. On the other hand, it is an abuse when the aristocracy, outside of the princely organism of power, stands in opposition to that power.

Absolute monarchy can and should develop institutions which lend a moral guarantee to territorial rights and public spirit, just as territorial representation offers a legal guarantee of this. Certainly an assembly of the estates of the realm with mere advisory capacity such as has been suggested for this goal, is not an option. On the one hand, a periodically sitting assembly elected by the country [vom Lande gewählte] cannot be restricted to advice and opinion without injury to the country itself, and, on the other hand, such an assembly will not remain restricted to this, for its council already has in it a power of decision, and it would be easy for it to gain for itself the right of consent, and thus to put an end to the absolute monarchy. But the institutions of moral guarantee suitable to absolute monarchy are the representation of small spheres, *district* and *provincial estates,* and the *council of state.* These organs are by the nature of the case restricted to advice; the very unity of the <330> territorial government cannot tolerate a right of consent of district and provincial estates, and the council of state by its very nature is there to provide advice, just as the territorial representation is there to consent and to deny. It is therefore no injury either to these organs or to the territory for them to be restricted to advice, nor can they ever gain for themselves the right of consent.

These institutions therefore are fully compatible with absolute monarchy and harbor no threat to its existence. Both, however, require proper cultivation. Besides advice, the district and provincial estates can most excellently be entrusted with their own administration of affairs within their sphere, while the council of state can be extended beyond the currently customary form by estates-oriented elements, should the king appoint notables from the landowning class and industry to it, in addition to notables in the civil service. Consultation [Befragung] on the part of the council of state may also serve as a formal precondition for the validity of the laws, even in the absolute monarchy. Apart from the broad association of the council of state, a privy council composed of a few persons can be set up for the more important matters of statesmanship, especially regarding foreign affairs. Of course, these institutions cannot replace the participation of the people in the great public questions and the experience of political self-worth, which are specific attributes of the territorial representation; but the district and provincial estates-oriented representation and self-administration do provide participation and security in these more restricted affairs, and the council of state provides public reassurance that the concerns of the state and the traditions of politics, which hitherto effectuated the well-being of the country, continue to be maintained.[167] On the other hand, popular representation as **<331>** pretense, such as is indispensable to imperialism, is neither essential to nor salutary for legitimate absolute monarchy.

---

[167] It is even tolerable to absolute monarchy that a power of legal hindrance against royal orders exist, as long as the king reserves the right to set it aside through an extraordinary ruling. So for example in the ancient French monarchy, the parliament could reject the registration of laws on behalf of the king, upon which they depended for their validity, as legally inadmissible; but the king was allowed, after repeated rejections, to appear personally in Parliament and to command the registration (*lit de justice*). The interpretation provided by the minister of Charles X to article 14 of the Charter of 1814, that the king enacts [erläßt] "decrees beneficial to the execution of the laws and the security of the state" would have led to a similar result. The dispensing power of the king of England, although it is only a tempering of parliamentary monarchy, would, through the expansion given it by James II, have founded a tempered absolute monarchy. All these shadings and transitions indicate that absolute monarchy and monarchy with territorial representation, each of which properly conceived and arranged, do not contrast in their innermost being but are distinct phases of one European monarchy.

Chapter 15: The Republic

§. 130. The Sovereign Popular Assembly

<333> The republic is the form of state according to which the supreme power (sovereignty) is vested in the *collective* [Gesammtheit], be it the collective of a special class (*aristocracy* in the broadest sense) or of the entire people (*democracy*). But in the republic, even in a democracy, the supreme power is vested in the collective not as a mass of individuals but in their institutional order, in the aristocratic or democratic assembly, as, and to the degree that, it operates according to the laws regarding composition, proceedings, and position vis-à-vis the magistracy. Even the republic, even a democracy, does not rest on "popular sovereignty." Even in it, the state is over the people, not the people over the state. In this manner alone is the republic a possible form of state. For it is the law of nature that unity should prevail, and only through the institutional order does the collective become a single uniform and enduring subject. Still, this artificial unity of the republic cannot supersede the natural, living unity of monarchy. Firstly, the various decisions of the popular assembly are not meshed with each other as are the king's; while it decides war, alliance, appoints field commanders, those who vote for war do not yet know what the choice will be regarding a field commander or the vote regarding an alliance. Secondly, the popular assembly is incapable of fully exercising its sovereignty, in that it needs a magistracy which is comprised not merely of civil servants, as in monarchy, but to a certain degree is itself a bearer of sovereignty, representative of the state. Accordingly, the republic cannot exist without a surrogate of royal power.

The distinctions in the developed monarchy which characterize representation, the people being subjects <334> and represented, must here, because the people are self-ruling, take their place in sovereignty itself, and in participation in it. In monarchy the nobility, initially alone, or at least in the main, comprises the imperial diet, and only then do the other estates participate; in the republic, rule is initially exercised exclusively by the nobility, and in its development it progresses to participation of the other estates; an estate of wealth is added to an estate of birth; the numerous popular class gains access to rule through various combinations, and so arise the distinctions of aristocracy, timocracy, democracy, the distinctions of the *comitia curiata, centuriata, tributa;* and the more recent history of the republic shows that the republic has an "estates-oriented" and a "representative" type, no less than does monarchy.[168]

§. 131. Municipalities are Natural Republics

The republic is the natural constitution of *sovereign municipalities.* In accordance with their tasks and interests, local orientation and community require a republican establishment, just as territory and the state are monarchical in accordance with theirs (§. 7). Where a local community, a city, becomes sovereign and thus a state, the city establishment appropriately and naturally takes on the political establishment. In the development which it requires and assumes for this, it becomes the republican form of state. Republics arise from cities, from local communities. In that the state is to belong to the nation, not to the individual city, there therefore does never arise an isolated republic; if there is a republican bent in a nation, that nation will divide itself by individual cities into republics; but these cities have a bond with each other, they manifest themselves again as members of a larger republic, or at least this union is recognized by them as their task. Republics, and virtually only republics, have the inner drive toward the federative state. All of this is **<335>** completely and undeniably established by the examples of the ancient republics, of Switzerland, of Holland. But no less so by the example of North America. *The republican constitution of North America has its ground and its possibility simply in the fact that there* (in particular New England, the model state of North America) *the states were founded not by peoples, as in Europe, but by local communities,* just as today there exists an independence of local communities there unheard of elsewhere. This utterly dissimilar historical origin of the states is decisive over the long term for the completely different character in the two parts of the world. Just so does North America demonstrate the general republican urge toward the federative state. This explains the entirely counter-natural, and thus failed, attempt to make of France, a kingdom that from the beginning was established by peoples and as a state, a republic, and a simple one in centralistic manner at that. A republic of France is as unnatural as, for instance, a kingdom of Nuremberg would be.

---

[168] This is to be distinguished from that which I above (§. 63) termed representative democracy.

§. 132. Advantages and Disadvantages

The republic has the advantage of developed legal order, apart from which it could not exist, and the self-activity and self-worth of the citizen, thus their awakening to political interests, public spirit, capacity for sacrifice. Upon this is based especially the brilliant period of citizen virtue in the ancient republics, which are the object of admiration for all times, to which one must ascribe not merely the republican constitution but also the particular mentality [Sinnesweise] of those peoples.

On the other hand, the republic suffers above all from a lack of uniform firm authority and power. For this reason, as a rule (excluding states particularly gifted for this) it usually has a less consistent and sustained development of power externally, and insufficient power to maintain the estates and parties within moderation and limits internally. In this manner, the nobility and the people in the ancient republics conducted an unremitting struggle for supreme power in that the nobility tried to exclude the other estate, while the **<336>** latter tried to make itself the equal of the nobility, and thus to abolish it. This struggle comprised the greater part of the life and history of these states, and the outcome, in that it killed a member necessary to the public order, tended to be the decline or collapse of the republic. Party strife, civil war, finally the collapse of order, therefore were held to be the most fearful dangers to the republic. For this reason, and because of the natural drive of states to monarchy, there was an awareness among the leading men that they, and not the incapable crowd, were called to rule; there as well was the temptation to pursue power in excess of the legally permissible, and vice versa, there was among the people an awareness of the facility with which the constitution could be overthrown, and thus jealousy against those leading men (ostracism). In these republics, there was always the fear of kingship as a more powerful entity which they could not handle should it be erected among them. Even in the republics of Lombardy, the Netherlands, Switzerland, such party strife manifested itself, leading, as the most recent history of Switzerland shows, to the fall and change of government, to civil war, while in monarchical states this strife either does not exist or is bridled by the higher power of monarchy from violent outburst, and cannot ever rise to the level of a war of annihilation. But even apart from this disadvantage in result, the republic, and in particular democracy, is in itself a less endowed, less complete, and therefore to that degree less perfect form of state than monarchy, at least monarchy developed in all of its elements. The very fact that it lacks monarchy, that is, its essence as a republic, is its defect; for the elevated regard, the visible majesty, the personal center and bearer of unity and the honor of the nation, and, accordingly, the ethical motives of piety, personal devotion, as well the natural love for ruling authority are absent to it.

Accordingly, the republic is by no means the most perfect constitution, the ideal state, which, were it feasible, should exist everywhere. It is the sense of human complacency, Promethean hubris, the Stoic idea of ethical fulfillment, which views the republic as political fulfillment. On the contrary, monarchy is the natural, normal constitution, which in its full development is of a higher character. The republic is the vo- <337> cation of certain states only by way of exception. But it is no less authorized according to God's order, no less legally justified, and, where a state has this vocation, no less a salutary constitution, the equal of monarchy.

Moreover, the republic has brought a general truth to awareness and existence, one of world-historical importance: the institutional character of the state, that the state has its own conditions and demands to follow, its own inner laws, and not just the personality of the ruling authority, be it monarchical or republican; and furthermore, this personality of the ruling authority is itself only a member of the institution. Such a character is entirely lacking in monarchy of ancient times; at that time, it existed only in republics or in monarchies which already carried the germ of the republic within themselves, and for this reason the republic was rightly considered the higher condition, alone worthy of the human race, a requirement of civilization. In more recent history, it was especially the Puritan republic in England[169] which showcased it. But in terms of its nature it is in no way restricted to the republic. Monarchy can and must also be won over to it, not merely the constitutional, but also even the absolute. And this has truly occurred. The monarchies of Europe bear this character to a high degree, and it is a false royalism that would deter it. *In fact, the concept of the state itself is republican in this sense,* and Europe's stage of civilization can no longer allow itself to be robbed of it. For this reason, the shrill contrast between

---

[169] [Stahl is here referring either to the Cromwellian republic or to *New* England, in which case the absence of "New" is a mistake. From statements he made elsewhere, it seems that the latter explanation is the more probable.]

monarchy and republic as existed in ancient times, in which each form of government established an entirely different form of civilization, no longer exists. The best and truest of that which the republic contains has been imbibed by monarchy.

§. 133. Institutions for the Rightly Ordered Republic

The mainspring of the republic is love for the legally ordered polity, faithfulness to the law, devotion to public goals and fellow citizens, temperance in the pursuit of power and riches, jealousy of any superiority of a personal will and any interference from its favor and bias. This is what Montesquieu understood by "virtue." The essence of the republican mentality is precisely the richness of the institu- **<338>** tional bond of the state, just as the essence of the monarchical mentality is richness of the personal bond. The new state-oriented monarchy, even without territorial representation, strives to unite both, just as the perfect state truly is built upon both.

The right ordering of the republic requires above all a traditional, historically established constitution. This is a requirement of all forms of state, but precisely the most to those in which veneration for the laws is to make up for the lack of a strong ruling authority. The continuity of the development and the sanctity of historical law was the strength of the Roman constitution, in the same way as it is for the republic-leaning English constitution; and that which gives the North American republics their greatest support is their constitution being based upon a tradition brought over from England, whereby the three factors in it – governor, senate, and assembly – are not merely as old as the foundation of the colonies, but, according to the local imagination, virtually as old as the Anglo-Norman race itself, which is why that people has the opinion of its necessity, believing that the state cannot in fact be anything else. What a contrast does the republic of France form with this, where one makes a new state constitution any time at the drop of a hat! The essence of the true republic is the commitment to a given, inherited, legal order, to the body politic in the specific form, and subjection to it. The true republic is therefore as contrary to and irreconcilable with the liberal mentality as monarchy is. What liberalism actually pursues is government by committee [ein Kollegialsystem], not a republic, and it deludes itself when it fancies its doctrine realized in the republic. **<339>**

The right ordering of the republic furthermore requires a proper formation [Bildung] of the sovereign popular assembly; for the republic this poses the same problems and the same difficulties as the territorial representation does for monarchy, the same succession of aristocratic and democratic power, the same predicament following the fall of the aristocracy, the same substitution by property qualification, and here as there the proper solution exists only in preserving all elements having life force and natural strength, and, in the popular assembly, drawing from all an aristocratic elite, on a democratic basis, i.e., in combination with the entire population.

The right ordering of the republic, finally, requires a *strong magistracy*. That is to say, understood more deeply, it requires a substitute for uniform sovereignty, a substitute for kingship. Thus, already in the ancient republics the magistracy assumed from kingship not merely the executive but also the sanction of laws (veto), whereby the popular decision is conditioned by proposal, preconsultation, preapproval on the part of the supreme magistracy, c.q. [bez.] the council or senate (προβούλευμα, *auctoritas senatus*). Above all, what an independent power of government and regard did Rome's supreme magistracy have! It was not distinguished from kings by content but by the duration of power and the plurality of its bearers. By contrast, the weakness of Athens consisted in its incomplete executive, insufficiently concentrated in the magistracy but exercised in large degree by the popular assembly itself, which, e.g., decided regarding peace, alliance, the plan of military campaign, received foreign emissaries and allowed them to negotiate before it and in competition with one another, chose all officials, especially judges and ambassadors. In North America, the magistracy has developed into a surrogate of royal power in supreme degree. Here were consciously imitated the relations of England's constitutional monarchy, and the president of the congress (or the governor) therefore exercises all monarchical functions. He concludes treaties (including treaties of peace and alliance), appoints emissaries, ministers, consuls, judges, officials, officers, with the advice and consent of the senate, and can alone, apart from the senate, remove them at his pleasure, excepting judges. In fact, his right regarding legislation is, in terms of form, less, but in result more effective than is that of the king of England. His veto does not unconditionally prevent the law, but makes necessary repeated votes on both houses, each requiring a two-thirds majority. Such usually approximates the effect of prevention, and for that reason the President of North America exercises the veto effectively and often, while the king of

England does not exercise it at all.[170] Just as monar- <340> chy had to imbibe a trait founded in world-historical manner by the republic – the institutional character of the state – so can the republic not exist without the monarchical trait of a strong independent magistracy. Authority over the people, and at the same time lawfully regulated internal relations, are the foundational pillars of all polities.

§. 134. Aristocracy

Aristocracy is as a rule the start, the initial shape, of the republic. In accordance with the general nature of the aristocratic element of the state, it provides a security of order, maintenance, and dignity, by virtue of which it has existed and flourished through the centuries. The shadow side is oppression of the people at large or the discouragement which the fundamental exclusion from power entails. Montesquieu rightly saw in aristocracy that its mainspring, the condition of its existence, is *restraint* on the part of the ruling estate. This is why the fall of the aristocratic regime commonly has its ground in the aristocracy using its possession of political power as a means of deriving base pecuniary advantages (e.g., in Rome) or in some other overbearing way, instead of being satisfied with that possession as their great and honorable vocation. As time progresses, however, the aristocratic constitution requires restraint likewise in institutions, i.e., that the nobility have a bond with the other classes (*connubium*) and recruit from their ranks, and that the other classes, when they mature and rise, be granted an appropriate portion in the body politic [öffentlichen Wesen]. A great example of this is the Roman centuriate constitution, through which the wealthy classes, which by virtue of their equipage formed the core of the armed forces, became <341> the center of gravity of the popular assembly, although the ancient entitled nobility nevertheless maintained its powerful position through its special

---

[170] Should one look to the actual power relation, one should not compare the president with the king of England but rather with his ministers, which shows the essential agreement. The president on the one hand and the ministers on the other, as long as they are in office, exercise that office fully independently with true monarchical position, and only thereby is the republic possible in both states. Only their continued position in office is under the higher power of the people, which in the one case is conducted through voting in Parliament, in the other through periodic elections, which makes the constitution republican.

centurions, through the influence of its clients, but mainly through the consent reserved to the all-patrician senate. By contrast, Solon's legislation in Athens, instead of supporting the aristocracy, eliminated it at one blow by restoring democracy in general principle and transferring what was left over as far as advantages are concerned from the blood lines to the wealthy (τίμημα).

A trait of true aristocratic character, and a true support thereof, comes also from the smaller circles in the state being founded in *personal,* not in material or local, togetherness [Zusammengehörigkeit]: thus, the old four phyles in Athens, based in descent; thus the *right of citizenship* in modern Europe, determined not by place of residence but of origin. It establishes a clan spirit [Sippschaft], fellowship [Genossenschaft], and thus an aristocratic feeling even in the lower circles.

§. 135. Democracy

Democracy is the weakest, least secure of all constitutions. Apart from the helplessness and awkwardness, and thus weakness, of popular rule, it releases all the passions and ignoble drives of the masses and delivers the state over to them. Of course, what is being discussed here is not the democracy which obtains in "small simple tribes persevering in ancient mores, engaging in farming or livestock" (Bluntschli) but democracy among true, significant states. In ancient times, its victory over the aristocracy was perhaps a momentary bright spot, but this was ever the precursor of the approaching fall of the republic through despotism or foreign conquest. The Athenian democracy is the decisive example in both respects. In Rome, even after the laws of Licinius the constitution was not yet democratic but mixed; true democracy began first with the Gracchi, but this also spelled the downfall of the constitution and mores. What a chain of horrors does Roman history consist of from that time until the fading of the republic into the empire. The political **<342>** thinkers of ancient times, Plato, Aristotle, Xenophon, Cicero, etc., all opposed democracy. In the republics of Christian Europe, the epoch of the collapse of the aristocracy for the most part began in recent times, since 1789, whereby a part of them have vanished, the remainder are waiting to see whether democracy, which has replaced it, will be able to maintain itself. Only in North America is there a specimen of democratic constitution. But it is also exceptional circumstances which support it there: the origin of most of these states from trading companies or religious communities, thus an egalitarian [gleichheitlichen] population without aristocratic elements, the broad, open stretches of land together with sparse populations, the principle of independence in all of the body politic, the manifold restriction of powers by the Union, the support from inherited English institutions and legal forms, the strong organization of executive power, in the southern states the transfer of base activities to a slave mass. Nevertheless, there as well the leading men, above all the greatest of them, Washington, resisted democracy, and a party of conservation still resists it today, expecting from it the most extreme breakdown. Above all, however, the duration of the American constitution is not yet lengthy enough to provide a definitive proof of the durability of democracy.

A basic question of the times is whether pure democracy is possible, i.e., a constitution in which the citizens [Staatsgenossen] in themselves, thus by virtue of their personality, apart from any requirement of birth, rank, landholding, wealth, are all equal participants in the legislative assembly. The possibility should by no means be denied. Are only outward relations, and not people themselves, truly to count as political values [Werthe]? But those outward relations are the *natural guarantees* of the public position, and when they are lacking, *ethical guarantees* must be provided in their place. Such an ethical guarantee in Sparta was provided by public education and the life order which permeated everything; in Rome, it was the censor. The highest ethical guarantee is the Christian faith, and church discipline as the effect and characteristic thereof. It is upon this that America's primeval democracy, the democracy of the states of New England, is founded, and this basis is yet firmer than any and all require- <343> ments of property qualification or landholding. The tradition from this commonwealth based upon Christianity and church discipline, the habituation to legality and obedience stemming from it, is perhaps itself yet the strongest glue of the American democracy.

By contrast, pure democracy in the usual sense, whereby people without either natural or ethical guarantees are all equally entitled to a place in the sovereign popular assembly merely by virtue of their human countenances – this pure democracy is simply impossible over the long term.

Everything here said about aristocracy and democracy is fully applicable, as is self-evident, to the monarchical states in relation to territorial representation and other powers under the sovereign.[171]

---

[171] Regarding the characteristic nature of various republican forms of state, see in particular Bluntschli, *Allgemeines Staatsrecht* [General State Law], vol. I, pp. 169f.

Chapter 16: Public Opinion and the Press[172]

§. 136. Public Opinion as Consciousness of the Nation

<345> As an ethical-intellectual kingdom, the state necessarily is based upon the ethical-intellectual consciousness of the nation, which has no determinate organs and external demarcations but which permeates the community as a single spiritual element. This element is the indispensable bearer of the state organism: no state can exist without it, and none ever has. But that it should be elevated to *actuality,* i.e., that it should not merely support the state as a whole, the regard of its ruling authority, and, moreover, only come to the fore in special catastrophes, but should constantly accompany all individual measures, that is what we specifically call the *power of public opinion*, and it is peculiar to our time that it already exists to a higher degree than ever before, and that its development and recognition is demanded as a requirement.

This developed power of public opinion has a dual significance (τέλος): *firstly,* that the government is obliged to gauge itself continually against public opinion, which excites the government's ethical-intellectual strength and direction, since the situation becomes difficult if it either does not assuage public opinion or is not morally elevated over that opinion; *secondly,* that the people itself, the free act of whom is to be the state as an ethical kingdom, becomes a jointly deciding and confirming actor regarding the ship of state. In both respects, it is a higher realization of the idea of the <346> state as a personal kingdom, and thus a true advance of the times.

§. 137. Public Opinion as Restraint

But the power of public opinion is neither in and for itself and apart from its content the fulfillment of the idea of the state, nor should it become either the exclusive power or a power superior to all others. Rather, rule in alignment with true ethics and insight is a yet higher goal than rule in accordance with or in

---

[172] I give this chapter with slight modifications from the second edition of 1846. The question regarding maintenance or abolition of censorship then formed a main object, a question which now has been decided. In this third edition, I have only added one section at the end.

tandem with public opinion; and the state, as a given thing, in its continuity – constitutional authority, traditional law – is a power which, in terms of time, is earlier, in terms of validity is higher, than momentary public opinion. The sound condition is therefore for public opinion to develop, be active, exercise a stimulative force on the government, not, however, to overpower the government, to draw rule to itself. The fulfillment of the true inward formative principle of the public condition – which stands over both authority and contemporary public opinion – is the final goal. But this principle of the public condition has both of these as its organs, and it is therefore proper that neither suppress the other, but that each maintain its position and mutually correct each other.

Public opinion is unsuited in every respect to be an authority over the government, to be a direct and positive determining power in the state. It is no less subject to passion and misjudgment than is the prince, and, in fact, tends much more to dissolution once it comes to power. It is not a formative principle, for it everywhere has only a general uncertain urge, not a view of determinate organization and government, and, as it is suffused with the rightness of its goal, so does it consider the ephemeral, in fact most counterproductive means to be just as infallible. It is without any restricting element, such as is not even lacking in despotic monarchy, for the prince as true ruler is ever restricted by public opinion, but what is to restrict public opinion when *it* is in power? It is without an appointed representative and organ; should it be recognized as positive guideline, it is not for all that the true, harmonious, enduring sentiment of the nation which decides the issue, but rather the shock of immediate excitement, the **<347>** battle cry of a passionate and thus energetic party in the state, or, in the calmest situation, the opinion of those who run the daily press. Therefore, there is no worse principle than the government having to serve public opinion.

Public opinion should however serve as a restriction and touchstone for the government. Without public opinion, the government not only treats the people, which itself is jointly to decide, which is held to be the bearer of the ethical kingdom of the state, as a mere passive object for obedience, but it also misconstrues the goals truly called for by the times. For the general pressure of public opinion, even when erroneous in its stated form, is still not lacking in a deeper, true motive: this hidden principle of formation of the times must be recognized by the government as its law, even when it resists its set doctrines, and whether it will help can only be proven when its results in the end satisfy minds. The prevailing attitude is therefore not mere inert matter for the government, which as such sets conditions for the use of means, like a pupil setting conditions for the teacher, but is likewise a source for properly recognizing the goal itself; and it is not merely a command of prudence to take it into consideration, but also of ethics, to wit, human modesty, whereby the appointed ruler does not simply allow his own judgment regarding the true and beneficial to prevail, but considers the great (objective) movement of the times as a sign from above, from a higher power, which he is to serve.

Accordingly, true wisdom of state is for the government not to be skittish about opposing public opinion when it comes to individual measures and goals, even temporarily to break with it entirely, and yet not to separate from it altogether and enduringly, not to cease having in it a solid footing – that it be firm and unmoved where the existing protects against public opinion's deceitful crush, but cautious and even modest where it wishes to introduce something new or bring back something vanished – that it guard itself less against political disapproval than against ethical offence – and above all, that it, where God's Word and command are imperative, not let itself be put off by the raging of public opinion where it otherwise remains within the limits of the law. Even if the approval of public opinion were <348> the final goal, which it by no means is, such would not be achieved if the government fulfills that which the loud voices of the day demand. He who would set the critic straight will ever suffer the same lot as the man in the fable with the son and the donkey.[173] Surely the last thing the government which directs itself to the press will receive is its praise. But the government which according to conscience pursues what is right and appropriate will also win over public opinion in its resistance, and in the end hold the field.[174]

The appropriate condition of the constitution, accordingly, is for the government to have an independent, secure position which can resist public opinion, but that public opinion truly be a power, and, in particular, a power for hindrance.

---

[173] [One of Aesop's fables, the moral of the story of which is, try to please everyone and you will please no one.]

[174] An example of this is offered by Prussia's politics in the oriental question [i.e., regarding the Ottoman Empire and the Crimean War].

Here is the innermost point in which my doctrine diverges from the most moderate and worthy representatives of the liberal principle, with whom I otherwise often agree in results. They would like for public opinion – i.e., that which is truly of the people and not of the journalists – that which is enduring, not momentary – to be irresistible, either legally or with factual certainty; they would like an independent administration but only on the basis of complete surrender to public opinion in matters of principle, which is why they advocate the unconditional right to refuse tax revenues in case of emergency, parliamentary government, trial by jury, the greatest possible strengthening of any influence of popular movement and popular expression (unrestricted popular assembly, association, petition). I on the other hand demand for authority the position to be able to resist public opinion even in matters of principle, where conservation and not an intent to innovate is concerned. In their case, everything in the state indeed comes down to a single power, to the opinion of the majority or the agitation; I wish for two powers, the independent, in fact primary power of the constitutional government, and, as secondary power, public opinion. The former is to be restricted, hindered by the latter, but **<349>** not determined, coerced by it; the latter is to be a true *power of conservation*. This end is served by the guarantees of the monarchical principle. Should one consider the past and present external condition to be unjustified in relation to the inward conviction of the current generation, there is no guarantee it will be so considered in the future. When however the currently living are allowed to destroy all that exists without limit, who is to ensure that they do not thereby irreversibly abbreviate the inheritance of future otherwise- and better-persuaded generations? Shall any period of time have the unrestricted disposition over institutions which are bestowed as goods and as a bond for all generations? If such is the case, should it not be desirable that the traditional and existing also have a powerful representation in the times?

In this manner, the power of public opinion which stems from the conception of the state as an ethical kingdom – a free ethical community under a given ethical authority – is distinguished from the power of public opinion which stems from the conception of the state as a contractually bound mass of free individuals, from the doctrine of popular sovereignty.

§. 138. Censorship versus Freedom of the Press

With the development of public opinion comes its power, since the real power of the state lies precisely in the people from whom public opinion comes. The means of this development is partly given automatically and cannot be hindered, such as, e.g., the improved education and heightened interaction of people, and partly depends upon political institutions.

Such a political institution above all is the institution of territorial representation. In itself, it is already the most significant and qualified organ of public opinion, and its official proceedings both awaken the political interest and judgment of the collective and pressure the government to sound itself out against it. Here, therefore, appears the final innermost purpose of this institution, which has only become clear in its most recent national and state-oriented **<350>** form. It is not so much that the territorial representation or the people should have a greater influence on the ship of state, but that, through being sounded out against the territorial representation and the public judgment, an understanding of the matter at hand becomes the determining power, so that measures are taken which have an inner justification (hence not derived from the principle of then-current opinion), and so that only those who are up to affairs (not necessarily sharing the orientation of the majority) actually deal with them.

Be that as it may, the specific and most powerful means of developing public opinion is *the press,* in particular *the daily press.* Given complete laissez-faire here, public opinion and its passions would develop to such a degree that no government and no order could exist. The latter, therefore, require a protection against the press. This is not disputed. Regarding the manner of this protection, two systems of contrary character have been developed in history, the old-continental and the English, and the verdict between them is among the most animated political questions of our time.

The measures of the government against corrupting writings originally arose, and continued in their development, in the protection of religion; the state did not yet have need of them. Since Christianity became the ruling church, it was held to be necessary, as was already customary in ancient Rome, to condemn, to burn, and to prohibit upon pain of punishment, anti-religious books. This was first exercised by the Emperor (Constantine against Arius), then, through the spiritual power, through the councils, later through the Pope. When book printing made for such a powerful expansion that the prohibition of books and their suppression proved insufficient, the institution of *censorship* was developed – in particular under Alexander VI and Leo X (1515) – whereby no book could be printed without prior perusal and approval (imprimatur) by the spiritual head, which also had to be expressly printed in the front of the book. In addition, punishments continued to exist both for the writer of anti-religious books and for the reader of prohibited books, as was especially maintained by the Inquisition; the latter prompted the preparation <**351**> and publication from then on, by the Curia, of a list of these books (*index librorum prohibitorum*), as was ordered by the Council of Trent.

As a result of the Reformation, censure was also introduced by the secular power, but mainly for ecclesiastical objects, in particular with the intention of restraining the bitter battle of the pens between religious parties, which threatened to frustrate all future reconciliation. The Imperial Ordinances of Nuremberg (1524), Speyer (1529), Augsburg (1530) ordered that no writing be printed without prior perusal by persons appointed to that end by the secular and spiritual ruling authorities, that the printer and the location of printing be mentioned, etc. These orders were included in the most recent public welfare ordinance [Polizeiordnung] of 1577. The writings the suppression of which was the purpose of the censorship, in line with the above-mentioned intention, initially were mainly diatribes (whereby the intent was invective against the other confessions and their adherents), although the Imperial ordinance of Augsburg 1548 also mentions those "not in accordance with the doctrine of the Christian church and the Imperial ordinances"; the Peace of Westphalia prohibited attacks on the treaties of religion in the German empire; finally, the coronation charter of Leopold II did so regarding everything incompatible with the doctrinal books of both religions, good customs, tranquility, and the current constitution of the empire.

The imperial laws were often unenforced by the territorial princes, who were repeatedly admonished, often without result. Often they themselves enacted ordinances regarding censorship. Censorship was sometimes oppressively exercised – Moser complained of additions the censors afforded themselves – although occasionally, the territorial government acquiesced in an excess of the press, if its interest was not involved. In particular, censorship was exercised in various spirits in accordance with the party to which the territorial prince belonged: in Catholic countries against Protestant writings, in Protestant against

Catholic, later in archiepiscopal against papist writings (e.g., Mainz's prohibition on the writings of Bellarmine), in papist-oriented territories, against the writings of the <352> episcopalists. Besides censorship, of course, there was also, to the degree that it should still be necessary, subsequent confiscation of writings and punishment of the writer (not, as with Catholic clerical censorship, the reader as well); in particular, the imperial public prosecutors were obligated to take action in the imperial courts against books and writers when territorial ruling authorities did not perform their obligation. But appeals against unjust censors were also upheld by the imperial courts. Among the Protestants, the conflict followed as to whether censorship regarding dogma did not infringe freedom of conscience. Those who rejected any ecclesiastical control of doctrine (Thomasius) had that much more reason to reject censorship regarding it. On the other hand, it was generally held that the printing of inflammatory or immoral writings was inadmissible. First during the period of "Enlightenment" did one arrive at the point of resisting censorship in general. Since the end of the 18th century, the voices of writers, and public opinion in their train, were lifted ever higher in favor of freedom of the press. Among the most serious extensions in favor thereof is that which was already exercised in many countries, whereby censorship was dropped, and a mere public-welfare-oriented oversight over the spread of printed books was exercised, with confiscation of those found to be injurious.

In England, matters took a different turn. There too, the original mode was censorship, exercised in especially hateful and oppressive manner. Already under the Plantagenets, criminal cases in exceptional situations were brought before the privy council, contrary to the rule of Magna Charta. Henry VIII expanded this into his own tribunal comprising high crown officials and bishops, which decided over political and ecclesiastical offences without jurors – the Star Chamber. This hated, extraordinary tribunal stood over the press, performed both censorship and punishment of press-oriented offences, and maintained both in strict, even horrific manner. When Charles I was forced to sacrifice this to the Long Parliament, press offences, in accordance with the common law, fell to trial by jury. But censorship continued unremittingly under the Long Parliament and Cromwell. Charles II needed a law of censorship, not to create this institution, <353> but to regulate it again and more strictly, in particular to determine the organs for it, since he could not make use of those of the Commonwealth; the designation of these organs remained essentially the same. This is the Licensing Act of 1662. It was only approved for a term of years, since devotion to the Restoration was not unconditional; and, after repeated renewals, even under William III, it was finally revoked in 1694. Herein, then, existed freedom of the press, not through direct implementation, but indirectly, through non-approval of the extension of the censorship law. Thus, in the moment that freedom of the press came about, something in the line of other guarantees against misuse of the press was not thought of; rather, the punishment for impermissible attacks on state and church or on private individuals – "libel" – remained in their previous relation. Now there was and is no law in England regarding the concept and extent of libel, and therefore, what is decisive is the extremely manifold doctrine and practice. Traditional practice, to which judges adhered, was usually the strictness of the Star Chamber, until finally the Fox Bill of 1792 authorized the jury in libel cases, not merely with regard to determination of fact (whether the defendant was the author of the writing and its spread) but the legal concept, i.e., regarding the qualification of the writing as libel, through which a freer movement of the press arose. From that point on, the character of freedom of the press in England has been decided. Pitt's modified statute (1798) concerning the obligatory inclusion of publication information and responsibility of the publishers, printers, etc., at newspapers, serves to keep legal prosecution from being frustrated, and since then has been imitated everywhere.

In France, freedom of the press was one of the first demands and deeds of the Revolution. But it soon succumbed to the power of the then ruling party, to wit, Napoleon's. First the Restoration, by means of the law of June 9th, 1819, laid the basis to ensure its continued existence through appropriate measures against misuse, and the July government completed this work through the law of September **<354>** 9th, 1835.[175] Censorship was ruled out by the Charter of 1830, when the press was brought under the jury. Safeguards against the press, in accordance with the laws of 1819 and 1835, are as follows:

---

[175] The institution of the press in France rested on both of these reasonable laws until the February [1848] revolution led to a condition first of lack of restraint, and then of absolute governmental control of the press.

- Thoroughly developed and strict determinations of punishment regarding crimes, offences, and transgressions of the press (especially 1835)
- highly significant bond pledges for periodicals (50,000–120,000 francs) with the further determination that every proprietor must himself be the holder of one-third of the security sum (since only property binds one to the existing order)
- joint liability of all participants
- issue of a copy of every new edition to the officials (prefect, mayor) upon appearance, although without them necessarily being able to halt the spread thereof
- immediate confiscation of writings by the investigating judge upon lodged accusation
- definitive suppression of writings as a result of conviction, with heavy penalties for their further spread
- the obligation of journals immediately to insert opposing articles from the government, or from any private individual attacked or mentioned (*lendemain*), and, especially, without cost to private individuals, as long as they remain within the length of the offending article.

Accordingly, there are two opposing ways to combat the abuse of the press. One is to prevent the spread of injurious writings – *censorship* or *confiscation;* the other is to allow the spread of writings while punishing the guilty author – *freedom of the press* and *press tribunals.* Confiscation, suppression of writings might also occur in the latter way, but only in consequence of conviction of the author and after dissemination has already occurred, thus without the latter being hindered; on the other hand, any restriction of a writing merely due to its quality (general injuriousness, danger) without the author being found guilty and punished is ruled out. In the former method, the press is the object of administration, of public welfare, namely care that injury not occur through it; in the latter, this is not the case at all, but **<355>** merely the object of legal procedure, and criminal procedure at that; the question is whether an offence which has been incurred is to be punished; any effect on the press is not taken into account at all. The two methods are characterized as the preventive system and the repressive one, which however only expresses the outward phenomenon and not the inward principle. Censorship, by the way, is not the only element of the repressive system, confiscation is as well, even after lengthy dissemination, as long as it occurs independently, and not merely in consequence of penal judgment.

The character of the English and the old continental press establishment thus stand in shrill contrast the one to the other: the former is a purely penal institution, the latter a purely public-welfare institution. But not only are a multiplicity of specific applications possible within these basic characters (e.g., whether the press tribunal is more appropriately a jury or a panel of judges), but even modifications through which the institution of one character approaches that of the other. Such modifications have been implemented in recent times.

A modification of the English pure penal character regarding the press is namely the French institution, according to which government authorities receive a preliminary copy (*au moment de la publication*) and are able to effect a provisional confiscation via the judge by bringing a charge. This joins concern for public welfare with criminal procedure. On the other hand, in recent times a modification of the continental public-welfare system has been implemented such that an appeal can be made from a judicial or administrative-adversarial sentence against public-welfare preventive activity. This includes the appeal to the council of state regarding confiscation of books in certain south German states, and the appeal against censorship orders in daily newspapers to a "supreme censorship court" specially set up for this in Prussia.[176]

When, in this manner, modifications to both press systems are **<356>** possible, by mutual rapprochement, nevertheless the fundamental opposition forms an unbridgeable gap between them: namely, no restriction on writing apart from punishment of the author in the former, mere dealing with the writing in the latter. The press ordinance in the former case is ever an ordinance regarding the guilt of an author, while in the latter case it is an ordinance regarding the permissibility of dissemination of a writing. The choice between the two therefore cannot be evaded.

The penal system of the press is now typified as *freedom of the press*, the opposite being the lack of the same, and with reason; for, although the extent of free reporting in either system depends upon the standard used by the lawful

---

[176] These institutions, described and discussed in more detail in the second edition, no longer have any interest, since they have everywhere given way to freedom of the press.

judge over the press (judges or censors), and therefore the press often can be unrestrained under censorship and suppressed under press tribunals, even so, the penal system does preserve two great advantages: firstly, that enunciation of the thought and thereby an effect on the public (even when extremely limited, as with the French establishment) cannot be hindered, should the author be willing to incur the punishment; secondly, that in relation to time and circumstance, the author's sphere of criminal liability can never and will never be as broad as the sphere of mere suppressibility of writing.

§. 139. The True Character of the Press and Censorship

The current established viewpoint, that censorship of the daily press is something simply and everywhere reprehensible, something intolerable, is part of the one-sidedness of the age, which takes freedom into account everywhere, authority nowhere.

The unconditional requirement of freedom of the press is based simply upon the private-legal viewpoint, the inalienable right of the individual everywhere to express and convey his thoughts (Blackstone; *Declaration of the Rights of Man,* 1789). Yet an unrestricted right of this sort is just as arbitrary a claim as is the unrestricted freedom to do anything one wishes which does not directly injure another. But the press is not a communica- <357> tion of thought like any other; it makes use of the effective means of dissemination which lie in the institutions [Anstalten] of human community. When, accordingly, individuals have the right to speak their minds, they still have no inalienable right to these means of the community and may only lay claim to the use thereof under the restrictions entailed by the consideration of the well-being of the community. Is the preventive prohibition on bearing arms not also a restriction of my natural rights of freedom and property? And who disapproves?

Furthermore, the unconditional postulate of freedom of the press is put forward from a political viewpoint which claims that it is the cornerstone of the constitutional system. To wit, the press is the final, highest control both for the legislative and the executive power, and it is therefore contradictory and absurd to put it under the oversight of the government over which it itself is to exercise oversight. The argument can be turned around: it is just as contradictory that those who are to govern are to be under the oversight and criticism of the governed, without protection, as would be the case with a court comprised of the governed (jury). One therefore can only consider the freedom of the press to be the necessary cornerstone of the constitutional system when one conceives this system in the sense of popular sovereignty, according to which the government is virtually to be made subservient to public opinion. In reality, however, the significance of the press in the constitutional state is not that the newspapers directly control the government, but that the general political education which they foster promotes the control to be exercised by the nation as a whole; but such is not affected by individual flawed strokes of censorship. Control in terms of specific cases is the concern of the territorial representative body, for which reason the publication of their proceedings should undergo no restriction. To consider the disordered inorganic element of the daily press to stand as a higher power over the government and the ordered representation of the people is a reversal of natural relations, the more so that daily journalists by no means are pure representatives of public opinion, i.e., the nation in its collective estates, but are themselves rather an individual specific estate with specific estate interests, and precisely those which are least materially bound to the public order and **<358>** public well-being, but which, through this peculiar activity, often externally forces its viewpoint onto the other estates, even when foreign to their position.

Against this, it should be taken into account that the political press, especially the daily press, is a form of public communication; it makes use of an organ because it is not an individual speaking to an individual but an individual speaking to all, to the entire nation, and by virtue of the daily appearance of the papers, accompanied by their simultaneous immediate examination by all, just as if in a popular assembly instituted for that purpose; and it has as its object, not the affairs of the individuals (the writers), but the public condition, and not even this generally, but the interests and government measures immediately at hand; the power which it possesses for this, by general acknowledgment, is incalculable. Such an ongoing public address from such a factual power regarding the public condition in a continuously-assembled ever-ready popular assembly falls, both according to general concepts and consideration of result, within the sphere of the supervisory and preventive activity of the state, not the mere punishing activity, if it is the organically ordered government that is to rule and not the disordered popular mass. The latter cannot make up for the disadvantages of its abuse. For in the case of general excitation, it is scarcely possible to follow up the countless violations with indictments, and it leads to the necessity of letting most go unpunished, and, beyond this, to the consequence that the yardstick for the judicial assessment of press abuse becomes looser the longer it takes. Even in the case of punishment (especially with public legal proceedings), the regard of the government is undercut by the fact that its injury is an object of public proceeding, and the accusing government often receives a much harsher criticism from the defense, which must be granted greater leeway, than from the initial offender.

Add to this the real tendency of the daily press. The question of censorship is not just about the possible opinions that can be expressed in the press and should not be restricted, but about the very specific intentions that the political daily press is currently pursuing. These undeniably **<359>** are: the rejection of revealed religion, and the church founded upon it, in favor of the religion of reason; then, the complete freedom [Ungebundenheit] of the individual (freedom of trade, freedom to parcel out an estate [Gutszertrümmerung], etc.); finally, the rule of the people, i.e., the propertied citizen class (*bourgeoisie*), over the king. This class is the source of all the institutions they advocate, so-called "constitutional state law" (which is something entirely other than a real constitutional constitution [konstitutionelle Verfassung], even the English), trial by jury, etc. Above all, however, the way in which public authority is discussed, and the opposing views and the men who represent them are judged, is based on this. Censorship only aims to hinder the latter tendency; ecclesiastical opposition is as good as unrestricted in the Protestant states, and the efforts in favor of individual freedom everywhere have their way. Censorship is only used to guard against the authority of the government being entirely disparaged, and to keep the institutions which along with monarchy are deemed intolerable, or regarded with misgivings, from being overrun by the press. The daily press is generally nothing other than a daily call to action: let us take up the reins of government, let us bring to bear only our (the people's) will in the state and make the king into the bare executor thereof. Newspapers of contrary tendency have difficulty maintaining themselves in any decisive number if at all, because readers and customers wish to read about how they are to command, not how they are to obey.

The question is whether the monarchy can maintain itself apart from censorship against this daily self-congratulating independent power. We do not wish to decide this *a priori;* history shall bear witness. In England and France, it is boasted, freedom of the press exists without harm. Certainly, but since when?

Since the intention was attained to make the king constitutionally a mere servant of popular opinion. There, of course, censorship is no longer required. Now that the reader of and buyer of dailies, the bourgeoisie, the gentry, themselves predominate in the government, the press must as natural law (to be marketable and to <360> strike a chord) represent the existing order and not seek to overthrow it. In fact it is now the ruling class which is strongly inclined, not to give up freedom of the press in principle, which could be dusted off if needed for the sake of the political position, but in practice to restrict it as much as possible. Did not the king of France receive the September Laws [of 1835 restricting freedom of the press] from the popular representation? And does not a ministry there remain at the helm which is accused of restricting the press through unconstitutional influence on the jury court? The constitution there could only be threatened by freedom of the press from another side, namely, when the proletariat would wish to snatch rule from the propertied [Besitzern] and set in motion its press to that end. The danger of the Chartist and proletarian press is not of the same degree to the power of the possessors as is the liberal press to the power of the monarchy; for, on the one hand, the proletariat cannot provide its press with the same level of income and recognition, and, on the other, the propertied, who beyond that always have the king on their side as far as this matter goes, themselves as mass are much more secure vis-à-vis the proletariat than is the monarch, who over against the citizenry has nothing other than faith in his authority. The current storm in favor of freedom of the press is therefore partly nothing other than the citizenry struggling with monarchy over the supreme power and calling out to the latter: thou shalt put off thy suit of armor, the better that I might do battle.

It therefore cannot be doubted that underlying censorship is a significant need for the maintenance of monarchy, not in its unrestrictedness but in its independence. This is not to deny its abuses.

One well-founded objection against censorship concerns the danger to free spiritual development which lies in its essence as a communication-restricting institution. Censorship in its historical origin is connected with the viewpoint that the government is to lead in the development of thought, and, in particular, is to prevent the emergence of false doctrine. In this sense, censorship was introduced by the Papists and in the same sense, albeit less despotically, it has been imitated by the secular ruling authority. This or that opinion <361> which runs counter to the ruling religion or the viewpoint of government is not to be expressed; and such an orientation, with which censorship began, may yet cling to it. The present time struggles against this, and rightly so, and to this in particular is attributable the inherited aversion to it. Just as the ruling authority by no means has as its task the leadership of thought, so can the task of censorship not be to influence the press in this sense. The significance of censorship therefore ought not to be sought in providing protection against the *subversion of the true conviction* but only to provide protection against agitation, against *assault on the foundations* of the existing order. This is true for church and state. Therefore, in this respect the representation of every political viewpoint and every judgment regarding daily occurrences and measures must be free; only passionate agitation and disrespect is to be prevented; and in this respect every religious and anti-religious doctrine must be expressible, while only frivolous assault and agitation of lower vulnerable classes against the faith is to be prevented. It is this maxim by which in Germany today virtually no scientific works and books undergo any censorship, and the confiscation which exists against them is exercised in the rarest of cases. May one complain of restrictions on the religious press when the works of Strauss and Feuerbach are freely available? Books in general have a gradual effect on the process of the development of ideas, which in turn determine church and state. This truly spiritual element may not be subjected to preventive influence, and in Germany is not subjected to such. On the other hand, newspapers have an immediate, external effect, not on the formation of thought but on passions and deeds; should the ruling authority here act preemptively, it does not exceed its sphere. This eliminates the objection that sickly and mistaken orientations also arise and expand apart from freedom of the press. This cannot be denied, and their origin and expansion are not to be restricted. But without freedom of the press, they do not come suddenly to external power, allowing them to shake or even topple the existing order, so that, without leaving destruction in their wake, they in time likewise can again be eliminated. It is impossible for medicine to preclude **<362>** the course of disease with all of its manifestations, but it is possible for medicine to alleviate it and to keep it from the most honorable members, so that the crisis does not destroy the body. Censorship acts something like this.

The other well-founded objection to censorship concerns the *arbitrariness of its exercise.* Should this mean the necessary *indeterminacy of its norms*, then the objection would be of little weight. Certainly, the boundaries between permissible discussion and impermissible agitation, between appropriate rebuke and disrespect, cannot be drawn by general definitions, and therefore a great deal of fortuitousness and thus inequality of judgment is unavoidable even with exemplary censors. But the same thing is true with freedom of the press regarding claims of private injury in press tribunals. Even the libel laws, even the concept of injury is necessarily subject to the same indeterminacy, and on the same grounds. The effect and meaning of a speech cannot be sharply delineated as can the effect and meaning of an act. For this reason, every judge will come to the same conclusion as to what constitutes theft, but not as to what constitutes libel or slander. The same degree of fortuitousness and inequality likewise prevails in many other spheres, for example in examinations for public office. The boundaries of capacity and incapacity or the degree thereof are not conceptually delineable, and is it any greater an evil that the notion of a journalist is unfairly deleted than that a candidate for legal or educational office is unfairly rejected?[177] Should one combat not this fortuitousness of censorship norms but the arbitrariness in their basis – should one find the anomaly in this, that the public welfare, of which censorship is an attribute, is conducted in terms of instructions of service rather than laws, and even the individual specific act of the censor depends upon the special instructions of the supreme administrative official or the prince himself – then the objection is entirely **<363>** justified; but it can also be remedied. For this reason, back in the first edition (1837, p. 230) I recommended a separation from "the person of the king," and the placement of censorship under *"independent officials,"* as a way out of the impasse. This was later realized in Prussia in a developed fashion through the *supreme censorship court.*

Should censorship cease to be a bare affair of public welfare and become an affair of administrative justice (§. 138), the objection of arbitrariness can no longer be made. Censorship arranged in this manner, its legally pronounced maxims protecting not against erroneous thought processes but only against agitation, exercised not in terms of public welfare but adversarially under

---

[177] More or less firm specifications and thus equal exercise can be fostered both for censorship and for press tribunals, not through bare general laws but by leaning on precedent.

administrative law [administrativ-contentiös], is anything but an intolerable institution. Despite countless mistakes in particulars, which cannot be avoided, it nevertheless on the whole does not stint the daily press in its appropriate free outlook. The most free-thinking men of earlier times, a Plato or a Luther, would have considered it completely natural. It compares to English freedom of the press something like the way a more classical play compares to a more romantic one. In the former, the state is made into a principle and the individual is ensured freedom within his indispensable edifice, while in the latter, individual freedom is made into a principle, with restrictions calculated merely by himself (his guilt), and from this the harmony of the whole is nevertheless to be maintained. This in general is the distinction between the character of our continental, in particular German, states, as opposed to the English.

§. 140. Practical Inevitability of Freedom of the Press

Regardless of this principled justification of censorship, a certain dampening of energy in the written representation of concrete authorizations and interests and the discussion of concrete events and measures is inseparable from it, and freedom of the press ever remains a good, like any condition of unrestricted, unhindered activity and development. Therefore, to the degree that it does not endanger higher interests, it is a goal to be pursued. But **<364>** the time appears fast to be approaching that freedom of the press with the appropriate guarantees is to be preferred to the preventive system, even for the protection of the public authority. The value of any institution is determined by the esteem it finds in public life, and its outcome depends upon that esteem. With the currently reigning sentiment, the point has been reached that censorship no longer is capable of fulfilling its task. While censorship itself is forced onto so broad a base that it virtually no longer hinders the opposition at all, the imagination of the public is that nothing can prevail against censorship, and, therefore, that the most significant things that can be said against the government and existing conditions are left unsaid. Thus does the existence of censorship give the opposition press a strength which it would be incapable of lending to itself, and it could in the end be better to sacrifice the tiny remainder of protection afforded to the regard for the ruling authority and the observance of a calm tone, which censorship is still capable of maintaining, in exchange for the fruit yielded by the consciousness of being unrestricted. It would bring the further advantage that, through the requirement to put up a bond deposit, the mass of local papers, which embody the most complete superficiality, would have to shrink, and the worse part of the news editors would no longer be shielded from well-deserved punishment by the protection of the censor. In fact, since one would rather remain well inside the boundaries of security, an orderly maintained press tribunal could have a better effect than censorship now does. Accordingly, while I cannot recognize a legal-philosophical necessity for freedom of the press, I do recognize a political one. Although it is often maintained that freedom of the press is the only allowable condition theoretically, while censorship is factually an unavoidable evil, I would say the reverse is true: censorship is a justifiable condition in theory, but freedom of the press is factually an unavoidable risk, which, when successful, of course brings with it an incomparably more welcome situation than what exists under censorship.

The guarantees of freedom of the press would include both a press law, as strictly determined and severe as possible (such as that **<365>** of September 9th, 1835), and judges over the daily press, of quality and position similar to the Prussian supreme censorship court. To which we add all the provisions of French press legislation.

It nevertheless remains the necessary course that censorship should only be entirely eliminated when constitutional relations can maintain their fixed enduring order. One does not put fermenting juice in flimsy skins, lest they burst. Historically, freedom of the press everywhere followed, not preceded, the establishment of constitutional relations, as was the case in England and France.

The German constitutional situation therefore corresponds to the two ways, according to the shape which relations take, either censorship under the given guarantees for freedom and the rights of writers, or freedom of the press under the given guarantees for order and for monarchy. On the other hand, freedom of the press in the English fashion, i.e., *press tribunal with trial by jury,* is not well suited. This form of freedom of the press is not the cornerstone of the constitutional constitution [konstitutionellen Verfassung] in general, but the cornerstone of the English constitution, or the parliamentary principle, namely, complete self-government of the nation, with the repression of royal power: for this reason, it contradicts the monarchical principle, which up until now has formed the center of our constitution. The protection of the existing order against the press is rightly put in the hands of the people (jury) when the people form the center of gravity of that order; but when the government is to remain the center of gravity of that order, means of protection against the power of the press must exist which do not depend upon the pleasure of the governed. Should these (the people, jury) have complete and absolute disposition of the degree to which they will allow calumny of the government and incitement to resistance, then, obviously, a government which does not place itself unconditionally under the will of the people is impossible. Freedom of the press, with mere trial by jury, transforms the monarchical constitution into the popular-rule or parliamentary one; this is an inevitable consequence. One might be of the viewpoint that the position of the king to the people as contained in the English and French constitutions is desirable, but one cannot be of the viewpoint that free- **<366>** dom of the press in those countries is compatible with the position of monarchy in Germany.

§. 141. Freedom of the Press since 1848

These were my considerations in 1846 regarding the then-pending questions regarding freedom of the press and censorship. The catastrophe which I characterized as the intention and achievement of the daily press did come about. The monarchy succumbed to the citizenry, or via the citizenry to the popular mass, and only through the favor of special circumstances was it reestablished. Freedom of the press, at the time "an unavoidable risk," is henceforth an existing institution, and it is the case even more for it than for territorial representation, that the task is not to defeat it but to conduct it properly, in order that it truly be "an incomparably more welcome situation than what exists under censorship." Even the safeguards against freedom of the press in Germany were mostly introduced in the manner I then extolled in the French legislation, in particular "provisional confiscation"; this "happy combination of public welfare with criminal procedure" has become a main element of protective equipment against the press. Trial by jury for press offences, against which I warned, does exist in Prussia (until 1854), albeit under certain restrictions. Its introduction for all criminal procedure made this virtually unavoidable anyway. Also, the measures which have been taken more frequently and have even been consented to by the chambers since the abolition of censorship – refusal of mailing licenses, withdrawal of bookselling licenses, suppression of an entire magazine in the case of repeated convictions – may in greater or lesser degree draw into question the compatibility of it with the strict concept of freedom of the press; they are, at any rate, a confirmation that freedom of the press truly is "a risk," and that it is not possible "to follow up the general agitation of the daily press with (individual) indictments"; the massive agitation of the public spirit demands a weapon of defense that also works on a mass scale. The prior treatment therefore retains an unchanged validity, even for the current situation.

On the other hand, now that freedom of the press exists, at- <367> tentiveness must in particular be directed to the proper attitude of the government to it. In this respect the following should be emphasized:

Firstly, petty police harassment, by which daily papers are destroyed by roundabout methods (repeated confiscation and withholding of issues, etc.) are to be avoided even in the case of the worst presses. It is precisely energetic interventions with legal means, and, thereby, a stronger, more just course of action by the government in accordance with the necessity of the matter, which at the least will compel the moral esteem of opposing public opinion, which is the only worthy and likewise the only secure and enduring defense against the evil.

Secondly, now that the struggle of the minds has been thrown open, the government has the task of *cultivating the good press* – through appreciative treatment, promotion of the truly meritorious and worthy men therein, contribution of official announcements to daily newspapers, etc. In response, the question has been posed, what is the good press? Is it that of one's own party? Who is to judge? My answer is this: "Where faith in the Christian revelation, and faithfulness to monarchy, form the foundation of sentiment and the living mainspring, there is the good press, regardless of whether gold, silver, wood, hay, or stubble is built upon it" (First Chamber, March 17th, 1854).[178] Accordingly, it is to cultivate the *loyal,* the *conservative*, not merely the *governmental* press, not the press which "supports the individual momentary measures of the government, but which promotes the sentiment upon which alone the government at all times can exist." The guarantee of its independence is therefore the supreme means to cultivate the good press. This requires scrupulousness and self-denial on the part of the government, and self-denial is the greater because, should the government behave in the opposite way, i.e., should the government suppress the good press in the case of conflict, because that sort of press is always unpopular,

---

[178] For republics, of course, faithfulness is to the constitutional ruling authority and the authority of the institutions. But an antimonarchist such as Thomas Paine belongs to the bad press even when he lives and writes in North America.

<368> it not only will promote its own measures but on top of that gain in popularity. For this reason such restraint will make the least sense to governments. But this scrupulousness and this self-denial are among the most urgent demands. The countless papers, brochures, and books which form the daily reading matter of the population, the ideas of which they breathe in like the breath of life, are, with few exceptions, the opposite of those which I characterize as the good press. They make it their task, in accordance with the euphemistic expression, to realize the system of 1789. This is a gradually acting corruption, and it cannot and shall not be steered by state measures – censorship, confiscation, judicial prosecution – these free spiritual forces are not amenable to such crude tools. Can one halt the sirocco with barriers? To counter it, an equal spiritual power is needed, an equally powerful breath, which purifies the most rarefied air.

It is therefore crucial for the future that a place be opened for and that development be promoted of such a healing spiritual power. In earlier conditions, the press was scarcely counted within the sphere of government concerns. Now, at least in the larger states, it is certainly a highly significant concern. But the mere *public welfare-oriented*, even the mere *parliamentary, treatment* of the press, which the governments are accustomed to engage in with zeal, since they establish a ministerial (official, quasi-official) press, is not enough; but what above all is required is the *pedagogical treatment* of the press. It is a part of national education, and, accordingly, is to be considered not as bare means for the government, but as itself one of its highest goals; the organs are not to be left to the external public-welfare order but to be supervised and led by more profound statesmen, who are devoted to education and ethical sentiment.

There are currently cabinets that understand how to set all the pens in Germany in movement for the goals of power and influence, and therefore doubtless have great external success. But a government which likewise calls for and inspires the journalistic forces for the divine order would effect an inward and enduring blessing, the likes of which, as with all true blessings, would likewise benefit the **<369>** other peoples.

Finally, freedom of the press as has now been introduced, which is only to be distinguished from the previous condition by the *means of operation,* ought not be viewed as a *change in standards.* In particular, the opinion must not be given room that in consequence of freedom of the press all opinions have an *equal* right in the press. Here as well only *freedom* counts, not *equality.* Even unchristian and republican viewpoints are to have *free* expression in the press in our Christian and monarchical states, but not *equal* to Christian and monarchical viewpoints, and in particular, not equal in the struggle against its opposite. One ought not be of the opinion that while the polemic against democratism and nationalism is unrestrictedly open, therefore in equal degree must the polemic against monarchical loyalty and Christian faith be unrestrictedly open, or else the former must also be restricted – that writing against the German Catholics and Reform Jews may only be done in the tone in which they write against the Christian church – that that which was permitted against the national assemblies of 1848 ought also to be permitted against the German governments – that if one may mock the voting right of all free-born natives, one may do the same regarding the sanctity and inviolability of the king. Private opinions and private pursuits in the state and in the press are free; the public institutions of the ruling authority and the church are not just free, but sacred. The tone of indignation, of mockery, of speech to agitate the mass, is allowable against the former, and between them reciprocally, but never against the latter.

Chapter 17: The Declaration of Rights

§. 142. Purpose of the Declaration of Rights

With regard to the state, man has not merely duties of obedience and performance but also rights, and these rights are not derived merely from the state order but are founded in the higher order of the ethical world, no less than is regard of the state itself. The state order only gives these rights, in the same way as it does the power of the ruling authorities, their specificity in terms of content and range. The object of these rights of man are, firstly, the *freedoms and goods of their independent existence,* which should not cease in the state, such as life, natural liberty, the entire sphere of individual life vocation; no less, however, the *freedoms and goods of their social existence,* that is, the action upon society to which man is called, and the material and ethical performances of society upon which he depends, thus, at the same time, his protection in the state and his enjoyment of the state itself. So, for example, not only does freedom of development belong to its sphere, but also freedom of the press and the capacity for state offices, not merely security against detention but also prompt justice. With the higher development of the state order, these freedoms and goods are not simply to be factually granted but also fundamentally recognized as rights, and they, to the degree that they are brought into doubt or are refused, are expressly guaranteed, namely through stipulation of boundaries which the ruling authority may not infringe in its pursuit of the public welfare. This is the significance of the "declaration of rights." They are thus the rights of the subjects acknowledged by and expressly safeguarded from the power of the state. They form a legal restriction on the government, a moral one even on legislation. By virtue of them, man is not a mere subject of the state, but also a citizen; he has a sphere in **<372>** which he is not so much subject to the state but rather in which the state is obligated to him.[179]

[179] In ancient times, the term "citizen" (*civis*) indicated a participation in state power; here, it signifies entitlement vis-à-vis state power. In the former case, the concept only held for the specific form of state of the republic, while in the latter it holds for every form.

On the same grounds, declarations of rights are to extend to the institutions which are subordinate to the state but which nevertheless have inviolable rights with respect to it, be it by virtue of immutable divine order, such as the church, be it by virtue of natural historical order, such as local communities and corporate bodies of estates [ständischen Korporationen], each according to the requirement thereof.

Ancient civilization knew nothing of declarations of rights. Such were impossible in the despotisms of the orient, given the unrestricted power of the ruler, nor possible in the Greek republics, since unrestricted devotion to the state was precisely those polities' innermost mainspring. Even in Rome, where the citizen had an independent sphere of private law and private freedom, these were not recognized as a demand of his rights vis-à-vis state power, and not expressly emphasized as such. There were therefore corresponding laws (such as e.g. those which were given at the Sacred Mountain after the secession of the plebs), but no declarations of rights. In the final analysis, what was sacrosanct was not one's own right brought to recognition but the laws which were effectuated. It may have been the same in result; it was not so in spirit. The declaration of rights in this specific sense, that the ruling authority secures a sphere of inviolability to its subjects, not only under itself, but at the same time, as it were, opposite of itself and beside itself, is an achievement of the Germanic spirit. Here, man is not merely a part in the architectonic construction of the state but of an absolute independent existence, and kingdoms are erected upon original independence which they restrict but do not abolish. The declaration of rights finds its deeper ethical foundation in Christianity, because Christianity elevates men, in accordance with their innermost exis- <373> tence, over the state, and binds them directly to God. Recent times have brought the concept of this to awareness and intensification – the concept that its content and goal is not merely to protect the subject against the abuse of the ruling authority, but to preserve the full personal existence of men within the state order. But because it has lately been wrongly implemented, it now requires sifting and rectification.

§. 143. Historical Development

Although in the earlier continental condition, in particular the German one, the recognition of the rights of subjects was not lacking, it did not have breadth, especially for the lower classes; and guarantees (territorial freedoms, etc.) were distributed more to the estates and territory [der Landschaft] than to individuals. It is from England that the "declaration of rights" takes its flight over the world.

The occasion in England as well was the general German custom [Sitte] by which the prince repeatedly confirmed the already existing law of the land, in particular when it experienced opposition. But in England, the law of the land contained, more than was customary elsewhere, the freedoms and securities of individuals (e.g., trial by peers in Magna Charta), and it was chiefly the confirmation of these that later received a particular character there. While it elsewhere was usual only to confirm "rights and freedoms" in general or, when it was wished to emphasize specifics, only the relevant documents (charters), the English parliament put together a list of specific rights and freedoms gathered from the documents and traditions, and had the king confirm them apart from the original written confirmations, directly in terms of content, and thereby also with a new interpretation and stipulation favorable to the country, first under Charles I (*Petition of Right*, 1627) and then under William III, with the renowned *Bill and Declaration of the Rights and Liberties of the Subjects etc.* (1689) which in England was the culmination, and which became the model for other kingdoms. **<374>**

Two traits of this declaration of rights are especially to be emphasized as characteristic: firstly, it contains rights of individuals (e.g., trial by jury, right of petition) alongside the rights of Parliament (e.g., its consent for the raising of an army), both being the position of the subject over against the king. Secondly, it only concerns existing rights usually committed to writing in previous documents, and the solemn declaration of them only had occasion and purpose because they were disputed or disregarded, and now again were guaranteed, or, in doubtful points, decided in favor of the country. The violations which led to the *Declaration* are mentioned in it, and rights which were not violated, such as the right of assembly, which one nowadays views as a chief right, are not included in it. Because of this, the pledged rights are absolutely positive-legal (concrete), and as far as meaning and extent are concerned, entirely specific and clear.

The North Americans followed the English example of declaration of rights when they constituted themselves as independent states, yet with an essential modification, by virtue of the influence of philosophical concepts at the time. They made rights of *men and citizens* from rights of subjects and Parliament, thus on the one hand systematically properly distinguishing between the rights of individual citizens and the attributes of Parliament, but, on the other hand, beyond a number of those concrete practical rights, which in accordance with their inherited English nature they still mainly had in mind, they stated entirely general doctrines or deductions by state decree, such as: "That all men are born equally free and independent, and have certain natural, inherent and inalienable rights, amongst which are, the enjoying and defending life and liberty, acquiring, possessing and protecting property, and pursuing and obtaining happiness and safety"; "That government is instituted for the common benefit, protection and security of the people."[180] A parallel to this is offered by the roughly contemporaneously drafted, albeit under entirely **<375>** different circumstances, Prussian Civil Code. Such general provisions, albeit not very many of them, and additionally the English rights – right of petition, assembly, freedom of the press, jury, security against home search etc. – are included in the constitutional documents of virtually every state in North America. The Union document itself did not at first contain such rights; only later (1791) were many added to it, of a practical nature, and without any general clauses. The Union document in its contemporary form can therefore, by virtue of its sobriety and reasonableness and restraint, serve as a model in the manner of stipulating such rights of citizens.

The French constitutional assembly was thrilled with these North American philosophical proceedings and followed them with the greatest exaggeration. While unceasingly and solemnly protesting that it was not metaphysical but practical rights which one wished to establish, the *Declaration of the Rights of Man and Citizen* at the top stated empty and furthermore erroneous natural-law deductions such as: "Liberty consists in the freedom to do everything which injures no one else; hence, the exercise of the natural rights of each man has no limits except those which assure to the other members of the society the enjoyment of the same rights." In actual practical stipulations, the French declaration does not contain that secured position of subjects which is preserved in the English, but the system of dissolution which the Revolution understands by freedom and equality: abolition of the peerage, guilds, corporations, feudal rights, etc. In various charters, the title of the rights of man went through a multiplicity

---

[180] [These two clauses are contained in the *Declaration of the Rights of the Inhabitants of the Commonwealth or State of Pennsylvania* (1776); Stahl does not cite a reference.]

of versions, until finally, in the Charter of Restoration [1814], the theoretical torrent was mostly set aside, being restricted to a few practical provisions, and its example was followed by the German constitutions prior to 1848. These likewise contain a few general, often trite clauses, for example equality before the law, and then a few practical rights and freedoms, the value of which largely depends upon whether, outside the relevant articles of the constitution, any laws exist to secure them in more appropriate and extensive manner, e.g., the inviolability of property, the guarantee of proper judges. The German act of confederation **<376>** contains a declaration of rights for the subjects of all German territories, certainly of an extremely restricted but an absolutely practical-juridical character, e.g., freedom of emigration, the right of appeal to higher courts [Sicherung der drei Instanzen], equal political rights for fellow Christians.

Then came the catastrophe of 1848. In the wake thereof, in certain German states the declaration of rights, or the section in the constitutional document concerning the rights of the citizen, was often expanded immeasurably through new concessions, on top of which the Belgian constitution was copied as a new model; finally, the "Fundamental Rights of Germans" were proclaimed for all of Germany by the National Assembly in Frankfurt, which both in extension and, in part, in subversive influence, outdid everything which of that sort was extant in history until then. These "Fundamental Rights of Germans" are nothing less than the complete implementation of the principle of the March movement.[181]

§. 144. Limited Scope of the Declaration of Rights

The result of this historical development is as follows:

Rights of subjects vis-à-vis state power are to be recognized and inviolably maintained (e.g., freedom of conscience, protection of property, freedom of emigration, certain inviolabilities over against prosecutorial and police power, a certain sphere of free public activity of the press and associations, similar rights of the church, local communities, etc.).

Committing these rights to written documents – "declaration of rights" – is good and beneficial, be it as special legislative act or a section in a constitutional document, be it in confirmation of already existing rights specifically set down

---

[181] A thorough demonstration of this is provided in my book *Die deutsche Reichsverfassung nach den Beschlüssen der deutschen Nationalversammlung* [The German Imperial Constitution According to the Decisions of the German National Assembly], pp. 62f.

in other laws, or in expansion or new conferment. Nevertheless, the rights must be specific (concrete, **<377>** positive) and clearly characterized and delimited and of contemporary stipulation – not doctrines, general principles, promises (§. 83) – and the declaration should only contain individual rights which to that point were disputed or not afforded, not an exhaustive codification of all the rights of subjects.

In the character of their validity in the state, rights are not to be declared as being derived from "human rights" and thus apart from, in fact even against the law of the state, as "inalienable and imprescriptible," but rather in the character of having their basis and goal in human right, i.e., not merely in protection against the illegality of the ruling authority but in the guarantee of full human personality within the state order. Therefore, in the present they have their significance not merely in the prince granting them to the entire territory, as in the past, but in the state granting them to the citizen. Accordingly, the declaration of rights currently should reasonably contain only that which is the right of every citizen, not, as with the English declaration, also that which is the right of the territorial representation. For both together characterize the right of the country over against the king, but only the former the right of men over against the state.

The declaration of rights ought to proclaim the entitlement and freedoms of subjects only as stipulations within the state order, so that the other stipulations in the constitution, e.g., regarding the power of the ruling authority, the church, etc., exist as equally fundamental beside and even over them, as in England. It is an error when the rights of citizens are themselves proclaimed as the foundation of the state so that all others – ruling authority, church, etc. – no longer have any independent validity, but are measured only against them, as called for in the French declaration: "The aim of all political association is the preservation of the natural and imprescriptible rights of man," thereby actually bringing other state orders (e.g., the property qualification for the active right of citizenship) into doubt as to whether they do not in fact contradict human rights; actually, the **<378>** entire edifice of the previous order counts as non-binding, in that there was in it no postulate of human rights. It is likewise an error when the declaration of rights comprises and settles the entire state order, as occurred with the "Fundamental Rights of Germans," which contain the fundamental characteristics of the entire administration of justice, schools, territorial constitutions, etc.

In terms of its result, the declaration of rights is to be a protection of men from the state, not a sacrifice to men of the state. For this reason in particular, the guarantees against prosecutorial and police power are only a means to the *freedom of the individual subject,* that he not suffer unjust punishment or detention, that he not depend in his endeavors upon the caprice and narrow-mindedness of government officials; they are not, as the change [Bewegungs-] party seeks, a means for the *power of the people as mass,* that the government not take action against associations and assemblies, have nothing on traitors and agitators, thus a means to conduct unrestricted opposition, unrestricted revolution, in order for the people to become lords over the ruling authority. But even apart from this sphere of mechanical order, the protection of personal freedom is not to become so unmeasured as to threaten the common goods of the nation. In fact, these common goods should instead be considered in the same manner as a right of citizens, and an authentic declaration of rights therefore ought not, as have those from 1789 until now, guarantee the corruption of such relations but rather maintain them and secure structured bonds, so, for example, not the unlimited divisibility and alienability of landholding but the integrity [Uneinziehbarkeit] of certain landed estates [Höfe] and exclusive succession, not the equal capacity of all for the office of teacher but the Christian school, etc. If the country once needed guarantees regarding the arbitrariness of ruling authority, the restrictedness of institutions, and the oppression of conscience, so nowadays is it much more in need of guarantees regarding the danger of anarchy, destruction, dechristianization.

These are the general viewpoints with regard to the declaration of rights. The decision about which rights in particular are to be guaranteed, and to what degree, can only be derived from the nature of the **<379>** object concerned. The discussion of this is therefore given in its proper place throughout this book. Such also depends upon the ethical capacity of the population (Book III [*Private Law*], §. 11).

The declaration of rights and the territorial representation are the two aspects of constitutional monarchy. Both are political truths and goods. Just as the territorial representation is not to be defeated but transformed from a power of subversion and opposition into one of maintenance and loyalty (§. 124), the task here as well is not to refrain from guarantees of rights but to put the guarantees of true rights in the place of false ones.

Chapter 18: The People and the Doctrine of Popular Sovereignty

§. 145. The People Subordinate to Authority and Law

<381> The position of the people, individually as well as collectively, as the previous discussion clarifies, is, initially, that it is subject to the state, this ethical-legal order, and to its constitutional ruling authorities.

Both the sovereign and the law (the constitution) have their regard, not through the people, but over the people, and independent of it.

With monarchy, the king is an independent power elevated over the people plain and simple, and a king under the sovereignty of the people is an absurdity[182]; this is no less true in a republic, even in a democracy, regarding the ordered popular assembly and the magistracy, each in its specific sphere. Here as well, the constitutionally established and constitutionally active assembly is the sovereign, while the people, apart from this assembly, are a mere obedient mass, just the same as with monarchy.[183] **<382>**

In the same way, laws and the constitution are a power over the people; they do not exist as an outflow of the popular will, and therefore cannot be revised through the popular will, but only through constitutional authority, in the way it itself delineates.

On the other hand, the people have just as much a right to this ethical-legal order as they have an obligation to it, and the representation of the people exists

---

[182] The ludicrousness of this notion was criticized most trenchantly by Louis Philippe, who when he was called away by a popular movement and returned from the balcony to the hall, assured his anxious company: "it was only the sovereign who wished to have a few words with the king."

[183] So, for example, the Zurich revolution of September 1839 may be justified by the necessity of circumstances, but that is another question of the same order as with the French July revolution; in terms of the *principle* of the republican constitution, by which such a justification has been attempted, it can never be justified, as if here the popular will is sovereign. Factually, of course, in the republic one is more inclined to excuse a revolt against the other party, which, having a few more votes, elevated its will to law, than a revolt in a monarchy against kingship. This puts the weakness of this form of government on full display.

to this end; but they also have this right in no less degree where such representation does not exist. In the same way, the individual has a right as well as a duty vis-à-vis the state; he is just as much a citizen as a subject, and therefore specific guarantees of the independence of his individual existence should exist (see the previous chapter).

§. 146. Popular Sovereignty as Lawlessness

The polar opposite to this position of the people to the government and to law is the doctrine which, previously in germ, finally was advanced with complete resolution by Rousseau, the doctrine of the "sovereignty of the people." According to it, the people are not merely over, for instance, the *king,* but over the *state* instead of under it. The state itself is there only through the will of the (unconstituted, dispersed) collective mass, and only as long as, and in the manner that, the people suffer it. For, according to Rousseau, the will of the collective mass (*volonté générale*) not only has the right [Fug] arbitrarily to abolish the government (king, senate), to withdraw its commission, but also the right arbitrarily to eliminate constitutional law. On its terms, the incontrovertible state-legal principle is that the people are not bound to fundamental law (*lois fundamentales*), and in fact cannot be bound to it.[184] This doctrine was propounded after Rousseau by Sieyès.[185] Its application followed immediately, in the Revolution. **<383>** Initially the French people as sovereign did not consider itself bound by the historically received constitution, king, and general estates, but gave itself a new constitution, against the will of the rightful authorities, as if it had begun its existence as a state right then, for the first time. But directly it considered itself not to be bound by this constitution which it had given itself. For example,

---

[184] "... par où l'on voit, qu'il n'y a ni ne peut y avoir nulle espèce de loi fondamentale obligatoire pour le corps du peuple, pas même le contrat social" [by which we see that there is not, nor can there be, any kind of fundamental law binding on the body of the people, not even the social contract]. Rousseau, *Contrat Social,* I. 7.

[185] "Il serait ridicule de supposer la nation liée elle même par les formalités ou par la constitution, auxquelles elle a assujetti ses mandataires" [It would be ridiculous to suppose that the nation itself is bound by the formalities or by the constitution to which it has subjected its representatives]. Sieyès, *Tiers état,* ch. 5. In the way that many absolutists consider the constitution to be a mere set of instructions for the king, Sieyès views it as such for the collective mass.

in the negotiations concerning the first accusation against the king, this constitution was no longer acknowledged as the authority for decision as to whether the king was accountable; only the current wish of the nation was.[186] The same mentality was evidenced in all petitions to the convention; by the same mentality the convention was forced to suppress the Girondists, etc.[187] The result of this conception is, then, that the existing constitution can be arbitrarily changed at any moment, that even without change it can be ignored, and that the lawless popular will of the moment decides against the constitution; it is permanent insurrection. Therefore, since popular sovereignty was proclaimed in France in 1789, there has been only a de facto legal condition there, apart from the short period of restoration. And this would also have been Germany's lot should the National Assembly have attained its intention of establishing the imperial constitution by virtue of the sovereignty of the German people against the lawful ruling authorities of Germany. **<384>**

Rousseau did assert that he wished not only for freedom but also for order and the regard for law,[188] and the entire party of liberalism and the Revolution

---

[186] "La nation vous a revêtu de sa confiance, vous connaissez son veu, ne tergiversez pas" [The nation has placed its trust in you, you know its will, do not procrastinate]. Buchez, *Hist.* XI. 22.

[187] Buchez and Roux provide a horrific report of this way of thinking in their work on the French Revolution, in which they recount the murders of Foulon and Berthier by the mob and then continue: "En principe d'ailleurs, on n'osait pas dire, que ce ne fut pas là de la justice, puisqu'il était enseigné, que toute justice émane du peuple, et que c'était a lui a nommer les juges" [In principle, moreover, no one dared say that this was not justice, since it was taught that all justice emanates from the people, and that it was up to them to appoint the judges]. Certainly, when the collective mass is sovereign in France, then that bestial mob in Paris was authorized to consider itself sovereign in its sphere [Strecke], and when such a sovereign, the people, cannot be bound to a constitution, how can it be bound to forms of justice?

[188] "Vous y verrez partout la Loi mise au dessus des hommes, vous y verrez partout la liberté réclamée, mais toujours sous l'autorité des loix, sans lesquelles la liberté ne peut exister" [Everywhere you look, you will see the Law placed above men, and everywhere you will see freedom demanded, but always under the authority of the laws, without which freedom cannot exist]. Rousseau, *Lettres de la Montagne,* VI.

repeats this after him, up to the present day. But therein lies the error: law which is the mere product of liberty (*volonté générale*), which exists merely by the will of those who obey it, is no actual law. In terms of their concept and nature, order and law can exist nowise other than as an independent and original necessity, and freedom can exist only through them and in them.

The idea that the people would have a greater respect for the laws if they made them themselves, and these existed only as a product of their will, is also a delusion. On the contrary, the people have respect for the laws only by considering them to be, not their own work, but something given from above. That which one produces himself he has under himself; it is not an object of awe; so it is with the self-made king, the self-made constitution. The way this lies in the nature of the case is confirmed everywhere in history. In the revolutions of France, Spain, and Portugal, the people gave themselves their own constitution, and nowhere in history has there been less regard by a people for their constitution as there. In England, the constitution was not given by the people but is the work of centuries, something existing over the people, which is why it is venerable there: one touches on it only with awe.

§. 147. Popular Sovereignty is Self-Contradictory

As is the case with every untruth, the doctrine of popular sovereignty is not even in agreement with itself, not even capable of implementation in terms of its own principle and standard. It is already impossible to determine the will of the people. What is to be recognized: the decisions of the chamber, the declarations of journals and associations, or the shock of insurrection? Even with universal suffrage in the primary assemblies, given **<385>** that the composition changes through death and accession to voting age, the final result will no longer be the will of the present people. There is, further, the undeniable consequence that if the popular majority is not bound to the given ruling authority and fundamental law, then the minority and the individual are not bound to the popular majority. For then the law of majority vote is itself a sort of fundamental law. And thus it is not the will of the people, but the will of each party, and of each individual, that is sovereign.

Finally, the concept of sovereignty upon which this doctrine is constructed is obscure from the start. For sovereignty is precisely state power in its center, by which it, in uniform manner, joins, supervises, leads the functions which unfold in manifold directions; it cannot (as Rousseau asserts) be separated from government and exist apart from it, but is itself the innermost moving power of government. Therefore, only a self-conscious being unified in itself can be sovereign, and therefore only a personality can be so in the fullest sense. Even the popular assembly in the republic has the capacity for sovereignty only through the artificial imitation of this unity, by means of ordered forms, and through a supplementation by the natural personality of the magistracy (§. 130).

It is actually impossible for the collective mass of individuals, that is, the people, to be sovereign apart from the unity of its constitutional order, by which it is already subject to authorities. This is why, with the doctrine of popular sovereignty, one understands sovereignty not as a power *in* the state organism, which is what the concept truly is, but a power *apart from* and *over* the state organism. Thus also, not a power restricted by law, which is what sovereignty always is (§§. 74, 75), but a power completely unrestricted, arbitrary. The people is not to be sovereign, i.e., state power, but a power over the sovereign or state power and over the laws of the state, authorized to dismiss state power at any moment and appoint another, to abolish the law and issue another. Popular sovereignty, thus, is a power of the people, not to rule the state, but continually to eliminate the state and constitute it afresh. And **<386>** herein lies the self-deception of the originators and the proponents of this doctrine in their opinion that the people can exercise an absolute power accruing to it apart from and over the state order, which yet is something ordered. For where are order and law to come from, when its essence is not to be bound to order and law?

Popular sovereignty is the denial of order, not merely in factual consequences, but already in the concept itself. With it, one does not proclaim, as he fancies he does, another relation of rulership in the state, but the abolition of the state, societal chaos.

At its deepest level, the doctrine of popular sovereignty is precisely the reversal of the ethical world-order. Because the people do not subject themselves to any order or personal authority as something given over them, the human will is the lord of the ethical world rather than an obedient member thereof.

§. 148. The Principle of Legitimacy; or, Continuity

We characterize the fundamental principle regarding the relation of the people to the state, as discussed above (§. 145), as the *principle of legitimacy.* This and only this is the opposite of popular sovereignty. It expresses the sanctification of the lawful (legitimate) ruling authority and order by God, and the binding or subjection of the people to it.[189] <387>

---

[189] Since popular sovereignty is not a principle of sovereignty in the state-legal sense, i.e., the supreme power within the state organism, but of the power of the popular mass outside of and opposite the state organism, its opposite cannot be *princely sovereignty.* For in the conception of princely sovereignty, sovereignty is understood precisely in that state-legal sense as the supreme power within the state organism, which unites and leads everything. The point of comparison is therefore lacking. Hence the sovereignty of princes allows restriction through other organs of the state organism, while the sovereignty of the people, being opposed to the state organism, is of necessity unrestricted and unconditioned. This is also confirmed by the fact that princely sovereignty extends only to monarchy, while popular sovereignty extends to all forms of constitution. The opposite of princely sovereignty is not popular sovereignty, but the *sovereignty of comitia.*

Accordingly, a higher truth over popular and princely sovereignty is not to be sought in *state sovereignty.* This is not any kind of conceivable concept at all. For a power outside of and opposite the state organism, as in the concept of popular sovereignty, as stands to reason, cannot be ascribed to the state. But even the supreme power in the state organism, which comprises and leads everything, such as in the concept of princely sovereignty, cannot possibly be ascribed to the state, but only to a specific organ, a living being, to which, then, the other organs are subordinate. The question is: where is the supreme head of the state, the center within the functions of the state? To this question one cannot give the answer: the state. One may erect the *state principle* as the higher truth between the patrimonial principle and the popular-rule principle, as has been done from the beginning in this book, but one may never do this with state sovereignty between princely sovereignty and popular sovereignty. (Compare my review of Maurenbrecher in the *Richter'schen Jahrbüchern* 1841.)

Finally, a distinction cannot be made in terms of constitution whereby *popular sovereignty is valid in the one state and not in the other.* In terms of the various constitutions, power within the state organism can fall to a different subject. Whether sovereignty is of the prince or of the comitia varies according to the constitution. But the power of the people over the entire state organism is either everywhere legally valid, or it is nowhere so. Precisely the first proclaimer of popular sovereignty, Rousseau, stated the

From another angle, however, this principle may be designated as the *principle of continuity:* the state (thus its ordered constitution) passing through all ages as one and the same, and thus binding and ruling even the actual present, as a power in it. This principle is not a *political maxim,* as is the principle of *conservatism,* but a *state-legal principle.* It is not expressed in whether the constitutional ruling authority intends to proceed with changes carefully or prudently or recklessly; **<388>** it is expressed in this, that none other than the constitutional ruling authority can lawfully carry out changes and can do so only on the basis of existing law. But there is certainly a general higher notion equally underlying the scientific conception of the historical viewpoint, the political maxim of conservation, and the state-legal principle of continuity, and that is the concept of the connection between times and the higher invisible power over men and generations which effectuates it. It is the notion that the state is not a society [Gesellschaft] of contemporary participants, but an ethical kingdom over them. This notion generally, and especially the principle of continuity, is lacking in the ruling orientation of our age, both for state and church. The will of the majority of those now living takes the place of the uninterrupted uniform institution. According to the one conception, the state is one through all times, while according to the other, it disintegrates into pure atoms of moments of time, of which not one is connected to the other; for the state of the previous moment does not bind the people of current moment. In this manner, the recent doctrine of state is *atomistic,* not merely respecting men, but also moments of time.

---

matter entirely clearly, that it is not a form of constitution, but a general supreme legal principle for all constitutions.

German national sovereignty, in the sense of a higher power of all of Germany over the individual states, can have the sense that this higher power of the collective mass befits the German people, as was truly intended with the solemn proclamation of the same, in which case it is the same false principle as popular sovereignty; or it can have the meaning that this higher power is attributed to the German collective state, in which case it is no political principle, but a state-legal one, which one day held true but, since the dissolution of the German empire, no longer does so. Since the state as a collective had no organ, it would have been the result of the constitution intended in Frankfurt, not the starting point.

§. 149. The Element of Truth in Popular Sovereignty

Nevertheless, the doctrine of popular sovereignty is based on a truth the fulfillment of which is the vocation of modern times. Although the people is not to be the sovereign, it is to be the *fellow bearer* and *guarantor of the ethical kingdom, which is the state.* This is expressed in the *dignity of the people,* which the prince must recognize, just as the people are to recognize the majesty of the prince. It is expressed in the right of disobedience to illegal commands (passive resistance), in the right to reject every innovation it has not approved. It is expressed most of all in the development of the independent action of the people, participation in the formation and safeguarding of the public condition, in the establishment of an estates-oriented constitutional constitution [reichsständisch-konstitutioneller Verfassung], and, even where this is lacking, in the power of public civility [Gesittung] and the ordered business of the government, **<389>** rooted in the public legal consciousness. Thereby is the prince no longer a bare power over against the ruled people, but joins together with it to form a spiritual unity, an interleaved [in sich gegliederten] yet national-spirit-filled kingdom.

The Reformation already paved the way for this higher position of the people which distinguishes the present time. Through it, in the area of religion, the congregation, which to that point was only passive, a merely ruled, obedient entity, having the ecclesiastical power (bishop, pope) opposite it as an external power, was itself recognized as bearer and seat of the Holy Spirit, from which the ecclesiastical power itself derives its regard, according to which the congregation then also jointly passes judgment over doctrine, is subjected to no establishment of doctrine apart from its own consent, and so joins together with those who have power over it, for the sake of praiseworthy order, into an undivided spiritual community. This by no means eliminates the church as a power over the congregation; the congregation by no means becomes sovereign. By "church," namely, I do not mean the embodiment of all congregations as against local congregations but, in contradistinction to the people joined into the collective congregation, the objective institution to which is given the Word of God, the sacraments, the divine authorization [Vollmacht], the God-ordained offices, the antecedent testimonies of faith, the historical rule of order, etc. This church as institution over the congregation (including the collective congregation) was factually recognized and paid homage to by the Reformers, although, in terms of theory, they were not as aware of it; later times, on the other hand, renounced it, retaining only the congregation of believers, and finally only the congregation (the collectivity of those externally belonging to the church association), into the will of which they subsumed the church – this is the *collegial system* [Kollegialsystem], the analogue of popular sovereignty.

The same truthful requirement of the times and the same aberration also exists in the area of politics. The nation, the political collective community, is to be elevated from passive obedience to active (free self-acting) obedience. It is to help engender every new law given and sanctioned by the higher authority, in <390> order for such not to be a mere command over it but at the same time to exist as the expression of its own, ethically reasonable will. But instead of this, it releases itself from obedience to the existing law and the existing authority. It ought to become the living carrier of the ethical order, of the state; but instead, it makes its will into the lord of the ethical order. It ought to be elevated to the level of the constitutional ruling authority which holds sway over it, to be allied therewith; instead, the latter is subordinated to it. While the collegial system destroys the church over the congregation, the doctrine of popular sovereignty destroys the state over the people. In this way, the congregation and the people itself becomes ruler, and an unrestricted ruler at that.

Our appreciation of the relationship of the people to the state gains its deepest confirmation in the Christian worldview. God wishes for the transformation of mankind, the saints are to reign in Christ with God, and they reign in that they obey. What in the eternal kingdom is the unity of the divine-human, is, in the external temporal kingdom of the state, which is the silhouette of the eternal kingdom, the unity of ruling authority and people. The former remains the higher, but the latter is to participate in rule. The ethical fundamental relations remain the same in all stages. Authority and self-acting (free) obedience, man as co-bearer and co-originator of the ethical order under which he stands, this is both the primeval law and final goal of the ethical world.

Chapter 19: Of the Right of the People to Rebel

§. 150. Rebellion Cannot Be Justified, Yet Is To Be Expected

<391> Rebellion [Empörung] is the application of physical violence against the ruling authority, either to coerce specific measures or forbearances from it, or to depose it. The former is usually called *active resistance,* the latter *rebellion* in the specific and eminent sense. A cardinal question for the societal condition, especially in our time, is whether the abuse of the ruling authority gives subjects the right to rebel.

In terms of the *foundations of law,* rebellion is inadmissible. For it is nothing other than the inversion of the legal order of the state. Through it, the subjects make themselves into judges, a higher power over the ruling authority.

This cannot be justified by asserting that when the ruling authority violates the bond with the subjects, "the contract," the subjects for their part are authorized to abrogate it. For the relation between ruling authority and subjects is not analogous to a property contract or a treaty between two nations. It is not a relation of equality, in which either party may judge whether the other performs his part, but one of regard and obedience, and it is not a relation which stands only under the rights of the participants, so that its annulment by the innocent people only affects the guilty ruling authority; rather, it is a higher, necessary bond over both, each of whom are just as much affected by its annulment as by the injustice which led to that annulment. When in consequence the ruling authority violates the order of the state, it by no means follows that the subjects for their part may also violate this order.[190] **<392>**

---

190 "Yes, you say: what about when a king or ruler obligates himself by oaths to his subjects to rule in terms of introduced articles, and does not keep them and thus is obligated to vacate rule? As is said, that the king of France ought to rule according to the Parliaments of his kingdom, and the king of Denmark must swear to particular articles, etc. To this I answer: it is fine and fair, that the ruling authority rules in terms of laws and maintain them, and not according to willfulness. But add to this that a king promises not only to maintain the law of the land or article, but God as well commands him to be pious, and he also promises to do that. Well then, when a king maintains neither

Just as ill-founded is the justification that the ruling authority, because its regard is founded in the law, loses that regard when it rules in opposition to the law. For the ruling authority is an independent, original power in the state, not merely an instrument of the law (§. 72), and therefore its regard depends on whether it is appointed according to the law, not whether it rules according to the law, and in any case it has no judge in the matter, in that, outside of itself, no one is supremely authorized to stand over or maintain the law.

Neither can rebellion be justified as self-defense, for self-defense is only justified against unlawful power, not against the unlawful use of lawful power; otherwise, it would have to be accorded against every partisan verdict of a competent court.

Just as, in terms of its essence, revolution is against the order <393> of the state, so does it also lack any order and legal limits. It cannot have any legal norm over its admissibility; rather, when it is considered to be admissible under some condition or other, so is it simply a matter of the caprice of the people to judge whether the condition exists.[191] It cannot have a lawful organ; rather, some

---

God's law nor the law of the land, is one then to attack him, judge and avenge them? Who commanded you to do so? Another ruling authority must step in between you, who questions both of you and condemns the guilty, otherwise you will not evade the judgment of God, in that He says: vengeance is mine, judge not....

"Well then, it may certainly be that the king (of Denmark) is unjustified before God and the world, and that the law is entirely on the side of the Danes and of Lübeck. That is one aspect [ein Stück für sich]. There is moreover another aspect, that the Danes and Lübeckers came on as judges and overlords of the king and punished and avenged [gerochen (*sic*)] that injustice, thus taking upon themselves the administration of justice and vengeance. This is the point as far as the issue and conscience are concerned. When the matter comes before God, He will not ask whether the king was unjust or just, for that is obvious; He will ask: You lords of Denmark and Lübeck, who commanded you to execute such vengeance and punishment?" Luther, *Works,* Walch edition, 10, p. 584; cf. 11, p. 2419. [*Whether Soldiers, Too, Can Be Saved* (1526).]

[191] "Furthermore there is behind it an evil consequence or example, that, where it is sanctioned to murder or drive away tyrants, a general willfulness takes hold wherein one reprimands as tyrants those who are not tyrants, and murders them as well, whatever the people have a mind for." Luther, *ibid.*

individuals or masses always elevate themselves ahead of others to this end. It can have no lawful process, as can two countries at war with each other; rather, the means through which it aims to attain the right is always the path of unruly power and cunning.

Rebellion is however likewise inadmissible according to the principles of *morality and religion.* Christian ethics requires that injustice rather be suffered than resisted or avenged, indeed suffered unconditionally, whereas resistance is only possible in an unlawful course of action.

Christian ethics do not admit the violation of a divine command, even for the most noble goal. The murder of a sentry or a princely valet, performing their duties innocently and trusting in peace, or of the tyrannical prince himself, fall under the eternal verdict "Thou shalt not kill," even when the most brilliant era of the fatherland is thereby inaugurated.

Christian ethics do not admit of taking matters into one's own hand apart from vocation; but in the state-order, no one has the vocation of establishing it against the ruling authority ("Who commanded you to execute such vengeance and punishment?"). Therefore, no one can consider the evil that arises from the omission of rebellion to be his fault, because each may say: rebellion was not my office; but the evil that arises from rebellion, even the evil because it is an act of violence, must be recognized by every one of its instigators as his work and his fault.

Christian ethics do not admit of high-handed premature ac- **<394>** tion against the divine arrangement; it recognizes in tyrannical kings the punishment for the frivolity of the people, and, accordingly, rebellion manifests itself as the unlawful means of thwarting a just judgment.[192]

Above all, Christian ethics has the special and express command in the Holy Scriptures of obedience to the ruling authority as ordained by God (Romans ch.

---

192 "If the ruling authority is evil, well then, God is there, and He has fire, water, iron, stone, and innumerable ways to kill. How quickly He slayed a tyrant and would do so as well, but our sins do not allow it. For He speaks in Job thusly: 'He allows a knave [Buben] to reign on account of the people's sin.' We can see just fine that a knave reigns, but nobody wants to see that he reigns not because of his knavery but because of the sin of the people." Luther, *ibid.*

13), while rebellion is the extreme opposition to such obedience.[193] Additionally, it is most noteworthy that this command of obedience was issued precisely under Nero, as if to make it even more clear, by drawing the unparalleled contrast precisely with the ruling authority which stands in world history as the pinnacle and prototype of tyranny.[194] **<395>**

---

[193] The word ἐξουσίαις refers to the ruling authority, the personal superior possessing power, not the mere legal order existing over us. That one owes obedience to the order and not to the person of the ruling authority is the principle of the constitution of 1791, not of the apostle. There has been an attempt to attribute this meaning to Romans 13 in recent times. Against this, see my speech in the proceedings of the Stuttgart German Protestant church assembly [Stuttgarter deutschevangelischen Kirchentags], 1850, p. 52.

[194] "The question is whether it can be fair, that is, whether a case can occur, that one in opposition to this law may be disobedient to the ruling authority and struggle against it, depose or bind it? .... The heathen, because they knew nothing of God and did not recognize that the secular regime is God's order (for they viewed it as a human happiness and act), here considered it not only fair but also praiseworthy to depose, slay, and drive away useless, evil ruling authority. But we are not here asking what the heathen and the Jews did, but what is right and just to do; not only before God in the spirit but also in divine external order of the secular regime.... No such case has yet manifested itself to me in which it was just, and I cannot imagine any at this point either.... Where e.g. a prince, king, or lord becomes insane, it is just that he be deposed and kept in a safe place. For he is no longer to be considered a man, in that his reason is lost. So you say a raging tyrant actually is also to be considered insane or even worse than someone out of his senses, for he does much more damage. This is difficult to answer, for such reasoning has a powerful appearance and would compel equity [will eine Billigkeit heraus zwingen]. But still I must say that it is not the same with an insane person and a tyrant. For the insane person can do or suffer nothing reasonable, and there is no hope of such because the lamp of reason is gone. But a tyrant does much of that sort: therefore he knows when he does injustice, and conscience and insight is still with him, and hope as well that he may mend his ways. Therefore the ruling authority is not to be resisted with outrage [Frevel] and riot, as the Romans, Greeks, Danes, and Swiss did; but we have other ways." Luther, *ibid.* The argument which has been popular from Knox to

The objection is made that, according to this doctrine, all constitutions are useless, that God provided poorly for His world and His order, because while a wealth of laws and institutions exists, everything depends upon the whim of a man to overthrow it all, and when he does so, no one has the duty and right to hinder him. But this is not the case. Rebellion certainly is inadmissible according to law and the Christian ethical command; but, factually, it is the necessary consequence of tyranny, and as such a factual consequence, it is by all means founded in the divine economy and providential guidance. God does not yield His order to the tyranny of a king, but maintains that order one way or another, in accordance with the degree to which men come to terms with it. In terms of His will, He maintains it in purely divine ways. If the people fulfilled His command, if men were like the Lord's apostles, law and justice would be maintained without rebellion, just as the church would be maintained without any act of violence, regardless of any oppression. God allows no tyrannical king, or, when the people persevere in patience, He will in the end intervene. "If the ruling authority is evil, well then, God is there, and He has fire, water..." (Luther). However, now that the peoples do not measure up to divine holiness, God maintains His order according to the world's laws, He overcomes injustice by violence, since the peoples fail to **<396>** overcome it through patience and faith; He uses the wrath of the peoples as a means against the injustice of kings, as He uses the tyranny of kings against the injustice of the peoples, and in this manner maintains His order, exercising His discipline without there being, humanly speaking, any justification for the occurrences and actions through which this is accomplished.

Accordingly, it is not to be feared that rulers have gained encouragement to caprice and tyranny from this doctrine. It is said to rulers and subjects: "the peoples *shall* not rebel," but it is not said to them, "the peoples *will* not rebel." On the contrary, as often as a king says to his subjects: "my father hath chastised you with whips, but I will chastise you with scorpions" [I Kings 12:14], so often will the peoples defect from him; this is the way of the world from the beginning.

Macauley, derived from the parallel between tyrannical and insane princes, accordingly was already decisively refuted by Luther. Charles I, James II, Louis XVI, were doubtless not insane; if however the borderlines are doubtful, it is a matter of uncertainty regarding facts, not of the ethical command.

Rulers must always consider what *will* transpire, not what *should* transpire. Unfortunately, it cannot be arranged that the Christian confession actually keeps rebellions from happening.[195]

§. 151. The Admissibility and Requirement of Passive Resistance

The matter is entirely different with *passive resistance* than with rebellion. Passive resistance consists in refraining from what the ruling authority commands and not refraining from what it forbids, as with the first Christians, who, contrary to the command of the ruling authority, did not sacrifice to the gods, did not refrain from preaching the Gospel, contrary to the prohibition of the ruling authority. Accordingly, it is fundamentally distinct from active resistance, in that the latter is an assault on the power of the ruling authority, a hindering of its actions, while the former is only a refusal of one's own actions, either of omission or of comission. It is also essentially distinct <397> from the renouncement of obedience, for it only resists specific commands, and does not withdraw the regard of the ruling authority in general.

Passive resistance is admissible, even commanded, under certain conditions. For man is not simply and in terms of all his actions under the state, but likewise immediately under God. When, therefore, the command of the ruling authority runs against the command of God, the subject has the duty to refuse his obedience in accordance with the statement: "We must obey God rather than men" [Acts 5: 29] (cf. Exodus 1:17; Augsburg Confession of Faith, V. 29.). In this, he has no effect on the state, he does not stand in judgment over the ruling authority, he executes no decision over it, but only stands in judgment over his own conscience. Where, however, the dividing line between obligation to the external command of the ruling authority and obligation to the inward command of God lies, cannot possibly be made known to man by the state, neither by its laws nor by its ruling authority, for such is precisely the boundary of the state; such can only be made known through the command of God Himself, as perceived in one's conscience. It is the power of personality which, through the immediate bond with God, likewise is ever over the state, in which the authority of the state

[195] "Furthermore, tyrants are in danger that, through God's decree, subjects rise up and slay or drive them off. For we here teach those who wish to do right, which are few; in addition, there are yet the heathen, godless, unchristian masses which, if God should so decree, unjustly oppose the ruling authority and cause disaster" (Luther).

finds its resistance; it is not a resistance in the state order itself. For this reason, the rule holds true here as well: "Render therefore unto Caesar the things which are Caesar's; and unto God the things that are God's" [Matthew 22: 21]. What concerns the state, what affects the state, change of ruling authority, paralysis or abortion of its power, no one dare intervene there who is not appointed to that end by the state order, there the ruling authority of the state is absolutely the highest authority; on the other hand, as far as the subjects' own actions and omissions are concerned, there God's command and His voice in conscience are the highest authority.

It is also, however, a command of God to submit to all legal order as a matter of conscience, and it therefore is also part of the sphere of passive resistance for the subjects not to allow themselves to be used as instruments for unjust oppression or abolition of the legal order (see above, p. 219, note). The degree to which this holds **<398>** for officials, judges, ministers, military personnel, is decided according to the specific official position; but the duty of obedience has its limits in every case.[196]

§. 152. The Right to Rebellion for the Sake of the Church

Just as only the Christian revelation brought the reprehensibility of rebellion to full recognition, so only in the Christian epoch of the world can the opposite be found: its fundamental justification and ethical glorification. Because pagan antiquity did not have this awareness of guilt, it did not have this drive to apology. Rebellions occurred often with them, but of a naive character, natural help against pressure, or natural satisfaction of a passion. Even the celebration of tyrannicide was only valid regarding the result, the salvation of the state, not as a political principle. But even in the Middle Ages rebellions in a manner of speaking run parallel to Christianity, the commandment being proclaimed but without being brought to bear on the rebellions. These rebellions largely manifested

[196] On account of one's own right and freedom (e.g., unlawful taxation, denial of established rights) the ruling authority may be opposed with passive resistance, although not in the same manner as on account of divine command. Passive resistance on behalf of one's own right is only a solemn witness against injustice, and cannot go further than to compel the ruling authority to apply coercion, while passive resistance on behalf of the divine command is a refusal of obedience within this sphere, and is justified even in evading the coercion of the ruling authority.

themselves not even as the salvation of the state, but as the defense of one's own good right. They were the consequence of independence or the aristocratic sense of equality vis-à-vis the king (§. 77). The concept of the state and the ruling authority (sovereign) was not yet fully developed.

First through the Reformation did the question of rebellion, like all questions of Christian ethics, come to awareness and decision. The Reformation emphasized the divine right of the ruling authority independent of the church, and, from this, the unconditional damna- **<399>** bleness of rebellion, with an emphasis and development of thought which hitherto had not existed. Thus, Luther, Calvin, and the entire phalanx of Protestant theology. Against this, *rebellion on principle* also began from the other side, beginning at the Reformation. The distinctive character of the subsequent, as against the preceding, is the origin in an investigation of the final ground of social order, and in a fundamental reversal of the relation of ruling authority and people, now proclaimed as doctrine. It thereby manifested itself in awareness of the proffered prohibition and precisely in opposition to it, with a claim to ethical justification, in fact ethical necessity, and thereby included the ongoing reversal of the relation of ruling authority and people in itself.

From this time on, rebellions are *revolutions.* The Puritan movement and the Catholic Liga movement were driven by the notion that the people are called to be the protector and avenger of the true faith and the divine command, even against the king. Therefore, the former preached the dismissal of the idol-serving king, the latter that of the heretical king or the king who did not sufficiently root out heresy. Thus, for decisive crises, the people of the faithful are set as a kingdom of God (kingdom of saints or Catholic church) over the king, and rebellion is the fulfillment of a divine task. Finally, the political movement since the end of the previous century is driven by the notion that the people are directed by reason unceasingly to subject the ruling authority to its will, by its own right and for its own sake. Consequently, rebellion is the result of everlasting arbitrary power of the people over the ruling authority, which in fact is the holy command that it protects; it is *revolution in absolute sense.* This is the world-historical ground upon which, in various ages, the scientific justification of rebellion ever moves.

The most extreme of the justifications of rebellion was attained in the doctrine of Rousseau, which is the consistent development of the notion of revolution. According to it, the people have a right of *arbitrary rebellion.* For, in terms of it, the ruling authority (*gouvernement*) is nothing other than a task or command which the people as sovereign ruler imparts to certain persons, and dismissal of <400> the ruling authority – which is known as rebellion – is nothing other than the retraction of this command, which the ruler must have the right to, whenever he wishes. The concept of ruling authority is abolished, as is that of rebellion. The inversion of the state order putting the subjects over the ruling authority, which is the fact of the matter in every rebellion, here becomes the idea of the state order itself. A moderation of this consistency of doctrine, albeit of little difference in result, is when the right of the people to rebel is restricted to the case of *violation of its rights,* as stated in the constitution of 1793, and maintained by Lafayette until the end of his life: "When the government violates the rights of the people, then the insurrection of the people and every individual part of it is the holiest of its rights and the highest of its duties." Or, as one elsewhere is in the habit of saying: if the prince violates the contract, the people are no longer bound by it. By this principle, the people are not, as in the other case, an arbitrary ruler, but are still the sovereign judge of their ruling authority.

Behind such a watered-down doctrine of revolution lie the doctrines that emerged from the Puritan and hierarchical movements, not so very long ago. Within the Reformed church, the right of rebellion because of tyranny was implemented by the writers of the age of religio-political struggle, thus Buchanan, Milton, Hubert Languet,[197] and achieved its most energetic and momentous representation in Knox. It maintained that, because in the words of the apostles the ruling authority is established for the good of man, man has to oppose a tyrannical government that uses its power to suppress the good. It especially maintained that the people, once a majority has confessed the true faith, must judge and put to death the king engaging in idolatry, i.e., hearing Mass (Mary Stuart), in accordance with God's command (Deuteronomy 17:5).

Within the Catholic church, the right to rebellion was mainly taught by the *Jesuits.* While hitherto the Catholic doctrine in general was that the secular ruling authority was *of God,* with the dispute only concerning whether *immediately* from God or *mediately* through the <401> Pope, the doctrine was spread mainly

---

[197] See Vol. I, p. 292 [*The Rise and Fall of Natural Law,* pp. 238ff.].

through the Jesuits that the ruling authority was *of the people.* It distinguished: the existence and necessity of *the power of the ruling authority in general* certainly is grounded in God's order, but the right of the *particular* ruling authorities (*this* king) is grounded simply on the will and delegation of the people, and from this they logically drew the conclusion that the people could retract this right on "just grounds" and arrange the ruling authority in another manner. Thus e.g. Lainez, Suarez, Bellarmine. In particular, Bellarmine taught, in line with Knox, that it is not permissible for a Christian to tolerate an unbelieving or heretical king over him.[198] Apart from this, already from the Middle Ages a doctrine of tyrannicide, i.e., the right and duty of each individual to murder a tyrant apart from any form of law, in fact even treacherously, runs through Catholic theology and moral teaching. It was derived from the teaching [Bildung] of classical antiquity, was especially stimulated by Johannes Parvus, and finally derived its extreme representation in the notorious book of the Jesuit [Juan de] Mariana. It also played an important role, both theoretically and practically, in the struggle between monarchy and Liga in France.[199] These individual trends and parties in the church-affiliated doctrines of the right of rebellion and tyrannicide nevertheless ought by no means be seen as the doctrine of the church itself, either Reformed or Catholic, but only as aberrations thereof.

§. 153. Rebellion in Exceptional Cases

Nevertheless, within the true Christian doctrine of the impermissibility of rebellion there is also a nuance [Schattirung], <402> namely, the viewpoint which rejects rebellion *without exception.* It was in particular asserted by the episcopal church of England and the Tories prior to the dethronement of James II. Absolute non-resistance had been the shibboleth of both parties up to that point.

---

[198] See my lectures, *Protestantismus als politisches Princip* [Protestantism as a Political Principle], p. 25, and chiefly my writing, *Die katholischen Widerlegungen* [The Catholic Refutations], p. 9, where all of this is fully presented from the sources. The opposition Catholic party refuted this doctrine (e.g., Petrus de Marca, *de concord. sac. et imper.* lib. II. cap. II).

[199] See the further discussion of this in my *Katholischen Widerlegungen,* pp. 15 and 20.

This is also essentially Luther's position.[200] Against this, another viewpoint, which likewise recognized as a fundamental principle the impermissibility of rebellion against a tyrannical ruling authority, nevertheless maintained its permissibility as exception in the most extreme emergency, when the ruling authority occasions the overthrow of the entire legal order, when he destroys the entire physical or ethical existence of the nation. One such emergency was considered to be the undertaking of James II to overthrow the entire state constitution and state-church of England. Much more so was the Turkish hegemony over the Greeks, which threatened life, property, and feminine chastity. This is the viewpoint of many Christians, and many loyal men, in particular after the stricter of the older Tories themselves repudiated their previous position by the action of 1688. It is implemented by Burke in cosmopolitan manner and divested of its Christian motives.[201] It is distinguished essentially from those which allow rebellion on "just grounds" (Bellarmine et al.). For it demonstrates the reserve regarding the lawful ruling authority, the duty to suffer injustice, and only considers impermissibility without **<403>** exception, like many other ethical truths, to be incapable of attainment. It justifies rebellion not from a right of the people or command of the state order, as do Lafayette, Milton, Bellarmine, but only by necessity, not as principle, but as isolated act. It therefore rests on the ground of Christian principles, and, in particular, no practical interest exists to contest it. This is clear from the above discussion (§. 151). For it is not servile subjection

---

[200] "No such case has yet manifested itself to me in which it was just, and I cannot imagine any at this point either" (cited above, p. 394, note). Only in Luther's table talk is an expression found in favor of the permissibility of rebellion under special circumstances. But apart from this, which might also admit of another signification, a statement overheard in someone's table talk surely cannot be taken in consideration against the innumerable specific and exhaustive argumentations he himself published, all in the same spirit.

[201] "When things are in that lamentable condition, the nature of the disease is to indicate the remedy to those whom nature has qualified to administer in extremities this critical, ambiguous, bitter potion to a distempered state." Burke, *Reflections on the Revolution in France* [in *Select Works of Edmund Burke.* A New Imprint of the Payne Edition. Foreword and Biographical Note by Francis Canavan (Indianapolis: Liberty Fund, 1999), Vol. 2, pp. 35–36].

that is the intention but opposition to a tyrannical ruling authority by the refusal of obedience and the witness to law and protection and the word of rebuke, not with bodily violence, and it stands exactly on faith. The living God cannot be left out of account with it. Truly, if it were possible for a people to suffer injustice and at the same time to bear witness to what is right at the risk of their lives, it would thereby triumph over all oppression, both through the natural effect of moral greatness and through the immediate assistance of God, which is promised to such faith, and this triumph would be enduring while rebellion usually only provides relief from the momentary pressure, only to fall into another, one perhaps even more unbearable. This has also been confirmed by history. The Huguenots turned to weapons and their faith is suppressed in France up until this hour. The first Christians allowed themselves to be killed and their faith attained the victory over the world.

The debate as to whether there are exceptions whereby rebellion is nevertheless justified is, as with all casuistry, of little value and decided with difficulty. This much is certain: Christian sacrifice which opposes injustice unarmed, only with the word, is more heroic than rebellion. Precisely because of this, however, it cannot very well be set up as a general requirement. For this reason, when a people brought to the extreme in the end resorts to violence, one may not judge whether it has sinned against God's command. And vice versa, one ought not to pass judgment and carte blanche as if they had acted rightly and in a godly manner in the affair; and least of all can characteristics and principles be established for the case in which such action is justified and allowed. The Gospel, in that it commands obedience to the ruling authority, does not mention any exceptions; but neither <404> does it declare that there are no exceptions. Accordingly, it is to be acknowledged that there are conditions of exceptional nature in the providential leading of the peoples in which rebellion by no means is justifiable objectively and in terms of sure identifiability, but in which human judgment is withdrawn from the general command and stands simply in the conscience of the participants and under the tribunal of God. Even with the most extreme concession, this can only hold true for such situations where either (as with James II) the existing legal order and its goods, or (as with the Turkish hegemony) the natural indispensable rights, life, chastity, etc., are to be protected against the ruling authority, not however where new religious or political notions are to be brought to hegemony against the existing legal order. Highhandedness and rebellion are never justified for this. The great revolutions that passed over the kingdoms of Europe since 1789 thereby unconditionally incur their condemnation, regardless of the debate over permissibility.[202] <405>

§. 154. The Revolution Cannot Be Celebrated[203]

It is an evil thing in our age that revolutions are made, and made without necessity, and it is by far more evil that they are celebrated. How dare a civilized people formally declare an act to be a service, and surround it with public glorification and reward, which demolished the eternal law of human society and the primeval right of states, by which the state and its order are guaranteed and sanctified! Rebellion is a violation of divine and human order, and its celebration is a mockery of this order. After all, there may be cases, as discussed above, where the pressure of physical or ethical necessity so powerfully incites insurrection that it befits no one to stand in judgment over its authors, and the result of which seems to be justifiable, as if it had been a natural necessity. But it is never for that reason an ethically pure act, it never ceases to be a demolition of the deepest foundations of social order. For this reason, no noble people with pure,

---

[202] As is self-evident, it is no rebellion when the supreme ruling authority is opposed by the resistance and force called to such by the constitution itself. It was no rebellion when in Sparta the ephors brought kings before their tribunal and even put them to death through the broader court [den weitern Gerichtshof], or when the German territorial estates opposed the territorial lords with armed resistance which was vouchsafed to them in the territorial charter [Landesfreiheiten]. This was the basis upon which Luther resigned himself to the decision of the Protestant princes to oppose the emperor with force. Legal experts found that the princes, in terms of the German constitution, were *co*-ruling authority, and hence authorized to this end, in fact even obligated to do so, in order to protect the subjects. This was also proper for all the princes, the emperor and the empire were the highest ruling authority, sovereign, in Germany, not so the territorial princes individually. Luther with entire justification left this question to the legal experts and the individual judgment of princes; it was a question of the particular constitution as to who the ruling authority in Germany is, not the supreme question of Christian morality as to whether one may resist the ruling authority.

[203] To appreciate the following, it having been first published in the summer of 1848, see my treatise *Die Revolution und die constitutionelle Monarchie* [The Revolution and Constitutional Monarchy].

undivided conscience can arise from a rebellion, and woe to it when it forgets the holy bonds it has broken, albeit of necessity, on account of freedom!

Mindful of this, how can it celebrate the Revolution? What undissipated person would celebrate a divorce: and the sundering of the supreme social bond, the separation of people and ruling authority, is to be celebrated as a festivity? Is it rightly demanded that praiseworthy bravery demonstrated in civil war forego the deserved laurels, yet those who battled against the hereditary prince and the army, the bulwark of the fatherland and the state order, may parade them? That the French people in 1830 had so little feeling for the ancient royal house, with which it for centuries shared joy and suffering, fame and humiliation, the fearful sins of which it long since made up for with its own, that that house was to it as when an invading barbarian chief is driven out of the country – that is a heavy bur- <406> den of debt, and its nemesis truly did not fail to materialize!

The innermost moral principle of the political condition is destroyed by the celebration of revolution, and the consequences of such corruption of morals therefore are never a long time in coming.

If street-fighting is once proclaimed to be service and honor, why should it not be repeated at every future occasion? This time around it was for the overthrow of the old system, the next time it will be for general suffrage, for a republic, for communal goods. Those now content because the result accorded with their viewpoint will have to put up with it when one day it is turned against them. Louis Philippe could not complain of February 24th after celebrating July 29th, and there is no telling by what right the uprising of May 15th and June 24th in France was punished, because the right thereto was derived from the uprising of February 24th, and there is no telling why the Berlin city council did not ask the fighters at the arsenal, who rose up for general arming of the people, for their credentials in order to receive their recompense, as occurred with the fighters for the other rights of the people. If one is of the opinion that the Revolution would not have triumphed unless it had the will of the entire population behind it, one can observe the still-novel example of several hundred men removing the monarchy from France, the people of which did not have such in mind and were not consulted in the matter. Or if one is of the opinion that it was only the one specific rebellion, in terms of its results recognized by the nation, that was celebrated, not rebellion in general, then one must ask what the standard is, and who the judge is who in the moment of action – which is all that matters – will know ahead of time whether the revolution will find recognition or rejection? Had not the official usage in all of Europe already settled it, that when an uprising is defeated it is termed "insurrection" but when victorious it is termed "glorious revolution"! This reorganization of the medieval law of the jungle [Faustrecht] is what the enlightened 19th century has achieved!

And it has already extended this law of the jungle, sanctioned for relations in the public sphere, to the private sphere as well. One says that the tenant farmers who forced their landlords to dispense <407> with tribute payments misunderstood freedom; yet they did not misunderstand it at all, but only applied it to their situation. If the princes had political concessions extorted from them by the masses taking to the streets, or in exchange for the concession of a limited tax which was prohibited by the sworn constitution, or, finally, by the barricades, why should one not do something similar to gain property concessions? Certainly, the right to participation in public power is no greater than that to a satisfactory subsistence. By what may one oppose the lawyer who defended some Berlin tailor journeymen for destroying a clothing warehouse by arguing that they had only asserted their social convictions by means of self-defense (!), and so had done nothing different than the combatants of March 18th? As long as one does not stop celebrating and rewarding the action that caused the entire edifice of public order to collapse, so long should one not wonder when, throughout the levels of society, the bonds of obedience and law dissolve. France has given the main, disastrous example of elevating the Revolution, which in the most favorable case should have been consigned both to the past and to oblivion as a tragic necessity, to festivity, and to maintain it as a continuous brilliant presence in the popular consciousness, for which reason France has not been able to emerge from the chain of riots and revolutions. Did they in France not greet with jubilation the new day of every new revolution since 1789, as is taking place at this moment in blinded Germany, and did any of those revolutions fulfill expectations, and not much rather put it into much worse straits, requiring a new revolution?

And what is the latest result, the freedom of 1848? The freedom of draconian laws against assemblies, the freedom of the suppression of journals, the freedom of civil war and states of siege, the freedom of uncertainty of life, of property, the freedom to escape abroad for he who is able, yes even, which in

France says a lot, for him to have the phrase "the glorious February revolution" fall silent! For this one should not seek this or that ground, the plight of the laborer, the mistakes of Louis Philippe and the like; this all had only one ground, that of political depravity [Entsittlichung]; but political depravity is nothing other than the recognition and **<408>** celebration of the Revolution.[204]

§. 155. The Validity of Usurpation

Just as rebellion can be either simple unsophisticated rebellion or fundamental rebellion, i.e., revolution, something similar is true regarding *usurpation.* Simple usurpations, in which a violent person ousts the previous ruling house and founds a new one, are in evidence throughout history, and incur no judgment on earth. On the other hand, usurpations erected on the *foundations of the revolution* and thereby *perpetuating* them, until now have not been able to found any dynasty. Cromwell could not transmit his power to his son.[205] Napoleon and Louis Philippe had to ascend to the throne in their own person, the former after the first-born destined for the diadem was removed.

As the Revolution of 1789 is the pure type of revolution, so is also the empire of Napoleon I the pure type of such establishment of a monarchy on the basis of the Revolution. Napoleon's power was acquired without the (greater or lesser) guilt of a Cromwell, William, Louis Philippe. He did not make the Revolution but only quelled the anarchy that he encountered. Salvation from this anarchy was his mission from above, his title to power. The Brumaire was not the overthrow of a legitimately established constitution but the foundation of an authority in the chaos of mutually destructive constitutional efforts. In the Republic, therefore, his power was lawful, ap- **<409>** pointed, well-founded, by no means a usurpation. It first began to be unlawful with the attempt to found

---

[204] Coups d'état stand in a certain parallel to rebellion, but do not, as does the latter, overturn the relations of ruling authority and subjects, although they do go against the legal order. See §. 90. A distinction should be made as to whether a coup is going against a historically legally rooted constitution or against an ephemeral one, just as with rebellion against a legitimate monarchy versus a de facto ruling authority. With the former, the oath is decisive, while with the latter, it is the character of the violation.

[205] William III does not belong in this lineup. He did not proclaim the principle of revolution (popular sovereignty), but only founded an approximation to it, and this reluctantly. But he also lost the adopted heir chosen to be the bearer of the new order.

a hereditary empire upon the Revolution. Thereby did he violate the right of the lawful royal house, and himself became the world-historical representative of the principle of revolution against the principle of legitimacy. From the start, he took his power in this new form no longer from the power and mission granted him from above, but from the hand of popular sovereignty, and in the world-historical struggle with the Bourbons, most evident in the hundred days, he placed himself absolutely on the ground of popular sovereignty, a ground which does not exist. It is noteworthy: the step from lawful power to unlawful, if this viewpoint is the proper one, was the settlement of the lifelong consulate with the right to name a successor, which is only another name for heritability, for the sake of which he also initiated the procedure for general suffrage. On the day in which he, in his new dignity, with pompous procession took possession of the presidency of the senate, the session was mainly devoted to trappings of monarchical devotion. After these ceremonies, and probably also more as a symbol of the government, five *senatus-consulta* or senate resolutions were presented. Among these, the last, and thus the end of this symbolic session, was the union of the island Elba with French state territory.[206] It is as if Providence wished to indicate what the final result of this first step would be.

In all of this, it has not entered my mind to wish to establish a law of divine world judgment. God's ways are inscrutable and His mercy and forbearance are unlimited, and we are not judges of the degree to which Godfearing guidance of government can reconcile the unlawfulness of its origin. But I wish only to establish a fact of history: it speaks with a wondrous impression, which one cannot ignore.

---

[206] Thiers, *Histoire du consulat et de l'Empire*, III, p. 555.

PART FOUR: THE ADMINISTRATION OF THE STATE

Chapter 1: The Military

§. 156.The War Power as the Basis of the State

<411> [The external power by which the state maintains its rule against subjects and against foreign states is a necessary side to it, as ethical kingdom, in fact the first, i.e., antecedent side, for upon it rests all rulership. States everywhere begin by building warmaking powers, and the war power is the first thing that uneducated folks think of when they consider a state or a people. This power is not merely a means to upholding public order, but is also an ethical activity of the nation, in that it is based on the most extreme sacrifice, ethical courage, unconditional devotion, as the spirit of individual citizens as well as the army as a whole (see above, p. 67). While the civil association of the state is organic, by which the members have their own determinate life originating in themselves, the military association is mechanical, in that what counts is the action of the whole outwardly, and all parts are valued only to the degree that they contribute to this. This is why it requires unconditional subordination.]

§. 157. Universal Military Service to be Preferred

[The truly developed state has a standing army based on universal liability for military service of subjects, in all its parts directly subordinate to the sovereign. Universal liability for service is well-founded because the state's task is to maintain itself as a power; this <412> power being inherent in the nation, the individuals, being members of the nation, ought to fulfill this task. This is the only legal grounds for liability for service.]

[The appropriate implementation of this liability for service [Waffenpflicht] is truly universal service [Waffendienst], better than conscription. It fulfills the requirement for equality of burdens, allows all members of the state to participate in the manly honor of arms, and preserves the capacity of the armed forces. Conscription requires shorter periods of service than a volunteer army, as does universal military service, which can easily meet them. Division into active duty and reservists is not ruled out by universal service but rather promoted by it, albeit only as a factual not a legal condition. Whether the advantage to the armed forces provided by universal service outweighs the disadvantage of shorter periods of service is a technical matter. It is of pure unconditional value to the ethical-political relation. It increases the traits of subordination, lawfulness, punctuality, and self-assurance and honor among the entire population, brings into the army a trait of civilization and decency, and binds all classes of the nation into the highest community and equality.]

[The vassal army of the Middle Ages was based on private duty and faithfulness, not public duty. Because the hierarchy was based on personal commitment to an immediate superior, the army could be split up by the decisions of the overlord's immediate generals. In the end, duty was subject to personal judgment at all times. Even though the bond of feudal troth was noble, it could not serve to base a public army because the organic bonds were insufficient to achieve the mechanical unity required.]

[An army of foreign mercenaries (as in the Italian republics) is degrading. The people hereby lose the esteem that they gain by being the bearer of power. The identity of state and army is lacking. The army has no moral impulse, while the state has no security over its army.]

[An army formed from recruitment is not the same as a mercenary army, for most of its members are natives. But an army should not depend on chance or free will, the recruiting contract **<413>** contains something unethical, while it makes sacrifice and vocation an object of purchase, and also leads the government to resort to unworthy machinations, and puts the dregs of society in uniform. An army formed from recruitment assumes the existence of universal liability for military service in the form of a militia to defend the nation and, in extreme need, the summons of everyone capable of bearing arms (last reserves). Fundamentally distinct from the older militia is the newer institution of national guard, first introduced in France. It supports the army against foreign threats but is exclusively charged with putting down domestic disorder and rebellion, to the exclusion of the army. In principle, a national guard is based on popular sovereignty, or at least republicanism. The units are built locally, the officers are largely determined by local communities. It is the armed community, and can be used by the local community even against the king. The rationale is apparently protection of life and property when public order is shaken, but it really stems from the revolution principle of protection of life and property apart from the government.]

§. 158. The Representative Body and the Army

The influence of the territorial representation with regard to the army may never extend to the command of the army, as in England was claimed by the Long Parliament for the militia; since the restoration of the monarchy, it has been constitutionally excluded except with reference to the existence or formation of the army. This influence can vary in type and degree. The English parliament annually grants military authority, i.e., laws against mutiny, desertion, etc. (bill of mutiny), and allows the army to exist. The Hungarian estates authorize troops in a manner similar to taxes. The older German estates everywhere authorized the funds when money had to be raised for the maintenance of troops, but often also for recruitment among their subjects and for the increase of the troops beyond the district contingent. In France, by law (March 1818 and March 1832), that is, with the chambers, the entire conscription system, not only the duty to serve, but also the entire procedure for recruitment down to the details, the way the lists are prepared, the personal call-up, the examination for physical unfitness, as well as the advancement, and, moreover, the annual contingent are determined by law together with the chambers. According to our current German constitutional law, in case of doubt one must assume that the provisions for the formation of the army are to be agreed upon by the territorial representation, to the extent that they contain new burdens on subjects for the state, hence namely compulsory service itself or the extension of it, along with the burden of billeting, because only to that extent do they contain legal principles (§. 112). But the procedure of levying the army is often determined by law, because the military burden of the citizen depends indirectly on the state, just as the rules of procedure are treated as laws because substantive law is conditioned by them. On the other hand, the entire organization of the army, the principles of advancement, as well as the size of the contingent, that is, the actual use that the government makes of the established duty of the subject, belongs, as an emanation of the power of government and not of the legislative power, to the sovereign alone. Of course, exceptional laws for civil or penal legal cases always fall to the territorial representation, not, however, in their capacity as military laws, but as judicial laws.

§. 159. Oath to the Sovereign or to the Constitution?

[Just as the sovereign alone has command of the army, in fact his position as sovereign (as executive power) is based on such, so does the army swear an oath to him alone. This does not obligate the army without limit. Regardless of the oath, the military does not allow itself to be used for actions outside military ethics and honor. It will not allow itself to be used to overthrow the legal order. In the Revolution, the oath was sworn to nation, law, and king, thus putting the king in a subordinate position and calling the army to judge whether the king was faithful to the people. Then it is the people which is the supreme lord of the army. This lies behind the army's **<414>** oath to uphold the constitution. The meaning of the latter has since taken on a less stark significance, by which the oath is taken to king and constitution, and not to the people. Hence the army is bound to uphold the constitution and not give heed to the king when he violates the constitution. In this case the army's oath to the constitution parallels that of the civil service's oath. But in this sense as well it is reprehensible. The civil service's oath to the constitution stems from the fact that it implements the constitution. The army does not do this, but only carries out the sovereign's commands, which it then would take upon itself to judge in the light of the constitution, leading to insubordination, divisions, and so putting the power and order of the state into question. The army's oath to the constitution is also the highest injustice against the army. Disobedience of the civil servant is not the same as that of the soldier, since the service rendered by the one is not indispensable like that of the other is. If a civil servant refuses to carry out an order he may resign his post. But for a soldier to do so is to commit treason.]

Chapter 2: Finances

§. 160. Sources of Public Finance

<415> [Sources of state finances are firstly demesnes, the original source as property of the prince. Secondly, sources of wealth which are found in concentrated masses and are not quickly renewable: mines, forests, alluviums [Flußerzeugnisse], etc. These are usually held by the state out of concern for general necessity and preservation for future generations. Many commercial activities are perhaps better put in the hands of the state than individuals, such as the postal service. But they must serve the interest of the community as a whole. Lotteries are entirely unethical and unworthy. Thirdly, charges levied on various services, such as appraisals, stamps, etc. Fourthly, taxes.]

§. 161. Rationale of Taxation

[The justification for taxation lies purely and simply in subjection: the members of the state must contribute to the state's upkeep. The justification is not a quid pro quo for the protection of property. For this reason the form of taxation should not be patterned on the insurance business, whereby I pay a premium for my property to be insured, but in terms of the nature of the state, the particular nature and inherent law of national wealth [Nationalvermögens]. Taxation therefore has a dual principle: the relation of the wealth-creating society as an organic whole, and the relation of individuals as entitled personalities, everywhere ends in themselves.]

[By the first principle, taxes are to be levied on the wealth-creating society, the first consideration of which is the harmonious condition of sources of income and opportunities for enjoyment. <416> There is a national or social wealth which is not the sum of the wealth of individuals, but which exists as a whole, which is society's originally and solely, as something undivided and also undeveloped, partly as mere possibility of specific wealth, which first becomes wealth for separate individuals and first takes shape in their possession. This is the possibility of wealth acquisition and wealth enjoyment which lies only in society. For the possibility of acquiring wealth, i.e., the possibility of acquiring general wealth assets, not merely to enjoy the fruit of one's land, live in a house, make clothing and shoes for oneself, but through these means to obtain means (money) to satisfy all one's needs, this is obviously a function of social wealth, individuals do not have it, only society does and preserves it for individuals. Likewise the possibility to enjoy wealth, i.e., through his acquired general wealth – money wealth – to gain individual satisfaction, is a function of social wealth. The community affords this to individuals. This social wealth is the actual object of taxation. Taxation thus falls on society as a whole and its wealth, and upon each individual to the degree that he participates in its wealth, in the possibility for acquisition and enjoyment. Taxation on the former is direct taxation, or more accurately acquisition taxation (property taxes on land and homes, tax on business), on the latter is indirect taxation, more accurately consumption taxation (duties, customs). Social wealth encloses the individual's wealth analogously to, in nature, the organic body and an element: the body takes up the element and processes it into a certain substance, but gives a part of the processed substance back to the element. But the reciprocal action of individual wealth and social wealth is not like a natural law, but a legal relation, with personal obligation and duty from free independent property.]

[This yields the yardstick for taxation, which is not the size of actual acquisition by individuals but the relation of the various possibilities of acquisition and enjoyment in the state and the participation of individuals therein. Sources of income should be taxed in accordance with capacity to bear, such that working capital not be undermined, that one producer be weakened thereby and so fall prey to another, but that the burden be shared equally. Articles of consumption <417> should be taxed so as to maintain the ability of subjects to acquire them, and the more so the more necessary they are (luxury items should be more heavily taxed). Regarding individuals, direct taxation should be applied in accordance with possibility of acquisition, indirect in accordance with participation in actual enjoyment. Thus the owner of larger or better lands, or those better situated for exports, is taxed more heavily because of the greater possibility for acquisition, regardless of whether, in actuality, cultivation is good or bad, the harvest is good or bad, the market is good or bad. The craftsman or merchant is taxed more highly according to whether the manner and size of his establishment offers better opportunities for income, regardless of the actual utilization of those opportunities. Hence, valuables are not a source of income and thus not to be taxed, but the importation and sale of valuables as objects of enjoyment are subject to duties.]

[Taxation should not be derived from the income of individuals as isolated subjects, but from the large organism of the social economy. The aim should be to keep from taxing individuals as much as possible, rather only to anticipate the necessary sums from the social wealth prior to its becoming private wealth, and since it always is likewise private wealth, the trick is only to affect the social component of private wealth and to leave unaffected private wealth as such, with the result that the taxed does not feel the tax as an individual but as a part of the public. Thus, land tax is not felt when it is ancient, for the buyer or heir received the property at a discount, for them, therefore, it is not taxed at all; but the tax must be in proportion to the yield of the good, so that the property owner does not feel as an additional burden that labor which he performs, which is also for the tax man. Consumption taxes are not felt when they are held to a minimum for the individual; this also removes all difficulty for the impecunious without having to resort to an income tax.]

[Regarding implementation, it is important to see how a tax on business and consumption works. Simply applying an abstract principle, a rigid percentage, without regard for differences in practical situations, cannot be the method here. A branch of industry can appear to be taxed too highly, but can bear it if it is in a condition to **<418>** pass the burden on to its customers; conversely, a low level of taxation can be too high when it nevertheless is burdensome and causes products to be sold too cheaply just to come up with cash. The question is not how taxes arithmetically relate to one's current amount of wealth but what effect they will have on one's future creation of wealth. Proper and appropriate taxation is better founded on economic than juridical considerations.]

[This is the primary viewpoint of taxation, which is taken from the organic nature of social wealth and is aimed more at the future result of wealth production than at present possession. A secondary viewpoint is consideration of individuals, who bear the burden of public charges equally, thus consideration of individual incomes. This principle is based on justice, but even so remains a secondary principle. The wealth of individuals is never isolated, never a dead stationary possession, it is a continuous acquiring activity, and thus in continuous reciprocal action with other wealth-acquiring forces. It is therefore a superficial concern with justice and equality merely to take the sum total of possessions or income into account, and not the entire wealth position, the possibility of the individual's recourse to others, the consequences to the source of income, the consequence to the individual's life-requirement from the effect of taxes on prices, etc.]

[This secondary principle, the measure of income, is applied firstly in itself in a tax disregarding source of income and consumption: the personal tax (family, property, class tax), which takes as standard wealth in its isolation and at rest. Such a tax should only be supplementary, applied together with but not in replacement of the primary principle.]

§. 162. Equitable Taxation

[Contrary to all historical existence in larger states and all conditions of reality and feasibility, the rationalistic doctrine of state posits the wealth or pure income tax as the only one in accordance with reason. All others, especially consumption taxes, it rejects. Just as it views people and state as an aggregate of individuals, so it views **<419>** national wealth as the mere sum of private wealth, the sum of each individual's annual income; it lacks the concept of national wealth as original unity, as power of wealth creation lying in the community itself. It thus assumes individuals to create wealth in isolation, apart from the state, and to have to pay taxes only for legal and public-welfare protection. Taxes are thus based on reimbursement for every protection, as for services rendered. The more wealth one has protected (insured), the more tax (premium) he must pay. All tax on possibility for acquisition and enjoyment is unjustified, since unprotected by the state, and the great elementary envelopment and reciprocal relation between national and private wealth disappears, and so does consideration of the effect of taxes on future national and private prosperity. This can be called the atomistic finance theory. The theory is legally untenable because its principle precludes it from determining whether taxes should be levied according to the amount of wealth or of pure income, or whether for the mere protection of property or also of life and limb, since the former requires unequal assessment, the latter equal assessment. To implement a pure income tax on the basis of justice or fairness, thus according to taxable capacity, is likewise untenable, for capacity depends not only upon income but also upon outgo, thus the costs of living, family size, home, health care, etc., and how are these to be measured? Thus income tax does not answer to equity either. It is impossible and uncalled for that human establishments do away with the inequalities of the divine distribution of fortunes.]

[The requirement for so-called equality of taxation included in modern constitutions along these lines is unclear, for it does not indicate whether taxation should be assessed in terms of capital wealth, opportunity of acquisition, actual income, taxable capacity (thus income plus outgo); it is a chimera, and, in terms of result, is an impossibility. Equality of taxation in the sense intended here still therefore has to be discovered, and it will not be discovered.]

Chapter 3: Public Welfare

§. 163. Public Welfare and the Role of Government

<421> Public welfare administration [Die Polizei] is the care of the common good. It must preserve the common life in all its relations, material and spiritual, and to promote it according to its aims. It is therefore the manifestation of the wisdom of the state, for wisdom is the power and intelligence which brings the fullness of the manifold forces to fruition and, in mutual promotion, to perfection. This activity of the state is necessarily founded in its nature and is as little dispensable or accidental as is justice. For the state, being a kingdom and a divinely ordained government of men, must bring this wisdom to manifestation, just as much as justice, and must strive for the goals set for the human community and, through it, for the individual. For this reason, public welfare manifests itself in the states as soon as justice does (e.g. care for ethical standards, education, religion).

The public welfare is the richest field of state administration; whatever is the aim and interest of human existence belongs to it, and is particularly its most positive endeavor. Justice is only preservative or restorative, and intervenes only in case of violation; finance has its limitations, and should not go to infinity; the military should merely hold power, not use it, unless by necessity. The public welfare, however, is the real and constant political activity. Constant development, promotion and increase is its character; it is its vocation to draw more and more of the common interests into its sphere, to satisfy them in an ever higher manner. Its activity is creative in accordance with this task and must therefore be free. The law may set constraints to the public welfare administration but must not determine the content of its orders and activities. This should be left to the spirit and the free judgment of its guides and providers, who consider all concrete circumstances and results. **<422>**

§. 164. Public Welfare Restricted to Common Life

According to the nature and purpose of the state as discussed above (§. 39), only the *common life*, not that of the individual, can be the task of the public welfare, thus only the *common well-being*, not the well-being of the individual. The common life and the common well-being are not the life and well-being of all the individuals for themselves but in their communal life, hence of the individuals only in so far as they are members of the community, not insofar as they have an independent individual existence and destiny, an independent individual aim and pursuit. Hence, it is the task of public welfare to ensure that public safety exists, that the nation advances in prosperity and education, that ethics and respectability are preserved. On the other hand, that the individual should be careful and safeguarded (lock his room, avoid traveling through suspicious forests), that he should live in prosperity, that he should acquire higher education, that he should be ethical in his relations with his family and friends – such is his own business, and no one can compel him to it. But he must allow himself to be secured as far as is necessary for general security (home guard, passport system, etc.); he must allow his prosperity to be promoted as far as is necessary for general prosperity; he must participate in educational institutions and allow his children to participate as far as is necessary for the nation not to remain barbaric; he must practice respectability and ethical behavior as far as is necessary to preserve and keep alive the image of ethical behavior and respectability in the nation. He himself is also subject to the care of the public welfare for his personal welfare, insofar as it concerns that which is unavoidable according to human nature and therefore also belongs to the welfare of all in the same way, the negative (not-capable-of-not-being [Nichtnichtseynkönnende]),[207] into which the sphere of individual freedom and choice does not extend. Thus, for example, the individual is saved from death even against his will, the insane are housed, the poor are fed even against their will, and so on. Accordingly, the aim of the public welfare is not the weal (the end) of the institution of the state – that belongs in the constitution – but of the people, but only in their community, to the exclusion of individual welfare in the strict sense, for which public welfare may never directly provide, but only indirectly, insofar as it is necessarily included in the common well-being.**<423>**

Furthermore, according to the same discussion of the nature of the state, public welfare can only be directed towards *external* preservation and *external* promotion. It has merely to order, prevent, and eliminate externally, to establish

---

[207] [A reference to Schelling's concept of the negative as opposed to the positive; cf. *The Rise and Fall of Natural Law,* p. 81.]

and support by external means; by its order it cannot replace the internal source of forces, nor command it. The state is not ordained to do this, which is why it has no factual capacity for it; to awaken common life inwardly is after all only God's business; the state cannot call forth the forces and activities, it can only direct them where they exist; it cannot positively mark out the way for them, for that is marked out by their inner living impulse; it can only cut off the erroneous one and come to the aid of the true one, to which nature impels, by external stimulation and support.

Public welfare must guard against *over-governance,* that is, against substituting its own guidance for that of the governed, and against wanting to generate the forces and aspirations of common life itself and to predetermine their course, instead of allowing and externally promoting common life as it arises from within. Doing so extends public welfare beyond the purpose of the state, which consists in *external* promotion, into the realm of creation and inward guidance, which is not of the state. Similarly, the wisdom of man consists in recognizing the gifts and inclinations which nature has given him, purifying them, preventing them from going astray and giving them the goal to which they themselves urge, but not in thinking out and prescribing for himself the gifts he should have. Likewise the wisdom of the state.

Thus, for example, the public welfare must not prescribe the nature of national commerce, but must allow it to exist and flourish according to the natural opportunities of the country, and only come to its aid. It must employ competent teachers and deter frivolous ones, but it must not dictate the course of science, nor the manner of teaching and treatment (e.g. through compulsory textbooks) to the individual teacher. If significant artistic genius manifests itself, it should provide the external means for it to express and fulfill itself; it should not presume to promote and introduce art where no artistic genius is forthcoming, etc.

§. 165. Controversy Stemming from Improper Definition

The nature of public welfare is so extremely simple to the unbiased mind, for it is so natural that the state should have as its task the promotion of the general well-being (*publica utilitas*), and that the real activity of public welfare seeks and strives for nothing else is so obvious, that there should hardly be any doubt about it. If nevertheless there is never so much dispute and uncertainty about anything as about the nature of public welfare, the reason for this lies only in the widespread philosophical and political mindset [Bildung] by which the entire state is oriented to the individual and his individual purposes, and because it is unable to appropriate the true and existing to its point of view, it proceeds to the insoluble task of subordinating the public welfare to a concept that fits into its system. The ordinary and consistent (philosophical) doctrine of this kind conceives of public welfare only as the prevention of violations of rights. For it can recognize only the protection of rights as the purpose of the state, i.e., it cannot tolerate any area that is not related to this; but the only relationship in which the public welfare can still be brought into line with the rights of individuals is precisely that of preventing future violations. This, however, is only one of the many and varied tasks and services of public welfare. Its care for prosperity, education and ethical standards must then either be regarded in the most unnatural way merely as a means of ensuring that fewer crimes against life and property are committed (Kant), or one must substitute a separate contract for these purposes, separate from the general state contract (Groos), <424> in which case, however, one would logically have to allow everyone to withdraw from the benefits and obligations of this subsidiary contract without prejudice to his right of citizenship.

The view recently put forward by Mohl also belongs to the same point of view, even if its result is the opposite to that just described: the purpose of the state is to remove the obstacles that stand in the way of the all-round development of the individual. While the removal of obstacles that arise from the unlawful will and actions of other people is the task of justice, those that have their cause in the force majeure of external circumstances are the task of public welfare. But just as the state does not have the individual as such directly as its purpose and does not merely accomplish negative things (e.g. administering justice, punishment, which is something quite different from protection against injury), so also the public welfare. It would certainly not be appropriate, for example, to regard the establishment of educational institutions as the clearing-out of unculture or of overpowering external circumstances inimical to learning, and how can the individual's restriction in his freedom for the sake of his or others' development (i.e., for ethical reasons) be justified, since the consequence of this point of view demands that a restriction be imposed solely for the sake of freedom itself and for no other purpose? This theory also leads us, contrary to all real existence and contrary to the inner nature of the matter, to regard measures for public safety as objects of justice. The protection of individual freedom from public welfare measures that seek to make individuals happy even against their will is a well-founded pursuit; but this follows not from the fact that public welfare has only negative things to do, but from the fact that it has to promote only public life directly, not the individual as such, and therefore only externally.

Those who seek the essence of public welfare in the perfection of mankind, in the promotion of ethics or of temporal happiness (e.g., Moser), are guided by a correct view, but the scientific foundation is lacking, and the consequence of their doctrine would therefore certainly lead to all-embracing public welfare activity which would devour the private freedom of men. Among the older writers, as a rule, no scientifically sharp or exhaustive designation is to be found at all, but whatever strikes them as the main object of public welfare, that they designate as the essence of the same; thus for some security, others trade and industry (Kreitmaier, Beckmann), for Justi prosperity, external discipline, the comforts of life.

§. 166. Branches of Public Welfare Activity

In the common well-being, which is the task of the public welfare, various interests, needs and goals can be distinguished, the satisfaction and achievement of which together constitute the common well-being. The various branches of public welfare are based on this. The first goal is the peace of the state, the protection against all undertakings against the existence of the state or against the right and peace of the subjects, against all violent acts – the *police* [Sicherheitspolizei]. Erected upon this basis come the positive concerns first for physical welfare, food (poor relief), prosperity (national economy), health (medical care), comfort and the like, then for the spiritual welfare, for ethics and respectability, education and culture [Bildung], for religion and the church. All institutions begin in history in their sacred form and then gradually distance themselves from the divine source and become secularized, until the day comes when they once again, albeit in the appropriate development, attach themselves to the religious center. Thus in the states of the ancient orient and classical antiquity, public welfare was concerned only with its highest sphere, the care of public religion, public morals and public education, and in the earlier times of the European states **<425>** this was the most important matter, so far as the state was at all active in public welfare, and even more so through the church. But since the care for physical welfare has become a task of the public welfare administration, as is right and necessary, it has more than justifiably pushed back those higher goals, so that now the material interests, the care for prosperity (some time ago also for increasing the population) have become almost the most important focus of attention in most states.

Furthermore, intellectual [geistigen] interests, the promotion of culture and science, have become alienated from religion and have thus lost their true and supreme meaning.

§. 167. Punishment of Violations

The public welfare administration also exercises *penal power*. This is not something taken from the administration of justice, but lies in its own nature. Since it promotes community life in accordance with its aims, it must not only compel those who disobey, but also castigate those who resist, instill fear and inflict harm on those who oppose the attainment of its aims, and inculcate in them the impermissibility of opposing actions. This is the essence of all guidance, encouragement and training. Just as the head of the household does not exercise criminal justice, yet cannot educate and encourage his children without punishing them, so too must the public welfare administration in its own way.

Public welfare punishment is therefore of a completely different nature than that of the justice system. Its meaning is not punishment in the truest sense, but rather *chastisement* so that the offender will refrain from doing the same in future, for the *deterrence* of others and the *reproval* of the offence, that is, the real, emphatic mitigation of the reprehensibility, and it is not imposed because of a violation of the legal order but because of a violation of the common well-being, because the measures taken for public safety, prosperity, or public morals and respectability, etc. have been violated. If some public welfare violations appear to have the character of a violation of the law (e.g. theft as a public welfare violation), this is only apparent. For the insignificance of the object means that the act cannot be viewed as a violation of the legal order, a rebellion against the rule of the state, but is only considered in terms of its detriment to the common well-being. These transgressions are therefore by no means criminal cases which are transferred to the police authorities for external expediency but are in their inner nature public welfare transgressions. However, the line between these offenses, where they have this or that character, can only be drawn by positive legislation, in the case where the difference is a quantitative, not a qualitative one. <426>

§. 168. Public Welfare or Judiciary?

Lately calls have come to separate the police (inappropriately called legal police or preventive justice) from the sphere of public welfare and relegate it to that of the judiciary, because it prevents *violations of the law,* and the prevention of such violations is precisely the nature of the administration of justice, just as voluntary jurisdiction[208] [freiwillige Gerichtsbarkeit] pertains to its sphere and not that of the public welfare. Wrongly! It is the justice of the state that is expressed in the administration of justice, but the justice the essence of which is the immutability and continuous grandeur of the legislative will does not consist in the fact that the law is not transgressed, hence not in the fact that rights are not violated, but in the fact that the legal order prevails against the one who has violated it, i.e., that the glory of the state or the right of the individual is restored after the violation. The administration of civil justice is therefore concerned only with the legal, not with the factual safeguarding of rights. That the subject's rights are not violated by legal means, that restoration is not denied, is its domain, but that the factual dangers which may threaten rights are eliminated is not a matter for the justice of the state but for its wisdom, not a matter for the administration of justice but for the public welfare.

Likewise the purpose of voluntary jurisdiction is only to protect against such violations that arise from legal transactions, not from merely factual acts. Voluntary jurisdiction is concerned to see that the transactions of a guardian in their legal correctness and legal authorization do not harm the ward, that the disposition of a testator, the contracts of parties are not overturned by legal means, that creditors are not deprived of their pledge by legal means. On the other hand, that thieves do not linger in forests and corners of towns, that gates

---

208 [Here is the only place in *The Doctrine of Law and State on the Basis of the Christian Worldview* where Stahl discusses voluntary (non-contentious) jurisdiction. This is a branch of the legal system that deals with matters where there is no dispute between parties, or where the state acts in an administrative or supervisory capacity rather than conflict resolution. It stands in contrast to "streitige Gerichtsbarkeit" which involves contentious litigation between opposing parties. Voluntary jurisdiction encompasses a wide range of proceedings, often handled by specialized courts like the *Amtsgericht* (local court). The court's role is to facilitate, register, or oversee proceedings rather than adjudicate disputes.]

and doors are kept closed, that gangs are not formed, that is a prevention against merely factual dangers, a matter for public welfare. The former is accomplished by legal institution and treatment, the latter by factual measures and factual attention; to the former belongs legal knowledge and accuracy, to the latter the wisdom of life and calculation of results. Herein lies the reason why it would be outwardly inexpedient to transfer the former to public welfare officers and the latter to judicial officers. Voluntary jurisdiction is not, of course, a direct manifestation of justice, but is merely a means directed towards it, in this respect a necessarily complementary element of the administration of justice, even if not the actual and ultimate task of the latter, but nevertheless indissolubly connected with it. To place it in the public welfare would be similar to referring evidence *ad perpetuam rei memoriam* [i.e., the preservation of evidence] to the public welfare. Where the administration of justice is to take place, it must be a matter of someone being judged. Voluntary jurisdiction does not judge directly, but it prepares for what will or could be judged in the future, so that it will be judged fairly.

Chapter 4: The Administration of Justice

§. 169. The Highest Branch of State Administration

<427> The administration of justice is the upholding of and the *manifestation of the justice of the state.*

[The justice of the state consists in its maintaining the rule of its order and the rights of its subjects (Book I [*Philosophical Foundations*], §. 51). The administration of justice is the activity by which violations of this order and these rights are restored against the violator. It thus concerns individuals, not a shared activity through general implementation (such as e.g. enforcement of the constitution). There are therefore two subjects whose rights are vindicated here: the state as the ethical divinely-sanctioned order on earth, and individuals. The restoration of the state order is achieved by punishing the violator, thus penally, while the restoration of an individual's rights is achieved by restoring a condition or an object. The former is criminal justice, the latter civil justice; the former is punitive, the latter protective.]

[Obedience to the state, and individuals' rights in the state, form the foundation of the state, and what actually is ethical about the state; therefore, the administration of justice is the highest, most indispensable, and most valuable branch of its administration. The majesty and sanctity of the state lie above all in the unshakeable maintenance of justice.]

§. 170. Due Process of Law

[The same justice which maintains the order of the state and the rights of subjects against the violator must also maintain the violator's right against those who would themselves undertake to restore these. This is owed him as a person. The infliction of punishment on <428> the violator is no infringement of his personality and right, but rather the satisfaction thereof. Justice can have no other consideration than guilt or innocence. All considerations of public or private good are foreign to it. The absolute entitlement of personality, that it only be measured by itself, that where its right is concerned it be subjected to no power it does not have to recognize as its own inherent law and being, is the essence of justice, and thus the character trait of the administration of justice.

Therefore guilt must be proven. The procedure of determining guilt or innocence must be established by law, above the will either of ruler or subject. This is due process. It is a struggle of two powers, the power of the state and the power of the personality of individuals which the state protects, in terms of the measure and purpose of that which is common to them, the law. As the administration of justice is grounded in justice, that which is peculiar to it is contrary to the other spheres of the state. Even in civil procedure, where the right of the violated is in conflict with the right of the accused, it is always the authority of the state which guarantees each of those rights and which the state puts into action. The judge, not the accuser, demands the accused to render account.]

§. 171. Judgment by Peers, Mediating Power of the Judiciary

[The real power maintaining justice is the court of law. The supreme principle establishing the courts is independence from the sovereign. This is the first guarantee of true impartial adjudication and the basis of all justice. This follows from the consideration that here it is not the spirit and personality of the ruler pursuing a result redounding to the whole, and thus deciding freely so as to attain that result, but the law, which is unwaveringly indifferent, existing as something ever present, having no goal in the future; in consequence, it is only an organ separate from the personality of the ruler, merely serving the laws, which makes the decision. And there is an even deeper ground. The law condemns the guilty, not simply because and to the degree that it is the law of the state, but also because it is his innermost being as citizen, a law inhering in himself. This is justice. This is the ground for his having to be judged by his **<429>** equals, not by a sovereign prince. He is thus judged by the standard of his equals, which is his own standard, which is what justice requires. This is the fundamental principle of the Roman administration of justice, and even more so the Germanic. Here, the ruler and legislator is always excluded from the court of law, while men who otherwise do not rule over the accused, judge him. With the Romans this was the *judex,* taken from the citizenry. In the ancient German situation, it was the collective community (jurors). With the strict separation of estates, only peers, members of the same estate, stood in judgment. With the division of labor and development of the law, there developed the educated judge, who is the equal of the accused and combines with this civic equality a deep insight into the law and an exercised power of judgment, upholding in the maintenance of justice the honor of his profession. Judges must not also have a power over subjects directed toward considerations of governmental expediency – which is why executive administration must be kept separate from the judiciary. In order to insulate judges from the influence of the sovereign, they must be established in their positions, irremovable.]

[Accordingly, the independence of the judiciary from the sovereign is founded on a similar notion to the popular representation. It is mediating power between the sovereign and the subject, in that it shares the position of both, subjection, yet rule. All political freedom rests on such mediating power. This power manifests itself differently in the popular representation and in the judiciary, in terms of the distinction between constitution and administration of justice.]

§. 172. No Separation of Powers, but Independent Exercise

[The independence of the judiciary by no means implies a separation of powers, a self-contained judiciary alongside and external to the government or princely power. The judiciary is the power of the ruling authority, thus the one ruling authority (the sovereign). For this reason the sovereign appoints, empowers, supervises judges, determines their districts, in case of default calls them to account, and they pronounce judgment in his name. The independence of <430> the judiciary consists in this, that in the administration of justice the ruling authority derives the content of the decision from the judgment of such independent, impartial men, devoted to justice.]

[There are therefore two moments active in the administration of justice: the power of the ruling authority (jurisdiction, Latin *jurisdictio*) which does not itself pass judgment, and reaching a verdict [Urtheilsfindung] (Latin *judicium*), which itself is no power, as little as is the verdict [Verdikt] of jurors. Therefore, the complete provision and spontaneous activity by which the law is fulfilled in civil and criminal cases lies in the power of the ruling authority, while only the verdict regarding questions placed before it lies in the judicature. They are naturally and fruitfully joined together in the German system of administration of justice. By contrast, in the French system they are separated, leading to the divestment of all power of the ruling authority in the judicature.]

Chapter 5: The Boundaries of Judiciary and Administration

§. 173. The Extent of Administrative Decision

<431> [The government with its functions interferes in all legal spheres of subjects, in their wealth, in their freedom, in competencies otherwise specially granted to them, and in this must proceed according to or within the laws, otherwise it forfeits its character as law-state. Should a subject claim to have been treated contrary to law and justice in this, the question arises as to who is competent to judge the case, the government or the courts, and, indeed, with regard both to what comes prior to the decision, thus whether the infringement occurred, and what comes afterwards, whether the decision came about lawfully, or whether restitution or compensation should be made. According to the nature of the state as ethical kingdom to which individuals belong as members, the only power which can judge regarding the lawful application of its power is the government; it cannot wait on the decision of the courts as a third power before it carries out its intentions, and even less may it be subject to the courts' judgment, command, and execution. The situation in which state power is everywhere subject to the intervention of judicial decisions whenever the subject charges violation of rights, is one in which the state as ethical kingdom ceases to exist; it has been degraded to level of a mere private party, its actions lose the character of a higher authority, its relation to the subject is no different than a creditor's authorization regarding a debtor. That which is part of administration cannot be subject to the judiciary, for that confuses the boundaries between these two branches of state power.]

[It comes down to defining the situations and conflicts to be <432> ordered and decided by the administration as opposed to the judiciary. Those relations in which the primary and absolute goal is the maintenance of the individual citizen in the rights to which he is entitled is the sphere of the judiciary; those in which the primary goal is a form and result redounding to the whole, is the sphere of administration, the civil service. The distinction with the right of individual citizens is not merely the common good in the sense of advantages to be acquired first by the collectivity, but no less the common order, the maintenance of the public condition, the constitution in its existing fundamental relations, the administration in its regular necessary course of business. Where the inner purpose is justice, it pertains to the sphere of the judiciary; justice is taken into consideration everywhere, including in the administration, but only as restriction and limit; but with the judiciary it forms the essence, the only goal. Administration pursues the common good while keeping justice in mind; the judiciary only keeps justice in mind. This is why punishment of violations and offenses pertains to the judiciary. Here the only standard is justice, the integrity of the innocent against any form of punishment is the individual's most absolute right, it can in no wise be the object of public obligation and sacrifice (as can freedom of corporeal services or property), and in no wise can it be viewed as a mere member of the collective order (as is right of citizenship, suffrage). Civil justice in general has its boundary with administration in terms of the separation of private from public law. In private law, the goal is the maintenance of the individual in his rights, while in public law it is the rule over men as a collective, binding them into a common existence. Where a conflict results not from a violation of individual rights but a violation of a right or authorization flowing from this common order and shared goal, then it falls within the sphere of administration. The term "administrative justice" is inappropriate to this. The purpose is not to attain justice but to maintain the common condition. Where the court speaks, it always concerns the case at hand, the protection of specific rights involved in that case, the persons involved. But where the case is not an individual one but a part of the general public condition, such as voting rights, **<433>** taxation, and the like, the courts cannot decide.]

[There are many social relations which do not fall simply into the one category or the other, but are of a mixed character, in which the activity of the individual is to be directed to an effect on the common condition, while also maintaining it among his guaranteed rights. For example, the right to an occupation in agriculture, industry, trade, is so essential to an individual's position and existence that the viewpoint of maintaining him in this right, the principle of justice, comes strongly to the fore, yet here it is precisely the occupational activity as a whole which is the object of higher common direction to a common result of prosperity and tending to public requirements. In terms of the latest viewpoints, trade and industry often has more of the appearance of public order than of private rights. Concessions are now given with a view to the whole, according to considerations affecting the entirety of industry, with authorizations to individuals only derivative, given out of the self-contained fabric of the whole. That is why decisions regarding conflicts over the extent of industrial concessions and such pertain to the authorities charged with maintaining the general condition of industry. Yet this condition can also be based on industrial rights, as an object of private law, thus of justice. It is otherwise with agriculture. Here private property is primary, with regulations and restrictions only functioning as modifications. The public viewpoint does not form the coherence, the center of the all landholding and farming activity. Therefore, matters of agriculture as a rule fall under the jurisdiction of the courts.]

[Personal status is especially amenable to being viewed from both viewpoints. Included here is the right of national citizenship, local citizenship, nobility. This belongs both to private and public law, in fact is the point at which both permeate each other, at which private law is enclosed and guaranteed by public law. The status of subject in the state is the authorization of individuals to the exercise of all civil, thus private rights in the nation, while that of noble usually includes a range of guaranteed private privileges. On the other hand it is part of the public condition to recognize one person as subject, another person as noble. In terms of German state law, per- **<434>** sonal status as a rule is considered a public, thus administrative matter.]

[Fiscal matters pertain indubitably and without exception to the sphere of justice. As fisc, the state is a mere private, legal person, a private wealth-holder like any other subject, for which what matters is determining who owns what. When a conflict arises between government and subject, what has to be done is to determine whether the courts have jurisdiction or the administration, whether it is a fiscal or a sovereign matter. As property owner and contracting agent, the state is a private actor subject to private law, as is any other such actor. But as levier of taxes it is truly something other, the state proper. The characteristic adhering to the fiscal side of the state is that the state here does not command the subject; where it does command the subject, it is no longer on the fiscal side but the sovereign side. The courts, then, have jurisdiction in fiscal matters, but not sovereign matters.]

§. 174. Exemption Rights

[There is a significant exception to this rule, having to do with so-called exemption rights. These are, as it were, private rights within the public sphere, which the state has to respect and cannot infringe upon, whereby such infringements fall under the jurisdiction of the courts.]

[*Rights of subjects vis-a-vis administrative dispositions.* This only concerns exemption rights. These form the limit beyond which the administration may not act. Major forms of such rights are:]

1. [Direct (positive) exemption of a right from sovereign exercise, i.e., a competence on the part of the subject which, because of its concept or purpose, forms an exception or restriction against this branch of state power and nowise is subjected to it. Thus, it is no exemption right when my property is assessed excessive taxes, but it is when in the face of constitutional or contractual freedom from taxation I am still assessed taxes. These exemption rights pertain to **<435>** the individual legal sphere: landed property, paternal power, business enterprise, exemption from taxation, exemption from military service. Constitutional positions such as peerage or essential rights of sovereignty, such as jurisdiction, cannot form part of exemption rights.]

2. [Indirect (negative) exemption of a right from sovereign exercise. This is mainly the case when the administrative power steps entirely outside its bounds, where it has no legal power, where the subject is not subjected to it. This holds true where the administrative power causes damages by way of fraud or negligence. Such damages may be pursued through the courts.]

[*The right of subjects vis-à-vis the upholding of the constitution.* In that constitutional relations above all form part of public law, which is the sphere in which subjects form a part of the whole, subjects stand under the authority of the state, and thus generally cannot be a party over against the state before a court of law. The various entities (corporate bodies, assemblies, offices) stand over against each other with rights and duties, yet not as private-legal subjects, but rather as public institutions.]

[*The right of subjects vis-à-vis legislation.* In the face of legislation, there is simply no right of exemption for subjects. There is a natural-ethical boundary in terms of law-ideas to the legislative power (§. 41) but not a positive-legal boundary, since the legislative power is the source of and ruler over positive law.]

§. 175. Acquired Rights

[Accordingly, this is our doctrine: in terms of the principle of state law which in Germany partly has developed and partly is being developed, the path of civil justice is open for rights in the private-legal sphere but not in the public-legal sphere, although there are exemption rights in the latter sphere. Only acquired rights can be the object of legal proceedings. On the other hand, the doctrine is now widespread that acquired rights alone make up the sphere of civil justice. The following discussion of acquired rights will demonstrate <**436**> the erroneousness hereof.]

[In terms of legal philosophy, the concept of acquired rights is opposed to that of innate rights; it is thus concerned not with that to which one is entitled in his existence as personality but only for specific conditions and in consequence of specific characteristics, actions, circumstances, for which reason the more appropriate designation is special as opposed to general rights (Book II [*Principles of Law*], §. 36). The concept of acquired rights furthermore, in terms of positive state law, which is what we are concerned with here, includes the independence and guarantee of those rights, it includes rights to which subjects are entitled to independently as his own, not merely in consequence and extension of the general legal order or disposition of the ruling authorities, and which in this character cannot (ordinarily) be removed and changed by state power; through which, then, as individual he assumes a legal sphere distinct and secured from the collective order. The expression "acquired" quite appropriately describes the appropriation of rights to the individual, while rights of another sort only entail the mere usage and exercise by the individual, and only those are secured to him, not their belonging to him (in a certain sense, his property in them). In this sense, acquired rights form the opposition to natural freedom (e.g., spatial movement); to general civil law (to be treated according to the law regarding taxes, conscription, in terms of the law to acquire, to be able to establish rights and advantages – to enjoy the favors and institutions of the state); to powers of the ruling authorities (business concessions, building permits); to rights derived from constitutional stipulations (right to family devotions, the right to submit petitions and complaints of the estates, right of emigration). These rights in turn are quite different in terms of state law. In particular, natural freedom can legally be restricted at any moment by the act of bare government power (decrees), but a right derived from constitutional stipulations cannot. Yet the criterion of independent attachment to the individual and the guarantee of this attachment is lacking to all of them. Regarding acquired rights, the consequence is, in correspondence to this independence and guarantee, both: firstly, that the laws which concern regulations amending the origin of such rights not

<437> automatically apply to those already brought into existence (thus, no retroactive force); secondly, that when such rights are abolished, that this comes out not simply as a mere change in the public legal condition but as the abolition of rights (as conflict of the public condition with opposing indefeasible entitlement), as an expression of extraordinary power (*potestas eminens*) of the state, which for the legislator can be manifest in reasons of consideration, which could even extend to protest, if not for unlawfulness, at least for material injustice.]

[It is part of the necessity of things, to wit, independent personality, that man must be maintained in the condition that certain rights have to be recognized as acquired rights, although the specific determination as to which rights in the public sphere are to be secured as acquired rights in this sense is a matter of positive law and can only be recognized in terms of positive law. The criterion of origin, thus that acquired rights require a specific special process while other rights do not, is by no means correct. The independent attachment which is the character of acquired rights does not have its basis in origin through a special act of acquisition but in the content and significance of specific rights. Therefore its distinguishing feature cannot consist in such an act of acquisition. This criterion at most is correct as compared with natural freedom, but not so as compared with rights from constitutional rules or government powers.]

[The sphere of acquired rights resides mainly in the area of private law, because it mainly concerns individuals assuming a distinct independent legal sphere over against the common condition of the state. Thus property, claims, rights of occupation. But there are also such in public law, as there should be, because here as well certain competencies best answer to the requirement of the respective institution when they take the character of unretractable independent rights of the person concerned. Above all, the princely right, the right to the throne or to succeed to the throne is an acquired right. Likewise, hereditary peerage is usually an acquired right. The rights of territorial estates can entirely or partly have the character of acquired rights. The exercise of sovereign rights such as jurisdiction can be due to the nobility or even to cities, just as city constitutions, <438> various forms of citizenship can be acquired rights upon which later laws have no retroactive effect, and which can only be withdrawn by abolition using the power of *potestas eminens*.]

[Every acquired right has a private-legal dimension: the independence of competence, its distinction and separation from the whole of the public condition, is something private.]

[This shows that the reach of legal proceedings is characterized not by the criterion of acquired rights but of the private-legal sphere. Rights in the public-legal sphere, even when acquired, are not subject to judicial decision.]

§. 177 [176].[209] The Sphere of Administrative Justice

[When, in accordance with the state-legal principle of modern times, both functions, judiciary and administration, are maintained in complete independence and coordination, this leads to the need for a neutral power for cases in which both relations are involved.]

[To wit, whereas the judiciary acts where the idea of justice is the ruling principle (in the sphere of private-legal or exemption rights), and whereas the administration acts where the idea of public necessity or utility is the ruling principle (in the area of exercise of sovereign rights), then there where both ideas act in equal manner, as independent and absolutely determining principles, a third form of action also arises, whereby officials keep in mind a judicial standing for both. This is the deeper meaning behind *administrative justice*, taking both words in a broader sense than their technical meanings.]

[The main instance wherein these principles are concurrent is in cases of conflict between them. A second instance is where subjects' rights are asserted which are not exempt from administrative power but yet are to be maintained in a certain guarantee against that power, which in a manner of speaking equilibrates that power. Here pertain, e.g., rights regarding the press. A third instance is where the **<439>** general result of performances is a public necessity, but where the distribution among individuals takes place in terms of justice. Thus, e.g., the distribution of reparations taxes, the total sum of which is fixed.]

§. 178 [177]. The Erstwhile Role of the Courts

[In earlier times, and especially in Germany prior to the dissolution of the Holy Roman Empire, another division between the judiciary and administration obtained. The private-legal coloring of the age led to the predominance of judicial

---

[209] [The original numbering of this section and the next were wrong; the proper numbering is given in brackets.]

proceedings, even in matters which now are considered public law. For example, conflicts between the territorial prince and the estates were decided in the courts. The only exception was that imperial powers, the imperial diet or the emperor and his officials, were not subject to such proceedings.]

§. 178. From Private Rights to Public Condition

[The theory of those times corresponded to the practice. "Violation of rights" was the criterion for legal proceedings, regardless of the sphere of law in which they occurred. Since the Empire dissolved, the German states have taken on a state-oriented character, and the theory is no longer entitlement but rather the legal sphere involved, whereby only private-legal matters are subject to judicial proceedings. This is the proper foundational division, but it is insufficient. Exceptions must be recognized in the public sphere. If not, then even criminal justice, the epitome of judicial proceedings, would fall to the administration.]

§. 179. Comparison with England

[In this third edition of this work, I cannot deviate from the position as outlined above. No other position is appropriate to the total structure of our legal condition. Our separation of the judiciary <440> from the administration has nothing to do with a division of powers, but only with a sharp distinction of the spheres which also characterizes our entire public condition in other relations. We separate administration and representation, even though the older territorial estates and the English parliament not only have functions of representation but also of administration. We unite civil and criminal justice and separate them sharply from public welfare, while the older concept of jurisdiction also included the entire police force [Sicherheitspolizei]. In England, criminal justice is joined to the police and separated from civil justice. If the division of spheres obtains, then the judicial competence can only hold for private-legal relations, yet in England this entire form of separation is non-existent.]

[In England, the sphere of the judges is not mere administration of justice, but also the king's peace, i.e., maintenance of public order as sanctioned by the king. In this capacity the high court orders and supervises the sheriff, who otherwise is an officer not of the court but of the executive and the public welfare. In this capacity, he often issues instructions to the fulfillment of legal duties to officials of the crown. In this, it is not subjective rights that determine the province of the court but the public order, and thus signals that the office of judges entails more than only judicial proceedings. Thus, in determining voting rights the judge does not adhere to judicial procedure, but rather acts the way an administrative official would here in Germany.]

Chapter 6: The Position of the Judge before the Sovereign and Officialdom

§. 180. Bound by General Rules, not Specific Directions

<441> [The judge stands under the ordered power of the sovereign, which is the sovereign's legislative power in the broadest sense, i.e., which yields general rules, both laws in strict and actual sense, and decrees. Both are norms for judicial application. But the judge does not stand under the particular instructions of the sovereign, such as intervention in a particular concrete case. He is obligated to obey the former, and to disregard the latter.]

[Regarding the laws, the judge is only to pass judgment regarding the existence thereof, not the validity thereof; whether the external characteristics, the proper form of enactment was followed, not the competence of the sovereign to make the enactment.]

[The viewpoint that the courts have to judge regarding the constitutionality of a decree, not of course in general to declare such null and void but to leave them out of consideration in a specific case, stems from the honorable sentiment for the independence of the administration of justice and the steadfastness of the constitution. Even so, I do not see how it can be upheld. The judge can only pass judgment over the form, not the substance, of decrees. The result of judges being allowed a material judgment as to the constitutionality of decrees is boundless confusion.]

§. 181. Coordination Not Subordination

[Vis-à-vis decisions of the sovereign and instructions of the administration, the judge is not in a position of subordination but of <442> coordination. Here it is still the case that the one keep from interfering in the internal functioning of the other. On the other hand, it is not contrary to coordination that the judge interpret and apply administrative regulations or dispositions in terms of his own judgment.]

Chapter 7: The Administration of Penal Justice

§. 182. Penal Justice as Restoration of Ethical Order

<443> [The ethical kingdom of the state being only an external (legal) one (§. 36), so likewise is its penal justice. Its order and rule are only violated by external deeds – crime – and are only restored through external, corporeally administered punishment. But in terms of its essence, this external penal justice can be none other than penal justice in general, thus also inward (divine) penal justice. This general essence of penal justice was already extensively discussed in the philosophical foundations (Book I [*Philosophical Foundations*], §. 54 and following). It is everywhere the unconditional supreme commandment that punishment follow upon violation. It is everywhere true that, where man desires to establish his will as a higher kingdom over the ethical order, the majesty of the ethical order must be restored over him through his being overpowered, his suffering. Here, though, it is the order of the state, the legal order, the majesty of which is to be maintained, and it is civil crime which violates it, and civil punishment which restores it. This distinguishes the punishment of the state from moral punishment, which is God's affair alone; for the state does not punish sin, but only crime, and its punishment is not eternal damnation and anxiety of soul, but a temporal and external evil.]

[The state is empowered and obligated to carry out this legal punishment, because its essence and its God-ordained purpose and imparted authorization is to maintain the external ethical order on Earth. The majesty of the state is nowhere more visible than in its exercise of punishment, yet nowhere is it more evident that this power is given it from above. This is by no means theocracy. The empowerment to punish, and the ethical commandments in terms of <444> which it is to inflict punishment, chiefly the Ten Commandments, are from God, and the guilty person must recognize, and must be informed, that he is being punished for violating God's commandment, by the ruling authority, which God put over him to this end. In this sense one may say that even civil punishment is for the greater glory of God (*ad majorem Dei gloriam*). Apart from this awareness, the death penalty and extended incarceration are barbarism. Therefore, in penal justice the close connection between the external legal order and the inward ethical world is manifest.]

§. 183. Justice the Primary yet not the Sole Motivation

[Although the significance of punishment can be none other than its being the necessary consequence of crime in terms of justice, it can also have other purposes than the vindication of justice. Exercise of punishment also protects the state against the danger to it harbored by crime, and when it does not maintain justice, it collapses (self-defense). Punishment not only renders harmless the evil portion of the population (prevention), it also keeps the entire population from crime through fear of punishment (deterrence). Punishment and the administration of justice also promote morality, both by improving the morality of the criminal and by confirming the proper sentiments of the population.]

§. 184. False Justifications

[Relativistic theories of penal justice all share the basic error of treating the person punished as means, injuring their freedom for the sake of a future goal of the community, either by forestalling his future crimes (prevention theory) or by deterring others (deterrence theory). This runs absolutely contrary to law and justice. These theories can only be founded either in the notion of a social contract (implicit agreement upon the founding of the state) or as a form of self-defense. But contract cannot justify what is inherently unjustified, and self-defense is no longer justified against someone whose crime has already been accomplished. To argue that this **<445>** would be allowable against a crime previously committed against the state would assume the lawfulness of punishment, which is what must be demonstrated. Punishment would not be legally necessary but only factually necessary, and the criminal would not acknowledge the verdict of an ethical power but only submit to superior force.]

[Absolute theories of penal justice, thus that punishment exists for the sake of justice, differ amongst each other according to the concept one attaches to justice. According to Kant and Hegel, the essence of justice and punishment is the logical consequence, while according to me (Book I [*Philosophical Foundations*], §§. 54, 55), it is the immutable will of the personal God and Lord to maintain His holy world-order. Regardless, in terms of the administration of civil penal justice, the result is hardly different, and the shortcoming of the former is not a lack of a theory of criminality but the entire system, in that it robs the criminal of the understanding that it is God's rule that is being restored, and that the same God also promises forgiveness to the penitent.]

§. 185. Crime versus Violations of Public Welfare

[The essence of penal justice as here laid out also yields the concept of crime and its delimitation. Accordingly, crime is the violation of the rule of law and state as the ethical order on Earth. Therefore, in order to establish a crime, the legal order must be violated, and in such a manner that bids defiance to its majesty, i.e., the power of the state to maintain that order. The legal order includes the integrity of the person, property, the order of the family, the existence of state and church.]

[However, immorality and sin, offences against the public welfare, disobedience and unlawfulness do not constitute crimes.]

[Regarding immorality and sin, this is not as such crime and therefore not subject to the penal justice of the state. For example, gluttony and drinking bouts, abuse of confidence, shameful betrayal of friends, malicious dissimulation, do not constitute civil crime. The false oath, as long as it only violates religion, is sin; the false oath sworn in a court of law is crime. Even so, by no means is it only **<446>** violations of the rights of others which constitute crimes. In the same way that the legal order is not restricted to the rights of others, but also has the existence of relations in accordance with higher commands as its content, thus also crime. Therefore, violations of the order of the family (adultery, incest, polygamy) are no less civil crimes than those against property. Even those crimes committed against others are not crimes because they violate those others' rights, but because they violate the legal order.]

[Offences against the public welfare are not crimes when not directed against the legal order, but only are such when directed against commands of the state to promote the public welfare. Upon this is based the well-founded distinction between criminal offence and mere offence against public welfare. Castigation, not punishment, is here in order. Everything which violates the command to promote prosperity, culture, sanitation, general security, etc., is mere offence against public welfare. On the other hand, the oft-cited concept of offence against the public welfare being actions which endanger the commonality is unsuited. The criterion of endangerment is unsuitable because only unlawfulness justifies punishment; furthermore, usually it is a series of such actions which endanger the public welfare, not just one in isolation, e.g., neglect of vaccination, exposure of dead bodies, vagabondage, while just as great a portion of public welfare ordinances concern not endangerment but positive goals such as prosperity, culture, mores, school attendance, observance of public propriety.]

[Regarding disobedience and unlawfulness: even those actions which violate the legal order are only crimes when they bid defiance to the rule and regard of the state. In this, crime is to be distinguished from mere disobedience against laws (such as the constitution) and unlawfulness. The state as external order only demands actions, not sentiments, and as such it is no violation of its majesty (as it would be with God) if one does not obey voluntarily, when he violates its commands. Crime is always a positive intervention in the public legal order or the rights of others, while disobedience and unlawfulness are only negative interventions. For instance, the for- <447> mer is established through the abolition or prevention of constitutional institutions (riot, bribery in voting), the latter through refusal to act (failure to attend sessions of the assembly, continued exercise of a non-competent estate right); the former through taking (theft, robbery), the latter through withholding (non-delivery of property, nonpayment of a loan).]

§. 186. Punishment: Definition, Kinds, Degrees; Correction

[Punishment must be an evil, for that is its concept. There is no subjugation of the will in its essence, or of personality, like unto that when it is made to suffer. In punishment it is intended that the delinquent feels pain, even when in specific instances such may be absent. Such an evil is above all the destruction of the criminal – capital punishment. The partial destruction of the existence of the criminal, bodily pain, is a further evil (mutilation, torture, beating) – corporal punishment. There is, furthermore, removal from the external world with the satisfactions it provides – imprisonment, and withdrawal of esteem by fellows, likewise a condition of our life-satisfaction – degrading punishment.]

[The greater or lesser the crime, the resistance to the majesty of the state, the greater or lesser the punishment, the authentication of the higher power of the state to the person of the perpetrator. Justice demands the proportionality of punishment with the same necessity as punishment itself, in that it demands in equal measure the majesty of the state and the inviolable security of the person. Were the act something in and of itself, then only the act would have to be rectified. But the act is an expression of the personality of the perpetrator, and it is in his subjugation, not the subjugation of the act, of which justice and punishment consist. But the perpetrator is more than just the act, he stands in obedience to the state in other relations, or at least must be assumed to unless the contrary is demonstrated, and as long as the higher and highest absence of regard for the rule of the legal order has not been confirmed for his part, to that degree he must be protected, preserved from punishment, and can only undergo punishment to the degree that the perpetrated act **<448>** manifests this resistance. For this reason, there is a hierarchy of crimes and, in accordance therewith, punishment.]

[The degree of crime is determined in terms of two criteria, the objective character of the act and the subjective character of the decision, thus in accordance with the degree of injury and the degree of guilt.]

[The degree of injury is based on: 1) the quality of the violated commandment or law; 2) the result of the act; 3) the causality of the act (not the will) to the injury.]

[The degree of guilt is based on: 1) the degree of freedom of the will, thus, full or partial accountability; 2) the manner of direction of the will (intent, direct, indirect, negligence); 3) the intensity of the criminal will (premeditation, violent temper, heinous calm regarding the act, etc.).]

[This hierarchy of crime accords with the hierarchy of punishment.]

[The protection of the life of man is the highest thing assigned to the state, the most sanctified component and content of its order, it being the highest thing man outwardly can injure. Man cannot injure God outwardly, but he can destroy God's image through murder, making that crime the highest form thereof. For this reason, murder demands the highest, complete punishment, the destruction of the perpetrator – the death penalty. Legislation which only punishes murder with imprisonment and not the death penalty does not maintain life in its full sanctity and therefore, far from being human, denies the esteem due human life, and is an unjust legislation.]

[Rebellion, high treason, are equal to murder, for the crime is against the state itself as institution, which protects the legal order and thus life. The death penalty is unjustified for other crimes; it can be excused as an emergency measure but can never be sanctified through the requirement of justice. Magnifying the death penalty through torture or mutilation is reprehensible.]

[Degrading punishments are not reprehensible in principle, although certain forms are callous and repulsive. Loss of esteem of fellows and an estimable position in society is the most natural evil <449> that follows upon crime.]

[Beatings are likewise not to be ruled out unconditionally. The absolute rejection thereof is based on the false principle of the Revolution, the divinization of man, in accordance with which man merely through his existence and quality as citizen has an absolute value and sanctity not conditioned by agreement with higher ethical law; for in other cases it is no degradation to people and citizens when the criminal, who demonstrates his lack of honor through his action, suffers degrading punishment.]

[In inflicting punishment, a chief consideration must be correction. Concern for the religious conversion of the convicted and, for the imprisoned, for acclimatizing to labor and the ability thereto, thus enabling a return to civil society, is one of the first duties of humanity and tasks of the state. Christianity cannot abolish punishment, not even the death penalty, but it can pursue correction as something as significant as punishment; Christianity can and should convert institutions of punishment into institutions of salvation.]

§. 187.[210] Pardon

[In the external kingdom of the state as well as in the eternal ethical kingdom, it is not merely justice which is to rule; mercy, love of the individual, must equally reveal itself, they are both part of the ethical power and are rule-ideas. Where punishment is done away with, mercy may still be found. Yet mercy is not imparted to the guilty by his equal, as is judgment, but can only come from a higher level, which has the original fullness of power, and it is not an affair of law – for judgment already contains the law – but of a free personality. This is the free right of pardon, which is accorded to the regent, and not the courts. Mercy does not abolish justice but works within it, where there are mitigating circumstances, in order to show love of the person.]

210 [In the original text, the section number is 145, which is obviously a mistake.]

WORKS CITED

Aquinas, St. Thomas. *Summa Theologica.* 1265–1274.

Bacon, Sir Francis. *De Augmentis Scientiarium* [The Advancement of Learning]. 1623.

Bluntschli, Johann Caspar. *Allgemeines Staatsrecht* [General State Law]. München: Literarische Anstalt, 1850.

—. *Psychologische Studien der Staat und Kirche* [Psychological Studies on State and Church]. Zürich and Frauenfeld: Ch. Beyel, 1844.

Boehmer, Justus Henning. *Introductio in jus publicum universale: ex genuinis iuris naturae principiis deductum adornatu* [Introduction to Universal Public Law]. Malae Magdeburgicae, 1719.

Boehmer, Justus Henning. *Maximes du droit publ. Franc.* [Maxims of French public law].

Bossuet, Jacques Bénigne. *Politique tirée des propres paroles de l'Écriture sainte* [Politics Derived from the Actual Words of Holy Scripture]. Paris: P. Cot, 1709.

Buchez, Philippe-Joseph-Benjamin, and P-C Roux. *Histoire parlementaire de la révolution française, ou, Journal des assemblées nationales, depuis 1789 jusqu'en 1815* [Parliamentary History of the French Revolution etc.]. Paris: Paulin, 1834–1838.

Burke, Edmund. *Reflections on the Revolution in France,* in *Select Works of Edmund Burke.* A New Imprint of the Payne Edition. Foreword and Biographical Note by Francis Canavan. Indianapolis: Liberty Fund, 1999. Vol. 2.

—. *Thoughts on the Cause of the Present Discontents.* London: Dodsley, 1784.

—. *Thoughts and Details on Scarcity: Originally Presented to the Right Hon. William Pitt, in the Month of November, 1795.* London: F. And C. Rivington, 1800.

Cicero, Marcus Tullius. *De Legibus* [Laws].

Cramer, Johann Ulrich Freiherr von. *Wetzlarische Nebenstunden worinnen auserlesene beym höchstpreisslichen Cammergericht entschiedene Rechtshändel zur erweiter- und Erläuterung der teutschen in gerichten üblichen Rechts-Gelehrsamkeit angewendet werden* [Wetzlar After-Hours in which selected legal cases decided at the highest court of the chambers are used to expand and explain the German legal scholarship customary in the courts]. Ulm: Verlegt Johann Conrad Wohler, 1755–73.

Dante Alighieri. *De Monarchia* [On Monarchy]. 1312–1313.

Filmer, Sir Robert. *Patriarcha: or, The Natural Power of Kings.* London: Printed, and are to be sold by Walter Davis, book-binder, in Amen-Corner, near Pater-noster-row, 1680.

Gerhard, Johann. *Loci theologici* [Theological Principles]. 1639.

Grotius, Hugo. *De jure belli et pac.* [On the Law of War and Peace]. 1625.

Hallam, Henry. *The constitutional history of England: from the accession of Henry VII to the death of George II.* Paris: L. Baudry, 1827

Hegel, G. W. F. *Grundlinien der Philosophie des Rechts* [Baselines of the Philosophy of Law]. Berlin: Nicolaische Buchhandlung, 1821.

Hobbes, Thomas. *De Cive* [On the Citizen]. 1642.

Jarcke, Carl Ernst. *Die ständische Verfassung und die deutschen Constitutionen* [The Estates-Oriented Constitution and the German Constitutions]. Leipzig: Weygand, 1834.

Kant, Immanuel. *Metaphysische Anfangsgründe der Rechtslehre* [Metaphysical Elements of the Doctrine of Law]. Königsberg. Friedrich Nicolovius, 1790.

—. *Zum ewigen Frieden* [For Eternal Peace]. Königsberg: F. Nicolovius, 1795.

Leo, Heinrich. *Studien und Skizzen zu einer Naturlehre des Staates* [Studies and Sketches Toward a Natural Doctrine of the State]. Halle: E. Anton, 1833.

Locke, John. *An Essay Concerning the True Original, Extent, and End of Civil Government.* London: Apollo Press, 1814.

Luther, Martin. *Sämtliche Schriften* [Complete Writings], vol. X. Edited by Johann Georg Walch. Halle: 1739–1753.

Marca, Petrus de; Stephanus Baluzius. *Illvstrissimi viri Petri de Marca ... Dissertationvm de concordia sacerdotii et imperii, sev de libertatibvs ecclesiæ Gallicanæ libri octo.* Paris: Apud Franciscvm Mvgvet .., 1663.

Maurenbrecher, Romeo. *Die deutschen regierenden Fürsten und die Souverainität* [The German Ruling Princes and Sovereignty]. Frankfurt am Main: Franz Barrentrapp, 1839.

Moser, Johann Jacob. *Familien-Staats-Recht derer teutschen Reichsstände. Neues teutsches Staatsrecht 12,1* [Family State Law of the German Imperial Estates]. Osnabrück: Zeller, 1967.

—. *Teutsches Staatsrecht* [German State Law]. Osnabrück: Zeller, 1968.

—. *Von der teutschen Reichs-Stände Länden* [Of the German Imperial Estates Territories]. Franckfurt and Leipzig, 1769.

—. *Von der Landeshoheit im Weltlichen* [Regarding Territorial Supremacy in Temporal Affairs]. Frankfurt and Leipzig, 1772.

Niebuhr, Barthold Georg. *Römische Geschichte* [History of Rome]. Berlin: G. Reimer, 1811–1832.

Puetter, Johann Stephan. *Institutiones iuris publici germanici* [Institutions of German Public Law]. Goettingae: sumtibus vidvae Vandenhoeck, 1776.

Rousseau, Jean-Jacque. *The Social Contract, Or Principles of Political Right.* 1762.

—. *Lettres de la Montagne* [Letters from the Mountain]. 1765.

Schelling, F. W. J. *Vorlesungen über die Methode des academischen Studium* [Lectures on the Method of Academic Study]. Tübingen: Cotta, 1803.

Schleiermacher, F. D. E. *Vorlesungen über die Lehre vom Staat* [Lectures regarding the Doctrine of State]. Abhandlungen der Königlich Preussischen Akademie der Wissenschaften. 1814–15. Berlin: in der Realschul-Buchhandlung, 1818.

Schubarth, Carl Ernst. *Ueber die Unvereinbarkeit der Hegel'schen Staatslehre mit dem obersten Lebens- und Entwickelungsprinzip des preußischen Staats* [Regarding the Irreconcilability of the Hegelian Doctrine of State with the Supreme Life and Development Principle of the Prussian State]. Breslau: Aderholz, 1839.

Sidney, Algernon. *Discourses of Civil Government.* 1698.

Stahl, F. J. *Der Protestantismus als politisches Princip* [Protestantism as a Political Principle]. Second unrevised edition. Berlin: Schultze, 1853.

—. *Die deutsche Reichsverfassung nach den Beschlüssen der deutschen Nationalversammlung und nach dem Entwurf der drei königlichen Regierungen* [The German Imperial Constitution According to the Decisions of the German National Assembly etc.]. Berlin: Hertz, 1849.

—. *Die gegenwärtigen Parteien in Staat und Kirche: neunundzwanzig akademische Vorlesungen* [The Current Parties in State and Church: 29 Academic Lectures]. Berlin: W. Hertz, 1863.

—. *Die katholischen Widerlegungen: eine Begleitungsschrift zur 4. Aufl. Meiner Vorträge über den Protestantismus als politisches Princip* [The Catholic Refutations etc.]. Berlin: 1854.

—. *Die Philosophie des Rechts: Bd. 1: Geschichte der Rechtsphilosophie* [The Philosophy of Law: Volume I: The History of Legal Philosophy]. Third Edition. Heidelberg: Mohr, 1854.

—. *Die Philosophie des Rechts: Bd. 2: Rechts- und Staatslehre auf der Grundlage christlicher Weltanschauung* [The Philosophy of Law: Volume II: The Doctrine of Law and State on the Basis of the Christian World-View]. Third edition. Heidelberg: Mohr, 1854.

—. *Die Revolution und die constitutionelle Monarchie: eine Reihe ineinandergreifende Abhandlungen* [The Revolution and Constitutional Monarchy: A Series of Interconnecting Essays]. Berlin: Hertz, 1849.

—. *Parlamentarische Reden* [Parliamentary Speeches], ed. J. P. M. Treuherz. Berlin: Verlag von Herman Hollstein, 1856.

—. *Reden von Stahl* [Stahl's Speeches]. Berlin: Verlag von Wilhelm Hertz (Bessersche Buchhandlung), 1850.

—. *Siebzehn parlamentarische Reden und drei Vorträge* [Seventeen Parliamentary Speeches and Three Lectures]. Berlin: Verlag von Wilhelm Hertz (Bessersche Buchhandlung), 1862.

Stein, Lorenz von. *Der Socialismus und Communismus des heutigen Frankreichs: Ein Beitrag zur Zeitgeschichte* [Socialism and Communism in Contemporary France]. Leipzig: Otto Wigand, 1842.

Thiers, M. A. *Histoire du Consulat et de l'Empire : faisant suite a l'histoire de la révolution française* [History of the Consulate and the Empire etc.]. Paris: Paulin, Libraire-Éditeur, 1845.

Vollgraff, Karl. *Die Täuschungen des Repräsentatif-Systems, oder Beweis: dass dieses System nicht das geeignete, rechte und zeitgemäse Mittel ist, den Bedürfnissen unserer Zeit zu begegnen, mit Andeutung der geeigneten, rechten und zeitgemäsen Reformen* [The Deceptions of the Representative System, or proof: that this system is not the appropriate, right and timely means to meet the needs of our time, with suggestion of appropriate, right and timely reforms]. Marburg: N.G. Elwert, 1832.

Wandelini, Joannes. *Juris regii ἀνυπευθύνου et solutissimi cum potestate summa nulli nisi deo obnoxia.*

Zachariä, Heinrich Albert. *Deutsches Staats- und Bundesrecht* [German State and Confederal Law]. Göttingen: Vandenhoeck und Ruprecht, 1841.

INDEX

N.B.: The page numbers below refer to the numbering of the original edition.

www.ingramcontent.com/pod-product-compliance
Ingram Content Group UK Ltd.
Pitfield, Milton Keynes, MK11 3LW, UK
UKHW021710190726
13853UKWH00001B/484